A History of Book Illustration

The Illuminated Manuscript and the
Printed Book

by DAVID BLAND

*With more than 400 illustrations in line, tone, and
lithograph – twenty of them in full color*

EVERY artist, graphic arts student, and bibliophile will welcome this scholarly and engaging book, with its abundance of illustrations selected from many centuries of book-making.

There have been many books on book illustration, but few of them have attempted to trace its development from the earliest days of the illuminated manuscript down to the printed book of the present day. Only thus can the essential unity of the two forms of art be seen, and the sameness of the problems that faced the medieval illustrator and still face the contemporary graphic artist be appreciated.

By picking out salient and typical books the author seeks to indicate the main lines of development and to avoid a mere catalogue of titles. In more than 400 illustrations he gives a bird's-eye view not only of the Western but also of the Oriental book. The impact of modern photo-mechanical processes is described in detail and the influence on illustration of reproductive techniques is stressed throughout. More than half of the book is devoted to the past 150 years, and the contemporary b[ook] through 1957 – as the end of a lo[ng] development comes in for its full attention.

A History of Book Illustration

by the same author

THE ILLUSTRATION OF BOOKS

To

MARY

1. *The Rohan Book of Hours.* French, 15th Century. $11\frac{1}{2}'' \times 8\frac{1}{4}''$. Paris. B.N. Lat. 9471

A HISTORY OF
BOOK ILLUSTRATION

*The Illuminated Manuscript
and the Printed Book*

by

DAVID BLAND

THE WORLD PUBLISHING COMPANY
CLEVELAND AND NEW YORK

Published by The World Publishing Company
2231 West 110th Street, Cleveland 2, Ohio

Library of Congress Catalog Card Number: 58–10061

First Edition

GBFF758

Printed in Great Britain

Author's Note

A history like this is bound to be founded on the work of others and I cannot claim any originality for it. I have tried to name those from whom I have borrowed and the titles of their works will be found in my bibliography. In addition I am deeply indebted to Dr. Walter Oakeshott, Dr. Otto Pächt, Dr. John White, Mr. Basil Gray, Mr. Charles Mitchell, Mr. Berthold Wolpe, Dr. Maurice Ettinghausen, Mr. Henry Pitz, Mr. Peter Floud and Mr. J. I. Davis for having read parts of my manuscript and for having made many helpful criticisms and suggestions. I also have to acknowledge with thanks the help of Dr. G. Hill, Mr. A. Zwemmer and Mr. F. Watson for lending me books to photograph, of Graphis, Urs Graf, The Penrose Annual, The Studio, Messrs. A. M. Rosenthal, Messrs. Faber and Faber and the Bodleian Library for lending me blocks, Messrs. Purnell and Sons and Messrs. W. S. Cowell for providing lithographed plates, Mr. R. G. Hawkins of Fine Art Engravers for taking infinite care over the reproduction of many intractable illustrations and Messrs. Robert MacLehose for their care in printing this book. Then there are innumerable publishers, libraries and illustrators (their names are given elsewhere), who have lent me material to reproduce, especially The World Publishing Company, the American Artist and the Limited Editions Club of America. I am grateful to the Librarian of the Victoria and Albert Museum for allowing me to photograph several of his books; but it is from the magnificent collection of printed books and manuscripts in the British Museum that most of my illustrations have come. Without that collection my book could never have been written and I acknowledge with pleasure my debt to the Reading Room staff who with unfailing courtesy have looked out thousands of books for me.

I am painfully aware of the risks of trying to describe in two short chapters the development over a period of nearly one thousand years of the illuminated manuscript in the West, and a great deal of this introductory section was bound to be second-hand. But I felt that the history of the illustrated book could not simply begin in the middle of the fifteenth century. In dealing with both manuscripts and printed books I have tried to avoid making a mere catalogue of titles by picking out the salient and typical books (not necessarily the best ones) which will themselves indicate the development of illustration. Consequently the omission of a book does not mean that it was unworthy of mention, simply that lack of space banished it.

It has not always been possible for the same reason to show complete pages in the illustrations but I have tried to do so in those cases where it seemed to be important. To obtain a larger image it has sometimes been necessary to reduce the margins slightly although I have tried to keep a pleasing proportion. And wherever possible the original page size is given. I would ask the reader to bear in mind that a poor reproduction may be due to a badly printed original, especially in the case of early printed books. The illustrations themselves are numbered consecutively, text figures, monochrome and colour plates, and are referred to by figures in square brackets. Manuscript locations and reference numbers will be found in the index at the end of the book.

Contents

List of Illustrations

An asterisk indicates a reproduction in colour. All measurements are in inches and apply to the full page size except where otherwise stated. Authors' names will be found under the illustrations themselves and manuscript reference numbers in the index.

Introduction

'And you who wish to represent by words the form of man and all the aspects of his membrification, relinquish that idea. For the more minutely you describe the more you will confine the mind of the reader, and the more you will keep him from the knowledge of the thing described. And so it is necessary to draw *and* to describe.'

Could there be a better justification for the illustrated book than this of Leonardo's? If it be agreed that he was thinking of scientific, rather than imaginative, illustration, it can easily be shown that there was no distinction in his day. The textbooks like *De Re Militari* which deals with the art of siege were as imaginatively illustrated as the *Poliphilo*.

Drawing and writing have in fact developed simultaneously from a common origin. Even today we can use the word 'illustration' indiscriminately of a graphic or of a verbal description. Each began as a means of communication and by degrees alphabets were built up of certain images. The process may be studied in the palaeolithic picture where the artist, wishing to show a herd of reindeer would draw only the first and last animals, indicating the rest by a few lines. So stylization came and with it the ideogram.

In a sense then all art is illustrative and in that sense illustration preceded literature. The earliest illustration was simply aimed to reach those who could not read, and this function continued right down to the fifteenth-century days of the printed block books. But here a distinction must be made between illustration and decoration, for while illustration came first it was followed, as soon as literacy developed, by its abstract counterpart, decoration. Throughout the Middle Ages, when manuscripts were written and illuminated for the learned or the rich, decoration was paramount. The fact that so many of these works were philosophical and did not lend themselves to illustration also had its effect. But even in the Middle Ages there were periods when the classical tradition was strong and when illustration assumed more importance than decoration—as for instance in the *Utrecht Psalter*. After the introduction of printing too there are strongly decorative periods; and so it goes on, first one stress and then the other.

In the medieval mind however it may be doubted whether there was any distinction between the two. The symbol, which is of such vast importance in the art of the Middle Ages and which persisted in the emblem books until quite recently, partakes of both illustration and decoration. It might be said that in those days they saw everything as an illustration but the result to us is usually decorative, almost abstract. Later on, in the early printed books the cuts seem to have been used partly as a sign-post to the contents. It is not until much later that we begin to find such definitions as Goethe's 'The artist must think out to the end the poet's ideas' which carry us much farther than Leonardo's into the realm of imaginative illustration. This type, of course, had long been practised and probably defined in early China but with the Romantic Revival it became self conscious and articulate in the West. So we come down to the present day and such dicta as that of Lynton Lamb, himself a book-artist: 'Illustrations can only be justified if they add to a book something that literature cannot encompass.'

Most historians of book illustration make a clear-cut distinction between the manuscript and the printed book. The former is often considered to be the preserve of the art-historian, its illumination more akin to painting than to graphic art. Yet, apart from the convenience of dealing separately with two such vast subjects, there are good reasons why they should be considered together. Printed illustration derived from the miniature, and if manuscripts were never produced in such large editions as printed books yet it is undeniable that they were copied with the object of producing replicas. The manuscript relied more on colour for its decoration but even this difference disappeared in the later history of the printed book. The important common factor is of course the *mise en page*. We have continually to consider how the picture is adapted to the page, how its depth is affected by the flatness of the type and so on. But the art-historian seldom takes into account the frames of the pictures which he describes.

Besides all this, the problems of the medieval book-painter were many of them exactly the same as the problem of the contemporary graphic artist—what passages to illustrate, whether or not to stick slavishly to the text and so on. Even in late classical times we meet an anomaly that persisted long after the arrival of printing; the better the illustration the poorer the text. Carelessness over the detail, even downright misunderstanding, are not modern phenomena. There is a curious instance in the *Utrecht Psalter* where the passage 'We are counted as sheep for the slaughter' is simply illustrated by two sheep in the foreground of the picture.

Weitenkampf has pointed out one way in which he thinks manuscripts differ in principle from printed books. The method of production by hand, he says, gives more unity to the finished work whereas any unity in the book of today is the result of conscious effort on the part of the designer. But at a very early stage there was a division between the writer and the decorator of the manuscript; moreover the early printed book was almost as much a hand-product as the manuscript.

If it be agreed that the illuminated manuscript[1] and the illustrated printed book have almost everything in common it must then be admitted that the illustration of both, especially the miniatures of the later manuscripts, should be considered within the framework of the history of painting. Not that painters with a few exceptions have much concerned themselves with books until fairly recently. They have usually rather looked down on illustration and in certain quarters the word has come to have a slightly contemptuous connotation. It is of course an 'impure' art, mixing literature with painting—but no more impure than opera which mixes literature with music. It has borrowed much from the other arts and crafts in every period of its history, from architecture[2] (seventeenth-century title pages), from flower-culture (late Flemish illumination) and from the art of the goldsmith which inspired the early copper-engravers. But generally of course it has followed the broad development of painting, with however a distinct time lag after the introduction of printing. Eric Gill was using the term too loosely[3] when he called Giotto the 'first great illustrator'; but it is significant that he should have named a painter who worked just at the time when a

---

[1] Morey defines illumination as the art of beautifying the object rather than clarifying the contents.

[2] Bradley says that many late classical liturgical books have decoration which reflects the architecture of the particular churches where they were to be used.

[3] He was also wrong in ignoring all the great miniaturists who preceded Giotto. The passage appears in one of Gill's letters in which he also compares illustration with programme music. He goes on to say that Giotto was hailed as the beginning of Christian art because he was the first great illustrator. 'And illustration is the only function of art honoured in an age in which men are no longer "partners with God in the *making of beauteous books*".'

distinction was growing up between book-painting and easel or panel painting. The major and the minor art have remained closely linked ever since and it must never be forgotten that it was from the minor that the major sprang.

The designation 'graphic artist' to describe one who draws for reproduction as distinct from a painter is a comparatively recent one, but there were always professional illustrators who even if they did not produce their own printing surfaces were expert in drawing for reproduction. These men have often produced magnificent work but the incursion of the painter, though technically the results may not often be as happy, is always to be welcomed as a reviving influence. The painter, for instance, has often been responsible for introducing colour into the book. He has often despised the study of reproductive techniques in the belief that it is the printer's responsibility to find a way to reproduce his work. And who shall say that he is wrong, for in this way technical progress is made. Such a state of affairs is preferable to what happened in the nineteenth century when the professional engravers sometimes dictated the method of drawing to the artist. It is easy to say that the artist must submit to the discipline of reproduction (and there is some truth in it) but the discipline must not be such that it stifles genius.

Perhaps the solution lies in the employment of intermediaries like August Clot and Roger de Lacourière who work for the peintres graveurs of the École de Paris. These men are both artists and technicians—but it seems that they are to be found only in France.

It must be admitted however that the painter-illustrated book is seldom as well integrated as the one illustrated by the professional. It is a fair criticism of the books of the École de Paris for instance that they are portfolios of drawings detachable from their texts—and in fact they *are* often so detached. But even this risk is worth running for the sake of the wonderful books that Bonnard and Picasso have given us.

It is interesting to speculate why the painter's interest in the printed book is of such comparatively recent growth. Rubens, Rembrandt and Fragonard all produced a few illustrations, while Hogarth and Blake produced many. But great names apart from these between the arrival of printing and the beginning of the nineteenth century are scarce. Joseph Pennell, writing in 1889, gives as a reason that their work was murdered in reproduction. This is unfair to, for instance, the brilliant French engravers of the eighteenth century whose proficiency we can check by many original drawings which survive; but it raises the important point that it is impossible to judge a drawing apart from its reproduction since the reproduction *is* the illustration. And yet often we shall have to make allowances for indifferent press-work (as opposed to poor engraving) in the case especially of early woodcuts whose quality survives the printer's lack of skill.

Another reason given by Pennell for the reluctance of painters to engage in book illustration is that it was simply not worth their while financially. The rewards of the illustrator have never been great and many have consequently been forced to turn out too much work. But to Pennell at the end of the nineteenth century things seemed brighter. 'Publishers today,' he says, 'are the greatest art patrons who ever lived.' His optimism however was hardly justified since most of the best books illustrated by painters in the twentieth century have been *éditions-de-luxe* or else published by private presses—just as the great illuminated manuscripts were executed for ecclesiastical or secular princes.

The chief effect of the publisher on illustration seems to have been to make it subject to fashion. Book illustration, in spite of its stylistic lag behind painting fashions, has nevertheless had fashions of its own which have ruled it quite rigidly. Even when the artist did not conform, the engraver who translated his drawing often adapted it accordingly.

Because the organization of the page and the relation between picture and text are at the centre of our subject we must omit consideration of the separate print and also of the album which has no text although it may be bound up like a book and even possess a title-page. This is a difficult, almost invidious, distinction to make in the case of the Japanese *yehon* and also perhaps of the early nineteenth-century English topographical book. But it is one which has to be made if our terms of reference are not to become too wide. For the same reason we have not considered it necessary to mention a book on account of a single good illustration if there is nothing else about it that merits attention.

For the sake of convenience this chronicle has been divided roughly into centuries, and within each chapter into countries. But distinctive national characteristics were slow in appearing. Although there were differences in the days of the manuscript there was also what might be called a changing international style; this persisted long after the introduction of printing, fostered by the interchange of wood-blocks between countries. Gradually national distinctions emerged until today it is possible to say in a general way that each country has its own style. Even in America, where we find an astonishing variety because of the large number of immigrant artists, national characteristics are beginning to appear which are quite different from England's.

England herself has long had a reputation for literary painting. And it has been said, 'the literary elements of a picture become illustration when physically associated with literature.' It is a literal quality, a faithfulness to the text which has generally marked English illustration, especially in its great period of the nineteenth century. It is a quality that easily degenerates into sentimentality and sentimentality is often apparent too in the judgement which Englishmen bring to their books. Charles Lamb for instance said he liked his Shakespeare with bad plates that did not try to emulate the text. And which of us can judge dispassionately the children's books on which we were brought up?

It may be the fondness for literary painting that has induced so many Englishmen to illustrate their own books. This is not a common enough phenomenon to rank as a national peculiarity but it is exemplified in at least two writers and artists of genius—William Blake and Edward Lear—quite apart from numerous authors of children's books where the dual function is common practice in other countries as well.

In France the matter has often been tackled the other way round. Rouault provided his own text for *Cirque de l'étoile filante*, Léger for *Cirque*, and Matisse for his *Jazz*. But these men, great as they are in their own fields, are primarily painters and would not make any great claims for their writings. Again, Vollard commissioned texts for illustrations which he already had; and as recently as 1946 Paul Eluard, writing at the beginning of *Le Dur Désir de Durer*, said, 'Je savais, en écrivant ces poèmes qu'ils seraient illustrés par des dessins de Marc Chagall.'

There is less risk of sentimentality in French illustration because it is less literary than English and because it nearly always takes precedence of the text. Champfleury said that a later age might smile at the importance the French attach to *petit art*, and it is a fact that illustration has always been taken seriously in France, certainly more seriously than typography. Italy was fortunate in that printing came to her during one of her greatest periods of painting and manuscript illumination, and she developed a strongly individual style of illustration which, alas, did not long survive. In Germany, on the other hand, the country where European printing originated, the tradition of painting was not so strong and the individuality of her less painterly style of illustration has survived better. The Netherlands with an equally strong printing tradition developed an international style in the seventeenth century which blunted all distinctive features.

The list could be extended indefinitely without taking in the countries of the Orient which all present individual traits not always distinctive to Western eyes. But Oriental illustration of the great periods before the nineteenth century, whether Chinese, Japanese, Islamic, Hebrew or Indian, is of course completely different from Western. In the Islamic countries illumination continued long after printing came to the West; and even in China and Japan where illustrations were printed centuries before Gutenberg or Pfister their design was always more closely allied to painting than in the West.

One special branch in which the Orientals excelled was the re-illustration of old classics. Most of the great Indian and Persian manuscripts fall into this class and innumerable Chinese books as well. In the West such works have great attractions for the publisher because they are out of copyright. But the danger is that they have all been illustrated before, often many times before, and this seems to have a more frustrating effect on the Western artist than on the Oriental. To re-illustrate a book that has already been well illustrated is a difficult task. Nevertheless certain familiar books always seem to attract the artist and in the following pages the same titles will be found to recur. In the days of the manuscript it was the *Physiologus* or Aratus or the *Psychomachia* of Prudentius, and of course the Bible or part of it. After the introduction of printing the Bible was still a favourite; then there were the Fables of Æsop (later of La Fontaine), *Daphnis and Chloe* (still a favourite with the private presses), Ovid's *Metamorphoses*, Boccaccio and many others. In our own days *The Pilgrim's Progress* still finds new illustrators. And if the book be as timeless as *The Pilgrim's Progress* the modern artist is often able to illuminate it afresh as Kauffer did for *The Anatomy of Melancholy*. But if not, he may merely produce a pastiche. Where, on the other hand, the author and artist are contemporary, as Delacroix was with Goethe and Bonnard with Verlaine, there is at least no danger of costumes and manners being unauthentic; and more important there is greater likelihood of sympathy and understanding between the two.

The book-illustrator, however, depends far more on his author than the author depends on him. True illustration can never be anything more than a dependent art. But within its limitations what a delightful art it is. The illustrated book, said William Morris, 'is not perhaps absolutely necessary to man's life, but it gives us such endless pleasure and is so intimately connected with the other absolutely necessary art of imaginative literature that it must remain one of the very worthiest things towards the production of which reasonable man should strive.'

1

The Beginnings in Roll and Codex

LATE ANTIQUE AND ORIENTAL ILLUSTRATION

The oldest illustrated book that has come down to us is an Egyptian papyrus roll of about 1980 B.C. The fact that it is Egyptian is accidental and is due only to the preservative qualities of Egyptian sand. It is known that there were books (written on wood) in China about the thirteenth or fourteenth centuries B.C. and some of these were probably illustrated; but none is left and the historian must rely on what has quite fortuitously survived. Survival has been made more precarious by the perishable materials that have been used for books—wood, leaves, leather, papyrus, parchment and paper. There are indeed Sumerian books on clay tablets of great antiquity but these are not illustrated; and nothing remains from the classical periods of Greece or Rome.

So it is to Egypt that one must look for the beginnings of the illustrated book, and in Egypt writing goes back to about the thirtieth century B.C. Our earliest illustrated roll therefore was likely to have had many predecessors which have now been lost. Even thus early it is possible to see the tension between text and illustration on which we shall often have cause to comment as this story proceeds. In this particular roll the little illustrations[1] run in a narrow strip along the bottom of the text to which they are obviously subordinate. In some later rolls we find them becoming larger or moving up to the top of the roll. But it would be rash to assume that therefore the illustration is becoming emancipated from the text, because we often find examples in one roll of all the three main types—the frieze picture, the column picture and the full-sized miniature.

The books which were most frequently illustrated at the time were the *Book of the Dead*, and because they were buried deliberately they have survived in some numbers. They contained a collection of prayers, hymns and magical formulae which were designed to secure the eternal happiness of the one in whose tomb they were placed. The length of the roll depended on the price that was paid for it, and often the portrait of the deceased is found at the beginning—a precursor of the dedicatory pictures in medieval MSS and of the portrait frontispieces in printed books. Otherwise the vignettes were usually in simple black outline without background or frame, and they were fitted into the writing columns with text above and below. These books were written in large numbers and were kept in stock by the undertakers, blank spaces being left for the names of the dead. With the eighteenth and nineteenth Dynasties we reach the most beautifully designed and colourful copies of the *Book of the Dead*; the *Hunefer Papyrus*[2] in the British Museum is an outstanding example [2]. But

[1] Called vignettes by Egyptologists, but not to be confused with what was later to be understood by that term.

[2] Manuscript reference numbers will be found in the index at the end of the book.

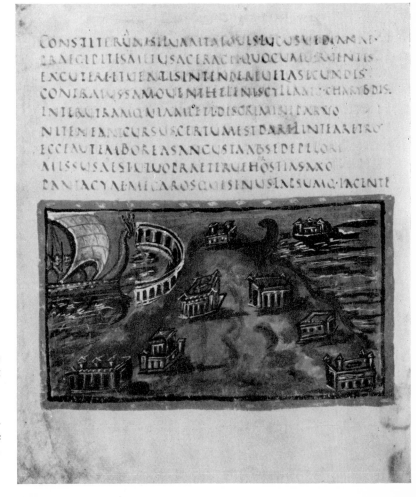

2. Egyptian *Book of the Dead. The Hunefer Papyrus. c.* 1300 B.C. Height 15½″. British Museum. Pap. 9901

3. *The Vatican Virgil.* Roman, probably 4th century. 12½″ × 12″. The Island of Sicily. Vatican Library. Cod. Vat. Lat. 3225

4. *The Ku K'ai Chih Scroll*. Chinese, 5th century. Height 9¾″. This picture shows how the Lady Feng protected the Emperor from an attack by a bear. British Museum

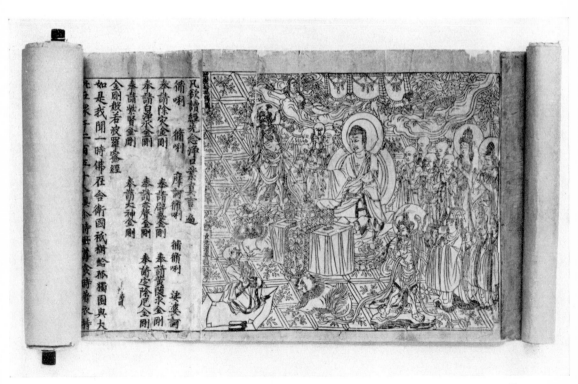

5. The printed frontispiece of the *Diamond Sutra*. Chinese, dated A.D. 868. Height 9¼″. British Museum

Egyptian art, like Byzantine later, was curiously static and although it seems to have reached a degree of technical perfection quite early, it developed little and remained strangely lifeless. It is interesting to note in passing that the best illustrated of these books are usually the least accurate textually; and this is a failing that has continued up to the present in all books where the artist predominates.

With the ousting of hieroglyphic (vertical) script by hieratic (horizontal) script, which read from right to left, we sometimes find pictures being placed on the right-hand side of the column and occupying only a part of the width of that column instead of extending right across it. Now at last we have some common ground with contemporary Greek illustration although our first-hand knowledge of this is woefully small. But we know enough to recognize the influence of the so-called 'papyrus style' which came from Egypt. We find in Greece the system of column-width pictures interrupting the text as well as pictures of only half the width of the column, and pictures too without background or frames. A distinction has been made between the 'papyrus style' of illustration from Egypt, characterized by illustration without frame or background, and the 'parchment style' with its isolated pictures. But it is more likely that the one grew naturally out of the other.

At all events it seems probable that Egyptian influences came at an early date, and where could those influences be exercised more naturally than in Alexandria, the book-centre of the ancient world? Yet, although we know so much about Alexandria with its great library and although we know much, too, about ancient Greek literature we have no rolls from the classical period and few illustrated rolls of any significance from any period. Our earliest example of the latter is a book on astronomy in the Louvre, dating from about 150 B.C.

The *Book of the Dead*, which has survived so wonderfully, was by no means the only type of illustrated book which Egypt produced. There were books on astronomy and magic, there were animal fables and there were erotica[1] (peculiarly dependent on illustration), and these profane books were more likely to have influenced Greek illustration than the *Book of the Dead*. Weitzmann believes that the Homeric poems and drama generally were frequently illustrated and on a large scale. His belief is based on pots, bowls or sarcophagi which would have survived better than papyrus rolls and which have a system of decoration that he thinks is derived from those rolls. From these he deduces that the Odyssey may have been illustrated by about five hundred pictures and the Iliad by about seven hundred, and he argues that only the roll could have contained so many pictures and therefore the roll must be the fountain which craftsmen in other media drew upon. He thinks it unlikely that because of its perishable nature the greatest artists were engaged on book-illustration. As in the Middle Ages the derivative works of art were often superior to their models. Greek art was always representational and the Greek illustrator of mythology may have found it difficult to adjust himself to an art that could not be based on personal observation.

Now this is an ingenious and attractive theory but it seems strange that not one of these illustrated rolls has survived. And in the absence of such proof it can only be a theory. Of the 1800 manuscript rolls dating from the first century A.D. which were discovered at Herculaneum not one is illustrated; which seems to prove at least that illustration was not common at this period. It is just as likely that, as Kurz believes, there was no literary illustration at all until comparatively late—say about the fourth century A.D. This would make the *Milan Iliad* [6] one of the first epics to be illustrated. But it was not the first example of classical illustra-

---

[1] A tendency to eroticism has dogged the illustrated book, particularly the luxury type, through the ages. It became more pronounced in France in the eighteenth century and it continues in the French *édition-de-luxe* today.

6. *The Milan Iliad.* Roman. Probably 4th century. $7\frac{1}{4}'' \times 8\frac{3}{4}''$. Noxix Aphrodite shows Zeus her hand which Diomedes has wounded. Hera and Athene laugh at her. Ambrosiana, Milan. Cod. F. 205, inf.

tion because there must have been scientific illustration long before; in fact Aristotle refers in his biological books to accompanying illustrations which have now disappeared. So Kurz distinguishes three stages—first, scientific illustration; then portrait illustration for which he cites Varro's *Imagines*, a collection of portraits of famous men dating from the first century A.D. and now lost; and lastly literary illustration.

The framework of this last is what is known as the cyclic method which probably came from the East rather than from Egypt and which was to continue right down to the end of the Middle Ages. It aimed at a series of consecutive pictures without specific attention to the suitability or otherwise of the subject for illustration. Static or dynamic situations were now equally favoured and the result was a cycle which could be 'read' almost as easily as the text—more easily by the illiterate.

Although there may have been prototype cycles which illustrated every part of all the great epics it was soon found that to illustrate a work like the Odyssey required so many pictures that some selection was advantageous. So the more important scenes were picked out or those which could be more easily illustrated. Usually these drawings were arranged in chronological order but they might also come in order of importance without any reference to time—a method which would have been obvious enough to one very familiar with the epic but which is confusing to the modern mind. Later on two or more stories might be combined or one abstract idea might become the thread on which scenes from various mythological sources were strung.

Weitzmann traces a similar development in the physical relationship of the miniatures which form the cycle. He distinguishes four stages: first there are the examples where scenes follow each other with no division. Then we find the picture being fitted into a decorative pattern; which implies the subordination of the text and often results in confusion for the reader. In the next step the balance is redressed and the scribe becomes paramount, assuming responsibility for the placing of the pictures. He leaves space for them in the text where there are passages that he thinks will require illustration; which makes the artist's task harder but is easier for the reader. The method is used in the few original codex manuscripts we possess such as the *Milan Iliad* and the *Vatican Virgil* as well as in medieval manuscripts copied from classical models. Lastly each scene becomes isolated though still not an entity but rather a unit from a cycle. It is not quite clear whether these stages are supposed to follow each other chronologically or whether they are alternatives. The latter seems more likely since the development of art has always refused to conform to a rigid pattern.

One characteristic these cyclic miniatures share with the Egyptian *Book of the Dead* which preceded them, and with almost all the illustrated books which have followed, right down to our own day. The picture is placed within the width of the column of writing and though it may be narrower, it hardly ever transgresses it and is often of exactly the same width. Now it is not extraordinary that this should be the usual practice in the printed book because there are good technical reasons why the block should be made to the same width as the type. But the freedom of writing and drawing is subject to no such restraint and, though long familiarity has made it seem an obvious practice to us, its first introduction must have been one of the great decisions in the history of the book.

Perhaps because the column itself provided an imaginary boundary these roll miniatures seldom have backgrounds or frames and in this they differ from the generality of later illustration. A three-dimensional illusion is made easier by a frame to isolate the picture from the flatness of the text but the illustrators of this time could not or did not want to achieve such

an effect. It is the more surprising because contemporary frescoes often have rich backgrounds. This suggests, as indeed is confirmed by the quality of the miniatures themselves,
that book illustration was considered to be of inferior artistic importance.

Some time in the second century A.D. occurred one of the most momentous events in the
whole history of the book, the introduction of the codex, or the paged book as we know it.
The papyrus codex was in use especially among Christians about A.D. 100 and Christians, too,
favoured parchment which supplanted papyrus about the fourth century, at the same time
that the roll virtually disappeared.[1] One would have expected that the coming of the codex
would have meant a radical alternation in the method of illustration but so conservative
were the scribes that the old system persisted for some time. Early codices were squarish
with several columns of writing on each page and pictures were fitted into the columns just
as before, without frames and without backgrounds. The advent of parchment, however, did
make a change. This material was made from the skins of cattle, sheep or goats, and it
offered a far better surface than anything that had hitherto been available. It would take
gouache whereas papyrus, as far as we know, had only been used for line drawing and water
colouring.

Unfortunately, this fourth century, so crucial in the history of the book, was also the time
of the great barbarian invasions and book production declined very sharply. But it was
nevertheless during this century that a European, as distinct from a classical civilization, was
born. The late antique period, which is the name given to the years between A.D. 300 and
700, played a vital part indeed in the evolution of medieval style. With the triumph of Christianity the classical tradition was under attack because the early Christians, like the Moslems, were opposed to all imagery. But the virtue of illustration as a factor in teaching was
soon recognized and quite early we find in Gospel manuscripts the pagan custom of inserting
the author's portrait at the beginning of each book. About A.D. 400 there was a return to
classicism in Roman Christian art which, though temporary, had a permanent effect.
Biblical scenes which hitherto have only a symbolical value develop into narrative cycles
filled with realistic detail. But generally speaking late antique art subordinates all forms of
realistic representation to another value which Kitzinger calls 'the abstract relationship between things rather than the things themselves'. This reaction, which recurs throughout our
history, is nearly always beneficial to the book, in which complete realism is neither possible
nor desirable. But during this particular period it is reinforced by a flight from materialism
and by the fact that the Christian artist, unlike the classical one, is seeking to convey a
message in his pictures.

In 1054 the Western and Eastern Churches had finally separated, Latin becoming the
language of the former and Greek of the latter. Monasticism arose in the East before the
West and with it appeared the scriptoria, which later were responsible for the wonderful
Byzantine illuminated MSS of the tenth and eleventh centuries. But long before that, the
Arab conquest of the seventh century had opened the door to the Orient.[2] It was indeed a
two-way traffic since Christian art had been carried eastwards by such heretics as the
Nestorians who flourished under the Sassanian kings of Persia (226–636). The Sassanids had
no prejudices against the representation of the human face or form, and it is believed that
in their time many richly illustrated Persian books were produced—though none has sur-

---

[1] It has survived however to the present day
for certain Hebrew works such as *The Book of
Esther* which in the early days was often provided
with miniatures, or later on with engraved illustrations.

[2] The art of paper-making reached Islam from
China in the middle of the eighth century and
until 1150 when the first European mill was started
in Spain all the supplies of the West came from
the Arabs.

vived. It is known too that Nestorian missionaries even penetrated to China; but a firmer link with the East seems to be provided by another religion, Manicheism, which was less kindly treated by the Sassanids. Its adherents fled to Eastern Turkestan where they are found as late as the thirteenth century. The founder Mani had himself decorated his writings with pictures and his followers held painting in high honour because of its use in religious propaganda. There are many references in contemporary literature to their magnificent manuscripts—but again only a few fragments are left to us.

In spite of our attempt to connect China with the West it must be admitted that the book-arts of both China and Japan grew up in complete isolation and in many ways far in advance of the West. Written Chinese is itself a form of illustration, a picture of the thing described, and the art of calligraphy has always been held in high esteem there. From the use of the brush in calligraphy to the use of the same brush for painting is a short step and what more natural than that the painting should accompany the calligraphy? A Chinese historian wrote of the early painter-poets 'When they could not express their thoughts [in painting] they made characters and when they could not express shapes [in writing] they made paintings'. In other words they had two languages which were interchangeable.

The quality of the brush-work, as well as faithfulness to tradition, were the criteria in both. Figure 4, which shows part of the fifth-century roll 'Admonition of the Instructress of the Palace' by Ku K'ai Chih, shows also that book illustration held a more honourable place here than in the West, for Ku K'ai Chih was a famous painter, as well as a civil servant. His roll is divided into nine groups, in which strips of vertical text appear between pictures of varying widths, design and illustration being thus nicely balanced.[1] Under the T'ang Dynasty which began some two hundred years later, painting was considered one of the highest intellectual activities and was practised by scholar officials, many of whose names have come down to us; whereas in Europe the illuminators of manuscripts are anonymous down to the late Middle Ages.

There is evidence that Chinese books were being written on wood in the thirteenth or fourteenth centuries B.C. Paper appeared first in China where it was traditionally invented by Ts'ai Lun about A.D. 105. But it was used in the form of a roll until about the fifth century, when it was folded into accordion pleats. China's greatest contribution however was the use of wood-blocks for text and illustrations (if contribution is the right word for a discovery that seems to have been made quite independently in Europe at least 600 years later).[2] The first use of wood-blocks seems to have been for printing textiles in about the seventh century. It is true that they were probably being used in Egypt for the same purpose at about the same time but it seems to have gone no further there. In China and Japan it led to what was virtually the beginning of book printing; and those who argue that printing is a European discovery are forced to equate it with the first use of the press—even movable types are now known to have been used in Korea, about 1390; earthenware types seem to have been used in China at least 300 years before that.

Block books in China thus preceded by several centuries illustrated books printed from movable types; whereas in Europe they were practically contemporaneous. But the Chinese language is hardly ideal for movable types. The lack of the printing press was more serious

[1] Ku K'ai Chih also illustrated in one continuous landscape a fairy tale called *Lo Shen* which exists in a late copy at Washington and *The Record of Eminent Women* which was reissued in the eleventh century with woodcuts and again in 1825.

[2] See, however, T. F. Carter, *The Invention of Printing in China and its Spread Westwards* (1925), for the fascinating possibility that block printing may have come to Europe from China via Persia.

because all the early woodcuts are printed by rubbing (in exactly the same way as the first European block-books) which accounts for the use of only one side of the paper; and rubbing can never give as good an impression as the press. In spite of this the famous *Diamond Sutra* of A.D. 868, the earliest printed book which can be dated, has a woodcut frontispiece which is a triumph of design and cutting and which would grace any European book of the fifteenth century [5]. The cutting is so good in fact that there is no doubt it had many predecessors. In the Tunhuang caves, from which it came, Stein discovered examples of coloured borders printed from more than one block, presumably of about the same date, and also another copy of the *Diamond Sutra* printed by an early form of lithography. The text was cut in stone from which rubbings were then taken.

Carter points out that printing has always been brought to new territories by expanding religion. Its first use in China was for the production of Buddhist pictures and texts, and Japan had been printing for centuries before any other sort of literature was attempted. From Japan, in fact, come even earlier examples of block printing than the *Diamond Sutra*, though they are not in the form of a book. These are the charms of which the Empress Shotoku ordered a million copies to be printed in 770 and of which some are still in existence. As Carter says, they represent in exactly the same way as the early European block prints 'the effort of the common man to get into his hands a bit of the sacred word or a sacred picture which he believed to have supernatural power but which he could not himself write or paint and could not afford to buy unless duplicated for him by some less laborious process'. It might be added that, as the common man could not read either, these charms would have had little real meaning for him.

The power of tradition in Eastern art to which we have already referred seems to have prevented any further great advance in the technique of woodcutting for few later cuts show any improvement on the *Diamond Sutra*. Perhaps tradition too is responsible for this book being in the form of a roll, although the Chinese type of codex had been in use for about 400 years. In other respects the Chinese were more adventurous, in the choice of materials for instance. Albums were often painted on silk [63] and quite often the pictures are found bleeding off the foredge of the book (i.e. with no outer margin) long before such a practice is ever seen in the West.

Returning to the West we find that by the fourth century the codex is well established and is becoming taller and narrower in shape, so that two columns of writing are usual on a page and sometimes there is only one. Thus the single column picture becomes the full-page one, or else perhaps two miniatures are placed side by side with an 'insertion motif' to divide one scene from the next, e.g. a pillar to represent a house. In a Roman *Kalendar* of the fourth century ornament makes its appearance as well as illustration, but generally speaking late classical manuscripts are illustrated rather than decorated.

Now at last we begin to find original manuscripts, not just fragments or copies, and some of them have illustrations of aesthetic not just historical importance. The *Vatican Virgil* survives in fifty pictures of unequal merit, the best of them pastoral scenes [3]. Some of the landscape backgrounds of these have considerable charm. They seem to have been painted complete, covering the whole picture area, the figures in the foreground being painted over afterwards. The colours of course, as in all early manuscripts, are opaque. A few of the pictures fill the whole page but most occupy the upper half only. One page which survives is divided into a number of rectangular frames, no doubt the ancestor of later pages of 'compartment' pictures; and we find the decorative element in the frames which surround them. The *Milan Iliad* [6] contains fifty-eight striking miniatures on parchment but there must once have been about 250. These are clearly related to contemporary Roman art because as illustrations to Homer they are full of anachronisms; for instance horsemen are shown where none are mentioned in the text; and this hardly suggests that they are based on a cycle with its roots in Homeric Greece. Another point of interest is that the pictures are framed with a simple line, which creates space and depth round the figures and adds a third dimension.

Soon the empty space within the frame begins to be filled with landscape. There is a famous *Genesis* in Vienna which was written in Antioch and dates from about the sixth century. Of this 'precious document of the junction of two worlds' Clark says that the artist known as the Illusionist 'was capable of true impressions of atmosphere, of the totality of landscape, even when his figures were formalized' in the Byzantine manner. It is painted on purple parchment with silver lettering and it shows a more systematic and unified arrangement of illustrations than has been found hitherto. The lower half of each page has been reserved for them and the text has been abridged to make it fit. This, together with its luxurious appearance, suggests that the buyer of the *édition-de-luxe* was already in existence, more interested in looking at his book than in reading it. From this manuscript we reproduce a picture designed for single column width to which a landscape has been added, making it as wide as the two columns of the text [7].

By the tenth century we find whole pages frequently given up to one picture, or two, one above the other. Often two pages of pictures face each other which means a big gap in the text.[1] But that is nothing compared to what we find much earlier in a sixth-century Gospel Book at Rossano [9]. Here all the pictures are collected into a cycle placed at the beginning of the book which can be 'read' without the assistance of the text at all. One would perhaps expect this to be a late development and its early occurrence shows how risky it is to assume an orderly chronological plan of development. This separation of pictures from text had the advantage of enabling the illustrator to work quite independently of the scribe, the binder bringing their respective sections together at the end. A medical MS in Durham Cathedral goes to the extreme of having no text at all, only pictures—but this is rare.

During the Romanesque period the three-dimensional method was dropped and the miniature returned to the same plane as the text, often with a patterned background instead of a landscape. But the full-page miniature begins to assume a different character from those in the text. The scale is often larger for one thing, and the restraint of the page of writing is less felt. This paved the way for the later medieval miniatures which are more in the nature of virtuoso paintings in books than illustrations.

Full page miniatures and column pictures were not the only sort; there were also marginal illustrations. These appeared after the invention of the codex for there was no place for them in the roll. They may have started as text illustrations and have been pushed into the margins, or the wide outer margins of the codex may simply have offered tempting space to the illuminator. But in many books, theological works especially, those outer margins were occupied by commentaries on the text and sometimes even these 'scholia' were illustrated.

As soon as we start to examine the subject matter and, to a lesser degree, the style of these various types of illustrations we find that the whole system is built up on copying. That is one justification for my dealing in one book with both manuscript and printed illustration—because this copying gave a continuity to versions of the same manuscript work which is comparable with the uniformity in copies of the same printed book, in spite of one being

---

[1] Weitzmann has shown how the illustrator's desire to arrange his miniatures in antithetical pairs occasionally led him to invent a scene that is not in the text to balance one that is.

done by hand and the other by machine. The average illuminator evidently did not regard originality as a virtue or more likely felt it was not for him to initiate changes. Often he went absurdly out of his way to find a model in some other quite alien MS, producing a result which seems grotesque to us. The evils of this continual copying are most clearly seen in the herbals, most of which go back to Dioscorides, who, we know, borrowed much of the text and presumably the illustrations of his first-century *Materia Medica* from Crateuas. That is as far back as we can go for Crateuas, Pliny tells us, illustrated his herbal himself. An illustrated *Dioscorides* [8], one of the handsomest Greek codices in existence, was given as a wedding gift in 512 to Juliana Anicia, daughter of the Emperor of the West. The work was copied countless times down to the end of the Middle Ages, and each time the pictures are farther from the originals, for it never seems to have occurred to the illuminators to go outside and look at the plants they were drawing. By the thirteenth century the drawings, although elaborately framed in burnished gold, were quite unrecognizable. And yet when Dioscorides had earlier been translated into Arabic and Persian he was given new illustrations which were far more naturalistic.

In studying these early illuminated manuscripts we meet the same titles over and over again. It must be remembered that the world's stock of literature was then vastly smaller but even so we are sometimes surprised at the books which were chosen for illustration. Dioscorides of course cried out for pictures but illuminated Gospels and Bibles were fairly rare before the Carolingian period. The *St. Augustine Gospel Book* at Cambridge which dates from about the sixth century and which had a certain influence on Anglo-Saxon illumination was among the earliest [15]. Then there were Boethius and Aratus (who wrote an astronomical poem) and also the *Psychomachia* by Prudentius, an early Christian poem which was much copied between the ninth and eleventh centuries. The plays of Terence were very popular and there seems to have been an unbroken chain right back to Roman origins from which scholars have been able to glean invaluable information about the classical theatre.

In all types of manuscript mistakes sometimes occurred in the copying of pictures and when they did they are often perpetuated because the illuminator seldom seems to have consulted his text. Sometimes a new format called for a new compositional scheme (perhaps extra space to be filled), another fruitful source of error. An interesting example of this is the birth of David quoted by Weitzmann. Now there is no account of this in the Scriptures, but it was often depicted, as if the illuminator was making up his own story. The reason may have been his desire to arrange his full-page miniatures in antithetical pairs. Or sometimes a miniature 'migrated' or was taken from one text and put into another. This might happen quite naturally as for instance in the compilation of a Biblical anthology when a miniature would be borrowed from a Biblical cycle—but it could easily be the wrong illustration.

But the fact that the subject matter of these illustrations was often copied slavishly does not mean that the style of drawing was always the same. That was dependent on the fashion of the period. Conventions enter into it too as when in later copies we find nude figures being clothed. Folds of drapery are one of the first things the experts look at when they are trying to fix the date of a miniature, for nothing was so much affected by stylistic fashions. In fact the style of the model and the style of the period in which the copyist works are far more important than any personal idiosyncracies of the artist. As we might expect, however, the better and more enterprising artists are less faithful to their models than the more mediocre ones and consequently the best illustrated manuscripts are no more accurate iconographically than they are textually. It is obvious that anyone who wishes to find the best reading of

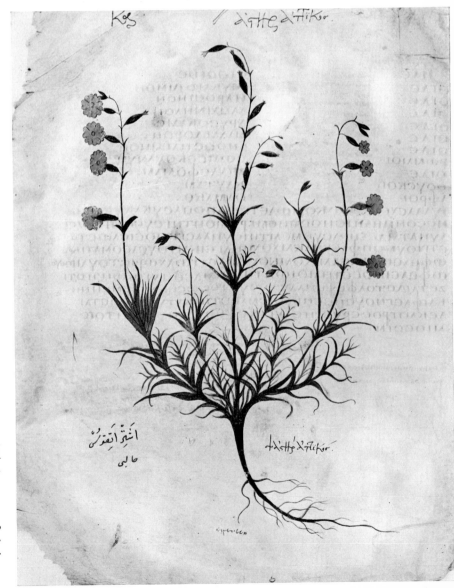

7. *The Vienna Genesis.*
Byzantine 6th century.
Picture area $7\frac{3}{4}'' \times 4''$.
Jacob blesses Ephraim and
Manasseh. Vienna. Vindob.
Theol. Gr. 31

8. Dioscorides: *Codex
Juliana Anicia*. Byzantine,
c. A.D. 500. $15'' \times 13''$.
Vienna. Cod. Med. Graec.
I

9. *The Rossano Gospel Book*. Byzantine, 6th century. 12″ × 10¼″. St. Mark. Rossano Cathedral

10. *The Menologion of Basil II.* Byzantine, 10th century, 14½″ × 11¼″. The scheme shown here of placing the miniatures one at the top and one at the bottom of facing pages is followed rigidly throughout. Vatican Library. Cod. Vat. Gr. 1613

the text will go back to the archetype, but on the other hand the archetype does not always or even often provide the best and most imaginative illustration. And before we pass judgement on all this copying we must remember that our concept of plagiarism did not then exist, any more than it existed for Bach or Handel. As in their music, we find among these miniatures, side by side with an old worn-out formula, a completely new and exciting work of art.

By the sixth century very little remained of the feeling for classical form. In any case the post-classical centuries contributed little that was new to the design and layout of illustration, though in decoration the story is very different as we shall see in Chapter 2. But the revival of decoration was to come from the North-west and was Celtic not classical in origin. Northern art, with its strangely Oriental affinities, had been abstract and ornamental from the earliest times and quite distinct from the art of the Mediterranean. In the meantime illumination everywhere was at a low ebb and the miniature of St. Luke that we show from the *St. Augustine Gospels* exemplifies this[15]. In the Eastern Empire classicism remained and gathered strength in preparation for the great period of Byzantine illumination when it was to return to the West.

BYZANTINE ILLUMINATION

In the year 330 Constantinople became the capital of the Roman Empire and the long strange history of Byzantine illumination began. Roman art, from the end of the third century, was in decline in the West. What took its place in the East was not merely a decadent form of the same thing, but a new blending of Greek, Roman and Oriental elements which, considering their diversity, made a surprisingly homogeneous whole. This marks the end of illustration (the object of which is to clarify) and the beginning of illumination (which seeks to beautify). And as decoration is less liable to development than illustration it is not surprising that Byzantine illumination lasted from the fourth to the fifteenth century with little change in composition, drawing or colours. Very few illuminated manuscripts remain from the fourth or fifth centuries, but from the sixth century we have enough, quite apart from surviving mosaics, to know that Byzantine art already had its own individuality, altogether distinct from that of Rome.

Its characteristics are a new use of colour which was probably borrowed from Persia and the contrast of lights and darks to form a pattern. The darks however are never produced by cast shadows. These disappear together with the desire for the third dimension. But there is enough of the Greek sense of proportion remaining to make a rather uneasy synthesis. As Morey says, Greek design 'depends for its harmony on the different but proportionate size of its units. Greek colour is local colour, used to pick out and emphasize form'. Persian art on the other hand 'may be naturalistic in detail but it is always ornamental in composition and its effect on the illumination of the Eastern Empire was to introduce an absolute colour harmony, by which we mean one to which the forms are subordinated, and a rhythmic design, whereby the eye, instead of resting on a stable unity is forced to move about the pattern by the alternation or recurrence of units that do not differ much in size or emphasis'.

Very soon, however, Byzantine illumination crystallized into forms which were prescribed by the Church. Here, even more than in the West, the Church was at the same time patron and sole producer of the arts; and rules were laid down by the Church which dictated the pose and colour and drawing of all sacred figure subjects and which were scrupulously obeyed. Thus early the method of portraying the Evangelists, for instance, was set for the

11. *A Greek Psalter*. Byzantine, 11th century. 9″ × 7½″. Marginal illustrations by Theodore of Caesarea. The close connexion between Byzantine and Islamic motifs can be seen here. British Museum. Add. MS 19352

whole of the Middle Ages. And Christ, who in classical times was portrayed as young and clean-shaven is shown by Byzantine artists as a mature, bearded figure in the way that He is usually portrayed today.

The angularity and elongation of form which is typical of Byzantine figure drawing appears very early and the Eastern Church's embargo on the representation of nudity must have had a great deal to do with this. Even the study of classical sculpture was frowned on. The human form does not in fact seem to have been properly studied by medieval artists until the advent of the Gothic. Byzantine illumination, with its astonishing power of continuity, twice formed a link with tradition when, in the West, that tradition was in danger of being lost. It was curious, and fortunate, that the first flowering of Byzantine illumination should have been in the sixth century when everywhere else the art was in eclipse. The second and more important renaissance also started when the West was relapsing into chaos after the dissolution of Charlemagne's Empire. It was then that the Byzantine Empire entered on its most prosperous period and between the tenth and twelfth centuries most of her best illuminated books were produced. The chief centres were Constantinople, Alexandria, Antioch and Ephesus and, as one would expect, books from the first two cities tend to be Greek and classical, from the latter two Oriental and decorative. In the interaction of West and East we find the Greek contribution of naturalism and elegance rather outweighed by the intensely dramatic art of the East, with its love of colour and pattern, and complete disregard of perspective. This Oriental cast came mainly from Syria but it was later reinforced by Persia who, although she was not to have her great period of illumination until after the Middle Ages were over, still made her own contribution of elaborate geometrical forms and arabesques thus early.

The Cotton *Genesis* which probably dates from the fifth century, and may have come from Egypt, is one of the earliest surviving Byzantine manuscripts, but unfortunately it has been much damaged by fire. Its miniatures, which are framed and are drawn to the width of the text, are classical in style and show a certain amount of gold. Gold lettering and purple stained vellum were to become a feature of Byzantine work and in the sixth-century Vienna *Genesis* we have an example of the latter [7]. The purple which was obtained from the murex shell had been used by Roman scribes and continued in manuscripts made for princely patrons down to Carolingian times. There is still a strong classical flavour in these pictures which belong rather to the Graeco-Roman decline than to the Byzantine Renaissance. But they are interesting because they are arranged continuously, i.e. successive scenes are shown in the same picture without divisions. There is one picture on each page in a rigidly uniform layout and the text is often abridged so as to accommodate it.

A very much more beautiful manuscript from about the same date and also now in Vienna is the famous *Dioscorides* of the Princess Juliana which has already been mentioned and which was to be copied countless times throughout the Middle Ages. This is a herbal written about 500 for the daughter of the Emperor and is one of the earliest preserved manuscripts with gold backgrounds and also a portrait of the author. Gold lines are used, as in the Cotton *Genesis*, to mark the folds of drapery, and colour generally is as brilliant as in any Byzantine work. Besides many small drawings of plants there are five large miniatures which in their figure drawing show a curious combination of classical and Byzantine styles. The border of one of these miniatures is obviously copied from a mosaic pavement of earlier date, an interesting pointer to one of the channels of Eastern influence in Italy where mosaics by Byzantine craftsmen still survive. The *Rossano Gospel Book* was even more potent in shaping the course of Italian illumination [9]. It dates from this period and it must have come quite early to Italy where it still is. It shows the Byzantine style almost mature, its figures elongated and no naturalism at all. The miniatures are segregated from the text and grouped together at the beginning. Probably this book once contained one of the earliest decorated sets of Canon Tables[1] which are to play an important part in medieval illumination. Perhaps because these vertical lists of references lent themselves to a special treatment or because they came at the beginning of the book, they are often among the most sumptuously decorated of all the pages of medieval manuscripts. Vertical columns topped by an arch act as framework for the lists, and above the arches doves and peacocks are often introduced.

Besides their Canon Tables the Gospel Books, which form the most important class of existing Byzantine books, often contain full-page pictures at the beginning, representing the four Evangelists, each of them enthroned under an arched canopy and holding or writing a copy of his Gospel. A fifth picture shows 'Christ in Majesty', enthroned on a rainbow with the earth at His feet; an oval aureole usually serves as a frame for this picture. And this scheme persists with very little variation in all the Gospel Books of the Middle Ages, not only in the East but in the West as well.

Another book which had an enormous influence, though chiefly in the East, was the cosmography of *Cosmas Indicopleustes*. It was written in the sixth century and the earliest manuscript is illustrated in the pure Byzantine style. It was later to be copied many times in Russia—for Russia and the Balkans came within the orbit of Byzantium of course.

In the eighth century the iconoclast schism brought about a serious decline in the production of books, especially those which were illuminated. Late, however, in the tenth century a revival of classical learning took place under the Emperor Constantine Porphyrogenitus which was to usher in the Golden Age of Byzantine illumination. Artists went back to classical sources for their illustration and invention seems to have been farther from their minds than ever. So many manuscripts have survived from this period that we are fortunate enough to have some which are probably very faithful copies of much older work; in fact our knowledge of classical illustration is almost wholly dependent on these medieval copies, which are far more revealing than the few and fragmentary originals that remain to us.[2]

The famous *Joshua Roll*, which dates from the tenth century, is not however a reliable indication of the antique method of illustration in spite of its archaic form [12]. Between the sixth century when the Vienna *Genesis* was written and the tenth century the continuous frieze was broken up into separate miniatures. And in the *Joshua Roll* we not only see the process at work but we have an object lesson in the danger of trying to lay down hard and fast lines of development; because both styles are here seen side by side. Weitzmann thinks that the painter for some unexplained reason transferred a series of separate codex pictures to his frieze which might account for the fact that some of the scenes are self-contained and are isolated by space on either side. In the *Paris Psalter*, a Byzantine codex of the same century, the miniature has separated itself even more completely as it had already done in the West; and the picture with a single figure has come into its own. But there are other manuscripts with lively marginal drawings in a realistic style which contrasts strongly with the monumentality of the *Paris Psalter* [11 and 13].

This period of Byzantine illumination yields many splendid books, particularly Bibles and Gospel Books. The Vatican has a Bible dating from the first half of the tenth century which

---

[1] The Canons of Bishop Eusebius are a set of ten tables giving parallel passages in the Gospels which usually preceded Gospel manuscripts.

[2] Such copies were being made for antiquaries as late as the seventeenth century.

12. *The Joshua Roll*. Byzantine, 10th century. Height 12″. Vatican Library. Palat. Gr. 431

13. *The Paris Psalter*. Byzantine, 10th century. 14¼″ × 10¼″. David with his harp.
Paris B.N. Cod. Gr. 139

14. *The Ostromirov Gospels*. Byzantine, A.D. 1056.
St. Luke. Saltykov-Shchedrin Library, Leningrad

15. *The St. Augustine Gospel Book*. Roman, probably 6th century. 10″ × 7½″. St. Luke.
Cambridge, Corpus Christi College. Cod. 286

shows the partial synthesis of classic and Oriental styles. And an even more interesting manuscript of the same period, also in the Vatican, is the *Menologion of Basil II* [10]. This is a collection of the lives of the saints and it contains over 400 miniatures painted by eight different artists, who signed their names in the margins. We must assume that the whole of each miniature was painted by the artist who signed it and yet there is a lack of stylistic unity within the miniatures themselves. Weitzmann thinks that this is because, the work being an anthology, several different cycles were drawn on belonging to the various texts which were put together. He calls it a polycyclic manuscript and believes that most of the illustrated Bibles fall into this class.

After the fall of Constantinople in 1453 Russia (soon to be freed from Mongol control) became the artistic and political successor of Byzantium. But long before then she was producing magnificent books in the Byzantine tradition like the *Ostromirov Gospels* (1056–67) [14], and the *Uriev Gospels* (1120–8). These all appeared under the Mongol regime which confined Russia within an iron curtain as exclusive as any she has since devised herself; and one result of this was that the Byzantine tradition was continued as rigidly as before. *The Manual of Dionysius*, which goes back to the twelfth century, laid down what subjects were to be illustrated from the Bible and how they were to be represented.

2

Medieval Illumination in the West

By the seventh century the Church, which had been the first to exploit the invention of the codex, had almost a monopoly of book production, and until the middle of the thirteenth century books were nearly all written in the religious houses. Whether they were always decorated there is a different matter and although it seems probable that, to begin with, they were, it is known for certain that later they were sent away for illumination, or it was done by visiting freelance artists. In these early days it was Gospel Books that were most frequently decorated but later we find secular books competing with sacred. In fact there was no competition, because our distinction between sacred and profane was not valid then. The use of classical models or styles, which often seems such a strange feature of Biblical illumination, simply means that for those fortunate beings everything in heaven and earth was a single order. As Swarzenski says: 'However great the importance of the book as the chief vehicle and agent of literary, artistic and iconographical traditions may have been for the Middle Ages, its evaluation and its unique position lie in its consecrated character. It elucidates the Christian myth that Christ is represented with a book in His hands; no other religion has given any of its gods this attribute.'

With this belief it is not surprising that they saw nothing incongruous in putting all their skill and lavishness into the decoration of sacred texts; anything less must have seemed wrong. The magnificent books of the Northumbrian School were far different in this respect from the fifteenth-century *Books of Hours*. The former were made for the service of God and their aesthetic appeal was incidental; the latter were made for the eye of some princely patron to whom the text must have been merely an excuse for the pictures.[1] For the Middle Ages the word was of far greater importance than the picture, and this attitude persists after the introduction of printing. Even though the miniature had by then emancipated itself and the book painting was almost independent of the text yet the printed illustration, in the block books for instance, is only there, one feels, to attract the illiterate.

The technical processes of illumination lasted with very little alteration from classical times down to the time of the Carolingian Renaissance. After the tenth century we notice the same fault which was apparent in the Vienna *Genesis* and indeed in the Egyptian *Book of the Dead*; the more beautiful the illumination the less accurate the text. In other words the scribes were becoming mere copyists while the illuminators were becoming painters. Middleton quotes a few amusing comments written at the ends of later manuscripts by the scribes which reflect not only the tediousness of the task but also the loss of a sense of divine duty; e.g. 'Scribere qui nescit, nullam putat esse laborem' (He who knows not how to write

---

[1] But many of the best Carolingian and Ottonian books were also made for princely patrons and contain portraits of them.

thinks it no labour) or 'Vinum scriptori reddatur de meliori' (Let wine of the best be given to the writer) or—significantly from a French monk—'Detur pro pena scriptori pulchra puella'.

At the beginning of our period there was the chaos and unsettlement that came in the train of the barbarian invasions of the Graeco-Roman Empire. Books could always be written and read in the most troublous times but the decoration of books was one of the first luxuries to be dispensed with when times were unpropitious. In the same way the copying of books was a mechanical task that did not require much skill or even a high degree of literacy. But the copying of illustrations was a very different matter and so an illustrated book when copied often became an unillustrated one. Fortunately however there remained a corner of the Western world to which neither Roman nor barbarian invaders had penetrated; and it was in Ireland that the illuminated book revived when everywhere else except in Northumbria it was at its worst. And from here it went with the Irish missionaries to Scotland and Northern England, to France and to Switzerland.

After St. Patrick's mission in the fifth century Irish missionaries went to Iona and from there evangelized Scotland, but when they reached Northern England they found in Northumbria religious communities newly established by missionaries from Europe. The clash of ideas and styles seems to have been amazingly fruitful, and it was from Northumbria that the greatest books of the seventh century came. The missionaries from Europe had brought with them Italian books illustrated with miniatures in the classical style, like that in [15]. But it was some time before the naturalism of this art had effect. The native genius, whether Irish or Northumbrian, was for pattern. And in the *Book of Durrow* (*c.* 670) which is one of the earliest books to survive from this period there are, for one solitary human figure, and that not very convincing, many whole pages of pure pattern—a thing unheard of in the south where ornament was only used to mark the beginning and end of a chapter or to frame a miniature [17].

This type of pattern is sometimes called Irish and the *Book of Durrow* itself was for long thought to have been written in Ireland. It is now believed to have come from England though probably written and decorated by Irishmen. The discovery of Anglo-Saxon treasure at Sutton Hoo in 1938 not only revealed the excellence of seventh-century Anglo-Saxon jewellery design, it also provided many striking points of similarity between that design and the decoration of the *Book of Durrow*. In England as well as Ireland the goldsmiths worked side by side with the illuminators in the same monastery and sometimes indeed both arts were practised by the same monk, who thus became the decorator of the inside and the outside of the book. This reminds us of the unity of the arts in those days. There was none of our modern division into major and minor arts, and the metal-worker was as highly esteemed as the painter. And while many of their stock designs were undoubtedly Irish in origin, many of them also had a classical ancestry. It has been pointed out that several of the spiral patterns found in Irish manuscripts are almost identical with forms in gold ornaments of the Greek Mycenean period 'showing the remarkable sameness of invention in the human mind at a certain stage of development, whatever the time or place may be'. Oriental influences also are seen in some patterns, no doubt derived from Eastern carpets and textiles which were now being imported for ecclesiastical use. Françoise Henry has drawn attention to similarities between the ornament in the *Book of Durrow* and Coptic and Syrian illumination; and she thinks that the Irish monks may have had Oriental models before them. But they never followed the rigid symmetry of the Moslem pattern-makers.

The original Celtic contribution was not so much the patterns themselves as the use of those patterns, particularly in the decoration of the initial. The importance of the initial in Western illumination can be traced back to sixth-century Italy; and in some of these early manuscripts it often dominates the whole page. Occasionally it is subservient to the miniature when the latter is placed above it, but more often the initial has pride of place at the top of the page; and it retained its importance for about 600 years after which it dwindled in size; but even then its tail or its branches often formed a border to envelop the text.

St. Aidan came from Iona and founded the Abbey of Lindisfarne in 635 and for the next hundred years Northumbria was pre-eminent in the art of book illustration as it was to be again more than a thousand years later in Bewick's lifetime. The clash of Irish and classical influences was echoed in the rivalry between the Celtic and Roman churches which was resolved at the Synod of Whitby (664) in favour of Rome. Thereafter, although Irish script continued to be used, classicism increased, helped by the many illuminated manuscripts and paintings that monks like Benedict Biscop brought with them from Rome. The *Lindisfarne Gospels* is the monument of this period and fortunately this great book has come down to us in wonderful condition in spite of falling into the sea during an invasion by Vikings. It dates from about 710 and was written in a fine black ink, much superior to the brownish ink used in contemporary Continental manuscripts. We have the names of the three monks who produced it, Eadfrith the scribe and illuminator,[1] Aethelwold and Bilfrith the binders. It is with the work of Eadfrith that we are here concerned and the most striking thing about it is the combination of the Byzantine figures of the evangelists with the wonderful pages of Celtic ornament. Irish illuminators seemed to be incapable of drawing the human figure and even in the later *Book of Kells* it is subordinated to pattern as if it was metal-work, and is almost unrecognizable. In the *Lindisfarne Gospels* classical and Byzantine influences are so strong that the book has been called one of the earliest links between Oriental and Occidental art. The use here of gold which is never found in contemporary Irish books must also have been revolutionary [18].

The *Book of Kells* is now generally agreed to have been written towards the end of the eighth century and there is little doubt that it originated in Ireland. It is remarkable for the intricacy of its decoration [19] which must be seen to be believed. Westwood calculated 158 interlacements in the space of a square inch and pointed out that all can be followed, none breaking off or leading to an impossible knot. The general effect of all this ingenuity however is often far from beautiful. The shapes of the letters are hopelessly obscured and some of the colour combinations are frankly hideous. It seems likely that several artists worked on the book, some good and some bad. There is nothing of the frozen perfection of Lindisfarne here but instead an immense vigour, and a demonstration of the somewhat perverse Irish delight in complication for its own sake which we find also for instance in the work of James Joyce. It is significant too that the text is far less perfect than in the *Lindisfarne Gospels*. The book represents the peak of Irish achievement however and none of the later manuscripts can come near it. Most of these later books, the ninth-century *Gospels of MacDurnan* for instance, were not intended to compete with the large altar books and were smaller and more portable. In them illustration naturally played a smaller part.

Meanwhile, Bede whose learning had shed so much lustre on Northumbria had died and his mantle fell on Alcuin who lived in York. But learning was not confined to the north of England, although the greatest illuminated books were produced there at this time. It was a West Saxon, Boniface, who became Archbishop of Mainz and founded the Abbey of Fulda

---

[1] Françoise Henry however believes that the separation of the scribe from the illuminator had already begun and doubts whether Eadfrith was really responsible for the illumination.

which became the centre of German learning. Already St. Gall in Switzerland and Luxeuil in Burgundy, founded by Irish missionaries, had produced many manuscripts of the Irish type, and these three monasteries had a great deal to do with the Carolingian Renaissance. In 768 Charlemagne was elected King of the Franks and soon after he summoned Alcuin from England to supervise the revision of church books. Perhaps too Alcuin was behind the reformation of handwriting which Charlemagne instituted after he had become Emperor of the West in 800. So it will be seen how great was Britain's part in this Renaissance.

Under the Merovingian Dynasty which preceded the Carolingian, Frankish and Lombardic illumination was decorative rather than illustrative, and what remains, e.g. the *Orosius* at Laon, is not very impressive in quality. Initials are fantastic, colouring is crude and the human figure is seldom attempted. The eighth-century *Sacramentary of Gellone* from the south of France has however a certain barbaric splendour. And we find the products of this native school continuing side by side with the more ambitious Carolingian works. Against this background Charlemagne set out deliberately to revive the spirit of the Roman Empire, the result being that most Carolingian illumination is imitative. The Ada school owed most to the late Latin style, the Franco-Saxon to Ireland and that of Tours went back to an earlier classical period than Ada. Only the later Rheims contribution was wholly original.

To begin with, however, the effect of the Carolingian Renaissance on illustration was utilitarian. It sought to teach, to clarify a text, and it naturally looked to the south, the home of illustration, rather than to the north, the home of decoration. As time goes on Carolingian books became increasingly elaborate and there are Byzantine touches in the gold lettering and purple vellum of such manuscripts as the *Evangeliarum of Charlemagne* which was written (*c.* 781) for the Emperor by a monk called Godescalc, and the *Ada Gospel Book* of about the same date with its elaborate purple-stained pages, produced for Charlemagne's sister. The *Harley Golden Gospels* in the British Museum (*c.* 800) which is all inscribed in gold, provides a very early example of an ornamental title-page [20]. Gospel Books were still the commonest type of manuscript just as they were in Byzantium but the Evangelists are now shown as youthful idealized types instead of the old men of Byzantine manuscripts. The general treatment of figures is flat (though there are occasional attempts at modelling) and the outlines seem to have been drawn first in red paint. Then the spaces were filled in with washes of colour mixed with a medium which gave a very glossy surface. Drapery was represented by lines drawn on top of the wash. And in some manuscripts a very splendid effect was achieved by the use of silver to contrast with gold.

Side by side with these rigid conventional portraits which owe so much to Byzantine art, there are also occasional miniatures which lean more to the Roman style in their illustrative tendencies. Although in the best manuscripts like the *Aachen Gospels* the figure drawing is light and brilliant, in most it is still clumsy; but generally the backgrounds make some attempt at naturalism. 'The old contrast between Greek realistic and Latin abstract art, between art aiming at a sympathetic representation of the outside world and art based on purely conceptual design presents itself in a new form as a contrast between the exuberant expression of human emotion and the purely impersonal ornamental display' says Kitzinger. Towards the end of the Carolingian period we find a mixture rather than a synthesis of the two.

Carolingian illumination reached its highest point in the ninth century during the reigns of Lothair and Charles the Bald. Decoration still surpasses figure drawing (the old Irish patterned figures are still to be found) but subjects for miniatures are becoming more varied. Now besides portraits of the Evangelists we find frontispieces showing Kings; there is for instance a Metz Gospel Book in Paris with a portrait of King Lothair. The Benedictine monasteries at Paris, St. Denis, Rheims, Tours and Metz are the chief centres of book production during this period.

Ascribed to the School of Tours during this century are the two earliest complete illustrated Bibles to have survived, the *Grandval* and *Vivian* Bibles. Weitzmann thinks that the miniatures are made up of several cycles, since it is unlikely that so large a book as the Bible could have had a comprehensively illustrated archetype. But there were cycles for each book —even for the Prophets—though none of these have survived. The effort of combining these different cycles, many of them in different styles, must have been considerable and it had its inevitable effect on the final result. But a book like the *Great Bible of Corbie* (*c*. 880) shows that a wonderfully rich effect could still be obtained in spite of varying styles [23].

These manuscripts, especially the *Vivian Bible*, show the disintegration of the cyclic system and the breaking up of the traditional interconnections between pictures which derived from the frieze. Miniatures are now becoming separate compositions and the artists begin (some 700 years after the introduction of the codex) to have a feeling for the page.

Some time during this century appeared the style of drawing which is associated with Rheims and its famous *Utrecht Psalter*. It consists of outline drawing, sketchy and vigorous, and while it is totally unlike the usual Carolingian style both styles are sometimes found together in the same manuscript. It is seen occasionally in classical manuscripts but its abrupt appearance now and sudden widespread popularity present one of the great mysteries of medieval art. With its unadorned impressionistic line, its fluttering draperies and its figures all in violent motion it must have produced on the contemporary eye an overpowering contrast to the static, highly coloured illumination of the time, the more so as it was applied to the same traditional subject matter [24].

Of the *Utrecht Psalter*, which is the masterpiece in this manner, Hanns Swarzenski says that its drawings rival those of Leonardo, Rembrandt and Van Gogh and thus have their place among the few genuinely original productions in the history of art. The fact that it was itself almost certainly a copy[1] of a previous manuscript does not alter this fact. The 180 drawings (there is one for every Psalm) are not themselves coloured, but coloured outlines and washes are often used in copies of this book [25]. Frames are never put round the drawings and where they are implied they are often broken through as it were by the feverish activity of the figures. Later there is a tendency to elongate and stylize but at its best the work is wonderfully vigorous and expressive. This style, which embraced not only drawing but all the decorative arts as well, had enormous influence throughout the whole of Northwest Europe and it helped to form the Romanesque and Gothic styles. When the *Utrecht Psalter* came to England at the end of the tenth century it was copied three times in 200 years, and each copy was a new work of art. But before that its influence was seen in the *Bury St. Edmunds Psalter* (now in the Vatican Library), which dates from early in the eleventh century. Here most of the drawings are marginal and how admirably the style is suited to this sort of thumbnail sketch can be seen in Fig. 21.

So far we have concentrated on book illustration in France and England because there the most far-reaching developments were taking place. But all this time beautiful manuscripts were being produced in Italy, Spain and Southern Germany. These however were still in the Late Antique tradition and what was happening in the north seems to have had curiously little effect on them. Of early Italian illumination little remains to enable us to judge its quality accurately. But we do know that Byzantine influence was very strong and

---

[1] E. M. Thompson pointed out that the text is written in archaic rustic capitals presumably to preserve the same relative positions of text and drawings as in the prototype.

16. *The Benedictional of St. Aethelwold.* English, 10th century. $11\frac{1}{2}'' \times 8\frac{1}{2}''$.
British Museum. Add. 49598

with it is also found the Hiberno-Saxon type of decoration. This is not so strange when we remember that there were Irish foundations like Bobbio in Northern Italy; and some authorities believe that this style originated in Italy and migrated to Ireland and Northumbria. Books like the *Bobbio Psalter*, now at Munich, however, have an almost undiluted Byzantine flavour.

By the tenth century we find manuscripts in all countries with whole pages occupied by pairs of miniatures, placed one above the other. Sometimes as in the St. Gall *Book of Maccabees* two pages of pictures face each other and the illustration is thus separated even more completely from the text. This segregation, which we noticed very early on in the sixth-century *Rossano Gospel Book*, had the technical advantage that the scribe and the illustrator could work separately and this no doubt was often done, their sections being collated later. Short inscriptions were then added to the drawings to identify them and so the explanatory caption or legend grew up.

During the second half of the ninth century Alfred was reigning in Wessex and his capital was Winchester. The northern part of England had repeatedly been devastated by Danish invaders and, although Alfred was himself a scholar and encouraged book production by importing instructors from France, the art of illumination had suffered a setback and took some time to recover. It was given the vital impetus by the monastic reforms which were started on the Continent by Odo of Cluny and in England by St. Dunstan. In Winchester, St. Aethelwold (who probably brought the *Utrecht Psalter* to England) was associated with St. Dunstan in his reforms, and the *Benedictional of St. Aethelwold* (*c.* 970) is one of the great books of this school [16]. It has 28 full-page miniatures, mostly scenes from the life of Christ and each framed with an elaborate border. The figure drawing in these shows a distinct advance on any previous English manuscript, but it owes little to the *Utrecht Psalter* except for a lightening of the rather heavy Carolingian style on which it is based.

Canute in the eleventh century did a great deal to encourage literature and art and for the latter purpose is said to have introduced large numbers of Roman manuscripts, presumably in the Byzantine style which was then so much favoured in Italy. But although due weight must be given to the Byzantine element in the Romanesque work of the following century, its influence in Britain as compared with the Italian and Ottonian Schools was curiously ephemeral, and by the thirteenth century that influence was quite thrown off. The *Pontifical of St. Dunstan* in Paris is a good example of early eleventh-century work, but it has no gold. Instead it has the drawings in coloured outline that were so characteristic of English illumination. Sometimes in manuscripts of this period we find the outlines filled in with colours, sometimes the outline is in brown ink shaded with colour. But it is essentially linear and it is in this type of drawing that English artists excelled. Another unfinished manuscript of this century in the Cottonian Collection gives us a valuable insight into the way the illuminators worked in stages on their books. This one contains some outline drawings tinted with colour; but most are painted with body colour in various stages and we can see that the colours of dresses were often applied without any previous outline. Afterwards the figures were drawn in outline and last of all the features were added.

The Norman Conquest, which had such a serious effect on our native literature, caused no break in the continuity of illumination. National boundaries as we know them meant so much less in those days and the only result was to bring the French and English styles closer together and to foster the Anglo-Norman school on both sides of the Channel. There were signs of this *rapprochement* before 1066 and it seems likely that the Conquest only hastened a

17. *The Book of Durrow*. Hiberno-Saxon, 7th century. $9\frac{3}{4}'' \times 6\frac{1}{2}''$. A decorative folio. Trinity College, Dublin

18. *The Lindisfarne Gospels*. Hiberno-Saxon, 8th century. $15\frac{3}{4}'' \times 12''$. St. Luke. British Museum. Cotton Nero D VI

19. *The Book of Kells*. Hiberno-Saxon, 8th century. 13″ × 10″. Trinity College, Dublin

20. *The Harley Golden Gospels*. Carolingian, 9th century. 14½″ × 10″. British Museum. Harl. 2788

21. *The Bury St. Edmunds Psalter*. English, 11th century. 12¾″ × 9¼″. Marginal drawing for Psalm LXV v. 12. Vatican. Reg. Lat. 12

22. *Exultet Roll*. Italian, 11th century. Width 11″. British Museum. Add. 30337

23. *The Great Bible of S. Paolo fuori le Mura*. Carolingian, 9th century. 18″ × 10½″. St. Jerome correcting the Bible. Rome

OLAVABOPERSINCV
LASNOCTESLECTUMME
UMLACRIMISMEISSTRA
TUMMEUMRIGABO
VIIPSALMVS
PROVERBIS

DISCEDITEAMEOMNES
QVIOPERAMINIINI
QVITATEM · QMEXAV
DIVITDNSVOCEFLETVSMEI
DAVIDQVEM
CHVSIFILII

CRVBESCANTICONIVN
BENTVRVEHEMENTER
OMNESINIMICIMEICON
VERTANTVRETERVBES
CANTAVDEVELOCITER ·
CANTAVITDNO
CEMICMAIORATRIC
DISIGIVMTISCAVD
KORVBLRAPIG
RADIIC

DNEDSMEVSIN
TESPERAVISALVUM
MEFACEXOMNIBUS
PERSEQVENTIBUSME
ENTERAME
EQVANDORAPIATVT

TVD SIESTINIQVITAS
INMANIBVSMEIS
SIREDDIRETRIBVENTI
BVSMIHIMALA · DECI
DAMMERITOABINIMI
CISMEISINANIS

ETGLORIAMMEAM
INPVIVEREMDEDVCAT
DIABPSALMA
EXVRCEDNEINIRAIVA
AEXALTARGINIRIC

24. *The Utrecht Psalter*. Carolingian, 9th century. 12¼″ × 9¾″. Illustration to Psalm VI.
University Library, Utrecht

lauabo persingulas noc
tes lectum meū lacrimis
stratum meum rigabo ;
Turbatus est prea oculus
meus. inueteraui inter
omnes inimicos meos ;

Discedite ame omnes qui
operamini iniquitatem .
quio exaudiuit dns uoce
fletus mei. exaudiuit dns
deprecationem meam.dns
orationem meā adsupsit ;

rubescant & conturbentur
omnes inimici mei. auer
tantur retrorsum&eru
bescant ualde uelociter ;

PSALMVS DAVID QVE
DNE DS MEVS
INTE speraui libera
me abomnibus perse
quentibus me &eripe me ;
Nequando rapiat ut leo

CANTAVIT PRO VERBIS
mihi mala·decidam meri
to abinimicis meis inanis;
Persequatur inimicus ani
mam meam &comprx
hendat eam

CHVSI.   ·VII·
Exurge dne ds meus inpre
cepto quod mandasti.&si
nagoga populorum circū
dabit te

25. Copy of the *Utrecht Psalter*. English, 11th century. 15″ × 12¼″. Illustration to Psalm VI.
British Museum, Harley 603

52

26. *The Bamberg Apocalypse*. German, *c.* 1020. Reichenau School. 11¼″ × 8″. The overthrow of the false prophet. Note the communication between the upper and lower registers. Bamberg State Library. Cod. Bib. 140

27. *The Maestricht Book of Hours*. Netherlands, 13th century. 3½″ × 2½″. British Museum. Stowe 17

28. *The Stavelot Bible*. Netherlands, 1097. 22¾″ × 15″. Written by Goderamus and Ernestus.
British Museum. Add. MS 28107

54

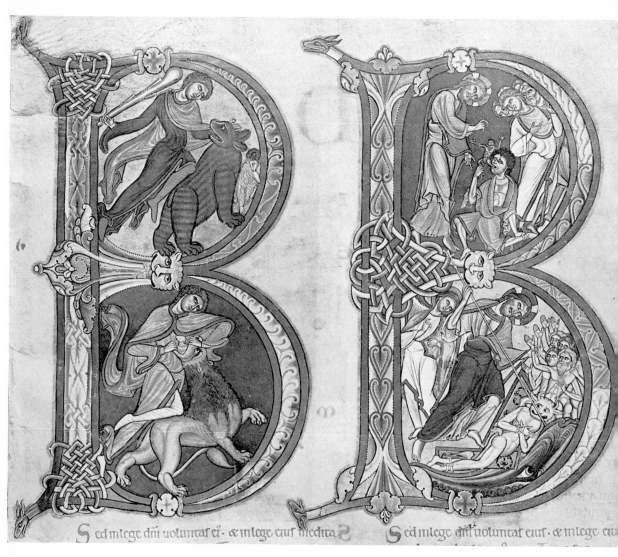

Sed inlege dni uoluntas ei· & inlege ein medita

Sed inlege dni uoluntas eius· & inlege ein

29. *The Winchester Bible*. English, 12th century.
$23'' \times 15\frac{3}{4}''$. The initial on the left contains Old Testament scenes, that on the right the New Testament antitype. Old Minster, Winchester

30. De Borron: *L'Histoire du Graal*. French, 13th century. $19\frac{1}{2}'' \times 13\frac{1}{2}''$. Paris. B.N. Fr. 95

natural process. Nevertheless it was the collapse of the Carolingian Empire that marked the end of a truly international manner and the beginning of national styles. English illumination, too, was so far ahead of French at this period that it gave more than it received in the exchange. Just before the Conquest the Harley version of the *Utrecht Psalter* had been made in coloured outline. Far from being a slavish copy it is a completely new work of art which in its rejection of all naturalistic illusion foreshadowed the Romanesque style [25]. By the time the next copy was made in the middle of the twelfth century Romanesque had arrived and the drawings have become solid and stylized, 'the triumph', as Clark calls it, 'of symbol over sensation'.

After the Carolingian period until almost the end of the tenth century there was a period of anarchy and disorder in France when few books were produced. Then, however, the revival of monasticism which had already had such a great effect in England spread from Cluny. *Beatus* manuscripts copied from a famous Spanish prototype (see page 81) are among the most important of this period; and Joan Evans has shown how great an effect they had on sculpture. She goes so far as to say, 'To the illuminated manuscripts nine-tenths of the sculptural innovations of the second half of the eleventh century can be directly traced.' It was in decorative initials rather than illustration proper that this period excelled and by the middle of the twelfth century even these had become monochrome in manuscripts, by the Cistercian Order of 1134.

Italian illumination, which had produced under Carolingian influences several fine books during the tenth century like the *Ambrosian Psalter*, was in eclipse during the eleventh century. Germany and Northern Italy were politically connected at this time so that it is not surprising to find echoes of Ottonian illumination in the manuscripts of Lombardy and Tuscany. In the Romanesque period the best work came from the great Benedictine monastery at Montecassino. Books like *The Life of St. Benedict* have, as one would expect, a strong Byzantine flavour. From Montecassino also came many fine examples of *Exultet* rolls on which was inscribed a liturgy illustrated with pictures. These latter were the opposite way up to the text so that they could be seen by the congregation while the priest read from the roll [22].

For the true inheritors of the Carolingian tradition we must look to Germany which now was also the centre of the Holy Roman Empire. Here in 962 Otto I became Emperor and was succeeded by Otto II and Otto III who gave their name to the Ottonian revival of the arts. It was a period of political aggrandizement for the Empire too and by the twelfth century it was the dominant power in Europe. The Emperors ruled from Bamberg which became a cultural centre, attracting many Greek artists. And to Bamberg from Constantinople, where Byzantine art was now at its peak, came Otto II's wife Theophanu.

But Bamberg did not become one of the great centres of Ottonian book illumination until comparatively late. From the Benedictine Abbey of Reichenau came the best German manuscripts of the tenth and eleventh centuries and its influence spread as far as Trèves and Hildesheim[1] where there were also famous schools. The Heidelberg *Sacramentary* was one of the most influential Reichenau books and its decorative work was copied *ad nauseam* during the following century. The *Egbert Pericope*, which is a more interesting work because

---

[1] Hildesheim was famous for its metal-work too, which is much more to our taste than its illumination. This was a period of integration of the arts in Germany. Contemporary murals and stained glass were often based on manuscript illumination, and books like the *St. Bernard Gospel Book* show a hard unyielding quality in their illustrations as if they were from the hand of a metal-worker.

of its miniatures deriving from Roman models, is much less typical of the Ottonian taste for heavy, isolated figures. This was a decorative period with its strapwork initials, its bird and serpent patterns, its vine stems and foliage, all of them showing an astonishing persistence. Monumentality is achieved by strict symmetry in the use of ornament and by reducing background to a minimum. It is, as Jantzen says, an art of the significant gesture rather than of naturalistic representation; and this can be seen in the reproduction from the Bamberg *Apocalypse*, another Reichenau book [26].

By now the *Pericope* had appeared, the collection of Gospel texts arranged not in their original sequence but according to their place in the liturgy. This made the insertion of author portraits impracticable and it forced artists to look for new illustrations. Rather than invent they usually had recourse to the old cycles.

From Ratisbon early in the eleventh century came the *Uta Gospels* in which, as Herbert says, the Gothic miniature of 200 years later is clearly foreshadowed and in which the symbolism is heightened by mysticism. This was perhaps the beginning of the Romanesque revival which resulted from the impact of Byzantine on Ottonian art. It did not appear in England until the twelfth century; but the results are curiously similar in both countries—largeness, severity and dignity together with a subtle beauty of design which often eludes at the first glance. There is another connexion too in the traces of the Northumbrian style of decoration which are found in German work of this period; only now the patterns of interlaced foliage have taken on a distinctly Teutonic flavour. In Germany particularly there is a love of symbolism which is seen at its best in the famous *Hortus Deliciarum*. This was a sort of philosophical and religious compendium which the Abbess of Hohenburg wrote and illuminated for her nuns and which is a forerunner of later Emblem Books. But more typical of the Carolingian tradition are the big Bibles like the *Arnstein Bible* in the British Museum with its huge initials and bright rather florid colours. Although it was produced under Cluny restrictions[1] it is nevertheless profusely decorated in a style that reflects contemporary architecture.

By now illuminated books were also being produced in the Netherlands. Later on Flemish illumination was to lead the world but at this time it followed in the wake of France, and it is often difficult to distinguish between German and Dutch or French and Flemish work. Enormous Bibles were also produced and the *Stavelot Bible*, which actually preceded the German ones we have just mentioned, shows the influence of the Rheims school as well as of Byzantium [28]. By the beginning of the thirteenth century Flemish artists had begun to demonstrate their superiority to those of Holland and Germany, although they were still behind French and English illuminators; and long before the end of the century they were producing books like the minute *Maestricht Book of Hours* in the British Museum that could hardly be surpassed anywhere [27].

The Romanesque style which came to fruition in Germany, France and England during the twelfth century is generally supposed to have been the offspring of the Ottonian schools of the tenth century and the Rheims style, unpromising though such a marriage might seem to be. Byzantine influences were strong in the German books and this made for solemnity and rigidity in illumination, for upright poses rather than diagonals which have been common hitherto. But fortunately the Rheims manner was powerful too, especially in England, and while it lightened the Ottonian style its own extravagances were in turn curbed. The synthesis which resulted has a powerful beauty and impressiveness of its own, not so im-

[1] See page 58.

mediately attractive as the Gothic which followed, but not so prone either to descend to mere prettiness. Its severity, or what seems severity to us, had no spiritual counterpart, for this was an age of devotional fervour which produced hymns like *Jesu dulcis memoria*. 'It seems to be,' says Morey, 'the maturity of centuries of growth, and the universality of the Romanesque manner in its larger aspect shows how completely it met the needs of European thought and feeling in the centuries of the Crusades.'

Byzantium and the West shared one characteristic in the tenth century which helps to account for the monumentality to be found in Eastern and Western books and which flowered 200 years later in the Romanesque style. This potent thing was the increasing influence of the Church, helped forward in the West by the reform of the monasteries. 'The need for expressing and propagating transcendental truth,' says Kitzinger, 'turns the scales against the classical tradition in art which came so much into prominence during the Carolingian period.' With the rejection of classical models came a new Biblical iconography in the typological system which interpreted the scheme of Redemption by means of parallels from the Old and New Testaments. This applied not only to Biblical illustration but to other works which we should think of as secular. All of them, even the Bestiaries, were made to contribute to this central doctrine of the Church.

There is no abrupt break in style between the eleventh and twelfth centuries in any of the arts except perhaps in architecture. From now on large scale painting and sculpture came into their own and the influence of their monumentality is seen in the organization of the book. Even the text page now has a fixed plan and its initials become 'historiated' rather than decorated. In the historiated initial text is intimately combined with illustration and the fusion of text, illustration and decoration is complete.

The *Albani Psalter* from St. Albans is one of the very first manuscripts in which we find the real Romanesque manner, but the *Winchester Bible* (c. 1160) is the great English monument of the period; and it is indeed monumental in every sense of the word. Perhaps, as Oakeshott says, it attempts too much and makes illustrations of what should have been wall-paintings. Like so many of the great books of the Middle Ages it contains the work of several hands and as it was many years in the making it shows at least two widely differing styles; there is the dynamic style reminiscent of the *Utrecht Psalter* with hot colours and everything in violent motion; and there is the Byzantine style, classical and static in cooler colours, using drapery to outline the body [29].

In the *Winchester Bible* there are initials that stretch the whole length of the page, nearly twenty inches. These contain actual illustrations and they are called historiated initials to distinguish them from initials which are merely decorated. Sometimes the illustration is fitted into the initial without affecting its structure, sometimes it is planned (or distorted) into the shape of the letter itself. This type of initial appeared first in about the eighth century and it continued side by side with the more popular decorated initial right down to Victorian times, when it was relegated to children's books.

The twelfth century was a period of developing technique. Decoration which, as far as we know, had always been carried out by the illustrator or miniaturist now began to demand its own practitioners. But in spite of their accomplishment the work does not seem to have been done by such skilled artists as the miniatures. Towards the end of the century an even greater innovation was brought about by the discovery that gold could be put on vellum by means of gold leaf with far more brilliant effect than fluid gold could ever produce. The leaf was laid on top of a smooth hard pad or mordant which not only set it in relief but also allowed it to be burnished.

As the century wore on the Rheims element seems to lose ground in England, though it was to reappear later in the work of Matthew Paris. There is little of it in the *Lambeth Bible*, which was roughly contemporary with the *Winchester Bible*; and when at the very end of the century the *Utrecht Psalter* is copied at Canterbury for the third time it is quite transformed. And it is preceded by a series of Bible pictures grouped together in a style that was to become popular in the following century. But things were different on the other side of the Channel where the Gothic style was already on the way. As if conserving her energies for her most glorious period of illumination France produced fewer great books in this century than England or Germany. No doubt Cistercian discouragement of illumination in the twelfth century had something to do with it too, but inasmuch as this concentrated attention on the calligraphic decoration of initials it may have been beneficial rather than otherwise. However in the middle of the twelfth century the Cistercians forbade even the decoration of initials, and illumination gradually passed into secular hands. Literature too became more secular; and a few manuscripts survive with lightly scribbled instructions to the illuminator on the illustration of unfamiliar subjects for which tradition afforded him no guidance. An early thirteenth-century *Treatise on Surgery* by Roger of Parma shows a curious combination of the sacred and the profane. In it are several pages of small pictures, nine to the page with backgrounds of alternating colours. The top row of each page shows scenes from the life of Christ while the lower two rows show surgical cases, delineated with an extraordinary degree of accuracy [32].

There has often been a remarkable coincidence between the architecture of buildings and the architecture of books; this is especially noticeable in the Middle Ages when all the arts were more closely inter-connected than they are now and when architecture and illumination were both practised by ecclesiastics. Just as the solid heavy Romanesque buildings gave way to the lighter airier Gothic so the same thing happened in illumination. The whole scale suddenly decreases and books become smaller and more delicate. The first Gothic churches that were built in the Ile de France during the second half of the century were not, it is true, any smaller than Romanesque churches which came before them, but they were totally different. By the last decade the Gothic style in architecture had been perfected and pointed arches were already appearing in manuscript decoration. Text and initials, which were distinct in Romanesque design, both assume a certain spikiness which has a unifying effect. Nor was it long before the fashion affected clothes for we find in these same miniatures the tall headgear of the women and the long pointed shoes of the men together with a general elongation of the human figure and an insistence on parallel verticals that is the artist's own contribution to the pattern. It is still a pattern rather than a picture, flat and two-dimensional like the stained glass of the time which it often closely resembles.

The leadership which France now begins to assume in the art of illumination and which was unquestionably hers by the end of the thirteenth century is one of the most striking things in the history of art. From France too came the idea of romantic love which appeared at the same time as the Gothic and which was to have a greater effect on literature, and so indirectly on its illustration. The magnificent *L'Histoire du Graal* in the Bibliothèque Nationale is one of the first romances to be illustrated. Other secular books, such as herbals and bestiaries, become commoner and a change takes place too in the layout of manuscripts. Hitherto the miniature had usually been fairly independent of the text and we often find a group of them all together at the beginning of a book. But now the miniature is often combined with an initial, serving the purpose of decoration as well as of illustration. Sometimes it is combined with the border and grows with it to occupy a whole page; only now the

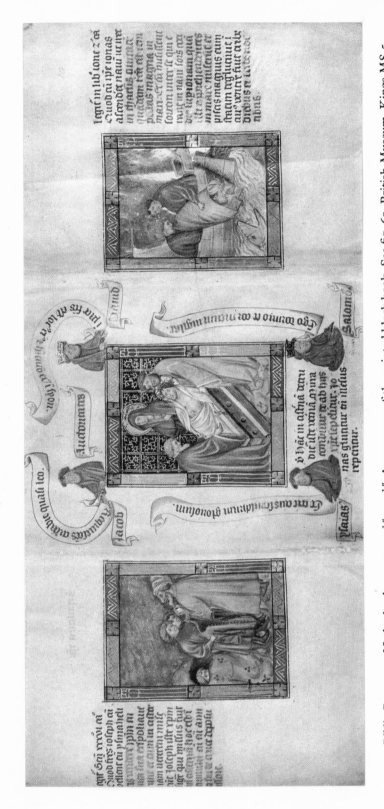

31. *Biblia Pauperum.* Netherlands, *c.* 1400. $7\frac{7}{8}'' \times 15\frac{1}{4}''$. A precursor of the printed block book. See fig. 69. British Museum. Kings MS 5

border lends it a decorative effect whereas before it was wholly illustrative. The simple full-page illustration became less common except in luxury manuscripts and the text itself generally occupies less space on the page [30].

The great French books of this period are those made for the private devotions of noble patrons; the *St. Louis Psalter* [33], the *Ingeburge Psalter* and the *Psalter of Blanche of Castile*. Now Bibles begin to appear with miniatures on a minute scale, precursors of the exquisite *Books of Hours*. And we find books specially designed for the unlearned and illiterate, books like the *Biblia Pauperum* [31], the *Golden Legend* and the *Speculum Humanae Salvationis* (in which each scene from the New Testament was paralleled by an anecdote from the Old Testament or from ancient secular history), which relied a great deal on their pictures. In these is seen a popular iconography which was to last on into the block book and the printed book. The *Bibles Moralisées* were far more splendid books with their whole text illustrated and their pictures enclosed in medallions.

At the beginning of the thirteenth century English illumination bore a very close resemblance to French. National boundaries had not yet segregated the art of one country from that of another and with monasteries still the chief centres of book production[1] and Latin still the universal language of learning there was continual interchange which helped to produce not so much uniformity as solidarity. To this may be traced those strange simultaneous changes of style which appear all at once in different places. Gothic appeared in England very soon after France and as in France it produced some fine service books like the *Windmill* and *Tenison Psalters* which are yet quite distinct from French manuscripts. In the latter there are borders containing some very accurately painted birds; and short lines in the text are filled out with bands of ornament so that the whole surface of the page is decorated—a custom that was imitated in some early printed books [34]. Many illuminated Bibles and psalters were produced during this century; very small ones similar to the French with tiny lettering and often with shortened text; and big ones with historiated initials which sometimes occupied a whole page. Backgrounds are formed of solid gold and there are architectural backgrounds too which copy the prevalent Gothic style. The thirteenth-century artist seems to have felt no more incongruity in a Gothic setting for a Biblical scene than the seventeenth-century engraver when he gave it a classical one.

Psalters were often prefaced with a series of Bible pictures in monumental style. Margaret Rickert has pointed out their connexion not only with contemporary stained glass but also with the wall-paintings of the time; and she says that this latter relationship is not found in French illumination. She concludes that both forms of art were probably based on cycles which were available for copying.

As the century proceeds we find more freedom of drawing and those delightfully informal marginal sketches or 'drolleries' which were never seen in the previous century make their appearance again and incidentally tell us a great deal about the costumes and everyday life of the time. With them we find a new feature which was later to become a characteristic of English work, the introduction of animal grotesques. Some of them, perhaps in imitation of the Bestiaries, are quite naturalistic; but their purpose is always decorative. St. Albans Abbey was famous for combining outline drawing with a monumental style, owing more to Byzantine than to Gothic art. This is to be seen in the work of Matthew Paris, who trained a school of illuminators at St. Albans and who is one of the earliest English illuminators to sign his work. His best known manuscript is the *Historia Anglorum*.

[1] *Scriptoria* appeared in the monasteries during this century.

The middle of the fourteenth century is one of the turning points in the history of illumination. Hitherto the manuscript had in some respects anticipated the printed book which was so soon to oust it, and the persistence of the cycle system points the similarity by emphasizing the continuity of manuscript illumination. The survival of that system up to this time is in fact quite astonishing and illustrations in bestiaries for instance were still being copied (at many removes) from the Latin *Physiologus* which was itself a translation from the Greek. Many of the books we have dealt with, like the *Utrecht Psalter*, were illustrated by men of genius and were truly original, even when they used the old iconography. But the great majority were more or less faithful copies of other books. Now however the time of the virtuoso had arrived and he disdained to copy other men's work. The *Books of Hours* painted for the Duc de Berry were not copies nor were they copied afterwards. This work was book-painting rather than illumination; and in it the pictures are of far greater importance than the text.

But with all that gain in technique there was a loss in feeling. Along with these superb books went a wholly inferior sort which can only be called mass-produced. Cheap *Books of Hours* for instance were turned out in large quantities to a set pattern in fifteenth-century France for the new bourgeois reading public. The production of books was gradually being secularized and even devotional books (which still comprised the greater part) were made less for the glory of God than for that of the patron or even the artist—who was fast losing his anonymity. Often he was known as a panel-painter as well, and for him illumination was only one way of making a living. That he saw little essential difference between the two arts is evidenced by the habit of painting frames for miniatures to make them look like panels. The natural consequence of all this was a general lowering of standards because speed became more essential when a man's livelihood depended on the amount of work he could turn out.[1] Here the monk had the advantage of knowing that his bread was assured besides the greater satisfaction of more selfless aims.

With illumination falling into secular hands it is not surprising to find Guilds growing up. These appeared towards the end of the thirteenth century and eventually it became as obligatory for an illuminator to join his local guild as it is for a printer today to join his trade union. Weale has given us some fascinating details about the Guild of St. John and St. Luke in Bruges—how those who wished to join had to submit a specimen of their work and how they were liable to a fine if they used inferior materials; limits were even set on the number of apprentices which could be taken.

Jean Pucelle was one of the first of the virtuosi illuminators in France, and in his work we find a wholly new conception of space—new that is to France though we find something similar in contemporary Italian painting. His *Hours of Jeanne d'Evreux* contains miniatures which begin to have depth and incidentally pose many problems for the illustrator with his flat page. In his best book, the *Belleville Breviary* of about 1340, there is a new naturalism too in the attitude of the Virgin to her Baby [35]. At this time many beautiful manuscripts of the Apocalypse were being produced both in France and England. But towards the end of the century English illumination declined, and French and Flemish were left paramount. This was the time when the great masterpieces of the Paris school were produced, the *Books of Hours* for the Duc d'Anjou and the Duc de Berry, the *Rohan Book of Hours*, the *Bedford Book of Hours* and the rest [1 and 39]. However disastrous the reign of Charles VI might be politically yet it turned out to be a glorious period for the arts in France. The unpopular

[1] This did not apply to those who worked for princely patrons on a salaried basis.

Duc de Berry took advantage of his relationship to the King to build up his wonderful library with public money. The names of some of the artists who worked for him are known to us—Pol de Limbourg who illuminated the *Très Riches Heures*, Jacquemart de Hesdin and André Beauneveu—and we know, too, that most of them were Flemish, and a few Italian. In the calendar section of the *Très Riches Heures*, which dates from about 1415, we find exquisite landscapes painted for their own sake and foreshadowing the work of the great Dutch masters in their truth to nature, yet still in the scale of the miniature [36]. Symbolism is beginning to decay. A new unity of light and tone makes its appearance.

Sir Kenneth Clark has pointed out that this 'sense of saturating light grew out of a school of manuscript illumination and first appears in miniatures. For in such small images a unity of tone is far more easily achieved and the whole scene can be given the concentrated brilliance of a reflection in a crystal'. What he calls the first modern landscapes appeared in the *Turin Hours* which was probably painted by Hubert van Eyck in about 1416. A section of this manuscript was destroyed by fire in 1904, but enough survives to indicate the astonishing leap forward not only in the painting of light but also in the importance of landscape in the miniature.

This startling change in technique and in subject-matter reflects a new attitude to life itself which is found also in the poetry of the time. The decay of medieval symbolism indicates a growing secularism, a turning away from things eternal and unchangeable to things temporal and fleeting. Men were becoming conscious of the beauty of change. They were, as Joan Evans says, 'peculiarly sensitive to things that were lovely because they were not lasting: to flowers that fade and to moments that cannot endure. . . . It is this poetic naturalism expressed first in poetry, then in the manuscript illuminations to poems and then in the manifold decorations of castles that sets the note for the imagery of ornament in the later Middle Ages.'

The *Bedford Book of Hours* (c. 1430) for all its magnificence and its four thousand vignettes looks slightly old-fashioned in comparison with the *Turin Hours*. But it is a wonderful book with its work by three different schools, Parisian, English and Franco-Flemish [39]. National styles begin to be distinct in the fourteenth century and by the fifteenth it is comparatively easy to assign illumination to its appropriate school. But it cannot be assumed that the illuminators themselves were natives because they seldom stayed long in one place.

Besides these devotional books many secular works appeared during the fourteenth and fifteenth centuries, and histories were especially popular. There were the *Grandes Chroniques de France* and of course Froissart who was equally fashionable in England. In these books we find warriors and others represented not in contemporary dress but in that of fifty years earlier than the date of the illustrations; and Middleton has suggested that this is because the artist wished to suggest antiquity and went back as far as his memory would carry him. Then there were the Arthurian romances, the books on natural science like Glanville's *Treatise on the Properties of Things*, the books on hunting, and the illustrated *Fabliaux* or short stories in verse. All these, whatever period they purport to describe, are invaluable to the historian because of their pictures of contemporary life and customs. This in fact is the beginning of genre painting.

Two interesting innovations now claim our attention, the first the use of grisaille, the second the striking development of the background and border. Grisaille is first seen during the fourteenth century in France and it lasts nearly to the end of the fifteenth century. By the time it appears the old system of pen outlines filled with flat colours was almost obsolete, and grisaille marks another step forward in the search for depth. It consists of painting in a

32. Roger of Parma; *A Treatise on Surgery*. French, 12th century. $7\frac{1}{2}'' \times 6\frac{1}{4}''$. British Museum. Sloane 1977

33. *The Psalter of St. Louis*. French, *c.* 1260. $8\frac{1}{4}'' \times 5\frac{3}{4}''$. Each miniature has a framework formed by a Gothic arch. Paris. B.N. Lat. 10525

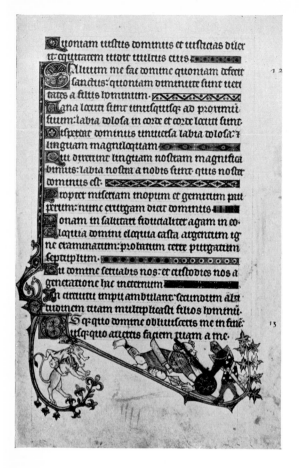

34. *The Tenison Psalter*. English, 13th century. $9\frac{1}{2}'' \times 6\frac{1}{2}''$. British Museum. Add. MS 24686

35. *The Belleville Breviary*. French, 14th century. $9\frac{1}{2}'' \times 6\frac{3}{4}''$. Illuminated by Jean Pucelle. Paris. B.N. Lat. 10483–4

36. *The Très Riches Heures du Duc de Berry*. French, 14th century. $11\frac{1}{2}'' \times 8\frac{1}{2}''$. A page from the Calendar painted by the Limbourg brothers. Condé Museum, Chantilly. MS 1284

blue-grey tone with highlights in white or gold, and in the hands of a master it is strikingly effective. In Italy it was called chiaroscuro and the principle was applied later to printed wood-cuts under the same name. Pächt suggests that it was an expedient to distinguish illumination from the richer effects of the panel picture and to place it in a category of its own, mid-way between painting and the graphic arts. That may be so, but it is of course found in manuscripts long before the introduction of printing.

During the early fourteenth century backgrounds were purely decorative. The typical background is a sort of chess-board of alternating gold and coloured squares. Towards the end of the century we find gold patterns on coloured grounds, but with the growth of land-scape painting and the discovery of the horizon a naturalistic background very gradually replaces this decoration, especially in Franco-Flemish work. So the miniature becomes just a smaller version of the panel paintings which the same artist was probably producing: a development that was not necessarily for the good of the book.

The border originally developed in the thirteenth century as a pendant of the initial and even when it grew to surround the whole page it still retained its connexion with the initial. From the bud of the pendant grew the 'ivy-leaf' border which was typical of fourteenth- and fifteenth-century French work. Usually it covered a very wide margin and sometimes there were leaves of burnished gold in the pattern which added greatly to its splendour. But it always formed an integral part of the text and it hardly developed at all. It was left to the Flemish illuminators to make their borders three-dimensional using the same perspective for border and miniature. And as naturalism thus increases, so symbolism declines.

In 1437 Philip the Good of Burgundy became ruler also of a great and wealthy land which included what is now Holland and Belgium. Here the Flemish school of panel painting in oils which is associated with the van Eycks had already grown up, itself an offspring of book illumination. Under its influence the third dimension, seldom found in miniatures of the previous two or three centuries, and never in borders, became common in books, and not altogether with the happiest results. The problem (which is as much the problem of the illustrator to-day) is to reconcile the flatness of the text with the depth of the picture; and Pächt has shown how one solution was found by the anonymous painter whose best work was done between 1475 and 1485 and whom he calls the Master of Mary of Burgundy. The name comes from the two wonderful *Books of Hours* which this unknown man painted for the wife of the Archduke Maximilian, one now in Vienna and the other in Berlin. In them and in his *Oxford Book of Hours* [37] is brought to perfection the technique of the 'scatter border'. This is an adaptation of the naturalistic still-life border which had already been used in the *Très Riches Heures du Duc de Berry*, and it consists of flowers, butterflies, jewels and so on, surrounding the miniature and, by means of shadows, giving its own feeling of depth quite independently of the miniature which it frames. The reader has the illusion that the border is nearer to him than the text and that the miniature is further away; and always 'the plane of the page is the central organizing factor'. Fig. 40 shows a famous miniature from the *Book of Hours* painted for Charles the Bold. In the foreground are the jewel case, the cushion and the open prayer book, all belonging to Mary of Burgundy. Framed by architecture is the crucifixion scene which has become almost the background and which is far less vivid and less real than the foreground. We have here the interpenetration of heaven and earth that is typical of fifteenth-century Dutch painting. The picture becomes an extension of the spectator's own world, the flat surface an open window.

These manuscripts also mark, as Bergström has pointed out, the beginning of still-life

37. *The Oxford Book of Hours*. Flemish, 15th century. Actual size. Illuminated by the Master of Mary of Burgundy. Bodleian Library, Douce 219

painting. Religious symbols have been separated from the miniature in the interests of naturalism and relegated to the border where they assume a disproportionate importance. To give them an independent existence in a separate painting was only a small step.

The book-painter in the Netherlands at this time was in fact a bold experimentalist and the easel-painters were content to follow in his path. This development had far-reaching consequences not only in the Ghent-Bruges school of illumination[1] which this Master founded but also in the art of Bourdichon in France and Glockendon in Germany. It seems to have had an immediate effect on the illuminators of the famous *Grimani Breviary*, one of whom was for a long time supposed to have been Gerard David.[2] That book was painted at about this time and it contains borders of startling naturalism, besides many fine miniatures [41]. And a hundred years later Georg Hoefnagel (who came from Flanders but did his best work in Bavaria) carried this decorative system to its conclusion in such works as the *Prayer Book of Albert V of Bavaria* (1574) and the *Missale Romanum* (1590). The idea of a framework has been abandoned completely, and the flowers and insects are the *raison d'être* of the miniatures. We feel that these were his chief interest; and he was in fact one of the founders of the Dutch school of still-life painting.

One great French illuminator who seems to have been unaffected by the Flemish fashion was Jean Fouquet. He was working in Tours during the second half of the fifteenth century; and in his hands the art of Tours becomes quite different from that of Paris which at this period is often indistinguishable from Flemish work. He uses mostly the ivy-leaf border but our attention is concentrated on his wonderful miniatures with their backgrounds of Loire landscape. Already the influence of the Italian classical Renaissance is seen in his architecture, which is emancipating itself from the Gothic, as well as in his handling of perspective. In his mastery of crowd scenes he is far beyond any of his contemporaries and his use of colour is always unerring. His chief books are the *Hours of Etienne Chevalier* and Josephus's *Jewish Antiquities* [42]. In the former we find again the conception of the miniature as something seen through a window. A strip of lettering at the foot which appears to be at right angles to the ground above acts as part of the frame. Jean Bourdichon also worked at Tours but a little later than Fouquet. His great work is the *Grandes Heures* of Anne of Brittany, which has more than a flavour of Flanders in its flower painting and in its very early 'scatter-borders' with their deep shadows. These incidentally surround the text only; the miniatures or 'histories' have plain frames [43]. But beautiful and accomplished as this book is we are already reminded that illumination is a dying art and that Bourdichon was a court painter first and an illustrator second. Under Francis I the Tours school moved to Paris where the Italian architect Rosso was enjoying great favour and the Italian taste for emblems had already taken hold. The *Hours of Anne of Austria* (c. 1530) was one of the last great French manuscripts and it shows a significant degree of over-ornamentation. By the turn of the century printing had established itself as the chief method of producing books and the illuminated manuscripts must have begun to seem an anachronism. Elsewhere in France quality had declined badly, and in some late French manuscripts we find transfers being used for the borders—a form of competition with the printer.

---

[1] This school is famous also for some of the very earliest examples of pure landscapes in its miniatures, i.e. landscapes which are not just a setting for heaven or for divine activities. These are painted with a beautiful and characteristic atmospheric quality and with a peculiar softness of colour.

[2] David, a master painter, is known to have belonged also to a guild of miniaturists. But this was probably exceptional and already a distinction seems to have grown up between painters and miniaturists.

During the thirteenth century when English, French and Flemish illumination was at such a high level, German work, unaffected by the Gothic style, continued with the old formulae. Consequently its quality inevitably declined. But in the fourteenth century an important Germanic school sprang up in Prague, which was now the capital of the Holy Roman Empire. Here under the patronage of the Emperor Charles IV was developed that distinctive style of decoration called Bohemian. There is Gothic architecture for instance in Princess Cunigunda's *Passionale* (c. 1312) but it is not French Gothic. For Charles was written the celebrated *Golden Bull* which contained all the constitutions of the Empire, and was copied many times in varying degrees of splendour [45]. For his son the *Wenzel Bible* was illuminated and though it is unfinished it is still a magnificent work. In the fifteenth century there was a steady deterioration such as indeed occurred throughout the whole of Germany. This was accelerated by the introduction of printing which seemed to be the signal for illumination of ever increasing gaudiness, e.g. the *Hildesheimer Prayer Book* at Berlin. And now the virtuosity enters which we shall find especially in France and Flanders during this period, when illumination partakes more of the nature of painting than of illustration. Already there have been many instances where the name of the illuminator is known but now he loses all anonymity and leaves us in no doubt about his identity. The books painted for Albert of Brandenburg early in the sixteenth century by Nicolas Glockendon and the *Prayer Book of William of Bavaria* by Albert Glockendon differ in nothing but dimensions, as Bradley says, from the works of the greatest contemporary painters. But as Bradley also points out, painters and illuminators seldom trespassed on each other's preserves because of the strict rules of the guilds.

In England printing seemed to kill illumination much more quickly. During the thirteenth century the Gothic style came from France and there was a general reduction of scale both for pictures and for text, together with a more delicate and freer style of drawing. But early in the fourteenth century the work of the East Anglian School begins to show some independence, with its flair for the illustration of exciting narrative and profusion of decoration which is sometimes carried too far. From it came some of the finest of all English manuscripts; and Margaret Rickert says that these manuscripts represent 'in all respects the most characteristically English phase of medieval painting'. East Anglia was at this time the centre of the wool trade and very prosperous, and as many books were now being produced for the laity as for the Church. *Queen Mary's Psalter* (c. 1330) is a magnificent example of this school, its first sixty-six pages a series of miniatures of Bible scenes with captions but without any other text [46]. These are outline drawings coloured with transparent washes, looking back to the *Utrecht Psalter* and quite different from the more conventional pictures which come later in the book. In the lower margins of these later miniatures however is a series of small tinted drawings of sports, hunting scenes and animals—a form of decoration that was carried much farther, almost too far in the famous *Luttrell Psalter*. Now the flowers in the borders begin to be of recognizable species, reminding us more of Flemish than of French work. We find too in borders that the conventional leaf pattern is developing into a pattern of feathery scrolls.

From about 1348 when England was ravaged by the Black Death until the end of the century there is a dearth of good books. French illumination was now at its peak but we lacked the princely patronage that fostered it there. At the end of this period however there was a revival, exemplified by such books as the great *Carmelite Missal* and the *Sherborne Missal* painted by John Siferwas and now in Alnwick Castle Library. A new influence can be discerned which seems to have come from Bohemia in exchange as it were for the benefits of the East Anglian style which had recently spread as far east as this. Bohemian illumination was now flourishing under Charles IV. Charles's daughter, Anne, married Richard II of England and among other things she introduced to the court the fashion of pointed toes which we find reflected in miniatures of the period. The representation of foliage too seems to be copied from Bohemian borders. But gradually French and Flemish styles prevailed and later work, apart from an occasional masterpiece like the *Hours of Elizabeth the Queen*, tends to be a reflection of foreign virtuosity, growing ever more florid. The new book-buying public seems often to have been content with flashy and inferior work and the more accomplished artists must have forsaken illumination for other branches of the arts. The death-blow given by the Wars of the Roses was indeed a *coup-de-grâce*.

In Italy the thirteenth century, though it was the century of Cimabue and Giotto, was not productive of many fine books.[1] Most of the early scribes there seem to have been French, just as, later on, the early printers there were German. Illustrated choir-books, some of them with initials more than twelve inches high, are among the most beautiful manuscripts of this period and production of these continued by hand until long after the introduction of printing. Fra Angelico is known to have illuminated some at Fiesole in the fifteenth century. [44] Law books from Bologna were famous all over Italy and beyond for their decoration and, curiously enough, their drolleries. Oderisi da Gubbio (whom Dante praised) worked on some of them.

Bologna led the other Italian cities in the art of illumination throughout the Gothic period. Miniature painting still held its own with large scale painting but in the fourteenth century Florence began to vie with Bologna and at the same time the miniature began to take second place. The broader style of the Florentines seems to show that they were panel painters first and miniaturists after. In Siena on the other hand artists like Tegliacci made no distinction between the two arts. Tegliacci may have been responsible for a wonderful Dante now in Perugia, one among many copies of the *Inferno* which was now being illuminated by masters of all schools.

The Gothic style as it was known in France did not greatly affect Italy as a whole. Byzantine tendencies still persisted, especially in Venetian manuscripts and are to be seen in certain antiphonals in St. Mark's Library. And Venetian manuscripts also show a definite Byzantine feeling throughout the period. In Lombardy however French influences were stronger, and the Gothic style lingers there. In the work of Giovannino de' Grassi we find spiky pinnacles similar to those in French manuscripts of the time. 'Giotto and his followers changed the course of art in many things,' says Morey, 'but they did nothing so extraordinary as their transformation of the form and formulae of the French decadent Gothic style.' Towards the close of the fourteenth century Italian artists were working in France on books for the Duke of Berry and so, although her own great period of illumination was not to come until just before the arrival of printing, Italy made her contribution to France's glory.

On the other hand the fifteenth century, particularly the period between 1455 and 1484, was an age of great achievement, in illumination as in the other arts. It was ironical that illumination flowered so much later in Italy than elsewhere and that it was at its height just

---

[1] It may be worth mentioning that an early thirteenth-century book of Astronomical Treatises in the British Museum is one of the oldest Western books written on paper. But after the introduction of printing, paper was used much more for manuscripts.

when printing arrived. It was bound to succumb but it held out for a surprising length of time. The effects of the Renaissance, which we associate with the revival of classicism in fifteenth-century Italy, were as potent on the printed book as on the manuscript. After the sack of Constantinople of course many Byzantine manuscripts reached Italy but they appear to have been valued more for their literary contents than for their illumination. Perhaps one reason for their comparative lack of influence was the close relationship between illumination and painting in Italy at this time. Just as in the north, painting grew out of illumination and then made itself independent. But in Italy, where the *quattrocento* was one of the most glorious periods of painting that the world has ever seen, the arts remained more closely allied and wherever there was a school of painting we find also a school of miniaturists, the influence of whose art is often to be seen in the altar-pieces of the time.

But the first generation of great Renaissance painters were more interested in monumental art and it was not until later that their influence began to be felt. There is indeed a monumental quality about the huge Graduals that were produced between 1463 and 1471 for Florence cathedral. At the other end of the scale were the little *Books of Hours* with exquisitely detailed borders by Francesco d'Antonio, notably the one executed in 1485 for Lorenzo the Magnificent which is known as the *Uffiziolo*, and Bishop Donato's *Lectionary* of 1436 in the Morgan Library with its host of little miniatures about two inches square [48]. Gherardo and Monte de Giovanni are celebrated for their landscape backgrounds in the manner of Fouquet, giving the page a depth more suitable perhaps to the mosaics on which they worked with Ghirlandaio and Botticelli. They also illuminated, for Matthias Corvinus, King of Hungary, Didymus's *De Spiritu Sancto* which has a text written by Sigismundus de Sigismundis, the most famous scribe of his day. Attavante, whose workshop produced the famous *Urbino Bible* (1476–8) for Federico di Montefelto, was highly esteemed in his own time but to us his pages seem too ornate even in that decorative age and his compositions too crowded. For Matthias Corvinus he too produced, among other manuscripts, a fine breviary in 1487; but it is certain that much of the work that came from his shop was not his. His followers in the early sixteenth century tried to outdo him and this marks the decline of Florentine work [53].

Italian manuscripts have always been famous for their calligraphy and there is a calligraphic quality about much of their ornament, especially of their initials. By now the roman hand was replacing the Gothic, anticipating the introduction of roman type by Jensen, the printer. Italian illuminators were more sensitive than most to the physical matching of pictures and text and the new style of writing had its effect on miniatures as well as on initials. The humanist book, which we are apt to associate with roman type and with printing, thus had its origins much earlier. There was an enormous demand for books, especially in Florence. Vespasiano da Bisticci, a famous Florentine publisher, employed numerous copyists and illuminators to produce the Greek and Latin classics for wealthy nobles, as well as liturgical works for the monasteries. We can trace the beginning of an antiquarian style in the humanistic book with its opening page framed in the Romanesque manner, a fashion that was even perpetuated in the earliest printed books. This subdued decoration was probably felt to detract less than true illustration from the literary value of the book which, for the humanist, was always paramount. It gives us too a curious side-light on what the Renaissance artist thought classical illustration was like.

If the Renaissance style may be said to have started in Florence it was in Ferrara that it produced some of its most original manifestations. The Este Court was from 1450–71 a scene of unparalleled brilliance and from here, between 1455 and 1461, came one of the

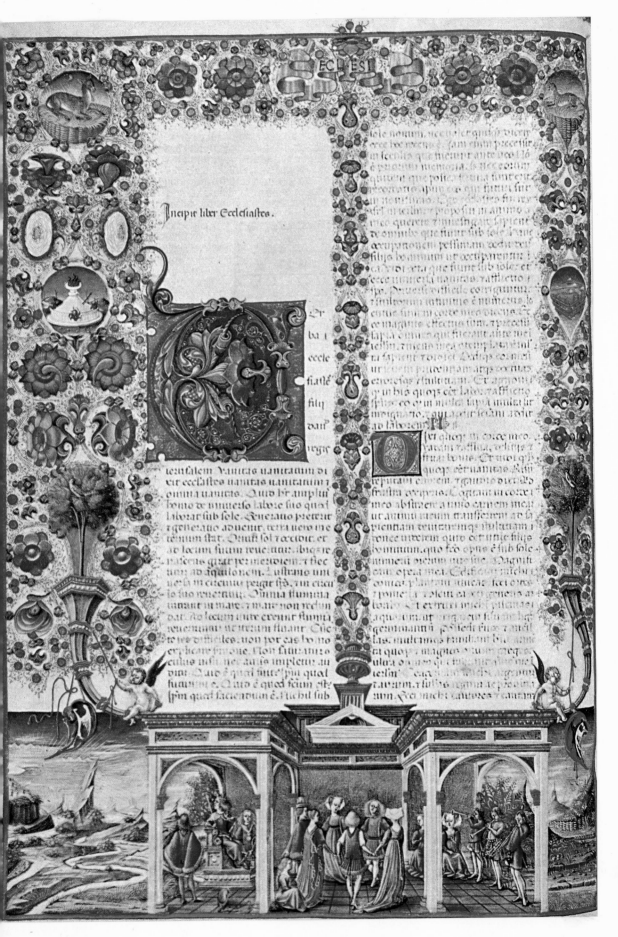

38. *The Borso d'Este Bible.* Italian, 1455–61. 14¾″ × 10½″. School of Ferrara. Illuminated by Taddeo Crivelli and others. Modena, Estense Library

great masterpieces of the Renaissance, the *Borso d'Este Bible* [38]. Crivelli, Franco de' Russi and the two or three others who provided the miniatures were all under the spell of Piero della Francesca who himself was painting at the Court. The little pictures embedded in the borders have in fact the same characteristics as the big easel pictures of the time.

De' Russi combined with Guglielmo Giraldi to produce a wonderful *Divina Commedia* in about 1480. One of the finest of all the many Dante manuscripts, its 110 large miniatures stand out even in such a rich period by their originality of conception [51]. There is also a fine four-volume Bible illuminated by Giraldi a few years before the Dante. The *Ercole d'Este Breviary* (1502) on which three artists worked, is the most notable late Ferrarese book, and here we find an imitation of the Flemish border which is a feature of Italian illumination in decline. Most Italian books of the time, irrespective of origin, have borders on the first few pages in which are embedded miniatures in medallion frames with a coat of arms at the bottom. But Ferrarese borders are even more elaborate, except when they imitate the twelfth century in antiquarian style with interlaced bands of white or gold which are thrown into relief by filling the interstices with alternating colours.

Bologna, long displaced from her former primacy, was now producing manuscripts that imitated those of Ferrara; but in the beautiful *Book of Offices of Giovanni II Bentivoglio* (1497) and the *Ghislieri Book of Hours* (which contains a miniature by Perugino) Bologna is seen to be reasserting her own individuality. In Padua at the end of the fifteenth century we can identify in Benedetto Bordone a great miniaturist who also produced wood-engravings. Many artists of this time must have worked for both manuscripts and printed books but it is difficult to identify them, for they never signed their engravings as they did their miniatures. In Verona Francesco and Girolamo dai Libri, working like Bordone under the influence of Mantegna, seemed to carry the art of illumination to a point beyond which it could progress no further.

In Lombardy the Gothic style lingered on long after everywhere else. The influence of Leonardo has been discerned in certain manuscripts from Milan such as the *Book of Hours* in the Fitzwilliam. But a far more important figure for the book is Belbello da Pavia, one of the greatest of all Renaissance miniaturists. His work in the second part of the *Visconti Book of Offices*, for certain Venetian choir-books and for a fine *Plutarch* [50] in the British Museum shows a love of brilliant colour, of minute detail and of exquisite landscape backgrounds. Salmi comments on the 'calligraphic bravura of his rapid, agitated and vigorous line'. His borders are often over-elaborated and when, as in the *Plutarch*, he dispenses with them altogether the miniatures benefit considerably. At the end of the century the famous *Sforza Book of Hours* came from Milan and to this book, rich as it is, Charles V later added some beautiful Flemish miniatures. The *Libro dell' Iesus*, also executed for the Sforzas right at the end of the century, has full-page miniatures without any ornamentation save for gold frames which emphasize their detachment from the book.

By the sixteenth century, with printing now well established, manuscript illumination was being practised only to please wealthy patrons by artists like the admired Giulio Clovio whose miniatures, inspired by Michelangelo and stippled with minute points of colour, have been likened to reduced versions of large-scale paintings. Nevertheless his *Book of Hours* of 1546 for Cardinal Alessandro Farnese is a *tour de force*. The page here reproduced [52] has been called 'probably the most original, elaborately conceived and delicately executed illustration to accompany the Litany ever attempted'. In it we can see reflections of the mannerist style which was fashionable in Italy at that time.

Illumination at this period was generally confined to religious books but at the same time

39. *The Bedford Book of Hours*. French, 1423–30. $10\frac{1}{4}'' \times 7\frac{1}{4}''$. British Museum. Add. MS 18850

40. Charles the Bold's *Book of Hours*. Flemish, 15th century. 9″ × 6″. A miniature by the Master of Mary of Burgundy. Vienna. Cod. 1857

41. *The Grimani Breviary*. Flemish, 1490–1510. 11″ × 8½″. Venice. Marciana Library. Lat. I, 99 (2138)

42. Josephus: *Jewish Antiquities*. French, 15th century. $17'' \times 11\frac{3}{4}''$. Painted by Fouquet.
Paris. B.N. Fr. 247

43. *Hours of Anne of Brittany*. French, 15th century. $11\frac{3}{4}'' \times 7\frac{3}{4}''$. Painted by Bourdichon. Paris. B.N. Lat. 9474

44. *Diurno Domenicale*. Italian, 1409. A Gradual illuminated by Fra Angelico and others. $26\frac{1}{4}'' \times 19\frac{1}{4}''$. Florence, Laurentian Library, Cor. 3

45. *The Golden Bull* of Charles IV. Bohemian, 1400. $16\frac{1}{2}'' \times 12''$. Vienna. Cod. Vindob.

46. *Queen Mary's Psalter.* English, 14th century. $10\frac{3}{4}'' \times 6\frac{3}{4}''$. A full page tinted drawing of a scene from the Creation. British Museum. Royal MS 2 B. VII

47. *The Commentary of Beatus on the Apocalypse of St. John.* Spanish, 12th century. $18'' \times 12\frac{3}{4}''$. Manchester, John Rylands Library, Lat. MS 8

48. Bishop Donato's *Lectionary.* Italian, 15th century. $10'' \times 7''$. New York. Pierpont Morgan Library. M. 180

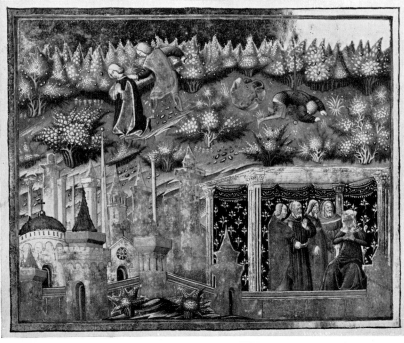

49. Petrarch's *Trionfi*. Italian, late 15th century. School of Florence. $8\frac{1}{2}'' \times 6''$. Pen drawings made in preparation for illumination in colour. Bodleian Library. MS Canon. ital. 83

50. Plutarch's *Lives*. Italian, 15th century. School of Lombardy. $13\frac{1}{4}'' \times 9\frac{1}{2}''$. Illuminated by Belbello da Pavia. British Museum. Add. MS 22318

Voi che siete in piccioletta barcha
desiderosi dascoltar seguiti
dietro.il mio legno che cantando uarcha
Tornate a riueder li uostri liti
non ui mettete in pelago: che forse

51. Dante's *Divina Commedia*. Italian, *c.* 1480. School of Ferrara. $19\frac{1}{4}'' \times 9\frac{1}{2}''$. Illuminated by Franco de' Russi and the Giraldis. Vatican Libary. Urb. Lat. 365

52. *Book of Hours*. Italian, 1546. $6\frac{3}{4}'' \times 4\frac{1}{4}''$. Painted for Cardinal Farnese by Clovio. An illustration to the Litany. New York, Pierpont Morgan Library M. 69

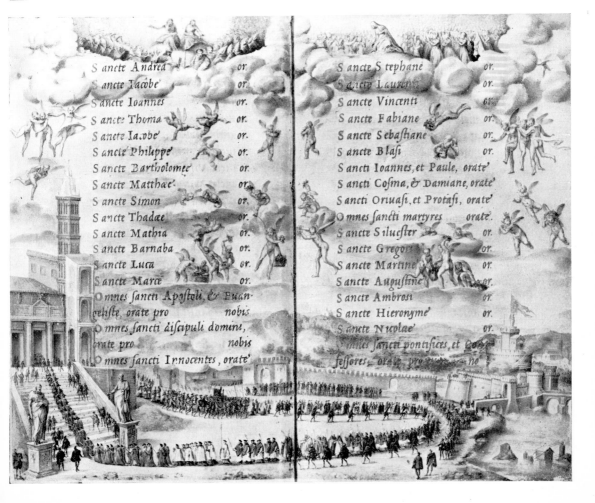

53. Sardi: *Anima peregrina*. Italian, late 15th
century. $14\frac{3}{4}'' \times 10\frac{1}{4}''$. School of Florence.
Illuminated by Attavante. Rome. Corsiniana
Library, MS 612

54. Codex Zouche-Nuttall. Mexican, *c.* 14th
century. $7\frac{1}{2}'' \times 10''$. Mixtec Migration story
and volcanic eruption, painted on deerskin.
British Museum

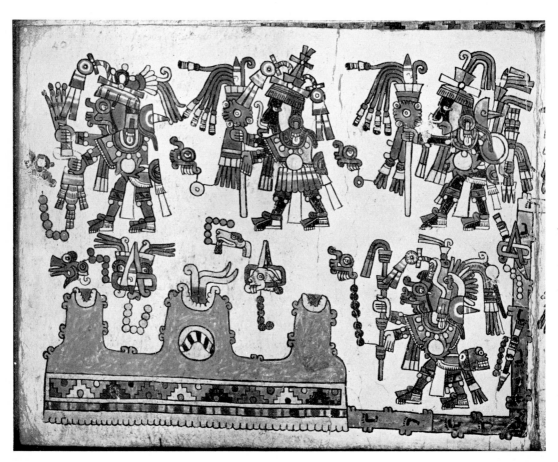

there was a curious revival of copying the classics and giving them new illustrations; Vasari for instance performed this service for the well-worn *Dioscorides*. At the opposite extreme from this antiquarianism are the occasional miniatures that seem to imitate the printed illustration. Could anything indicate more clearly the decline of illumination?

Spain has been left to the last, not because her work is any less interesting than that of other countries but because it was subject to alien influences and requires separate treatment. From the eighth to the eleventh century Spain was almost the only repository of the classical tradition which was lost elsewhere in the West. Moslem rule affected chiefly the south and as in Islamic countries it was tolerant towards Christianity and it encouraged learning. Cordova in fact became in the tenth century a centre of learning and a place of pilgrimage for scholars from all parts of the civilized world.

Mozarabic art is the name given to the Christian art which flourished under the Moslems; Mudejar art that of the Moslems who stayed after the Christian conquest and kept their own culture. The former was more productive of illumination but it had a great deal in common with the latter, particularly the richly decorative Oriental element. There are of course many early Spanish manuscripts which show strong Carolingian influences, particularly those of the tenth-century Catalan school. Two famous Bibles of this category may be mentioned, that of St. Peter of Ronda and the *Farfa Bible*—both of great beauty. But Spain's most original examples of illumination are Mozarabic and the most remarkable Mozarabic manuscript is the famous *Commentary of St. Beatus* on the Apocalypse. It was written in the eighth century and frequently copied during the next 400 years. Even in the eleventh century copy made at Saint-Sever in the south of France and illuminated by Etienne Garcia the Mozarabic character of the pictures is unchanged, the violent colours, the dreamlike atmosphere of the apocalyptic vision [47 and 55].

After the defeat of the Moslems the Oriental element in Spanish illumination gradually decreased, and it became less and less distinctive. It succumbed to the Gothic fashion in the thirteenth century, and there are one or two delightful books by Alfonso X illustrated in this style—the *Lapidary* and the *Book of Chess* for instance. Alfonso was a great patron of letters and with his encouragement the *Cronica General* was written and illustrated. From then until the introduction of printing Spanish illuminators contented themselves with imitations of Italian or Flemish work, the difference being that colouring is generally subdued in deference to the Inquisition. So we find, in the fifteenth century, miniatures with black backgrounds and draperies. But these restrictions were eased in the sixteenth century and under Philip II some of the finest Spanish manuscripts appeared. The introduction of printing was a very slow affair in Spain and Portugal, and illumination therefore persisted longer than in most other countries and perhaps influenced printing design more. The magnificent and enormous choir-books ordered by Philip for San Lorenzo of the Escorial between 1572 and 1589 were partly produced by Italians (Scorza of Genoa, a famous miniaturist of the time, was one of them) and display an Italian richness. The flowering of Spanish painting in the next generation must have owed much to these miniaturists—in whose work however one can hardly expect to see as yet the emergence of a national style.

Calligraphy was always highly esteemed in Spain, even more in Portugal, and many fifteenth-century manuscripts depend entirely on their writing for their beauty. Portugal was politically connected with Burgundy and Flemish strains are apparent in Portuguese manuscripts. Her greatest manuscript was perhaps the Bible of the Hieronymites which was mostly written by Italians. In Portugal as in Spain good manuscripts continued to appear

55. *The Commentary of Beatus on the Apocalypse of St. John.* Franco-
Spanish, 11th century. 14½″ × 11½″. A copy of the famous Spanish work,
illuminated at Saint-Sever in Gascony by Etienne Garcia.
Paris. B.N. Lat. 8878

long after printing arrived. The British Museum has a *Missale Romanum* dating from about 1557, its title-page reminiscent of contemporary engraved titles with its formula of Roman soldiers supporting a tablet.

When in 1519 Cortes arrived in Mexico he found a highly developed form of picture writing which survived long after the Spanish conquest. Many of the wonderful books which were written by this method were preserved by the Spaniards (though unfortunately many more were destroyed) so it seems proper to give some account of them here although they have nothing in common with European illumination at all.

The books themselves were folded rolls of deerskin or of tree-bark paper, and the pictures were painted in the most brilliant colours imaginable. The subject-matter was generally magic or history, going back in time to the era before the Toltec Empire. The magic books have been described by C. A. Burland but few of them survive, the best being the *Codex Borgia* and the *Codex Laud* at Oxford. Of the history books the best are the Aztec *Codex Boturini*, the Mixtec *Vienna Codex*, the *Codex Zouche Nuttall* [54].

These books are unique because they demonstrate the evolution of writing and its origin in picture. In those which have no writing, like the *Vienna Codex*, the illustration *is* the text, so to say. And there is a barbaric splendour in the colour and pattern as well as a more subtle skill in their disposition on the page. 'There is,' says Burland, 'an insistent rhythm in the pattern that is almost like music. . . . This is all exciting to the eye and at the same time regularized by its dependence on a very strictly observed code of proportion'.

Even in Spain and Portugal the illumination and indeed the production of manuscripts had virtually ended by the seventeenth century. Manuscripts like those which Jarry produced for Louis XIV are few and far between. It is a commonplace to say that manuscripts were killed by printing but this does not seem quite to account for the decay of illumination which relied on colour inaccessible to printers until the nineteenth century. That curious but often very effective hybrid, the printed book with painted decoration, was only a transitional apparition. The answer seems to be an economic one. Where, as in Spain, the Church continued her patronage, illumination flourished to a comparatively late date. But elsewhere lay patronage was not enough to arrest its decay.

3

Oriental Illumination and Illustration

ISLAM

It is convenient to discuss Islamic work here because our knowledge of it is almost wholly confined to the period following the downfall of Constantinople when Byzantine art practically disappeared. And while Islam may perhaps be called an artistic heir of Byzantium, yet her art derived also from all the other countries where the Moslems ruled—Syria, Armenia, Persia, Egypt and, much later, India. Syria we have already seen as a contributor to the Byzantine synthesis and her influence on Christian iconography was decisive for all time; but very few of her manuscripts survive. In Armenia we know that there was a time in the seventh century when many beautifully illuminated books appeared, but again we have nothing until the tenth century when the *Gospel Book of Queen Mlqé* [58] was produced. Until the thirteenth century there was a flourishing Armenian school producing decorative work of an astonishing intricacy but after the fifteenth century it decayed. In Persia we have already seen how illumination flourished under the Sasanids and how a link with Central Asia was formed by Manichaean miniaturists who fled eastwards from Persia. Although nothing remains of this glorious period except hearsay, the Sassanian tradition reappears after Persia was conquered by the Mongols in the thirteenth century. Egypt's offering was Coptic art, a primitive accompaniment of the Coptic Christian literature which poured forth from the great monasteries that were founded about the fourth century. It continued even after the Arab conquest in 641 for the Moslems seem to have been amazingly tolerant in such matters. As for India it was not until the beginning of the sixteenth century when the Mughal period began that there was any close intercourse, and then she received from Islamic illumination more than she contributed.

From the eighth to the twelfth centuries we have the extraordinary spectacle of Islam as one of the leaders of the civilized world in scientific thought and culture. It is said that some of their libraries contained over 100,000 volumes. Although very few complete illuminated books survive from this period (those that escaped the Mongolian invasion were destroyed after the Christian conquest of Spain) it must have been fruitful in that respect too. A thirteenth-century translation of Dioscorides is interesting, although it is of no great artistic value, because it shows Islamic care for Greek learning. But generally speaking the development of Islamic illumination was governed to an unusual degree by the Islamic religion. Orthodox Moslems were opposed to any representation of the human figure, or indeed of any living being whatsoever. Illustrators working under the patronage of the great sometimes transgressed the law however and 'transcribed the classics of love or of war'. But for obvious reasons they never signed their work.

The banning of representational art led naturally to decoration rather than illustration and

56. *The Maqamat of al-Hariri*. Baghdad School, 13th century. 15″ × 11″. The Procession.
Paris. B.N. MS 5847

as the copying of the Koran was an act of merit, such decoration assumed a calligraphic quality, and took the form of ornamental flourishes and so on. This attitude was also a bar to the spread of printing which might otherwise have reached Europe much sooner from China. From fragments which survive it seems that the earliest Islamic books of the ninth to the twelfth centuries had much in common with those of the Hiberno-Northumbrian school which preceded them, with their pages of pure decoration reminiscent of the *Book of Durrow*.

The calligraphy itself was of the utmost importance, for the meaning of the text was held to be dependent to some degree on the script in which it was written. A master in fact could add overtones to what he wrote and thus make his own addition which was more than a purely decorative one. It has been suggested that this may have been one of the reasons for the late arrival of the miniature in Islamic books.

Like the Bible in the West the best decoration and calligraphy were lavished on the Koran. Representational illustration is seldom or never found, but there is a wealth of ornament and colour, especially the combination of blue and gold. Many motifs seem to have been borrowed from Persian carpets and textiles, or at least the same designs are often found in both, and endpapers usually received far more attention than they did in the West. The Byzantine and Islamic genius was for borders made up from repeated units or motifs, a fashion that was not copied in the West until much later on. Apart from the Koran a few secular works have come down to us from this early period and they provide rare examples of representational art. There is for instance *The Maqamat* of al-Hariri [56] now in Paris. It is a picaresque story book and came from Baghdad just before the Mongol invasion in the middle of the thirteenth century. Its illustrations give us an invaluable picture of the daily life of the time, and they are displayed with an eye for the layout of the page. They show too a great gift of imagination and humour which is quite lacking in the elegance of later Persian illumination.

In 1258 Baghdad was captured by the Mongols and by the end of the fourteenth century they had established their rule over Persia and most of the Islamic area as well as China. The conquest brought with it an unspeakable trail of bloodshed and destruction but when it was over a more settled period began in which the arts of the book flourished again. It is at this point, Carter suggests, when the Islamic barrier between East and West was broken, that block printing came to Europe in the wake of the Mongol invasion of Poland and Hungary. But the Chinese stylistic influences that one would have expected to come with the Mongols, although they are discernible, do not really amount to very much; a Bestiary in the Pierpont Morgan Library, which goes back to the end of the thirteenth century and is the first dated Persian book, has some miniatures in the colourful Baghdad manner and others in the almost wholly monochrome style of contemporary Chinese ink-painting. The Demotte *Shah-Namah*, produced some fifty years later and now broken up, has richer colouring and heralds the beginning of the proper Persian style.

But it was not until the end of the fourteenth century that Mongolian influences were completely digested and curiously enough this happened at about the time of another terrible invasion from the East, that of Timur in 1386. In the manuscript of the *Poems of Khwaju of Kirman*, now in the British Museum, the true Persian book at last appears [57]. The chief Chinese contribution to these beautiful miniatures is the use of landscape but the handling of the landscape was to be peculiar to Persia for the next two hundred years. All its elements are conventionalized, the rocky background, the flowery foreground and the stiff figures. The fact that it is two-dimensional, without shading or perspective, fits it well for book illustration and it means that we do not feel any incongruity when we see part of the

57. *The Poems of Kwaju.* Persian, 14th century. 12″ × 8¼″. British Museum. Or. 18113

text actually inscribed on the picture. Our example shows how this was done by means of a small panel let into the painting and it suggests too that the calligrapher was of greater importance than the miniaturist.

It can be assumed that for a long time the calligrapher and the miniaturist were separate people; but now the division of labour began to be complete just as it was in contemporary Europe. Arnold distinguishes at least eight specialists: the painter, the leaf-cutter, the gilder, the draughtsman, the binder, the preparer of gold-sprinkled paper, the designer of borders and the master who supervised the whole. This supervision might be done, as in China, by the calligrapher, the most highly esteemed of them all—even princes are known to have been engaged in the meritorious act of transcribing the Koran, and to have designed if not executed the ornamentation of the page. In the Mughal schools which flourished in the sixteenth and seventeenth centuries further subdivisions of labour appear so that we find, for instance, specialists in the painting of faces.[1] Binding is outside the scope of this study but the splendour of Persian binding must be mentioned and particularly a later custom which developed in the sixteenth century of painting designs on the covers of books to give the reader some idea of the contents.

Under Timur, in spite of his warlike propensities, began the most brilliant period of Persian art and it continued to flourish under his successors. It is an efflorescence comparable with that of the Italian Renaissance which was taking place at the same time. But there seems to have been little artistic interchange between Europe and Asia. When Bellini was sent to Constantinople in 1479 to work for the Sultan he seems to have founded no new school. Turkish illumination then and later was a pale reflection of Persian and few books of note were produced in the cities which once were the centres of Byzantine illumination. But in Persia there was much more official encouragement and a great general interest in painting and literature. One would have expected that Western Europe, whose traders and explorers were at this moment everywhere penetrating the Orient, would have produced some effect on its book illumination. But it must be remembered that by now the printed book has made its appearance in the West and painting had already separated itself for good from book decoration.[2] In the East this step was not taken for four or five centuries and meanwhile, until the time when Western models did make their appearance and were responsible for some deterioration, illumination continued as it had always done. This, in fact, is my excuse for pursuing in this chapter the history of the Oriental book far beyond the chronological limits imposed on the accompanying chapters on Western illustration. There is little to be gained by treating them side by side.

Bihzad was one of the first Persian artists that we know by name, and was the most famous of this era. He flourished between 1470 and 1520 when poetry as well as art was at a very high level. It was poetry that was most frequently illustrated and Bihzad's illustrations for the poems of *Sa'di* and *Nizami* are a tribute not only to the artist's skill, but also to the literature that inspired it. Poetry, especially of the lyrical sort, is notoriously difficult to illustrate because it seldom presents a series of clear-cut situations like a novel or a history. It consists of intangibles and its images, however prolific, are often too nebulous or too subjective to be caught and pinned down by the artist. Bihzad's art and that of the school he founded was admirably adapted to the lyricism of Persian poetry. But far from being amorphous, it is minute work containing details that can be scrutinized under a magnifying glass. Every element is carefully thought out. For instance as the hero's love increases so the

---

[1] The same thing is found in English illumination of the eleventh century.

[2] For the curious influence of Western engravings on Mughal illustration, see below.

53. *The Gospel Book of Queen Mlqé.*
Armenia, 10th century. Venice. Mekhi-
tharist Library

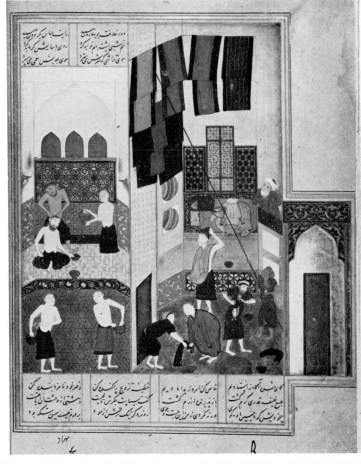

59. *The Khamsa of Nizami.* Persian, *c.*
1495. 7″ × 6″. A miniature by Bihzad and
Mirak showing a scene in a Turkish Bath.
British Museum. Or. 6810

60. An illustration to the *Chaurapan-chasika*, a poem by Bilhana in loose-leaf form. Central India, *c.* 1550. 6½″ × 8½″. N.C. Mehta, Bombay

61. *The Coruña Bible*. Hebrew-Spanish, 1476. 11½″ × 9″. Bodleian Library, Kennicott 1

62. Scroll attributed to Toba Sojo. Japanese, 11th century. Height 11¾". Kozaryi Temple, Kyoto

63. A drawing by Hsia Kuei on a silk album leaf illustrating a poem on the facing page by the Emperor Hsiao Tsung. Chinese, 13th century. 9¼" × 9¾". Boston Museum of Fine Arts

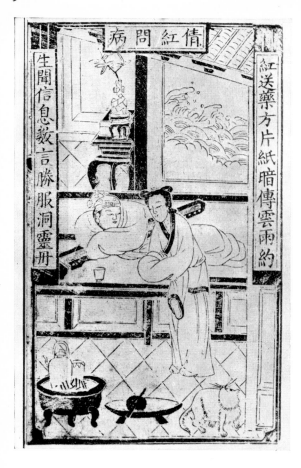

64. Wood-cut from the popular drama *Western Chamber* (1569) engraved by Ho-ching. 13″ × 9″.

65. Surprise encounter between two lovers, from a romance engraved by Huang Yu-lin, *c.* 1590. 13″ × 9″.

66. A wood-cut from a poetic drama engraved by Lui Su-Ming, *c.* 1590. 13″ × 9″.

colours grow warmer, and vice versa. The fleeting moods of the poetry have been translated by means of a system of symbols and, though later these were to become ossified, now they share the freshness of poetry. An important point that Arnold makes is that Bihzad had gone 'beyond the *horror vacui* of primitive art and knew how to make skilful use of empty spaces'. Perhaps he was indebted for this to China whose painters and illustrators had solved the problem centuries before [59].

The sixteenth century was an era of great painting in Persia and most of it went into books. One of the most splendid is the *Khamsa* of Nizami in the British Museum. It is a collection of five metrical romances which formed a favourite vehicle for illustrations during this period—Bihzad had already illustrated it in a much smaller format. This is a large book executed at Tabriz in the middle of the century. It has several fine frontispieces which were a feature of Persian books but what is more unusual is the remarkable marginal decoration that surrounds the text pages as well as the miniatures. This, like the Flemish borders that preceded it in Europe, takes the form of animals and flowers but there the resemblance ends. The Persian borders are two-dimensional in flat gold on a creamy background which gives the effect of a subdued pattern very different from the brilliance and depth of Flemish work. But the unity of the book is enhanced because the border does not distract the eye, and in addition there are other devices to tie the text to the pictures. Both are surrounded by a combination of ruled lines for instance; and though the panels so formed are not exactly the same size for text and illustration, as they were in many other contemporary books, still they help to balance the pages and teach us that it is easier for the calligrapher to achieve homogeneity in the books he designs than the painter.

The decline in late seventeenth century Persian book illustration is partly due to the habit of imitating European models, and partly to the decline of patronage. Moslem India, upon whose artists the Persian mantle fell, was subjected to the same influences in Jehangir's reign (1605–27) but seems to have assimilated them better. Mughal book illustration started by being predominantly Persian in character; and it was under the Emperor Humayun that book-painting received the official encouragement that seems to have been a *sine qua non* almost for its very existence. We know little of early Hindu painting but it was encouraged by the Hindu religion and its influence is plainly to be seen in work done for the Mughal emperors, who although they were Moslems, seem to have patronized it. The early Hindu books were on palm leaves or birch-bark, of which the former was used in parts of India until the end of the eighteenth century. It is not surprising then that few have survived on such an impermanent material, but we know that Gujarat had an outstanding school of illustration influenced by Persia, which flourished from the first half of the twelfth century until the sixteenth when many of its artists went into the service of the Mughals. Thereafter Hindu books are strongly influenced by the Persian idea. The characteristic oblong shape of the palm-leaf manuscript gives way to the upright Persian format; and the use of paper was copied from the Moslems too. What remains is the more important because it constitutes the essence of Hindu illustration. It is a special conception of the connexion between painting and literature, in which each play an equal part. The legends of Krishna and Radha provided a fertile source of poetry but as Gray says the pictures that accompany the verse no more 'illustrate' it (in the usual sense) than the verse describes the picture; 'both express the sentiment of the moment chosen' [60]. In the seventeenth-century Ragmala illustrations, music enters the partnership. Poems were written and pictures were painted on musical themes, so we have here perhaps the only moment in our history when the three arts combine.

E

To begin with, Mughal illustration shows few of these traits. Humayun, the second Mughal emperor, imported two Persian artists to supervise the illustration of the 'Romance of Amir Hamza' or the *Hamza-Nama*. It was planned as a very large work, measuring about 22 × 28 inches, and consisting of twelve volumes with a picture on every page. As many as fifty painters are said to have worked on it and it was not finished until after Akbar had succeeded to the throne in 1556. It is not surprising therefore that there are in it stylistic differences and that in the course of the work we can perhaps discern the emergence of Mughal characteristics, the chief of which seems to be a desire for greater naturalism.

This tendency gathered force under Akbar (1556–1605) who was a great patron of the arts. He could not read himself and delighted to have romances read to him from the 24,000 volumes which his library contained. He kept a staff of book-painters whose work was submitted to him every week and who were rewarded accordingly [67]. Among them were many Hindu artists, for Akbar was interested in the older culture and for him the two great Sanskrit epics, the *Mahabharata* and the *Ramayana*, had been translated and illustrated. Perhaps the Hindu contribution is seen in the illustrated books of animal fables that were produced during his reign. At this time, too, Western influence began to make itself felt and some of it can be traced to the presentation by Portuguese Jesuits to Akbar of a Plantin Bible with Flemish engravings. Later and especially under Akbar's successor, Jehangir, it is not uncommon to find in the background of a Mughal illustration a village transported bodily from a Flemish or German engraving or miniature.

Jehangir employed his artists to paint separate pictures (especially portraits) rather than to illustrate manuscripts and even though these pictures were often bound up into albums this step marks the emancipation of Mughal painting from book illustration. After his reign the prestige of the artist decreased and his work deteriorated correspondingly until the break-up of the Mughal Empire in the middle of the eighteenth century.

HEBREW ILLUMINATION

During the Middle Ages the Jews were so widely dispersed throughout Europe and Asia that one might expect the illumination of their books to partake of innumerable foreign characteristics. But their unique ability to keep their nationalism intact is reflected in the peculiar qualities of those books and this distinguishes them from those which were produced by their Gentile compatriots. Nevertheless, there is a distinct difference between Eastern and Western Jewish books. The former are less representational in their decoration and nearer to the Islamic books which were being produced in neighbouring countries. But although the ritual copies of the Bible had to be free of illustration and decoration, this veto did not apply to private Bibles, or to secular books. We know that the historian Josephus was originally illustrated, and Roth has said of the oldest surviving illustrated Pentateuch (which dates back to the tenth century), that its drawings are stylized enough to suggest a long previous development going back to the classical period.

In these Eastern books there is the same preoccupation with calligraphy that we find amongst the Moslems, and this often takes the form of enormous initial letters in gold on a blue background. The large solid areas of gold produce a splendid glitter quite different from the jewel-like effect of the smaller gold initials in Christian manuscripts. In East and West alike most of the decoration was lavished on religious books—Bibles, commentaries and, especially in fourteenth-century Spain and Germany, the Haggadoth, an order of service for Passover Eve that has shown a curious stylistic traditionalism in its illustration right down

67. *The Akbar-nama.* Mughal, *c.* 1602. 14¾″ × 9¾″. A miniature by Kesu and Chatar, depicting the birth of Salim. London, Victoria and Albert Museum

to the present day. In Western Jewish books representation is rare but it is commoner than in Eastern; and where it is found it is often based on local Christian illustration and may well have been executed by Christian artists. The finest books of this class are the Spanish fourteenth- and fifteenth-century Bibles, such as the *Coruña Bible* of 1476 in the Bodleian. In these the human figure seldom appears but instead we find pictures of ritual objects which are treated decoratively, and fulfil their function admirably. After the fifteenth century with the increasing persecution of the Jews, illumination declined everywhere except in Italy where it continued to flourish well into the sixteenth century.

CHINA AND JAPAN

The art of the book in the Far East developed in complete isolation in spite of that brief period in the thirteenth century when most of Asia was united under Mongolian rule. We have already seen in Chapter 1 how far ahead China was of the West in the use of wood-cutting, of paper, and of movable types; but the point is that none of these discoveries seems to have been developed. Until recent times both China and Japan[1] have lagged far behind the West in printing techniques and most of their illustrated books have been produced by hand. Furthermore their scroll-painting is such a large part of their whole artistic output that any survey of their book-painting is likely to assume much too wide a scope. In other words there was far less distinction than in the West between the painting designed to illustrate a text and the painting designed to stand on its own.

The distinction is even more blurred by the tradition of 'literary painting' which started with Wang Wei during the Chinese T'ang Dynasty (618–906) and continued for many centuries. Wang Wei was supposed to have been the first to combine the functions of painter and poet, a phenomenon that appeared habitually in no other country. Such a combination would seem to promise something outstanding in the way of illustration, because when a man attains equal eminence in the two arts (as Blake did) he is often able to fuse them in a way that would be impossible otherwise. But unfortunately for our subject neither these 'literary painters' nor their later successors ever practised illustration as we know it. Sometimes indeed they inscribed poems on their pictures and this was done even more often by other and later hands. As early as the sixth century we find instances of this subtle inter-relation between painting and poem, the former expressing pictorially the mood of the latter, as the Persian miniatures were to do some centuries later. But although in a sense this is illustration, it is not book illustration and it must not detain us here.

Another element that helped to draw painting closer to writing was calligraphy. As later in Persia calligraphy was held in greater esteem than painting and the writing of the text came to be of greater importance than its illustration. But, unlike Persian, Chinese calligraphy was practised with the brush which gave it a closer connexion with painting; and the Chinese ideogram was of course a picture of the thing described rather than an abstract letter-form, and so itself partook of the nature of the illustration. Scrolls continued in the East long after they had been superseded in the West and their capabilities for continuous strip-illustration (often without text) was fully exploited, especially in Japan. An eighth-century paper scroll is devoted to the life of Shakyamuni, the founder of Buddhism, and the eleventh century in Japan was the classic period of the horizontal story-telling roll, such as the Toba Sojo scroll with its wonderful nature painting and its satirical pictures of animals

[1] But see Chapter 6 for Japanese colour-printing.

behaving like humans, which had such an influence on the eighteenth-century impressionists [62]. But China's greatest gift to painting was the landscape.

Now it is true that pure landscape as distinct from landscape as a background for figures does not lend itself to illustration; but it can make an exquisite accompaniment for a poem in the manner already described, and to illustrate this we reproduce a picture from a fan-shaped album leaf painted on silk [63]. The painting is by Hsia Kuei who lived at the end of the twelfth century and the poem (here inscribed by the Emperor Hsiao Tsung on the facing page) was written long before. The subtle relationship of the calligraphy (quite apart from the sense of the poem) to the painting is more apparent to Eastern than to Western eyes. Another example of painting inspired by an Emperor's calligraphy is that of Ma Ho-chih who a few years earlier illustrated some ancient ballads inscribed by the Emperor Kao-Tsung.

All this time block books were appearing in China though most of them were unillustrated. The earliest record goes back to the year 594. The greatest variety of block printing, both of pictures and texts has been found in Turfan, an oasis in Sinkiang, 400 miles from Tunhuang, where Buddhists, Christians and Manicheans all seem to have rubbed shoulders. Nearly all the printing that has survived there, (the best of it dating from the thirteenth century), is Buddhist, for the Buddhists seem to have been the first to realise the value of reduplication. But generally the use of wood-blocks for texts seems to have been valued not so much for the opportunity it gave of including illustrations (as in European block books) as for the possibility of printing and reprinting texts without the intrusion of errors. It was this that gained the approval of scholars for a technique which was earlier regarded as a cheap substitute for the manuscript and fit only for the very poor. The great edition of the Confucian Classics which appeared in 130 volumes between 932 and 953, or the Tripitaka (the Buddhist canon) which followed soon after in more than 6,000 volumes, seem to have been printed in very small numbers which suggests that the authentication of the texts was of more importance than their availability to the masses—who of course could not read. It may well be that the rarity of printed illustration[1] in works of learning reflects the same scholastic prejudice as we shall find later in Renaissance Italy. It is certain that under the Sung Dynasty (960–1280) printing was reserved for works of great dignity produced under royal patronage, such as Po Ku t'u lu, the catalogue of bronzes in the Imperial collection, which is illustrated with many woodcuts.

The Yuan Dynasty, which succeeded the T'ang and lasted until 1368 was a time of Mongol domination and of intercourse with Islam. But although Chinese wares (and perhaps Chinese woodcuts) reached Europe there is little Western influence discernible in China.

At the end of the fourteenth century movable types suddenly appeared in Korea and soon after in Japan. But although both countries reached a high degree of skill in the production of printed books, the woodcut seems to have remained essentially a separate thing, and type and cut were seldom united in books of any dignity until the seventeenth century. When they do appear together they often achieve a striking unity which is due to the fact that the type itself and its letter-forms derive directly from the woodcut. There are a few early exceptions among Japanese religious books, namely the *Yudzu Nembutsu Engi* (early fifteenth century) and a biography of *Kobo Daishi* (late sixteenth century) both painted rolls with very large cuts, some of the illustrations being several feet long.

The Ming Dynasty which began in China in 1368 reacted against everything foreign and

---

[1] This refers to imaginative not documentary illustration such as diagrams.

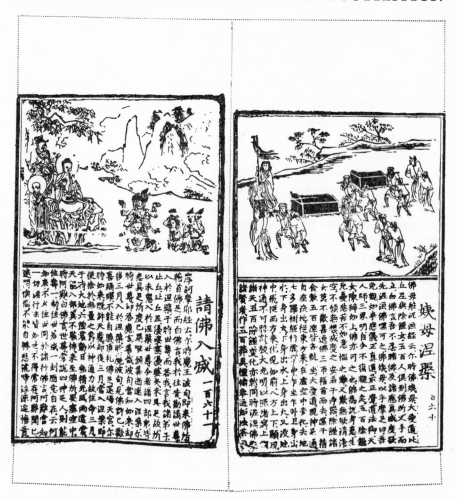

68. *The Life of Sakyamuni Buddha*. Chinese, 1486. 14″ × 8½″

looked back to the T'angs. A book of episodes in the life of Shakyamuni Buddha which dates from 1486 is reminiscent of the eighth-century roll on the same subject which has already been mentioned. The upper half of each page of this large book contains a cut,[1] so that the pictures can be read continuously as an alternative to the text. There is no feeling here for the double-spread picture which was later to become so common in China and Japan. The cuts, though crude, are more accomplished than European cuts of the same date [68].

During the first 200 years of the Ming Dynasty most of the illustrated books were religious in character. After about 1570 cuts are to be found in all sorts of books, classical, historical and literary, and a greater degree of delicacy and precision becomes apparent. There is much more flexibility also in the layout of the page. The double-spread picture makes its appearance and we also find groups of cuts at the beginning or the end of the book and suites, several connected pictures following one after the other, often in the middle of the text. We find cuts of a circular shape and another very curious arrangement that seems to

[1] This is a characteristic of the Kien-Ngan school of woodcutting throughout the Ming period.

be peculiar to the Oriental book is the picture divided into two, one half being printed on a recto and the other half on the verso overleaf; no white margin is left at the outer edge of the page.

There is much more experiment of this sort going on in China than in contemporary Europe and in fact for printing the late Ming period is a time of great innovation in spite of its reputation for conservatism. One development of the utmost importance that now appeared was colour-printing. It was used for lines of the text as well as for illustrations and the first book in this style was also one of the most important. This was Ch'eng's *Mo-yuan* of 1606 which was printed in five colours and which is especially interesting to us because its appendix consists of cuts of Western pictures taken from Plantin engravings by the brothers Wiericx.

The last hundred years of the Ming dynasty, from the middle of the sixteenth to the middle of the seventeenth century have been called the heyday of the Chinese illustrated book. Quite apart from colour plates many novels and plays are decorated with monochrome cuts in simple outline but of great beauty [64]. According to Mr. K. T. Wu they were usually designed and cut by the same craftsmen among whom the Huang family and the Wong family of An-Hwei province are the best known [65]. These book illustrations are even more dependent than contemporary painting on the *ti-pen* system, which involved the use of models created by famous artists. From these models tracings were made and then cut in wood after adaptations of position or movement. The painter in fact provided the *ti-pen* and the engraver did the rest—but it was the latter rather than the former who was the illustrator. This system lent itself particularly to the depiction of the same person in different situations such as book illustration frequently calls for. The employment of *ti-pen* has been compared to the use of Chinese characters by the calligrapher; it is not to be regarded as plagiarism. In a famous illustrated book of the Ming period, *Lieh-Nü-Chuan*, we can trace the use of the same basic models throughout but because of skilful adaptation there is no monotony here.

Towards the end of the sixteenth century the art of engraving reached its highest level especially in the illustration of poetic dramas [66]. Nanking now became a cultural centre of great importance, and the separate colour-print (nearly always the reproduction of a painting) overshadowed the coloured book illustration. It was from this beginning that the later and (to us) better known Japanese print was derived. In 1622 a treatise on painting called *Hsüeh-kuan Chu-p'u* appeared with many colour plates and thereafter a steady flow of such albums followed, some with prints in five or six colours. There is no intrinsic connexion however between the plates which are based on the designs of different artists and they can hardly therefore be regarded as illustrated books, even though each picture is accompanied by a poem. Colour is used in two distinct ways. The usual and more effective method is in flat contrasting areas; but we also find some prints and illustrations designed as a network of coloured lines. The two categories never mix. There was even a traditional order of priority for colours, so that the important parts of the picture were in one colour, the less important in another and so on, irrespective of reality.

Although so much wonderful work was done this was a period of *fin de siècle* art in China. The barbarians were invading the northern areas and the Ming Empire was about to fall. There is an air of decadence about many of these woodcuts comparable with the English atmosphere at the end of the nineteenth century. It is significant that many of the albums contain erotic prints and verses, and were privately produced—although they were often reissued for sale later. With the fall of the Dynasty in 1644 there was a moral change but painting traditions were by no means broken. In 1679 appeared a treatise called *Chieh-tzu-yüan Hua-chuan* which is a sort of encyclopaedia of Chinese painting and which was produced with a very high degree of technical skill. It is still being reprinted in China.

Under the Ch'ing Dynasty which lasted right up to the twentieth century the rigid copying of old masters produced sterility among the literary painters. Brush-work had become all important and with the insistence on tone rather than line one would expect the link between painting and calligraphy to be weakened. This did not happen however for the literary style continued to flourish and in 'the four Wangs' it produced the greatest masters of landscape in this period. One of them, Wang Yuan-Ch'i was appointed to superintend the compilation of *Shu Hu a P'u*, an encyclopaedic history of calligraphy and painting.

In the middle of the eighteenth century the Emperor Ch'ien Lung began an enormous literary project known as 'The Complete Writings in the Four Branches of Literature'. This involved transcribing all the rare books and manuscripts in the empire for the Imperial Manuscript Library and, though most of it was done by hand, a small proportion was printed from movable types under the superintendence of Chin Chien. In 1777 Chin Chien received permission from the Emperor to include among these books a manual written by himself on the use of movable types; and this was illustrated by a collection of woodcuts which combine decoration with their diagrammatic function in a most delightful way.

Returning to Japan we find that the seventeenth century marks the true beginning there of the printed illustrated book. Koetsu, the famous painter and calligrapher, was still producing rolls at this date with poems and pictures, but he was also largely responsible for the revival of printing. The remarkable series of illustrated books which he printed at Saga and which are known as the Saga-Bon are some of them inscribed by hand, some printed from movable types. The best known is the *Ise Monogatari* of 1608 which for a long time was thought to be the first Japanese illustrated book. It consists of two volumes on paper of five different tints and it contains 48 full-page cuts probably by Koetsu himself.

The earliest colour-printing in Japan dates from about 1627 and by the middle of the seventeenth century we find many illustrated books on all sorts of subjects, some with hand-coloured cuts. Sometimes as in China we meet that curious convention of printing a double-spread illustration and placing it so that the fold comes at the foredge of the book. This means that the first half of the cut is a recto page and the second a verso, so that the whole cannot be viewed at once.

After the middle of the century the design of woodcuts which hitherto seems to have fallen to artisans began to be undertaken by painters who evidently employed craftsmen for the actual cutting. Illustrations began to lose their archaic quality and with Moronobu the names of the illustrators begin to appear in print. Moronobu is generally taken as the founder of the Ukiyoye school of illustration and his work will be dealt with in Chapter 6. But there were many other sorts of illustrated books produced at this time particularly guide-books and Joruri-Bon, or popular ballad poems not unlike our chap-books. Moronobu himself illustrated examples of both types.

4

From the Introduction of Printing Until About 1520

The introduction of printing did not mean the immediate disappearance of the manuscript book although the latter was already declining in every country except Italy. For many years the two arts lived side by side in apparent harmony. Indeed the earliest printers seem at first to have aimed at producing books of the same sort as the manuscripts, perhaps even more elaborate and certainly no cheaper. The marvel is that they were able to compete at all. The new craft seems in fact to have arrived almost immediately at complete typographical maturity, though it must be remembered that as far as illustration was concerned it had behind it a considerable period of development. While a fair proportion of incunabula were illustrated, it is rather strange that the typography of the books printed before 1490 was on the whole so much better than their illustration which had had a longer start. But even their tightly filled columns of type were obviously modelled on the manuscripts. Later there was a tendency to cheaper books with a consequent decline in the quality of illustration.

There is no evidence that the early printers tried to pass off their illustrated books as manuscripts. A few copies of some editions were printed on vellum but most of them were on paper, the introduction of which into Europe was one of the great factors in the spread of printing. But several printers, Schoeffer for instance, started their careers as illuminators, and right up to the end of the sixteenth century we find books like the Italian *Life of Francesco Sforza* (1490) with illuminated borders surrounding printed text [91]; or less successful French ones like Vérard's where woodcut borders and pictures are painted over with opaque colours. The simplicity of the woodcut, which seems to us to fit it so admirably for its partnership with type, was evidently considered a defect by most of the early printers, to be remedied with a lavish application of colour. It is surprising that with the high degree of skill available from contemporary miniaturists, this colour should usually have been so crudely laid on. The reason is probably that, while a skilled artist would take enormous pains over a single initial, only a hack would undertake the task of colouring up the large numbers required in a printed edition.

While printed books with painted decorations are fairly common, it is rare to find manuscripts with printed illustrations. Some of the earliest block books (called chiroxylographic) have a hand-written text. There is, for example, the unique copy of the *Servatius Legend* in Brussels with its beautifully coloured woodcuts which probably dates from the middle of the fifteenth century [73]. Usually such illustrations were pasted into the manuscript, having been printed separately, but the British Museum possesses a Dominican Prayer Book where they are printed on the vellum alongside a pure miniature. This curious mixture of printing and illumination leads us to inquire whether the woodcut illustration was ever copied in manuscripts. One would expect it to be the other way round and in fact we shall meet many books with cuts based on miniatures. But the miniaturists also copied the engravers, and it is indeed hard to exaggerate the influence on art generally of the woodcut prints of the fourteenth and fifteenth centuries. It was as great as that of manuscript illumination in the Romanesque and Gothic periods. Joan Evans has given some reasons: the cuts were in the main traditional in subject; they were of little enough value to be easily acquired or borrowed; and being in simple line they provided an easy basis for working drawings in any craft, not only for illumination but also for tapestries and stained glass.

We have already seen how woodcuts had long been used in China and Japan, and in Europe too they preceded the introduction of movable type by many years. They were being used for playing-cards at the end of the fourteenth century and for printing patterns on textiles long before that. It is from the ranks of the textile printers rather than from the illuminators that the early woodcutters were recruited. To begin with they seem to have been their own designers, but it is probable that the division of labour between designer and cutter took place very soon; for by the end of the fifteenth century they were evidently quite distinct. The designer, who may well have begun as an illuminator, was considered to be of a higher social standing and so too was the metal engraver whose craft derived from that of the goldsmith. This is amusingly shown in Jost Amman's picture of *Der Reisser* at work with his sword hanging up behind him [119].

According to Hind the earliest dated woodcut is a Madonna of 1418 at Brussels; and it seems likely that 'image prints' began to be produced in Europe at the end of the fourteenth century. They were all of religious subjects, crudely cut in simple outline, and probably intended as charms. The famous St. Christopher of 1423 has some lettering cut at its foot that points the way to the later block books. But neither of these two cuts can compare with Chinese work of six centuries before and the chief fault of these early prints seems to have been in the method of taking the impression. This was done either by placing the inked block face down on paper and then hammering it; or else by placing it face up with paper on top which was then rubbed with a pad. The latter method was used in conjunction with a brownish ink for the earliest block books and it meant incidentally that only one side of the paper could be used for printing, because of the pressure marks on the other side.

Block books represent the first step in the use of woodcuts for book illustration—if not the first in time, then the first in logical order. In them the text as well as the picture is cut on wood, and it is very tempting to believe that they preceded the introduction of movable type. But although it is now held that the Haarlem *Apocalypse* was probably printed about 1420, Schreiber has pointed out that there are no existing block books which can with certainty be dated before 1455, so that we shall have to content ourselves with calling them the forerunners of printed books with illustrations—the fact that they were not printed in a press and in the case of the earliest have a text which is written by hand means they cannot properly be called printed books themselves. Most of them came from the Netherlands or Germany, and in the subject-matter of their illustrations they are very close to contemporary manuscripts. Van Eyck is said to have had considerable influence on the style of these cuts but they must have appeared unbelievably crude by the side of the simplest miniature, in spite of the addition of transparent colouring by hand.

Although these block books were produced in very large numbers they were confined to only a few titles, each of which went into many different editions or series differing from each other widely. The authors of the texts as well as the designers and engravers are nearly

69. The block-book *Biblia Pauperum*. Netherlands, mid 15th century. $11\frac{1}{2}'' \times 8\frac{1}{2}''$.
The New Testament scene occupies the centre flanked by the Old Testament parallels

all unknown. The *Apocalypse* series is one of the earliest and best aesthetically; and then
there was the *Ars Moriendi*, the *Biblia Pauperum*, the *Canticum canticorum*, and the *Speculum
Humanae Salvationis*. There was also the *Mirabilia Romae*, which Hind calls the most popular
guide-book of the period. It will be seen that nearly all of them were devotional books and it
seems likely that most of them came from religious foundations whose members realized
the didactic value of the picture. They were in fact issued as tracts. The *Ars Moriendi* in
which a dialogue of angels and devils is displayed on banderoles or labels issuing from their
mouths shows that the medieval preoccupation with death of which we talk so glibly was not

only the result of living close to war and plague but was also regarded as a salutary religious exercise. To the medieval mind it is perhaps our fear of the subject that would appear unnatural. A different and more macabre attitude appears in another series called *The Dance of Death* which was to be better known as a printed book later on. No student of early illustration can fail to be struck by the astonishing savagery of many of these early cuts. Any collection of reproductions showing them divorced from their context reveals a large proportion of scenes of carnage, men having their heads cut off, martyrs being sawn asunder and so on. All this was perhaps regarded as a means of enlivening the sacred texts.

The *Biblia Pauperum* and the *Speculum Humanae Salvationis* were a sort of harmony of scripture. In both the pictures are arranged under arches, in threes in the former, and in the latter in twos [69]. The fourth edition of the *Speculum Humanae Salvationis* (*c.* 1470) is of great interest because in it part of the text is printed from movable type in a press, which at one time led to the mistaken belief that true printing was introduced while the book was being produced. Nevertheless block books continued into the sixteenth century, and we also find their woodcuts, with the text cut off, appearing in later printed books. In the hands of William Blake their principle was revived some 300 years later but with metal taking the place of wood.

GERMANY

Thus we find a method of illustration, woodcut, ready to the hand of the very first printers. Like its modern counterpart, the line-block, it prints in relief, and is therefore an ideal partner for type. And crude though most of these block books were (and few of the cuts in contemporary printed books were much better to begin with) yet by the end of the century books were appearing like the *Hypnerotomachia Poliphili* which have never been bettered for balance of type and illustration.

Nearly all these early cuts were in simple outline and seem to have been conceived simply as a basis for colour. Most of them were probably based on miniatures, but towards the end of the century shading in line made the use of colour unnecessary and the true character of the woodcut begins to appear. Printing from wood-blocks in two or more colours is very rarely found but curiously enough it was used in Schoeffer's *Mainz Psalter* of 1457, probably the first printed book to contain woodcut decoration. Whether they were printed from wood or metal cast from wood, the initials in this book were a triumph for so early a work, especially in the register of colour. Gutenberg himself used hand drawn initials in his famous Bible; and after 1457 the Mainz printers seem not to have used woodcuts for some time.

It fell to a Bamberg printer, Albrecht Pfister, to produce the first illustrated books proper between 1460 and 1465, all of them now extremely rare. Probably his *Edelstein* by Ulrich Boner (1461) was the first of them [74]. The fact that the cuts in this book were printed *after* the text suggests that technical difficulties may have delayed the advent of the illustrated book in print. The first Italian illustrated book was printed about six years later; the first Dutch one about 1475, the first French one in 1478 and the first English one about 1481. So it will be seen that Germany had a good start and it was a start that she maintained until the turn of the century.

For a few years after Pfister's books were printed there was a lull which continued until Gunther Zainer produced several illustrated works in Augsburg. When in 1468 he arrived in that town (which significantly had sheltered a famous scriptorium) he was prevented from using cuts in his books by the local *formschneiders*.[1] Later he was granted permission on condition that he used members of these guilds for his work.

The result was a fine series of books that later were greatly admired by William Morris. Among them were a fine *Golden Legend* (1471), one of the earliest illustrated Bibles [75] with a series of historiated initials worthy to rank with manuscript initials, and an edition of the *Speculum Humanae Salvationis* which we have already met as a block book. In the latter the cuts are surrounded by a thick line which makes them exactly the same width as the type measure [76]. Thus the printer adopted the convention which we have already met in the very earliest manuscripts—and with even better reason because technically it is a great convenience for the printer to have his blocks fitting thus into the type. This would have mattered little if Zainer, like Pfister before him, had printed his blocks and type separately.

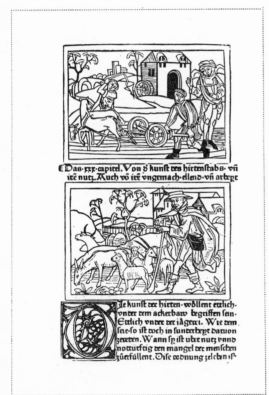

70. Rodericus: *Spiegel des Menschlichen Lebens*, 1477. $12\frac{1}{4}'' \times 8''$

But although this seems to have been his practice to begin with, by the time this book appeared he was printing both together. In his last and perhaps his best book, Rodericus's *Spiegel des Menschlichen Lebens* (1477) his cuts show a definite advance. They contain, a rarity for that time, small areas of solid black which add greatly to their interest—as well as to the difficulty of printing them [70].

Meanwhile at Ulm, where there was a tradition of woodcutting going back to the days when it was an international centre for the manufacture of playing-cards, Gunther Zainer's brother Johann was also printing illustrated books. One of them, an Æsop, contained perhaps the best illustrations that had yet been seen. It was to have great influence on subsequent editions of the ever-popular *Fables* and we find its blocks being used later by Gunther

---

[1] Hind suggests that they were engaged on block books and were jealous of illustrations in printed books.

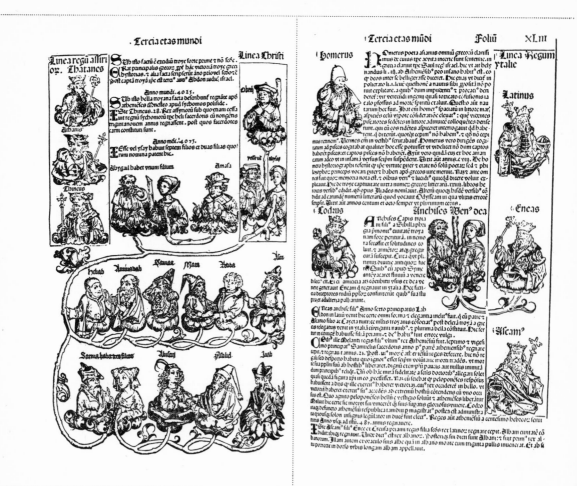

71. Schedel: *The Nuremberg Chronicle*, 1493. 18½" × 13"

Zainer at Augsburg, an early example of a habit that soon was to bedevil the illustrated book. Blocks were valuable property and if a printer could borrow them he would make shift to do so rather than cut his own, even if he had to get them from another country. The early English printers, for instance, were much addicted to borrowing blocks from Holland. Soon they were being used when they were quite worn out or even in books to which they did not belong. An edition of *Seelenwurzgarten*, printed at Ulm in 1483, has one cut which is used 37 times, and altogether 19 blocks do duty for 134 illustrations!

Before we condemn this practice out of hand we must remember that for most of these early printers the purpose of illustration seems to have been rather different from what it was for the manuscript illuminators, and from what we assume it to be today. Making a virtue of necessity, the printer treated his cuts almost as if they were stereotypes, and typically rather than individually. We find this in the famous *Nuremberg Chronicle* which Wolgemut helped to illustrate for the great printer Koberger in 1493. Kristeller pointed out the cuts are really there to help the reader find his way about the text. The picture of a city is that of a typical city and it does not matter if it appears on various pages where different cities are mentioned. In fact this is a marvellous book, a landmark in the history of illustration. It cannot fail to impress by sheer size and by the quality of its cuts. They take up almost as much space as the text with which they are integrated in a remarkable way. Most of the

roeste vander macht dat dye dinge wael ge
uallen waren·ende dye strijt dye geseyen weer
ende sprack maken wy vns enen namen ende
gaen wy oek vechten entegen dye heyden die
vintrent vns sint ende he beual den genen de in
sinen heer ware dat se gingen to Jammam·en
Goegyas quam vyt der stat ende sine manne
en entegen to striden ende se worden veriaget
Josephus ende Azarias bys to den eynde van
Judea·en vp den dage vielen vanden volke Js
rahel by twe dusent manne ende inden volcke
wart groete vluchte· want se niet gehoet en
hadde Judam ende sijn broder:mer se dachte
dat se starkliken doen solde:mer se ware niet
vander mane sade doer welke de verlossinge ge
schiet was in Jstahel·ende de mane iuda wor
de sere verheue in alle der van istahels anschou
wen en der heide darmen een namen horde en
se vergaderden sich to en dye en repen gelijk·
ende Judas ende sijn broder togen vyt ende be

streden de kinder Esau inden lande to den sude
wert·ende he sloech chebron ende ere dochter
ende ere muyren ende verbrande ere toern all
vm ende vm myt den vuer·ende Judas vpbrak
sijn tenten vm to gaen inder heydenen lant en
doerwandelen samarien Jnden dage vielen de
priestere ✶ Josephus en azarias·do se starkli
ken doen wolde ende sunder raet to de stride ge
ghen·ende Judas toech neder in azotum inder
vremder heyden lant ende warp ere altaer aff
ende ere gode roue verbernde he myt den vuyr
ende he nam der stat roue ende he keerde weder
der in dat lant van iuda

¶ Dat·vi·Capittell·woe Anthpochus starff
ende sijn soen na em regneerde ende wo he ver
wonnen wart doe he tegen dye ioden strept·

Die konink anthpochus doerwandelde
die bauenste lantschappen en hoerde dat
in perse was elimaydes een also eddel
stat·en also rijk in siluer en in golde· en dat in
een sere rijk tempel en dat binne gulde voehenk
sel en schylde en panzer de dar gelaten hadde al
lexander phylips soen een konink va macedoni
en de erst regneerde in greken en he quam ende
pinsde sik de stat to winnen en se to berouen:
mer he en mochte des niet want de binnen der
stat ware vername dat ende togen entegen de to

stride en ye vlo van danne en toech eweech mit
groter droeffheit en kerde weder to babiloni
en een qua de em boethhapde in perse dat dye
getzelde veriaget ware de inden lande va iuda
ware ende dat lysias getoge wart myt starker
macht en veriaget was vader ioden ansicht·en
se hebbe auerhant gehalt entegen se in wape
en in krafft ende in wel roeffs de se gewonne
hebbe vande getzelden de se verslogen·en want
se verworpe hebbe de vwerdicheit de gemackt
was vp den altaer binnen Jherusalem ende
dat se die helychmakinghe vmbgemuyrt had
den myt groeten hoghen murten als se thoe
voeren was ende oeck Bethsuram syne stat

72. *The Cologne Bible*, 1478. 15½″ × 10½″

small blocks are let into the type at the inner or outer edge of the page, while sometimes the branches of the genealogical tables run right in among the type in a way that had probably never been seen before and is certainly seldom seen today [71]. The usual cut extending across the page to the same width as the type is in a minority and full-page cuts are very rare. Altogether there are 645 separate blocks which occur 1809 times, but this repetition does not jar, indeed it is scarcely noticeable unless it is sought. It cannot therefore have seemed inappropriate to the fifteenth-century printer to use such blocks even in different books.

When it was not practicable to borrow blocks most printers had no hesitation in copying them. So we have a situation similar to that which we encountered in illuminated manuscripts, of copies at second and third hand becoming at each stage more unlike their originals. But, as with the manuscripts, it did not necessarily follow that the later versions were inferior, though they usually were. As the technique of woodcutting improved so the possibility increased of the copies being better than the prototypes—but better only in execution, seldom in conception.

A famous book which inspired more copying than usual was the *Cologne Bible* printed by Quentell in 1478. Its cuts are Netherlandish in feeling, not unlike those found in some of the block books; and they set the style of Biblical illustration for many years to come. The *Lübeck Bible* of 1494, though it contains better designs, was nothing like so influential. The illustrators of these and other early Bibles had the disarming habit of giving familiar local backgrounds to the Biblical scenes [72 and 79].

Until 1486 we are ignorant of the names of any of the early book illustrators. In that year was published in Mainz the *Peregrinatio in Terram Sanctam* by Breydenbach which was illustrated by Reuwich. Breydenbach was a Dean of Mainz who made a pilgrimage to the Holy Land as a sort of penance for the sins of his youth and he took Reuwich with him as a travelling artist. The result was the first truly topographical book with the first attempt to illustrate the thing seen at the moment of seeing [78]. It is at the opposite pole from the *Nuremberg Chronicle* although it is an earlier book. Also incidentally it is the first book to contain folding plates—one of them more than five feet long—and one of the earliest in which cross-hatching appears.

Just before the appearance of this book Schoeffer, working in the same city, printed two herbals which in their different ways also made history. We have already seen how in the early manuscript herbals the drawings became more and more stylized through slavish copying until they bore no resemblance to the real thing. Then at the end of the manuscript period came the revival of naturalism which flourished so vigorously in Flanders and Italy and produced the wonderful flower-borders of Bourdichon in France. Yet the printed herbals of this time are astonishingly like the earlier manuscripts and their cuts are completely stylized, even diagrammatic. This startling contrast between the miniature at its highest naturalistic development and the woodcut at almost the outset of its career is of course inevitable, and most marked even when the woodcuts were those which appeared in Breydenbach. Although there are examples in many early cuts of attempts at a third dimension the early cutters worked well within the limitations of their medium. They generally avoided backgrounds altogether at a period when landscape painting was just beginning to come into its own. We must not forget that the blocks were often small and little detail was possible; and also presses were so crude that fine lines had to be avoided.

Schoeffer's two herbals were the *Herbarius Latinus* of 1484 and the *Gart der Gesundheit* of 1485. In them he did not completely break with tradition for there are many of those curious diagrammatic illustrations which we find in other herbals of the time. But there is a

73. *The Servatius Legend.* c. 1460. 7″ × 5¼″. A chiroxylographic book of which only one copy exists. Its text was inscribed, its woodcuts printed and afterwards coloured by hand. Royal Brussels Library

74. Boner's *Edelstein*, 1461. 12″ × 8″. The first illustrated book printed from movable types

75. An initial from Zainer's *Bible* of 1477. 15½″ × 10½″

·LXXXVIII·

76. *Spiegel menschlicher Behaltniss*, 1476. 15″ × 11″. A Swiss version of the *Speculum Humanae Salvations*. Hand-coloured wood-cuts in a double-column arrangement. Bodleian. Douce 277

77. Grüninger's *Virgil*, 1502. 12″ × 8″

78. Breydenbach's *Peregrinatio in Terram Sanctam*, 1486.
12″ × 8½″

new feeling in many of the other cuts which pointed the way for Fuchs and Brunfels in the next century. Another printer who introduced innovations of a more technical kind was Johann Grüninger of Strassburg. His Virgil of 1502 which was superintended by Sebastian Brant is perhaps his best book and the cuts are interesting because, as Pollard says, they medievalize Virgil on the very eve of the Renaissance. They also present us with some of the earliest examples of the woodcut imitating the copper-engraving [77]. The tonal effects of the latter often seem to have made the woodcutter envious and prompted him to aim at qualities which are really foreign to the nature of the wood. But they also resulted in greater refinement and delicacy of cutting so that in the hands of a Bewick the woodcut (or more accurately wood-engraving) could almost compete with the line-engraving on its own ground. There was little of this in Grüninger's work of course but he was one of the first to use parallel lines for shading (not cross-hatching which was too laborious for almost all except the reproductive wood-engravers of the nineteenth century). Sometimes he also joined blocks together to make a larger printing surface.

We have already seen Michael Wolgemut as one of the illustrators of the *Nuremberg Chronicle*. In 1491 he helped to illustrate Stephen's *Schatzbehalter*, also printed in Nuremberg by Koberger. Here too an attempt at tone begins to appear in the cuts but it is obscured by the hand-colouring which is the rule in nearly all the surviving copies. There are in fact printed directions for hand colouring in the book itself.

From Lübeck came two important books, *The Dance of Death* (1489) and the *Lübeck Bible* of 1494. Although the latter does not seem to have been as successful as the *Cologne*

scholen dar inghan teghen der stete dar se stande wer
den Dirvmme iosue te sone nim eschete te prestere. vnte
sete to en. Gy scholen neme de archen des vorbundes.
vñ de anderen soue prestere scholen neme te vij. basst
nen ter ghuldene tarc.vñ scholen voregha vor der ar
chen des here. Vñ ok sete he to deme volke. Gy schole
ghan. vñ scholen ghewapet de stad vmmeghā.vor te
archen des heren toghāde. Vñ also iosue de worde en
dighet hadde. vñ te souen prestere myt soue basstnen
blesen vor der archen des vorbūdes des heren. vñ alle
dat volk des wapentē heeres vore ghink. vñ dat ante
re volke.sder strydbar mēne.vrolghede ter archen. vñ
allent ghaf en wedderlud den bassiūe. Vñ iosue had
de deme volke ghebate. segghēde. Werdet nicht rope
de.noch inwe stemne schal nicht ghehoret werte. noch
en schal vth inweine munde neen rete ghande werten.
beth de dach kamede werd in deme ik inw dat segḡe
de werde.ropet vñ gheuet enen stene van iuw. Hirvm
me ghink de arche des here in deme daghe ens vmme
de stad. vñ kerede wedderūme in de telde. vñ blef dar
Hirvmme also iosue des nachtes vpghestaen was. do
neme de prestere de archen des here. vñ souene van en
neme soue basstnen. ter ere brukynghe was yn deme
ghuldene tarc. vñ ghinghe vor ter archen des heren.
vñ ghinghe vñ weren blasende.vñ dat ghewapende
volk ghink vor en. vñ dat anders sstriddvare.volk vol
ghete ter archen.vñ gafslud myt ten basstnen. vnde
ghinghe vmme de stad des andere daghes ens.vñ ke
reden wedderūme in de telde. also deden se sos daghe
vmme Vñ in teme souede daghe alse de dach vpbrak
weren se vpstade.vñ ghinghe vmme de stad. also ghe
schicket was. souen werue. Alse de prester blesen mit te
bassiūe in deme souete vmmeghāge. do sede yosue to
allene israhelischen volke. Ropet.wente de here hefft
inw de stad ghegheue. vnte desse stad te schal vorvlo
ket sin. vñ alle dink de dar vnne sint. teme here.s scho
len bewaret sin.s Allene raab de schoke schal ere leuend
beholden. mit alle de mit ere in deme huse sut.wente se
behodde de bade de wy hadte vthghesant. Vnde gy
scholet inw hoden: dat gy nichtes antasten.s vā ghiri
cheyt to beholdede.svan den de inw ghebade sint.s de

me schal vorstoren.sedder deme heren offere. vñ werte
schuldich ter auertredinghe. vñ alle de telte israel sint
*s darūme.sin den sünde.s in der pine vmme de sunte
vñ lydende drosenisse. Vñ allent wat dar vñ gholde
edder vā suluer is.edder erne vate edder yserne. dath
schal deme here ghehilghet werden. vñ bilecht to syne
me schatte. Hirvmme also alle volk ropende was.vñ de
basstnen lutede. vñ darna so de stene ter velheyt. vñ
de lud in ten oren barstende was. vppe der stid vlle
te muren. vñ een islick steck vp doer de stede te teghen
em was. vñ se wunne de stad. v.i dodeten allent wat
dar inne was. vā deme manne an beth to deme wyne
van deme kunde an beth tho deme olden. De ossen vñ
ok de schape. vnde de esele sloghen se in deme scherpe
des swerdes. Vñ iosue sete to te twen mēnen dede vor
speers ghesane weren. Gy scholen ghū in dat hus der
schōken. vñ bringhet se dar vth.vñ alle de ere synt.al
so gy mit deme ede benestet hebben. vñ de iunghe mē
ne ghinghen dar in.vñ brochten dar vth raab vñ ere
olderen. vñ ok ere brodere. vñ alle ere inghedomte vñ
ere slechte. vñ leten se blyuen buten ten telde des isra
helitisschen volkes. vñ de stad vñ allent wat dar inne
gheuūden ward vorbrende se. sünder dat gold vnde
dat suluer.vnde de erne vate vñ yseren.de se hebbe ghe
hilghet in de schatkamere des heren. Vñ raab de scho
ken. vñ dat hus eres vaders. vñ allent wath se hadde
dat led iosue leuendich bliuen. vnde wanede midden
mank deme israelitescheme volke. bet in dessen iegh̄
wardighen dach.sso dat se sik gheue to der iodeschen
ee.sdarūme dat se behod hadde de bade.de he.s iosue.s
ghesand hadde dat se iericho vorspeen scholde. In tes
sid wüschede iosue. segghende. Vormalediet sy de mā
vor deme heren.de de yericho de stad wedder vp richt
tende vñ buwende werd. In sineme erstghebare sone
mote he setten de fundamentes.s dat is sin erstghebare
mote steruen.wen he de fundamente lechte.svñ in deme
latesten siner vryghebare kindere mote sete ere pot
te.s dat is de leste siner wighebare kintere mote sterue
wē he de porte richtet. vñ so scach dat adhiel de se med
ter buwede.s Hirvmme was de here mit iosue vñ sin na
me.s siu ruchte.sward ghebreidet in allene errike.

Bible, if we may judge from the number of times its blocks were copied, yet its oblong cuts, extending across two columns of type, were of very remarkable quality and far more advanced in feeling and technique than in the other book [79].

Basle was a centre of printing that owes its chief interest to the fact that Dürer may have illustrated some books there between 1493 and 1494. In those years two books appeared with some illustrations which were far above the average. They were the *Ritter vom Turn* (1493) and the *Narrenschiff* (1494). Landscape backgrounds appear in both and in other ways they show such a distinct advance on contemporary work that they may well have come from the young Dürer. If so he must have worked in close conjunction with Sebastian Brant, who as author of the *Narrenschiff*, is known to have taken a keen interest in the illustration of his own writings. These are perhaps the first intentionally comic illustrations in the printed book [80].

Dürer was the most considerable figure in the history of the woodcut. The greater part of his work, quite apart from his paintings, was not done for books at all but took the form of separate prints. He was one of the first known painters to turn his hand to reproductive work although he was soon followed by others; and it must be remembered that during his life-time his reputation depended far more on his prints which had an enormous circulation, and not only in Germany, than on his altar-pieces which were seen by comparatively few.

It is generally agreed that Dürer must have left the cutting of his blocks to others, but Hind thinks that he probably drew his designs on the wood first and then supervised their cutting. He was certainly interested in the technique, and the tones he could obtain from wood are far in advance of most contemporary work. But apart from technique he brought

80. Brant's *Narrenschiff*, 1494. 5¾″ × 3¾″

81. Dürer's *Apocalypse*, 1498. $15\frac{1}{2}'' \times 11\frac{1}{4}''$

to these problems the fresh mind and eye which has so often been the painter's contribution to the book. His work is always Gothic in its strength and directness, but it was mellowed by his stay in Italy. As we follow its evolution from the *Apocalypse* of 1498 to the *Little Passion* of 1511 we see the impact of Italian order and composition on the formlessness and congestion that are typical of Northern woodcuts. The change can almost be watched in one book, the *Great Passion*, which was begun about 1499 and completed about 1510. The contrast between the earliest and the latest cuts is quite remarkable and it has been suggested that it was partly a result of Dürer's conversion to Lutheranism. He stands at the turning point between the medieval art in which he was nurtured and that of the Renaissance into which he grew [81].

Dürer's chief works were the *Apocalypse*, the *Great Passion*, the *Life of the Virgin* and the *Little Passion*. These were all published between 1498 and 1511, in which year the first three were reissued in one volume with new title-pages. In spite of their slender texts they are not true illustrated books. The verses which Chelidonius supplied seem to be an afterthought; and the cuts themselves were sold as separate prints. But Dürer must nevertheless have taken an interest in the typography of these volumes as the use of roman type in the second edition of the *Life of the Virgin* and of the *Great Passion* seems to suggest. Roman had been in use in Italy for some time but its introduction into Germany at a time when Gothic was almost universally favoured must have been quite startling. There are also his title-pages and his works on measurement, proportion and fortification, subjects which preoccupied his later years. These are illustrated with cuts which are really in the nature of diagrams.

One of Dürer's greatest services to the woodcut was to emancipate it from hand-colouring. It is true that the illustrations of the *Theuerdank* which Burgkmair and others helped to produce in 1517 for the Emperor Maximilian's marriage are often found coloured, but the fact remains that they are better without, and that from this time the use of colour is on the decline. Dürer's interest in copper-engraving must also have had its effect on his woodcuts. His engravings, which he is supposed to have executed himself, and which were aimed at a more fastidious public than his woodcuts, were mostly reproductions of his other works, and as none of them were for books they need not detain us here. But the refinement possible to the graver must have prompted him to demand more delicacy from his woodcutters. And complaints of his about their work have survived.

Dürer's use of engraving and etching on iron belong to the next chapter, but his great contribution to the dying art of illumination must be mentioned here. This was the *Emperor Maximilian's Prayer Book* of 1514, the text of which was printed and the exquisite borders drawn by Dürer, Cranach and others in coloured inks. The unique copy is preserved at Munich, but it has several times been reproduced.

Before we leave Germany we must mention a variation on woodcutting which is of little more than academic interest. This is the relief metal-cut. It evolved no effects that were not obtainable with wood, and often it is impossible to distinguish books illustrated by this method from those with woodcuts. An early example is the German edition of *The Meditations of Cardinal Turrecremata* (Mainz 1479), a famous book first printed in Rome twelve years earlier with ordinary woodcuts. The so-called 'dotted prints' which mostly came from Germany during this period were printed from metal blocks but they are seldom found in books. It seems likely that the plates were not primarily intended for printing but were themselves used for wall decoration and impressions were only taken by chance. Two important and very early books were illustrated by this method however, the *Mysteries of the Virgin* printed by Pfister between 1460 and 1462 and *The Stoeger Passion* (? 1461), printed in Italy, probably by a German. Later the French used the method to provide dotted backgrounds for their little sixteenth-century *Horae*.

ITALY

In spite of the close intercourse between Italy and Germany, the Italian book remained unillustrated long after woodcuts were appearing in its northern counterpart. Sander suggests that one reason was the kinder climate of the south which fostered monumental rather than graphic art. The contempt of wealthy patrons like Matthias Corvinus and Lorenzo the Magnificent for the illustrated book as compared with the illuminated manuscript is well known. A contemporary biographer of Duke Federigo of Urbino wrote 'Every book in the ducal library is of faultless beauty, written by hand on parchment and adorned with miniatures. There is not a single printed book in the collection. The Duke would have been ashamed to own any such'. And it is significant that the presentation copy of the Landino Dante of 1481 in the National Library of Florence lacks all its illustrations.

But this does not explain the absence of cheap illustrated books. Perhaps among the earliest books with cuts only the block books could really be called cheap; yet they are almost unknown in Italy, at a time when they were being mass-produced in Germany and the Netherlands.[1] The reason may lie deeper and farther back in a different conception of the function of illustration which is as valid for manuscripts as for printed books. German miniatures, though often incidentally decorative, aimed primarily at an explanation of the text. They were coloured simply or not at all. Italian miniatures were first and foremost decorative and they flourished long after printing had triumphed elsewhere, sometimes even in combination with printing. With their elaborate colouring the miniaturists strove to outdo the printer in the one department where he could not compete.

But the printer had his answer even if it was later coming in Italy than in Germany. And although Italy owed her earliest printed books to German craftsmen the decoration of those books very soon assumed distinctive qualities, and in the last year of the century she produced a work that for beauty of illustration and typography surpassed anything from her northern neighbour. But apart from the *Hypnerotomachia Poliphili* the individual Italian cut was often surpassed by the individual German one. The difference was that the best Italian work all went into books whereas in Germany a large proportion went into separate prints. Dürer's output of the latter, for instance, greatly exceeded his book illustration. But the production of prints was a rarity in Italy. Where the Italians excelled was in the way they saw the page as a whole, treating the illustration rather as an ornament than as a picture in its own right; consequently they avoided the crude use of colour that is found in most other countries. Where their books are hand-coloured we feel that they had been designed for it, not that it has been added as an afterthought. We even find in some of the early books outline borders specially designed for the addition of colour. The *Aristotle* of 1483 printed by Andreas de Asola is an outstanding example of hand-colouring.

It is interesting to note that Ratdolt, who was also responsible for the first title-page and for some of the earliest Italian colour-printing, produced some of the first borders which stand on their own without hand-colouring. In Venice, where he worked, most of the early cuts were in simple outline and this style continued there long after hand-colouring had been abandoned. Generally speaking the Italian cut has a lighter line than the German one and is less crude and less archaic to our eyes. What it loses in vigour it gains in elegance, though the standard of cutting in Germany seems to have been a little higher. The super-imposition of Italian elegance on Gothic design is seen very early in Lorenzo Spirito's *Sorte* (1482). This is a book about fortune telling of which only a single copy of the first edition survives. It has some wonderful portraits of kings, four to a page, surrounded by architectural borders; and for its date the cutting of the blocks is extremely skilful.

After the *Stoeger Passion* the first illustrated book was Turrecremata's *Meditationes* (1467) the woodcuts in which were based on frescoes in Rome, but were almost certainly cut by a German craftsman. *De Re Militari* (1472) is usually agreed to be the first book with purely Italian illustration, and its cuts, though diagrammatic, are far in advance of their time. Sander says 'this book is among the most curious things which this fifteenth century, so rich in an astonishing capacity to create new things, ever produced'. Incidentally the illustrations were probably printed separately from the text; and they correspond very closely with the illustrations in a manuscript of this work which is in the British Museum. Their influence is seen in the Verona Æsop of 1479 which is interesting because of the 'printer's

---

[1] But Castaldi, a block printer who worked in Italy at the end of the fourteenth century, is supposed to have been given the idea by blocks which Marco Polo brought back from China. Marco Polo however never himself mentions printing in China, except of paper money.

82. Tuppo's *Aesop*, 1485. 9" × 6"

flowers' that are used in it for borders and also singly throughout the text.[1] Another far
better Æsop was published in Naples by Tuppo in 1485 and in this the cuts are surrounded
by elaborate *passe-partout* borders which were designed separately and could be used with
other blocks as well. This is an outstanding book in printing and illustration, the more so
because it was the work of an amateur. Tuppo was *persona grata* at the court of Ferdinand of
Aragon, a patron who seems to have shown more interest in printing than his princely
neighbours. It was perhaps in deference to him that the cuts in this book have been given a
decidedly hispano-mauresque cast [82].

A similar combination of cut and border, of illustration and decoration, is found in the
second of the two *Malermi Bibles* where the blocks are slightly smaller than in the first
edition and are rather clumsily made up to column width by strips of border on either side.
These are two famous Venetian products, the first being published by Giunta in 1490 and
the second (pirated) by Tridino in 1493. They are generally taken to exemplify the popular
and classical styles respectively, for it is supposed that Mantegna's influence can be seen in
the 1493 volume. It is said that many of the earlier cuts are based on the *Cologne Bible* but
they are wholly Italianized and most of them are infinitely superior, in their plain rule
borders, to the Tridino cuts [83 and 84]. These two styles are found side by side in contemporary work, often in books from the same press, which suggests that the woodcutters worked
independently of the printers. More important perhaps is the small size of these cuts of
which there are 386 in the 1490 edition. This was a natural result of the decision to
illustrate the text as fully as possible, so fully that the whole story is told by the pictures.

Monte Sancto di Dio, printed in Florence in 1477, is a landmark because it contains illus-

[1] Typographic unit ornaments seem to have   also from Verona. In this book a whole page is
been first used the previous year in the *Ars Moriendi*   thus decorated.

83. *The Malermi Bible*, Giunta, 1490. 12½″ × 8¼″

84. *The Malermi Bible*, Tridino, 1493. 11¾″ × 7¾″

trations engraved on copper. It is also the first book printed in Florence with illustrations of any kind; and von Rath has pointed out that in most of the nine European cities where copper-engravings were used to illustrate books they were the first illustrations of any sort to be printed there—in other words, wood replaced copper as soon as the printers realized how much easier it was to work. But during the seventeenth century copper was to rival wood and in the eighteenth it was to supplant it altogether. The two methods are of course quite dissimilar both in technique and in result. Woodcuts are printed in relief, in the same way as type, but engravings are printed intaglio from an incised line. This means that an engraving cannot be printed with type in one operation; if it is found on the type page it has been printed either before or after, but more usually engravings are printed on separate pages which are pasted into the book when it is bound. Very much finer and more delicate effects are possible in copper than in wood, and the illusion of tone is more accessible because cross-hatching is so much easier. On the other hand it has been argued that the relief method forms the perfect counterpart for type and makes a homogeneous whole; and theoretically this may be so. But all the same no one can deny a high degree of perfection to the best French books of the eighteenth century in spite of the separate process.

Engraved illustration is at its best in small books, which is perhaps why eighteenth-century books progressively diminished in size. Its sharpness and detail make their greatest effect in a small area and it was here the engraving scored over the woodcut and later stimulated the production of the wood-engraving. Line-engraving (in which the burin is used) is more formal and is better fitted for illustration than the later developments such as etching, stipple, mezzotint and aquatint which all aim at producing tone.

Engraving has an older and more honourable history than woodcutting. Before it was thought of as a method of printing it was a branch of the goldsmith's art, and right from the start the engraver has been a more independent artist than the woodcutter, working from a less detailed drawing where he has not been his own designer. The earliest book with engravings was Boccaccio's *De casibus illustrium Virorum*, published in Bruges in 1476, and engraving was used the next year for maps in a book from Bologna; but the first of any importance was Bettini's *Monte Sancto di Dio* (1477) printed by the German Lorenz. Here Baldini's illustrations are strongly influenced by Botticelli and were once thought to have been his work [85].

Another even more interesting book, the illustrations of which can definitely be traced to Botticelli, is Landino's *Dante* of 1481 which came from the same printer. Baldini's engravings are based on a wonderful set of drawings which Botticelli did for a manuscript of the *Divina Commedia*. This manuscript was probably commissioned by Lorenzo de'Medici and the drawings were in existence until the last war when most of them were lost. They are perhaps the only illustrations for Dante that in imaginative force can stand up to the text, for Botticelli is known to have had a great admiration for him and in this instance the poet and the painter were perfectly matched. We find a curious reminder of early illumination in the grouping of several scenes in one drawing so that successive actions are shown as if they happened simultaneously. A few were wholly or partly coloured. But although this suggests that these drawings were not specifically designed for engraving there is an interesting remark of Vasari about Botticelli: 'He illustrated the *Inferno* and caused it to be printed.' So it may well be that Baldini engraved the drawings for the first nineteen cantos of the *Inferno* with the painter's sanction and that the printer could not wait for any more. The difficulty of printing engravings on the text paper is shown by the fact that only the first two or three are printed in this way, and one of them is printed in the bottom margin because the printer failed to leave sufficient space for it at the top of the page. The remainder are pasted in on blank spaces left for them, and no illustrations at all appear after the nineteenth canto. There are eleven illustrations for which we have both drawings and engravings. The later are far from being facsimiles, but they are obviously based on the drawings. They are greatly reduced in size and are often reversed; and their function seems to have been not so much to decorate as to indicate the contents of each canto. The drawing and engraving for Canto X are reproduced here for purposes of comparison [92 and 93].

Both these books are often dismissed as inferior but they are important because they show the development of engraving in Italy. As Hind says, its growth there was more indigenous than the growth of printing which came from Germany. And though the engravers were not as proficient technically as their northern counterparts they show a keener sense of beauty

85. Bettini's *Monte Sancto di Dio*, 1477. 11″ × 8″. An early copper engraving

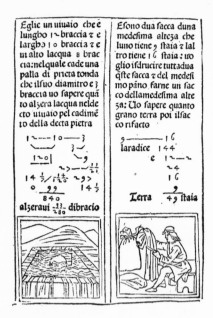

86. Calandri's *Arithmetic*, 1491. $5\frac{1}{4}'' \times 4''$

in their designs. Great painters like Mantegna and Pollaiuolo are known to have engraved (though not for books), and already we find this method being used to reproduce paintings, a practice that has seldom done justice either to painting or to engraving. It is unfortunate that so many of these early Italian engravings are badly printed for this makes it difficult to assess them.[1]

During the sixteenth century technical proficiency arrived and we find the debt to Germany being repaid by engravers like Marcantonio Raimondi (b. 1480) who had at least as much influence in Germany towards the end of the century as Dürer had in Italy at the beginning. He copied Dürer's *Life of Mary* on copper and even added Dürer's initials to the plates. Later he engraved a licentious set of small illustrations after Romano for Aretino's *Sonetti* which were printed direct on the text paper and these are said to have caused his banishment from Rome.

The first engraved title-page appeared in Florence in 1512 but although this was to become a commonplace in the next century it remained a rarity for many years. The bulk of early Italian illustration was printed from woodcuts and the period of its pre-eminence was from about 1490–1510. Italy was now divided into city-states and from almost every city of any size came work of wonderful quality, matching the painting of this astonishing era and identifiable with its place of origin. Venice and Florence particularly excelled. The difference between their books is broadly indicated by the distinction we make when we call Venetian painting sensuous and Florentine intellectual. Florentine books were smaller and cheaper and have not survived so well. They contained fewer illustrations than Venetian books but those are well disposed on the page. Florentine printers and engravers never lost sight of the double page spread (formed by the two facing pages of the open book) and we have the feeling that for them the text was of more importance than it was for the Venetians. Their cuts often have borders to isolate them from the text. In Venice illustrations generally took pride of place, the text being treated as subordinate. One good result was that cuts were less often used apart from the texts to which they belonged; and as the fashion was to employ

[1] They were printed by rubbing as were the block books. Where they are found on the text paper they seem to have been printed after the letterpress.

many small ones (of an average size of 3 × 2 inches) the cutters developed a minute technique akin to copper-engraving. But when Italian illustration began to decline after 1520 this skill often produced emptier designs than the less elaborate Florentine engraving.

From Florence in 1491 came Calandri's *Arithmetic*, one of the very first to be published, with its delightful little pictures in outline [86]; and in 1495 came Pacini's *Epistole et Evangelii*, one of the great books of the period with over a hundred cuts, many of which appear in later books [87]. From Venice came Ketham's *Fasciculus Medicine*, to the second edition of which, published in 1493, were added four new cuts sometimes attributed to Bellini [88]. They are cut in outline in the style which was to be used later in the *Poliphilo*. This was a distinct advance on the dotted backgrounds which seem to have been used in so many early cuts with the object of bringing the figures forward, but which so often have the opposite effect. The fact that this is one of the earliest books printed (or more probably stencilled) in colour may have had something to do with this choice of style because an open outline lends itself readily to the application of colour. Another work whose illustrations give a foretaste of Aldus's famous book is Giunta's edition of Ovid's *Metamorphoses* (1497). Hind says that these illustrations may have been designed by Montagna but this is only supposition and no books of this period except for the *Dante* of 1481 can be definitely linked with any famous painters. The great *Hypnerotomachia Poliphili* of 1499 seems to owe much to Bellini and its designer obviously had a good knowledge of classical decoration. Kristeller believed him to have been a sculptor rather than a painter. But it owes still more to its

87. *Epistole et Evangelii*, 1495. 10½″ × 7¾″

88. Ketham's *Fasciculus Medicine*, second edition 1493. $12\frac{1}{2}'' \times 8\frac{1}{2}''$

printer Aldus, and its presentation is an object-lesson in the enhancement of illustration by good typography, presswork and *mise en page*. The actual cutting of the blocks is beyond criticism and the use of white space in the pictures strikes one forcibly after the cramped and confused designs that were prevalent at the time. But it is the total effect of the whole book that is so impressive. It is a pity that apart from an insignificant *Hero and Leander* Aldus produced no more illustrated books;[1] the *Poliphilo* which he published on commission was not a financial success [89].

The text of the book was a strange hotch-potch, an attempt, as Goldschmidt has said, to bridge the gap between classical and vernacular literature, between the antiquarianism of the Renaissance and the romance of the Middle Ages. But it had a widespread influence (French and English editions were published later) and the emblematic element may have had something to do with Alciati's *Emblemata* of 1531, a book which started a craze lasting for 200 years.

Venice at the beginning of the sixteenth century was at the height of her fame, a city-state with her own army and navy, colonies and a world-wide trade. Titian was then her greatest painter and many of the beautiful books that poured from her presses seem to bear something of the imprint of his genius, e.g. the translation of Voragine's *Golden Legend* (1518). They suggest, too, a period of prosperity and peace. So we are surprised to learn of unsettlement from complaints in Aldus's prefaces, and we are reminded that the French armies under Louis XII were then overrunning Italy.

[1] But the Chatsworth Library has an exquisite copy of *Le Cose Volgari* which was printed by him in 1524 and afterwards illuminated by hand. This contains six full-page miniatures besides numerous delicate marginal decorations. It is an example of Italian skill in a hybrid form in which they excelled the French.

iuerfi loci appédeua. Gliqli rami & inqua & i la affixi, cú fupftitõe feruata finaal futuro anniuerfario ftauano. Et ritornato lo anno tute qlle arefa-éte fronde racogliédole gli facrarii fimpulatori, il facrificio icendeuano. Finalméte dappo tuto qfto feftiuiffimaméte pacto & fúma cú obferuan-tia celebrato gli ferali officii cú pce fupplice cum religione & cerimonie degli dii. qualúque malo genio fugato. Il fúmo facerdote Curione primo & pofcia dicédo le extreme parole, illicet . Ognuno licenteméte & fefti-uo ritornare poteua al pprio ícolato & læti remeare ad la domuitione.

Cú quefto tale ordine la mia magniloqua Polia facondaméte hauédo, & cú blandicelle parole tanta obferuantia digna di laudatiffima commé datione integramente exponendo narrato, & me compendiofaméte in-ftituto al fpatiofo & harenulato litore di piaceuoli plémyruli irruenti re lixo, oue era il deftructo & deferto tempio perueniffimo.

89. Colonna: *Hypnerotomachia Poliphili*, 1499. $11\frac{1}{4}'' \times 7\frac{3}{4}''$. Compare with 136

The chief change in the book brought by the new century was a stylistic one which seems to have come to Venice from Florence. The outline cut which reached its zenith in the *Poliphilo* gave way to the design with parallel shading. Another innovation which is seen in a few of the cuts in that book was white-line engraving, which also came from Florence. This consists in cutting the design in white lines against a black ground instead of in black against white.[1] It is the usual method today and has been since the days of Thomas Bewick. It has some affinity with copper-engraving in method though not of course in result. It appears spasmodically in early cuts of all nationalities but especially in Florence; and it reminds us that there the first experiments were made with copper-engraved illustrations. Frezzi's *Quatri-regio* of 1508 [90] exemplifies this tendency well and shows how the woodcut was beginning to anticipate the competition of the copper-engraving and was already striving after tone. This appears chiefly in the black backgrounds relieved with white dots or lines, against which the white figures are thrown into strong relief. The combination of white and black line in one block is often handled most skilfully, considering the date of the book. This is also one of the first books to show much thought about the placing of the blocks on the page. They

[1] But the first printed writing manual, Arrighi's *La Operina* which appeared in Rome in 1522, had its calligraphic examples cut in black line though white line would have been simpler and was in fact occasionally used later against a solid black background.

are mostly arranged in pairs on facing pages, usually at the foot of each page, and this adds greatly to their effect.

The Prince d'Essling thought that because the introduction of shading and tone coincided roughly with the beginning of the so-called decline of Italian illustration, therefore the one was the cause of the other. But perhaps it is wiser to believe that shading was an inevitable development of the woodcut under stress of competition with copper-engraving and in imitation too of the effects obtainable from relief metal-cuts. The same thing was happening in Germany where Dürer of course was working in both media. And the fact that Lucantonio Degli Uberti, a prolific illustrator of Venetian books, is known to have done so too suggests that such versatility was not uncommon. All this marks a change of direction for woodcutting but not necessarily a deterioration. We need not follow d'Essling in his dislike of the engraver's influence nor lament, as Pollard does, the end of the 'old-world' cut. The epithet, behind its sentimental connotation which gives it away, implies quite truly the astonishing change from the primitive to the modern which came so suddenly in the early years of the sixteenth century. Hitherto we have had the feeling that the designers of the fifteenth century were unsurpassed but that they were ill-served by the cutters. Now the technique has vastly improved but the designing is often not worthy of it.

In Florence the archaic style persisted in pamphlets like the Savonarola tracts and the *Rappresentazioni* (which were sacred and secular plays). They represent real popular art, of

Compa-
ratione.

giua anfiando come fa la cagna
ad cui ueder i fuoi figluoli fi nieghi
E lafo tucte & fol me per compagna
feco menoe & falfe tanto aderto
chella peruenne in una gran montagna
Alquanto andâmo li per un diferto
al fine uenímo in un prato fiorito
oue ella te di fiori hauea coperto
Ella gictoffi doue eri dormito
& cómincio ad dir con pianto amaro
O dolce fpofo mio oue fe ito
Douc fe hora O dolce amico caro
hor ti uedeffi innanzi chio mi parta
da che contra el partir non ho riparo
Da chebbe pianto li bene una quarta
di una groffa hora fu in un faxo fcripfe
col dardo fuo come chi fcriue in carta
Et li lo pofe & pofcia indi partiffe
& per uederti io credo mille uolte
giu per la piaggia mirando fafiffe
Iunon le nymphe fue hauea raccolte
& perche Lippea folla uera mancho
mâdato hauea a trouarla nymphe molte
La piaggia tucta non hauea fcefa ancho
che fu pigliata & menata ad Iunone
collanimo anfiofo & molto ftancho
Non ualfe ad dir che fdegno fu cagione

del fuo abfentarfi:che crefo era piue
ad fuidia el falfo che allei el uer fermone
Che non la feffe dalle nymphe fue
bactere prima & pofcia la mandata
ftrecta & legata al monte olympo in fue
Nel fuo partir mi impofe efta ambafciata
la qual tho decta & dixi digli quanto
da lui mi parto afHicta & fconfolara
Tanto ne gliocchi mi abondaua el pianto
quando la Driada quefto ad me proferfe
che non rifpofi per lo piagner tanto
Ma per leuie tanto afpere & peruerfe
con lei andai in fine alla pianura
oue Lippea di fior mi coperfe
Et racto corfi ad leger la fcriptura
la qual hauea fcolpita fu uel faxo
quando ella fece la partenza dura
Ella dicea perduto e il bello fpaffo
chauea di ueder te O dolce Drudo
partir côuiêmi & il mio chor ti laffo
Troppa Cupido ad me eftato crudo
egli chio non ti uteggia tha nafcofo
& di te mha ferito ad pecto nudo
Facti con dio O mio primaio fpofo
& ultimo ancho O me chio nô ho fpene
di riuederti mai nhauer ripofo
Che quel reame che Iunon fu tiene

90. Frezzi's *Quatriregio*,
1508. $10\frac{3}{4}'' \times 7\frac{3}{4}''$

the same sort that was later to be seen in the chap-books. Popular art is essentially conservative in form and the style of these cuts is found in certain illustrations of every country for the next 300 years. The printing and typography were poor but the cuts were often extremely lively. They usually had a border which was part of the block itself and additional borders might be added to bring its width to the same as that of the accompanying type. There were as a rule only two of these cuts, one at the beginning and one at the end and they picked unerringly on the best scenes to illustrate. Both these series continued well into the sixteenth century, and their illustrations are often found with texts other than those for which they were originally intended.

Another class of small popular book, in the production of which Italy owed more to France than to Germany, was the *Horae*. As we shall see these appeared in huge quantities in France at the end of the century and they began to be published in Venice from 1489 onwards. Many of them had borders of a French type but the best were those produced by Hamman which were decorated with something of Italy's native genius. Finally there were the little guide-books to Rome known as the *Mirabilia Romae*, descendants of manuscript guides for pilgrims dating from the seventh or eighth centuries, which we have already met as block books. These were very small but they often contain cuts of delightful quality.

THE NETHERLANDS

Although it was in the Netherlands that most of the early block books originated, that country seems strangely to have lagged behind her neighbours in the production of ordinary illustrated books. It must be remembered that block books were being produced long after the introduction of movable type and cuts from them sometimes appeared in the ordinary illustrated books of the time. In the earliest books the reflection of their style is often seen for instance in the *Dialogus creaturarum*, an attractive book of fables printed at Gouda in 1480. The delightfully humorous cuts display a lightness and fantasy that were quite foreign to German work of the time [94].

As we have already seen the second half of the fifteenth century was a great period for the book painter, both in the Netherlands and in France. In both countries there was a closer similarity than elsewhere between the design of miniatures and the design of contemporary woodcuts. But this seems to have been due to the woodcutters copying existing miniatures rather than to the miniaturists designing for the printers, and it therefore perhaps implies some lack of imagination. Flemish painters in fact seem to have been even less interested in printing than their German or Italian counterparts. Woodcutting must have appeared deplorably crude to artists like the Master of Mary of Burgundy.

It would have been strange however if the printers of the Netherlands, who were so early in the field, had made no contribution to the history of the illustrated book. In fact Veldener's *Fasciculus Temporum* is one of the very first books in which printed ornaments and borders occur. A French translation of Boccaccio's *De Casibus Virorum*, published in Bruges in 1476 by Caxton's master Mansion, is probably the very first book to be illustrated with copper-engravings, which in this case were pasted in. And *Le Chevalier Délibéré* (Gouda 1486) is one of the important early books from any country. This is an allegorical romance in verse and it also exists in several manuscripts. In one of them the author Olivier de la Marche gave detailed instructions to the artist both on design and on colouring. But this does not seem

LIBRO PRIMO DELLA HISTORIA DELLE COSE FACTE DALLO
INVICTISSIMO DVCA FRANCESCO SFORZA SCRIPTA IN LA
TINO DA GIOVANNI SIMONETTA ET TRADOCTA IN LIN
GVA FIORENTINA DA CHRISTOPHORO LANDINO FIOREN
TINO.

FRAN·SFOR·VIC·
DVX
MLI IIII

PATER·PATRIÆ

NE TEMPI CHE LA REGINA GIOVANNA SE
conda figliuola di Carlo Re regnaua:perche era suc
ceduta nel regno Neapolitano a Latislao Re suo fra
tello.elquale parti di uita sanza figliuoli:Alphonso
Re daragona con grande armata mouendo di Cata
logna uenne in Sicilia; Isola di suo Imperio.La cui
uenuta excito gli huomini del Neapolitano regno a
uarii fauori:& a diuersi consigli:& non con piccoli
mouimenti di quel regno:Impero che Giouána Regina per molti & uarii
suoi impudichi amori era caduta in soma infamia.Et desperandosi che lei
femina potessi adempiere lofficio del Re:& administrare tanto regno:fece
a se marito Iacopo di Nerbona Conte di Marcia:elquale per nobilita di san
gue:& belleza di corpo:ne meno per uirtu era tra Principi di Francia excel
lente. Ma accorgendosi in breue che quello desideraua piu essere Re: che
marito:& quella non molto stimaua:mosso da feminile leuita lo rifiuto:&
priuo dogni administratiõe. Questo fu cagione chel suo regno:elquale per
sua natura e prono alle dissensioni & discordie:arrogendousi e nõ honesti
costumi della Regina: ritorno nelle antiche factioni & partialita:& comin
cio ogni giorno piu a fluctuare & uacillare.Erano alcuni a quali nõ dispia
ceua la signoria della dóna:perche benche il nome fussi in lei:loro nientedi
meno com·idauono.Altri desiderauano che Lodouico tertio Duca dang io:
figliuolo di Lodouico elquale era nomato Re di Puglia:& di uio!ante:na ta
della Reale stirpe daragonia:fussi adoptato dalla Regina.Costui poco auátt
pe conforti di Martino tertio sómo Pontefice:& di Sforza Attendolo excel
lentissimo Duca in militare disciplina : & padre di Francesco sforza de cui
egregii facti habbiamo a scriuere era uenuto a liti di Campagna:Et cógiun
tosi Sforza:hauea mosso guerra alla Regina. Ma quegli che repugnauano
a Lodouico:metteuano ogni industria: che Alphonso fussi adoptato in fi
gliuolo della Reina: accio che in Napoli fussi tal Re:che con le sue forze &
di mare & di terra potessi resistere alla possa de Franciosi. Adunque in cosi
ueheméte contentione de baroni:& piu huomini del regno:Alphonso chia
mato dalla Reina in herede & compagno del regno:diuene nõ solo:illustre:
ma anchora horribile: Et el nome Catelano elquale insino a quegli tempi
nõ era molto noto & celebre se non a popoli maritimi:ma inuiso & odioso:
comincio a crescere: & farsi chiaro. Ma & da Lodouico & di Sforza tanto
ogni giorno piu erono oppressi:el Re & la Regina:che diffididosi nelle pro
prie forze:conduxono Braccio Perugino: el quale era el secondo Capitano
di militia in Italia in quegli tépi có molte honoreuoli códitiõi:& maxime

91. A painted border surrounding a printed page. Simonetta's *Historia dallo
Duca Francesco Sforza*. Milan, 1490. 14″ × 9½″

92. Dante's *Divina Commedia*. Italian 1480–90. Size of MS 9″ × 13″. Botticelli's drawing for Canto X of the Inferno. Vatican Library. Reg. Lat. 1896 A

93. Landino's *Dante*, 1481. Original width 6¾″. An engraving by Baldini based on Botticelli's drawing above

94. *Dialogus creaturarum*, 1480. $12\frac{1}{4}'' \times 8\frac{1}{4}''$

to have cramped the latter's style in the least because the big cuts with their almost precocious feeling for tone are full of vitality and observation. There were many editions of this book printed during the following century too.

FRANCE

As in Italy the earliest books were printed by expatriate Germans and the very first French illustrated book, the *Miroir de la Rédemption* (Lyons 1478), actually used cuts imported from Basle. But fortunately this was a time when the French miniature was flourishing and its influence soon made itself felt on the native cut. In Italy it was the classical spirit of the Renaissance that asserted itself against the German Gothic and produced such books as the 1493 *Malermi Bible*. In France the Gothic style still persisted and in fact flourished in the manuscripts as in building, but it was a very different thing from the German product. And the relationship between the woodcut and the miniature was even closer than in the Netherlands. We find many printed books with spaces left for miniatures and even cuts over which a completely different design has been painted. This last was a favourite expedient of Vérard, bookseller to King Charles VIII, and the typical first of a long line of publishers of *éditions-de-luxe*. He was a fifteenth-century Vollard without the latter's artistic conscience. He published manuscripts and printed books at the same time, and so it was an easy matter for him to mix them.[1] It is instructive to compare the sumptuous-

---

[1] He had himself been trained as an illuminator.

96. *La Mer des Histoires*, 1488–9. 15½″ × 11″

95. St. Augustine: *La Cité de Dieu*, 1486. 14″ × 10″. The angle of the block in relation to the type suggests that it was printed separately.

ness of the vellum copies of books printed for Charles or for our own King Henry VII with the mediocrity of the same books when they were intended for the ordinary buyer.

During this period two famous miniaturists were working—Fouquet and Bourdichon. It is tempting to see their hand in some of the best printed books of the time as Bouchot does for instance in *La Mer des Histoires*; but Sander's warning against making this assumption for Italian books must apply here too. Hind is more cautious and says that the illustrations of *La Mer des Histoires* and Augustine's *Cité de Dieu* are 'directly dependent on known illumination'. Apart from the *Books of Hours* and Marchant's *Danse Macabre* these two works are the most distinguished productions of the century. *La Cité de Dieu* was printed at Abbeville in 1486 by Jean Dupré, the Parisian printer, a magnificent set of four volumes though with comparatively few illustrations [95]. Dupré is known to have employed Venetian craftsmen and the finish of his cuts speaks well for their workmanship. He was an enterprising publisher and in 1490 he actually printed a *Book of Hours* in colours, though he did not venture beyond one colour for each picture. *La Mer des Histoires* which was printed in Paris is 1488–9 by Pierre le Rouge is a sort of universal history compounded with legend and going back to the Creation. Its two large volumes are famous for their magnificent initials and borders, obviously based on manuscript decoration which is not surprising since Le Rouge himself came of a family of illuminators. It is one of those books in which the trimmings and the *mise en page* are more important than the individual cuts (which are mostly small ones of column width and are often repeated) and the sum total is very impressive [96].

Guy Marchant was another great Parisian printer whose best books were the *Danse Macabre des Hommes* (1485) and *Danse Macabre des Femmes* (1486).[1] Hind describes them as 'perhaps the finest achievement of French woodcut in the fifteenth century' and in subject matter they are of course closely related to the block book series called *The Dance of Death*. These are poor men's books. To the under-privileged they must have brought some satisfaction, in a century marked by frequent outbreaks of plague, at the sight of Death's hand laid upon the great and the wealthy. Pope and Emperor, knight and lady alike are shown in this predicament. And it is one of the cases where a picture is far more effective than words even if all those for whom these books were intended had been able to read. How much more dramatic are these vigorous cuts than the verses that accompany them. Nothing could be farther from Vérard's books in intention and no cuts could be less imitative of illumination. With that influence shaken off the woodcut was free to develop in its own way and the *Danse Macabre* showed the way it was to go [97].

Its development is best seen in the great series of *Horae* which between 1485 and 1505 poured from the French presses and penetrated into every part of Western Europe. In these little books (they were nearly all about 6 × 4 inches in size) French art produced something quite peculiar to itself. We have seen how popular this type of devotional book was in manuscript; now, with printing, it reached an even wider public. It still indicated its origin however by means of its borders in which vignettes are embedded [99 and 100], a feature that is seldom found outside France, and which gives a rather congested appearance to the page. The vignettes in the Calendar section have lively little scenes of everyday life reflecting the occupations of each month—a convention borrowed from the manuscript *Horae*. Most of these books came from Paris and the best were printed by Pigouchet and

[1] Marchant also printed the delightful *Compost et Calendrier des bergiers* which had its first edition in 1491. Fig. 98 is taken from the best edition of 1499.

Hado mori medic⁹: medicamine nõ redimed⁹.
Quicquid agat medici pocio: Hado mori.

Hado mori: nõ me retiēt Viciosa Voluptas
Nec luyus auget Viueré: Hado mori·

O felip mortale genus: si semper haberet. Eternum pre mente deum): sinemqz timeret.

La mort
Medecin a tout voctre vrine
Voyes vous icy quamender:

La mort
Gentil amoureuz gent et frique
Qui vous cuidez de grant valeur

97. Marchant's *Danse Macabre*, 1491–2. 10½″ × 7¼″

Auril

Auril suis ou quel de Terdure
Soie et buissens font couuerture
Et la terre pareillement
A pres ie Veulz soudainnement
Que mes tresors seur soie . uuers
Et tout soient de mes ffe. . couuers
Mon temps si est doulp ~ gnin
Mais a la creue gist le Vo.

Je suis auil le plus iolp
De tous en honneur et vaillance
Car en mon temps fut enfranchi
Le monde du fer dune lance
Par la saincte digne souffrance
De dieu qui le monde crea
On en doit auoir souuenance
Car en mon tenps refusata

98. Marchant's *Compost et Calendrier*, 1499. 10¾″ × 7¾″

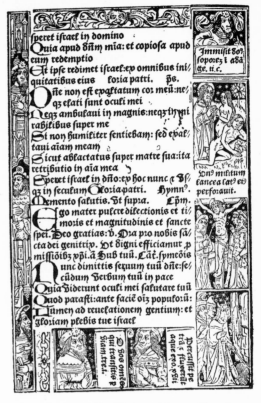

99. Pigouchet's *Hours*, 1492. $5\frac{1}{4}'' \times 4''$ 100. Dupré's *Hours*, 1488–9. $5\frac{1}{4}'' \times 4''$

Vostre.[1] Kerver was rather less prolific and often copied Pigouchet. Vérard himself produced a group for the King in 1490; they were called the *Grandes Heures* because, as one would expect of him, they were of a larger size than the average.

In these little books certain principles of design were consistently followed which are important because they set a style for many years to come. The double page spread becomes the basic unit, rather than the single page. This is an axiom that was later to be reaffirmed by William Morris and it is generally endorsed by designers today. But at the end of the fifteenth century, which was the heyday of the miniature, it cannot have been at all self-evident and indeed must have been quite revolutionary. The miniature, as we have seen, had become a painting in a book and as such its surroundings were of minor importance. But now the woodcut has to take its place in a planned page with margins in much the same proportions as ours today. A curious survival from the manuscript, however, is seen in the treatment of borders where they occur. They are invariably regarded as margins themselves and the page is cut almost flush with their outer edges. In other words they imitate the illuminated borders which were added to fill up the white spaces of the manuscripts.

In technique as in conception many of these cuts are excellent and often surpass the ones which are found in far more expensive books. In the earliest *Horae* they are usually in black-line and then a little later we find white-line designs on a dotted ground. This was the *manière criblée* and it lent itself to the use of metal instead of wood. It is often difficult to tell which material is being used but Hind points out how metal-cuts can be distinguished from wood by the fact that the straight lines of metal-cuts are liable to bend or curve slightly with

---

[1] Pigouchet also printed for Vostre a charming
little popular book which traces the life of a young
married couple. It is called *Le Chasteau de Labeur*.

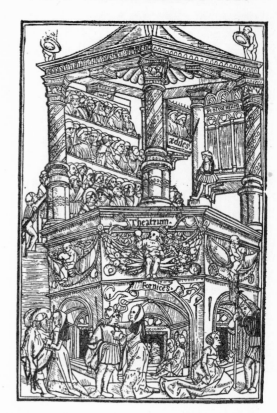

101. Terence's *Comedies*, 1493. 9¾″ × 6¾″

use whereas wood will rather break. Metal-cuts too seem often to print more faintly than wood. The next chapter will describe how in the sixteenth century the Italian fashion of black-line cutting returned to France and reached its highest point in the Horae of Geoffrey Tory.

Besides Paris there was only one other French centre of importance for illustration and that was Lyons, from which the very first French illustrated book had come. Lyons occupied a key position in the south which made it readily accessible from Germany and Italy. The result was a distinctive school of wood-engraving which combined German force and direct-ness with Italian polish. Guillaume Leroy printed several books such as the *Quatre Fils Aymon* in which the cuts show great originality and depend far less on illumination than most contemporary Paris productions. Even before printing the city had gained a reputation for the production of romantic literature and here the first of innumerable illustrated editions of the *Roman de la Rose* was printed in about 1480. But the best illustrated book to come from Lyons in the fifteenth century was Terence's *Comedies* printed by the German Johann Trechsel in 1493 [101]. These cuts have a delightfully humorous air that is more often found in German than in French work. They remind us faintly of the wonderful Holbein cuts which were to win immortality for Trechsel's sons when they used them to illustrate two books some forty-five years later. Another book with some technical interest was the first French edition of *Breydenbach* (1488) in which the maps are beautifully engraved on copper, and inserted as folding plates.

Mention must be made finally of another famous book that came neither from Paris nor Lyons. The *Roi Modus* is a treatise on venery, printed in 1486 by Antoine Neyret at Cham-béry, with remarkable hand-coloured cuts. Brun has pointed out their similarity to work done in Geneva but they are unusual for France.

SPAIN AND PORTUGAL

Long before the introduction of printing the Oriental element had died out of Spanish illumination and manuscripts had become imitative of Western work. The wonderful *Beatus* manuscripts, though frequently copied, seem to have been unique of their kind. It is not really surprising then to discover that the earliest book illustration is imitative too, chiefly of Italy, Germany or France. Spain's great period in art as in politics was not to come until the next century when illustration in other countries was generally deteriorating; and it was not until the very end of the fifteenth century that the Spanish style, which has been characterized as a combination of the decorative and the bizarre, began to appear. It is in the borders that we first notice an Islamic flavour—they are often designed in white line and cut in metal. But there is nothing bizarre about the printing of the texts. On the contrary these display a magnificent austerity which in a different way is just as typical of the Spanish book, and which was to set the style for the successes of the sixteenth and seventeenth centuries. This feeling for the printed page helps to make up for a certain poverty of illustrative invention.

The first book of any importance is Villena's *Los Trabajos de Hercules* printed at Zamora in 1483 by Centenera [102]. It contains crudely vigorous metal-cuts by a Spanish artist which have apparently been printed after the text. A similar overprinting of the text by a border occurs in some of Pfister's and Ratdolt's work and suggests that this may have been common

102. Villena's *Los Trabajos de Hercules*, 1483. 11″ × 8″

103. Ludolphus de Saxonia: *Vita Christi*, 1495. 14″ × 9½″. The first illustrated book printed in Portugal. A woodcut after a copper engraving by Master E.S.

practice at the time. Another interesting book produced in 1495 by Rosembach, a famous Barcelona printer, is worth mentioning for its title-page alone. This is Ximenes' *Libre de les Dones* the cuts of which exhibit a Greco-like elongation.

The *Vida de Santa Magdalena* printed by Joffre in 1505 only survives in one copy. It is one of the most remarkable books of the time with its fine borders which rather overshadow the cuts which they surround. It was followed, during the first 30 years of the sixteenth century by an impressive succession of books which will be described in the next chapter.

The earliest printers in Portugal were all Jews and they produced many Hebrew books. After them came German printers and it was one of these, Nicolas of Saxony, who was responsible for the best and first non-Hebrew book of the period, the *Vita Christi* of 1495 with its fine cuts [103].

ENGLAND

It must be admitted without qualification that England's early contribution to the history of the illustrated book was negligible. This was one of the very few countries of Western Europe where printing was not pioneered by Germans and possibly as a consequence both typography and illustration were retarded. It was perhaps a little unfortunate that Caxton (after starting in Cologne) learnt his trade in the Netherlands, where the general level of illustration was not as high as, say, in France or Italy; and he continued to borrow his blocks from the Netherlands for some years. Many *Books of Hours* were printed in France for English consumption, mostly before 1491, but they seem not to have made much difference to the design of the local product.

The truth is that the earliest printers had little interest in illustration as such. We have seen how the tradition of fine illumination had already died out in England, perhaps killed as is often said by the Wars of the Roses, but more likely by the rise of a new moneyed class of merchants who seem to have been content with the inferior work their increasing demand produced. A period of peace and prosperity paved the way for a revival of scholarship which as in Italy militated against the illustration of books. Caxton himself was primarily a man of letters, concerned more with his texts than with their presentation. The result was that English illustration began with a handicap that lasted almost until the nineteenth century.

The earliest illustrated book is generally supposed to be Caxton's *The Mirrour of the World* (c. 1481), with crude diagrammatic cuts. The captions for these cuts are written in by hand, a reminder of the chronic shortage of plant among the early English printers, which explains though it does not excuse their perpetual borrowing of blocks. Caxton's Æsop of 1484 is derived as usual from Zainer's Ulm edition but it is a very poor and distant relation. His second edition of the *Canterbury Tales* (1484) has cuts whereas the first edition was unillustrated; and though they are just as crude as those of the Æsop their inclusion may indicate the growth of a school of native engravers. He printed several *Horae* but most seem to have been without cuts. His best illustrated book was the *Speculum Vitae Christi* of about 1486 [104] which contains some small cuts of a delicacy hitherto unknown in English books (they may well have been importations of course). They are superior to the well-known Calvary in his *Book of Prayers* of 1491, which is marred by ill-fitting borders.

Machlinia's *Primer* of c. 1485 is a sort of *Horae* which shows in its borders some vestiges of French influence. And Pynson's best work is contained in a similar book some fifteen years later, the *Morton Missal*. Pynson has an importance in this history quite disproportionate to the quality of his work, because he purchased some Holbein blocks from abroad which influenced later English book design profoundly.

Wynkyn de Worde was Caxton's apprentice and successor. He was apparently more enthusiastic about illustration than his master and produced several editions of Caxton's books

104. Caxton's *Speculum Vitae Christi, c.* 1486. 9¾″ × 7″

illustrated with blocks borrowed from abroad. His best book was *All the Proprytees of Thinges* (1495) in which the cuts, though adapted from foreign ones, have some originality.

Lastly we have a curiosity, the *Book of St. Albans* (1486) on field sports. This work contains the earliest English examples of colour-printing from two or three blocks, produced within five years of the first English illustrated books, but it is not otherwise remarkable.

5

From about 1520 to the
End of the Seventeenth Century

ITALY

In 1530 Charles V was crowned Emperor of Italy at Bologna and most of the city-states
lost their independence. We have already seen how each of the major centres set its
distinctive stamp upon the illustration of the books printed there. But with this loss of
independence the books themselves begin to look more alike. Added to this is the slow
deterioration in the quality not only of illustration but also of printing which sank to a low
ebb at the end of the sixteenth century and affected the whole of the next century as well. In
painting too the freshness of the quattrocento was giving way to mannerism, which in turn
made its mark on illustration. Yet in spite of this the seventeenth century was noted for
many magnificent festival books and for innumerable beautifully engraved title-pages which
amply redeem it from the disrepute in which it is usually held.

During the first half of the sixteenth century there was an enormous increase in the number of books published but surprisingly little falling off in quality. A large output however
called into being a large organization concerned wholly with book production, and one result
was a certain facility in these books which makes them seem a long way from those which
preceded them by a few decades. In order to meet the increased demand for woodcuts groups
of reproductive engravers seem to have been fully organized by about 1520; and the natural
tendency of such groups is to follow slavishly whatever designs are given them. So we find
for instance a steady deterioration in the illustrations of the successive editions of Dante's
Divina Commedia, none of which unfortunately seem to have been based on the Botticelli
drawings.

The Giunta family, one member in Venice and two in Florence, was typical of the publishers of the day with their prolific output of liturgical works containing cuts in which outline design has completely given way to shading. These were generally large books, but the
tendency, as the century wore on, was to a smaller page. Although Aldus had published only
one or two illustrated books, the small unillustrated volumes which he introduced in 1506
had their inevitable effect on woodcutting style. Besides the limitation of the smaller area,
the growing popularity of italic type demanded a thinner and more lightly printed line to
match it.

The new style can be seen at its best in such books as Giolito's *Petrarch* of 1544 [109].
Giolito of Venice was the most influential Italian printer in the middle years of the century
and he set a new fashion with his initials, borders and illustrations. These employed cross-
hatching much more freely than hitherto and were copied by nearly all his Italian contem-

14 LIBRO PRIMO

Endimione
Cacciatore fu
amato da la
Luna perche
prima ritro=
uò il suo cor=
so Xenofon=
te.

I l bello *Endimion*, che tanto piacque
A te gran *Dea di Delo*, e fu sì caro,
Fu degno Cacciatore, e a lui dispiacque
Lasciar sua castità, che tanto amaro
Ninfe de Boschi e delle limpide Acque.
E tu con raggio piu lucente, e chiaro
Lui uagheggi d'amor con uoglie accese,
Adormentato e in Cacciatrice arnese.

Adone figli=
uol di Cinará
e di Mirra
sua figliuola
fu Cacciatore
amato da Ve
nere & ucci=
so da un Cin=
ghiale.

O quanto amaua l'alma Dea del Mirto
Il giouenetto Adon: che tante uolte
Su gli aspri Monti e in luoco horrido & irto
Seguia le Fiere, in longa fuga uolte:
Di lui piu lieto, o piu felice spirto
Non uiuea alhor, che le speranze tolte,
Con la uita li fur da quella fera
Che lui ferì, mentre bacciar lo spera.

La fama de
Cacciatori an
tichi.
Hispanico
Mar ditto
Esperio.
Lidi Eoi det=
ti Orientali.

L ongo saria, se Cacciatori Heroi
Narrassi, la cui fama alta e immortale,
Dal Hispanico Mar a lidi Eoi
Spiegar si uede ogn'hor le ueloce ale:
Mentre gli eterni Dei li penser suoi
Puosero, in farla inuitta e trionfale;
E di quei molti anchor trassero al cielo
Poi che l'alma lasciò il corporeo uelo.

DELLA CACCIA. 15

B en quattro uolte, e sei felice uita
Si puo dir quella de i gran Reggi antichi,
Che'l miglior tempo di sua età fiorita,
Viuean cacciando per li campi aprichi;
E la lor tromba fu mai sempre udita
A danno sol d'Orsi e Leoni inichi:
Contenti e paghi del lor patrio regno
Pensando l'usurpar quel d'altri indegno.

Laude de li
Re antichi,
che contenti
del suo atten=
deuano alla
Caccia e nõ
ad usurpar
quel d'altri.

B ell'era il ueder quei corcar sue membra
Fra l'herbe e fiori gia stancati in caccia.
Veder la Ninfa sua, che si rimembra
Del suo amator, e con desio l'abbraccia.
E'l longo faticar, che lo dismembra
Li liena, mentre il tien'entro le braccia.
Tal Pantea bella allo stanco marito
Fece fra Boschi così degno inuito.

Diletto de li
Re antichi
Cacciatori.
Pantea moglie
di Abradate
che in tutte le
imprese segui
tello.

105. Scandianese: *I quattro libri della Caccia*, 1556. 7¾″ × 6″. The woodcut here approaches the fineness of the wood engraving

poraries. His initials, of which he had several sets cut, each contained a complete scene rather like the historiated initials of medieval manuscripts, and they seem to have been immensely popular. One of his best books was Scandianese's *Libri della Caccia* (1556), a collection of poems on field sports with cuts that are wood-engravings in all but name [105]. The distinction between the two terms, which rests on the use of the graver on the end grain of the wood, and is discussed more fully under Bewick, is proved somewhat meaningless by work like this.

Giolito also seems to have set a fashion for small figures in his illustrations. The finer the work the smaller the compass in which it can be contained, as Bewick showed. But Giolito's solution was to combine several episodes in one picture. He issued twenty-eight editions of *Orlando Furioso* in the illustrations for which we can trace the beginning of this curious habit. It was carried to an almost ludicrous extremity in Valgrisi's edition of 1556 which has only one cut for each canto, each showing a series of scenes arranged in receding planes; for the sake of clarity names are attached to the characters [106].

Another innovation which was popularized during the early years of this century was the portrait frontispiece. Manuscripts of course had often been prefaced by a miniature of the author presenting his book to a patron and the printed book soon followed suit. The earliest example is said to be the portrait of Attavante in a Milan book of 1479 and it is difficult to say whether it is cut in metal or wood. This is significant because the portrait frontispiece

106. Valgrisi's edition of *Orlando Furioso*, 1556. 9" × 6"

was soon to become a prominent feature of copper-engraved illustration, and there was a period when wood and copper were evenly balanced as it were, and the relief method aped the effects of the intaglio. The effects may be seen in some later books also from Milan in which Leonardo's influence is apparent. The 1532 edition of *Orlando Furioso* has a portrait

107. Verdizotti's *Cento Favole*, 1570. 8" × 5½"

of the author attributed to Titian, but this is still a woodcut and was to be copied as such in many subsequent editions. A remarkable chiaroscuro woodcut[1] also attributed to Titian on the title-page of Aretino's *Stanze in Lode di Madonna Angela Sirena* (1537) shows the author dressed as a pilgrim and singing his own poem. Although not strictly a frontispiece it has the same function; but such a use of the title-page is rare. It was not until the next century that the engraved frontispiece came into its own.

The engraved title-page however is found quite early in the sixteenth century. A. F. Johnson says the first came from Italy and belonged to Aquinas's *Purifica della conscientia* printed in Florence in 1512. By mid-century it was fairly common, one of the most magnificent examples being Blado's title-page for Labacco's *Libro Appartenente a l'Architettura* (Rome, 1552). As befitted its subject-matter this title-page had an architectural motif, a very early specimen of what was later to become almost a cliché.

This book also contained other engraved illustrations and by the end of the century these too had become common in spite of the inconvenience and expense of printing them separately. One result of this separation was to make it easy to include in a book engravings which covered two pages. 'Double-spread' woodcut illustrations are rare for technical reasons. But engravings of this sort are frequently to be found in the big commemorative books of the seventeenth century in all countries; sometimes they are so big that they have to be folded. It is almost impossible that such illustrations, their margins bearing no relationship to those of the text pages, should be assimilated into the book. Sometimes however

[1] See p. 151 for a description of this technique.

the early engravings were based in design on early woodcuts;[1] for instance Francheschi's 1584 edition of *Orlando Furioso* has engravings by Porro[2] copied from the cuts in Valgrisi's 1556 edition previously described. A comparison will show how much clearer in detail the copper is than the wood. Another book Verdizotti's *Cento Favole* (1570) shows signs of a new technique being applied to wood for some of its delightful cuts seem to have been based on pen drawings [107].

The most successful Italian illustrations to appear in the second half of the sixteenth and the first half of the seventeenth century were the representational ones which belonged to books on architecture, anatomy or costume. There were many editions of Vesalius's *Anatomy*

108. Botero's *Alla Quarta Parte dell'Indie*, 1618. $8\frac{1}{2}'' \times 5\frac{1}{2}''$

as there were in the north. The *Speculum Romanae Magnificentiae* (1548–68) which deals with the monuments of Rome is perhaps the earliest of the engraved topographical books. And Vecellio's *Costume Book* of 1590 was a monument of the period. While mannerism had prevailed in painting technique was taking the place of imagination in printing, and we find this even in the Emblem Books which began with Alciati's Augsburg edition of 1531 and

[1] There were also books like the 1568 edition of Boccaccio's *Ninfale Fiesolano* with woodcuts based on earlier ones which have since disappeared. It is impossible to say whether in this case the original blocks were used or merely copied. But it is interesting to note that a fine new edition of this work was produced by the Officina Bodoni in 1940 with all these illustrations and some others from sixteenth-century works recut by Fritz Kredel.

[2] Porro's name is given on the title-page—one of the very earliest references to an illustrator there.

continued in full spate all through this century. Here where one would expect if any-where to find imaginative treatment one is often struck by the extreme realism just as one often is in the twentieth-century work of the Surrealists. When the symbol has so much weight of meaning to carry, it must be made plain beyond a doubt; and the process was hastened by the triumph of copper-engraving with its superior definition and clarity. A fine early Emblem Book with engravings was that of Bocchius published at Bologna in 1574.

Hofer in his *Baroque Book Illustration* has pointed out the injustice of the neglect which has been accorded to Italian work of the seventeenth century; for only recently has the baroque style become so sympathetic to us. It is true that it was a period of low standards in the books printed for the common man, but it was also a period when books of unprecedented magnificence were commissioned by princely patrons. This was happening everywhere of course, but Italian commemorative books are especially distinguished.[1] They are mostly volumes of large format dealing with opera, architecture or with some festival, the celebra-tion of which would reflect glory on the patron. Or there were funeral books like that pub-lished in Florence in 1612 for the Queen of Spain in which Callot's first illustrations ap-peared. (An interesting book because the engravings are arranged in a sequence showing events in the life of the Queen.)

Architecture which has always had an affinity with typography was never more closely linked with it than now. We have already noted the cult of the engraved architectural title-page by which the reader was led as it were into the text through a triumphal arch. This formula was soon to be used for all sorts of books however unsuitable, and by degrees other architectural ornaments found their way into the pages. It was a period of building on a grand scale and, just as Gothic architecture was reflected in the thirteenth-century miniature, so baroque architecture is never far from the seventeenth-century Italian book. Hofer says that the illustrators gave free rein to their exuberance in a way that was not possible to the builders themselves in their handling of real materials. The structure of these title-pages, like Piranesi's echoing and receding halls which were to be etched in the following century, have often the most tenuous hold on reality, but they are not the less wonderful or evocative for that. It was thus rather than in literature that the poetry of the baroque age expressed itself.

It was in Italy too that the style first attained its full stature in all the arts. Monteverdi's operas were produced from the very beginning of the century and from that impetus baroque music lasted well into the middle of the eighteenth century, long after the style had given way to something different in illustration. The same characteristics are apparent in all the arts which it affected—a deliberate excess, almost violence, and a use of ornament that was unrelated to structure.

Quite often the title-pages are the most interesting things in these volumes and more care seems to have gone into them than into other illustrations. To us they seem to be a more integral part of the book because, as the lettering of the title was always engraved on them, they form as it were a common meeting place for text and illustration. Like the other en-gravings they were printed separately from the text but whereas the illustrations proper bear little relationship to the typography and might be (in fact often were) produced for separate sale, the title-pages by virtue of their lettering, could not wholly ignore typographi-

[1] Woodcuts still persisted into the seventeenth century and Fig. 108 shows an illustration from an outstanding Venetian travel book of 1618.

SONETTO SOPRA LE SACRE CENERI
DEL PETRARCHA E DI LAVRA.

Laura, ch'un Sol fu tra le Donne in terra,
Hor tien del cielo il piu sublime honore :
Merce di quella penna ; il cui valore ,
Fa , che mai non sara spenta o sotterra
Mentre facendo al tempo illustre guerra ,
Con dolce foco di celeste amore
Accende e infiamma ogni gelato core ;
Le sue reliquie il piccol marmo serra :
Et le ceneri elette accoglie anchora
Di lui ; che seco ne i stellanti seggi
Fra Dante et Bice il terzo ciel congiunse .
Tu, che l'un miri ; e i bassi accenti leggi ;
A lor t'inchina ; e'l sacro Vaso honora ,
Che le sante reliquie insieme aggiunse .

A iii

PHILIPPVS IIII. Pulcher, Hat angefangen zu regieren/
im Jar nach Christi Geburt 1286.

Hat regiert 28. Jar/vmb das 12. Jahr seines Regiments/ wirt Rudolphi
Sohn Albertus zum Keyser erwöhlet/ der vberwindt Adolphum von
Nassaw das ander jar darnach/vnd im 14 Jar dieses Philippi Regiment/
hebt der Erbfeinde der Christen Ottomannus bey den Türcken an zu re-
girn.Philippus stirbt 5. Jar nach Alberto I. dem Keyser Anno Christi 1314.
                                                                    Weite

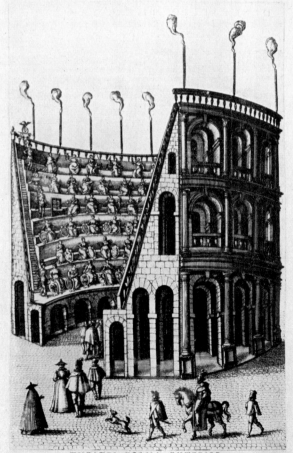

THEATRI FORMA EXTERIOR.

109. Giolito's *Petrarch*, 1544. 8″ × 6″

110. *Iconographia Regum Francorum*, 1576.
7½″ × 6″. Illustrated by Amman and Solis

111. Bochius: *Descriptio publicae gratulationis*,
1595. 15″ × 10″

A. IESVS *e naui ad Capharnaum docet.*
B. *Pater familias bonum semen seminans.*
C. *Dæmon zizania seminat ibidem noctu.*
D. *Seges maturescens.*
E. *Serui mirantur nata esse zizania, eaque volunt eradicare, & agrum a noxijs*

herbis perpurgare.
F. *Pater familias prohibet fieri.*
G. *Seges matura.*
H. *Pater familias iubet.*
I. *Zizania collecta comburi.*
K. *Triticum condi in horreum.*

112. Natalis: *Evangelicae Historiae Imagines*, 1593. 13″ × 8½″. The Parable of the Wheat and the Tares. Successive events are portrayed simultaneously and reference numbers are used. Engraving by the Wiericx brothers

cal considerations. Occasionally books were engraved throughout, text and illustrations, and then their homogeneity benefits enormously. This must have involved great labour and it was commoner in eighteenth-century France. But there are nevertheless such books as Fialetti's *Scherzi d'Amore* (1617) which are as charming as anything France had to show.

Title-pages were not by any means always architectural. A favourite variant was the banner which bore the title and was supported by mythological figures. A good example is to be found in the *Statuti dell' Ordine de' Cavalieri de Sto. Stefano* (1620) which was designed by Callot during his stay in Italy. Other title-pages might combine an illustration of the text with the lettering, as a sort of foretaste of the book's contents; or the lettering might be shown in a panel surrounded by a subordinate design; but though that design fulfils the function of a border it is never formalized and indeed it often takes on a life and activity of its own so that it finishes by overpowering the wording. An example is the title-page of Casserio's medical work *De Vocis auditusque organis* (1600) with its grisly surround of skeletons whose varied postures immediately steal our attention from the centre panel—a reminder too that the seventeenth century for all its magnificence was the century of the Thirty Years War and was no less concerned with death than the Middle Ages; and a book like Cavalcanti's *Esequie del Serenissimo Principe Francesco* (1634) with engravings by Stefano della Bella shows how characteristically it often concealed that concern under splendid trappings [113]. Della Bella, a pupil of Callot whom he later followed to France, was perhaps the most outstanding Italian engraver of the century; and in his work, as one would expect of a pupil of Callot, there is a great deal of etching. *Le Nozze degli Dei* (1637), made to commemorate a play performed for the wedding of Ferdinand II de Medici, shows him at his best.

113. Cavalcanti's *Esequie*, 1634. $7\frac{1}{2}'' \times 5''$. An engraving by della Bella

GERMANY

A description of Dürer's engraved work has been left until now because, although much of it falls within the limits of the last chapter, it seems to belong more truly to a later date, and foreshadows the work of the seventeenth and eighteenth centuries. Dürer, himself the son of a goldsmith, was an innovator in more than one craft and this certainly applies to his engravings. The series known as the *Copperplate Passion* (1507–12), though it does not exactly constitute a book, should be mentioned because it contains some of the earliest engravings by a known master. In addition to line-engravings he also produced a few dry-points and some etchings on iron, though none seems to have found its way into books. Perhaps the only work we can honestly claim is a plate of St. George, designed as a frontispiece for a history of that worthy.

But if his engraving was not done for books it had almost as much influence as his wood-cutting on later book illustration. Unlike the woodcuts his engravings were not only designed but executed by himself and most of them reproduced his own paintings. This was a use to which engraving was unhappily subjected a great deal in the eighteenth and early nineteenth centuries and Dürer seems to have been the first to use it so. But at least he used it only to reproduce his own work; and he himself must have regarded his engravings as of greater value than his woodcuts, since he did not delegate their execution to others.

Engraving however did not establish its hold on the illustration of German books until the latter part of the century, later than in Italy or the Netherlands. During the early years the woodcut, and Dürer's use of it, were paramount. And just as we have noted the effect of the Italian Renaissance on Dürer's own work, so we may expect to find its increasing effect on

114. Luther's *Passional Christi und Antichristi*, 1521. $7\frac{3}{4}'' \times 5\frac{3}{4}''$. A wood-cut after Cranach

Tem-
pel Salomo
nis.
2. Para. 3.

Marginal notes (left column):

a
(Dreiſſig ellen
hoch.) Im andern
teil der Chronica
cap. 3. ſpricht der
tert. Das Haus ſer
hundert vnd zwen
zig ellen hoch ge-
weſen / welchs iſt
von des gantzen
Hauſes höhe ge-
redt. Hie aber re-
det er vom vnter-
ſten gemach aller-
ne / welchs dreiſſig
ellen hoch war.

b
Die Fenſter ſo in-
wendig weit / vnd
auswendig enge
ſind / da kan man
nicht wol noch viel
hin ein ſehen / Aber
ſeer wol vnd viel
heraus ſehen.
Solchs reimet ſich
fein mit dem my-
ſterio Spiritualis
homo omnia iudi-
cat / et ipſe à nemi-
ne iudicatur. Ein
geiſtlicher Menſch
kennet alles / vnd
ſiehet wol aus / Aber
niemand kennet
jn. Das iſt meins
achtens / das der
Tert ſpricht / Die
Fenſter am Hauſe
waren offen vnd
zu / Wir hinnen
ſind ſie offen / die
dr. auſſen ſind ſie
zu.

Main text:

IM vier hundert vnd achzigſten jar nach dem auszug der kinder
Iſrael aus Egyptenland / im vierden jar des Königreichs Salomo vber Iſrael / im monden Sif / das iſt der ander mond / ward
das Haus dem HERRN gebawet. Das Haus aber / das der Kö-
nig Salomo dem HERRN bawet / war ſechzig ellen lang / zwen-
zig ellen breit / vnd ᵃ dreiſſig ellen hoch. Vnd bawet eine Halle fur dem Tempel / zwenzig ellen lang / nach der breite des Hauſes / vnd zehen ellen breit fur
dem Hauſe her. Vnd er machte an das Haus ᵇ Fenſter / inwendig weit auswendig enge.

Vnd er bawet einen Vmbgang an der wand des Hauſes rings vmbher /
das er beide vmb den Tempel vnd Chor her gieng / vnd machet ſein euſſer
wand vmbher. Der vnterſt Gang war fünff ellen weit / vnd der mittelſt ſechs
ellen weit / vnd der dritte ſieben ellen weit / Denn er legte Thramen auſſen am
Hauſe vmbher / das ſie nicht an der wand des Hauſes ſich hielten.

Vnd da das Haus geſetzt ward / waren die Stein zuuor gantz zugericht /
das man kein Hamer noch Beil / noch jrgend ein eiſen Gezeug im bawen hörete.

Eine Thür aber war zur rechten ſeiten mitten am Hauſe / das man durch
Wendelſtein hinauff gieng auff den Mittelgang / vnd vom mittelgang auff
den dritten. Alſo bawet er das Haus vnd volendets. Vnd ſpündet das Haus
mit Cedern / beide oben vnd an wenden. Er bawet auch einen Gang oben auff
dem gantzen Hauſe herumb / fünff ellen hoch. Vnd decket das Haus mit Ce-
dernholtz.

VND es geſchach des HERRN wort zu Salomo / vnd ſprach / Das ſey
das Haus das du baweſt. Wirſtu in meinen Geboten wandeln / vnd
nach meinen Rechten thun / vnd alle meine Gebot halten / drinnen zu
wandeln / So wil ich mein wort mit dir beſtetigen / wie ich deinem vater Da-
uid geredt habe / vnd wil wonen vnter den kindern Iſrael / vnd wil mein volck
Iſrael nicht verlaſſen. ALSo bawet Salomo das Haus vnd volendets.
Vnd bawet die Wende des Hauſes inwendig an den ſeiten von Cedern / von
des Hauſes boden an bis an die decke / vnd ſpündets mit Holtz inwendig / vnd
teffelt den Boden des Hauſes mit tennen Bretter.

VND er

2. Reg. 7.

Ia. 7.

his followers. A. F. Johnson has pointed out the enormous variety of woodcut illustration, borders and initials employed by German printers during this period; he estimates that there were about a thousand title borders, not necessarily designed for any specific books, but used indiscriminately. Many of these are found in tracts, for this was the time of the Reformation in Germany and of great religious controversy. Just as we find unexpectedly fine illustrations in the Savonarola tracts in Italy, so here immense care seems to have been expended on the decoration of the Lutheran ones. Luther himself evidently knew the power of illustration to reach his unlettered public. His *Passional Christi und Antichristi* of 1521 for instance is illustrated by Hans Cranach who, though a painter, evidently did not think it a prostitution of his art to illustrate something that we might regard as ephemeral [114]. Incidentally the popularity of these little pamphlets may also have been one cause of the diminished size of the average book-page.

Cranach also illustrated the earlier editions of the Luther *Bible* of 1534, or rather the earlier part of the Old Testament and the Book of Revelation—for some reason the other parts of the German Bible of that date were usually left unillustrated. Cranach's cuts are excellent especially when they are not spoiled by crude hand-colouring. Later editions of this Bible were illustrated by Lemberger in whose work we can discern the approach of the baroque [115].

We now begin to recognize the emergence of a class of professional illustrators, men like Beham, Burgkmair, Baldung and Weiditz. Hans Sebald Beham illustrated the *Biblische Historien* (1533) with a series of small cuts which influenced Biblical illustration in many countries for many years to come [116]. Burgkmair collaborated in the *Theuerdank* and in another of the Emperor Maximilian's books called the *Weisskunig* which was not actually published until 1775. Baldung produced a remarkable white-line cut for Kaisersperg's *Granatapfel* (1510) which is a foretaste of later wood-engraving. And Weiditz illustrated Brunfels' famous herbal of 1530, one of the first printed books in which the artist is duly credited, and the first printed herbal to make a real attempt at naturalism. Burgkmair and

116. *Biblische Historien*, 1533, illustrated by Beham. $7\frac{1}{4}'' \times 5\frac{1}{4}''$

ELIAS diuidit aquas pallio. Raptus in cœ‹
lum non inuenitur. Eliſeum irridentes pue‹
ri lacerantur ab urſis.

IIII.   REGVM   II.

Vng chariot de feu ardant rauit
Le bon Elie, & plus on ne le uid.
Enfantz ſont mortz, & des Ours ſuffoquez
Car ilz ſ'eſtoient d'Eliſce mocquez.

117. Holbein's *Historiarum Veteris Testamenti Icones*, 1538. $6'' \times 4\frac{1}{2}''$

Baldung also produced several chiaroscuro cuts though not many of these were used to illustrate books. Chiaroscuro was a technique, fairly common in sixteenth-century Germany[1] (and also in Italy), which seems to have derived from the chiaroscuro painting in Italian manuscripts and the *grisaille* of French and Flemish. It consisted of printing various tones of the same colour, or else very nearly related colours, from different blocks so that they combine to form one picture. It differs from ordinary colour-printing in that it avoids contrasting colours and the result is almost a monotone. The German practice was to cut a key block which would stand on its own and add the tones afterwards; Italian chiaroscuro prints, however, depend on the tones for their complete effect. But although colour-printing was used successfully in the *Mainz Psalter* of 1457 no form of it appears on any scale in books until the nineteenth century.

After Dürer Holbein is the most considerable figure in sixteenth-century illustration and in some ways he is more of a true illustrator because his cuts belong more intimately to the books in which they appear than do Dürer's. Although nearly all his illustration was done in Switzerland, he is of course technically German; but in his case national distinctions seem to matter even less than usual because his best books were printed in France from blocks cut in Basle. Basle itself was a signally cosmopolitan city at that time, on the direct route

[1] Jost de Negker of Antwerp is credited with the production of the first chiaroscuro prints in Augsburg about 1508.

between Italy and Germany and the great Erasmus[1] lived there. Thus classical influences are first felt here before they reach Germany or even France and they are fully apparent in the illustrations, borders and other decorations designed by Holbein between 1515 and 1526. Many of these were cut in metal and so preserved a characteristic sharpness, even after considerable use, which compares well with wooden blocks. Holbein's drawings for the *Encomium Moriae*, now preserved in Basle (but not reproduced until long after his death) are

118. Holbein's *Dance of Death*, 1538. 6″ × 4½″

said to have brought him to the notice of Erasmus. His Biblical illustrations were collected in Froschauer's great folio Bible published in Zurich in 1538, and many of them reappeared in the *Historiarum Veteris Testamenti Icones*, printed by the Trechsel brothers of Lyons in 1538. In the same year the same printers issued in similar octavo format Holbein's famous *Dance of Death* which was to be such a phenomenal success [117 and 118].

In their typography, their size and the placing of the cuts on the page these two little books are so harmonious that it is hard to believe that the illustrations were designed and cut so far from the place where they were printed and probably without any thought of the books' format. The printer of course deserves every credit for this but with such wonderful material he could hardly go wrong. In any book of reproductions these cuts stand out from contemporary illustrations as if they belonged to a different age. Even their small size is more sympathetic to us than the large and elaborate blocks which were more usual at that time. But it is their simplicity and clarity, achieved by the omission of all superfluous detail, that is most attractive to the modern eye. In the *Dance of Death* the backgrounds are skilfully varied between indoor and outdoor. There is little attempt at tone in either book and cross-hatching is not used. The page though small has ample margins, and the text consists of only a few lines so that the cut is able to make its full effect. And above all Holbein was well served by Lützelburger, his cutter in Basle, who must have translated his drawings superlatively well.[2]

[1] For his *Adagia* (1513) Urs Graf cut some of the very earliest architectural borders.

[2] It appears that the Trechsels received the blocks as part-payment for a debt from Lützelburger's heirs after his death in 1526.

In Basle at that time there seems to have been a school of *formschneider* who worked principally for export; and while some of their work found its way to Lyons before it was printed it was sometimes re-exported to Germany in its printed state; for in Lyons were printed many books for the Kobergers, the great Nuremberg publishers. And in further demonstration of the extraordinary freedom of commerce between the printers of those days we may note that many of Holbein's cuts found their way to England where they had a considerable effect on the course of English printing. From Basle in 1542 came the first of the great *florilegia*, the ornamental flower books as opposed to the herbals which dealt with useful plants. This was Fuchs's *De Historia Stirpium* with its hundreds of large illustrations in the new naturalistic style of Weiditz.

The most prolific German illustrators in the middle of the sixteenth century were Virgil Solis and Jost Amman. Solis is chiefly remembered for his two editions of the Bible, one in 1560 and the other in 1563 with cuts that are notable for their decorative quality. Amman worked chiefly for the Frankfurt publisher Feyerabend. His woodcuts are a whole age away from Holbein's and in them we see a striving after the effects of copper engraving. This in itself might not have been harmful for it brought a delicacy and minuteness of technique that could have been, and in the case of contemporary Italian cuts often was, beneficial. But combined with it was an accumulation of ornament for its own sake that usually accompanies a period of deteriorating taste. This is most noticeable in the title-pages that Amman designed for Feyerabend, but in his best-known work, *Eygentliche Beschreibung aller Stande auf Erden* (1568) he is comparatively restrained. We owe to this book those fascinating pictures of the printer and his associates that have so often been reproduced [119].

Amman also claims our attention as one of the earliest craftsmen to produce etchings on any scale. We have already noted that Dürer did some etching on iron and Urs Graf is known to have etched on copper in 1513. This process, in which the needle is drawn through the ground against very slight resistance, has always been popular with painters because of

119. Sachs: *Eygentliche Beschreibung aller Stande auf Erden*, 1568. 7″ × 5¼″.
The printer and the engraver. Illustrated by Amman.

the spontaneity which it commands. Italian etching which started with Mazzuoli in 1520 showed a much clearer grasp of the potentialities than German; but it is questionable how far this free sketchy quality is suitable for illustration. Until the present century few notable books have been produced with pure etchings and it is at least arguable that the formality of line-engraving is a far better consort for the formality of type. As Hind says, 'the genius of etching is the very antithesis of the formality of line-engraving'. In the next century Rembrandt was to raise it to the status of great art, but as yet it was hardly distinct from line-engraving because the earliest etchers only used acid to reinforce lines which they had already cut. Not many of Amman's etchings were done for books but he joined with Virgil Solis in 1576 to produce a volume of portraits called *Iconographia Regum Francorum*. Such collections were becoming fashionable at this time and this one has more right than most to be called an illustrated book because picture and text are printed on the same page. The portrait of each king is joined with a scene from his life in a way that reminds us of the economical combinations of contemporary Italian illustration [110].

By the end of the sixteenth century line-engraving had taken a firm hold on German book illustration. It had been slower coming than in Italy but in the end its sway was undisputed. Unfortunately it arrived when illustration was at a low ebb. Germany was divided into many small states and torn by dissension. The liberty of the press was curtailed as a result of the Catholic reaction and in many books we find careless workmanship, worn blocks, and poor paper. The slovenly way in which stock woodcut borders were fitted round title-pages is a fair indication of this. In every country title-pages were appearing surrounded by a most incongruous collection of cuts which neither fitted together nor even remotely resembled each other. The advent of engraving at least meant an end of the worn and ill-fitting blocks but it brought its own dangers, as we shall see when we trace its career in the Netherlands. Meanwhile it produced some very successful plates in the series of travel books, such as the *Collectiones Peregrinationum*, sometimes called the *Grands et petits voyages* which appeared in Frankfurt between 1590 and 1634. These were edited and illustrated by the three De Brys who themselves came from the Netherlands.

The Thirty Years War lasted from 1618 to 1648 and it brought to Germany grinding poverty, famine and plague as well as the other more immediate miseries of war. It is not surprising that there are fewer books of note—we may well be surprised at the number there are. Somehow there always seemed to be enough wealthy people to make a demand for the large volumes with engravings. These are mostly concerned with technical subjects—astronomy, mechanics, military science—and there are fewer books on the arts than in Italy or France. Most of these books are large and elaborate but occasionally we find less assuming ones like the Volckamer herbals, in some of which there is a curious combination of florid woodcuts for the head-pieces and simple engravings for the illustrations.

Woodcuts were also used to illustrate what must have been the most influential and in its way the most famous German book of the century. This was the *Orbis sensualium pictus* by J. A. Comenius which was published in Nuremberg in 1658 [120]. It was to all intents and purposes the first illustrated children's book and certainly represents the first systematic attempt to teach the young by means of pictures. Our reproduction shows how numbers in each picture refer to explanations in the text, and there are more than 150 of these illustrations altogether. Many of them remind us of the Emblem Books and in just the same way the objects shown somehow assume a life of their own when they are isolated from the usual background and shown in all their simplicity.

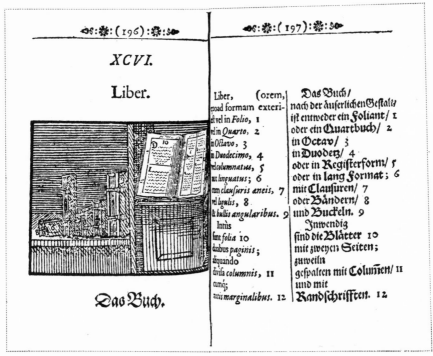

120. Comenius: *Orbis sensualium pictus*, 1658. 6″ × 3½″

The cuts in the first edition which were by Michael Endter were not very good. But it very soon became the most popular school book in Europe and editions are found in all countries, even Russia, appearing even in the nineteenth century. An English translation appeared within a year under the title of *Visible World* and this was provided with excellent engravings which are a great advance on Endter's cuts; but in spite of a more expert technique they preserve the delightful simplicity of their originals.

Simplicity however was not a virtue of seventeenth-century baroque illustration either in Germany or anywhere else. There is a family likeness between the engravings of Italy, Germany, France and the Netherlands but it must be admitted that the German ones are the most prone to over-elaboration and they are therefore the least sympathetic to us. Typical are the illustrations to *Ovid* by J. W. Baur (1640) which have been called a travesty of the classical spirit. Baur also produced in his *Iconographia* of 1670 a collection of miscellaneous engravings, many of them illustrations, of a sort that was often to appear later. Some of them, in particular the Biblical illustrations, have a few verses engraved on them, but otherwise there is no text and not much connexion between the pictures.

Baroque art, whether in music, painting or illustration, was primarily intended for the rich. And all this time humbler books were being produced, many of them with good engravings; but because of the troubled times they were seldom well printed and for the same reason not many have survived. The ubiquitous and very topical *Dance of Death* appeared in numerous editions throughout the century, and Emblem Books were as popular in Germany as elsewhere. Sometimes we find exquisite engravings in what are little more than pamphlets, for instance Puteanus's poem *Bruma* of 1619, where many of the pictures are about two inches square. They give a foretaste of the rococo age and its use of small engravings as vignettes. But the seventeenth century was not a time of innovation in Germany either in design or in technique. It comes as something of a surprise to find a mezzotint frontispiece in Hevenesius's *Fasciculus variorum exercitiorum* which was published in 1689, only a few years after the technique was first used in Holland.[1]

THE NETHERLANDS

At the beginning of the sixteenth century printed illustration in the Netherlands was overshadowed by manuscript illumination which was then at its height there. As in England the woodcutters lagged behind those of France, Germany and Italy. There was indeed a literal time-lag and fashions like mannerism which came at third hand from Italy via Germany, lasted longer in the Netherlands than elsewhere. Yet before the century is over we find a complete reversal and we might almost say that the Netherlands have taken the lead. This was due to the astonishing enterprise of the Antwerp print-sellers, men like Cock and Galle and the Passes, whose engravings found their way all over Western Europe and (almost incidentally) into contemporary books. It was from the Netherlands too that during the next century there came the first major technical innovation for about 150 years in the shape of mezzotint.

The supplanting of Bruges by Antwerp early in the sixteenth century as the book-producing centre of the country is indicative of the decline of manuscript-painting for which Bruges had long been famous. During the first half of the century we can recognize the gradual evolution in the iconography of illustration from the simple religious subjects, little changed from those which adorned the block books, to the worldly and sophisticated which contained profane elements even when they belonged to devotional books. This change has of course already been noted in Germany and Italy but it is especially apparent here. Its full extent may be seen if one compares the simple but moving cuts of a book like *Leven ons Liefs Heren* (1500) with the etchings in Plantin's *Images et Figures de la Bible* (1581); its early progress may be studied in the growing number of secular books like *Die Reyse van Lissebone* (1508) with its exotic cuts of foreign lands and *Loeflicken Sanck* (1515), a fine big book produced in honour of the Emperor Maximilian.

Biblical illustration resisted the new tendencies longest. In the two well-known Bibles with cuts by Jan Swart (1526 and 1528) it is noteworthy that the illustrator has gone back to early German sources for many of his subjects. As Beets has said these early illustrators would as soon have thought of altering the sacred text as the iconography. But the style of cutting has greatly changed of course and there is much greater simplicity and less overcrowding in Swart's work than in his models. One can even discern a development in the two years that separate his two Bibles. The second shows that Holbein's work was becoming known in the north.

Associated with Swart in the 1528 Bible was the Dutch painter Lucas van Leyden. These two, with Jacob Cornelis and van Alst were the important illustrators during the first half of the century. Most of van Leyden's work went into separate prints and he seems not to have attached much importance to the cuts he did for illustration, or to have cared when they were used in books other than those for which they were designed. The *Missale Trajectense* (1514–15) contains his best work which is made more colourful than Swart's by the use of crossed rather than parallel lines for shading. Cornelis, in whose work the Middle Ages seem to have no part at all, illustrated Alardus's *Passio Domini Nostri* in 1523. Unfortunately in many copies of this book his work has been spoiled by injudicious hand-colouring.

[1] See pages 220–221 for a description of this technique, and see also page 191 for an even earlier English book with a mezzotint plate.

121. A design and engraved title page by Rubens, 1635. Drawing $6\frac{7}{8}'' \times 5\frac{1}{8}''$. Title page $8'' \times 5\frac{3}{4}''$. Victoria and Albert Museum

122. *Missale Romanum*, 1613. $12\frac{1}{2}'' \times 8\frac{1}{2}''$. An engraving after Rubens

123. Gevartius: *Pompa introitus Ferdinandi*, 1641. $22'' \times 16''$

124. Thibault: *Académie de l'Espée*, 1628. $20\frac{1}{2}'' \times 15''$. Illustrated by Passe

125. Menasseh Ben Israel: *La Piedra . . . de Nebuchadnesar*, 1655. Actual size. Three etchings by Rembrandt

126. De Wicquefort: *Advis Fidèle*, 1673. 9″ × 7″. Illustrated by de Hooghe

127. La Fontaine's *Contes*, 1685. 6¼″ × 3¾″. Illustrated by de Hooghe

Peter Coecke van Alst, the master and father-in-law of the elder Bruegel, was responsible for one of the really important books of the century. This was *La Tresadmirable, Tresmagnifique & Triumphante Entrée du Treshaut & Trespuissant Prince Philipes, Prince d'Espaigne* to give it its full title. Modelled on a French book, the *Entrée d'Henri II*, which appeared the year before illustrated by Goujon, it was published in 1550 in French, Flemish and Latin simultaneously. It is not luxurious by the standards which were set by later commemorative volumes but with its representations of archways designed for the occasion by the architect Floris it marks the beginning of the baroque book in the Netherlands.

The fostering of the baroque style during the second half of the century was pre-eminently in the hands of one man whose books circulated all over Western Europe and affected design everywhere. This was Christopher Plantin who, although he was a Frenchman by birth, worked in Antwerp from 1535 until his death in 1589. The numerous documents so wonderfully preserved in the Plantin Museum give us the first detailed inside information we have since the introduction of printing about book illustration. Complete accounts are preserved there, giving among other things the names of the woodcutters and engravers who worked for Plantin and the sums paid to them. We have too a fascinating description of that remarkable book *Evangelicae Historiae Imagines* by Jerome Natalis which was finally published in 1593 after Plantin's death, and of Plantin's extraordinary efforts to get it illustrated for the Jesuits—which suggest that the famous illustrators were even more temperamental in the sixteenth century than they are now [112].

With Plantin the Renaissance spirit flowers for the first time in the Netherlands. As he came from France he naturally brought French styles with him but eventually he evolved a manner that was peculiar to himself. His earliest books contained woodcuts and his best illustrator in this medium was Arnold Nicolai, who, although he generally worked from the designs of others, nevertheless has a recognizable personal quality. Between 1564 and 1565 he helped to illustrate three Emblem Books for Plantin, the best known being that of Sambucus (1564) for which he cut designs made by many hands. The cuts are surrounded with elaborate borders, moulded like picture frames, and these help to give a unity to what could have been a heterogeneous collection.

One of the designers for this book, whose work Nicolai cut in wood, was Peter van der Borcht, Plantin's chief designer of copper-engravings. It is for his engraved rather than his woodcut illustrations that Plantin is chiefly remembered and 1570 is the date generally given when he began to use copper. But in 1559 there appeared under his imprint a famous commemorative book called *La Magnifique et somptueuse Pompe funèbre . . . de Charles V* for which he only printed the text. Jerome Cock designed and probably printed the engravings which go to make this one of the most magnificent books of a magnificent century. Thus encouraged, Plantin went on to use this type of illustration frequently. Copper-engravings as well as woodcuts appear in his great eight-volume *Polyglot Bible* of 1568 which is Plantin's greatest work. A few of the engravings are designed by van der Borcht but most are by Peter Huys. Some of van der Borcht's best engravings appeared in the missals and breviaries for which Plantin is justly famed and with which he continued the tradition of the previous century; in the *Hours of the Virgin Mary* of 1570 for instance and the *Missale* of 1572. These, with the *Breviarium Romanum* of 1575 set the style for such books right up to the end of the century. In Barrafelt's *Images et Figures de la Bible* (1581) there are etchings by the same artist. In 1595 he did some more etchings for a fine memorial volume published by Moretus, Plantin's successor, to commemorate the entry of the Archduke of Austria into Antwerp [111].

We have now reached the time when we begin to distinguish between designers and engravers by name. This is often difficult in the sixteenth and seventeenth centuries, but in the case of Plantin's books we are helped by his records. We know for instance that much of van der Borcht's work was engraved by the three brothers Wiericx who were among Plantin's most highly paid employees. (They were also very dissipated and time after time he helped them out of trouble, even out of the hands of the police.) It is clear that they designed as well as engraved, but they brought such virtuosity and skill to the translation of other artists' work that it is impossible to say where they are original and where they are not. It was they who in the end engraved the illustrations for Natalis which we have already mentioned, and how brilliant they are [112]. They did many engravings which were used in books other than those for which they were designed and some of them were even passed from printer to printer.

The engravers of the Netherlands were distinguished at this time for their splendid maps and atlases. The famous *Theatrum orbis terrarum* of Ortelius which Plantin printed is only one of many in which the engravings are enlivened by bright colours.

Plantin was not of course the only printer to produce illustrated books during this period though he overshadows all his neighbours. In Bruges in 1567 appeared a delightful little book of animal fables, Edward de Dene's *De Warachtighe Fabulen der Dieren* illustrated by Gheeraerts, one of the earliest Flemish etchers [128]. In this book Gheeraerts manages to

128. De Dene: *De Warachtighe Fabulen der Dieren*, 1567. $7\frac{1}{2}'' \times 5\frac{1}{4}''$. Illustrated by Gheeraerts

catch with extreme economy the characters of the various animals in a way that is only rivalled in Barlow's *Æsop* a hundred years later. Plantin paid him the compliment of imitating his etchings in the engravings of *XXV Fables des Animaux* (1578). Another book, which came from Antwerp though not from Plantin's office, is Goltzius's *Imagines* (1557), a book about antique medals. It is interesting because of its unusual technique. The black outline of the medal is engraved or etched in copper but the backgrounds are printed from wood, in a brown ink.

This conjunction of wood and copper in one picture is very rare but the combination of woodcuts and copper-engravings in one book became increasingly common towards the end of the century, especially after Plantin's death, when his widow and J. Moretus continued to run his press. We find too a tendency to smaller engravings—those in the Ovid *Metamorphoses* of 1591 are obviously modelled on Salomon's woodcuts in the French edition of 1557, with the addition of a Flemish flavour which does not improve them.

Perhaps the finest of the post-Plantin books is the *Graduale Romanum* which Moretus published in 1599. One of the illustrators of this was probably Philippe Galle who is better known as a print-seller. He and Crispin van der Passe (who illustrated many French books) and Jerome Cock were the leading figures in the great print-selling industry which had grown up in the Netherlands during the second half of the century. From its centre, Antwerp, engravings were circulated throughout the whole of Western Europe. Book illustration was affected not only by the fact that prints designed for separate sale were often so used but also by the large number of highly skilled engravers available. Much of their work however was devoted to the reproduction of paintings—many of Breugel's were popularized in this way—and this did not necessarily fit them to be good illustrators. Of course the great engravers like the Wiericxes were not content to imitate slavishly and we can discern a sort of reciprocal influence which they had on the contemporary painters whose work they reproduced and who like them were attached to the print-sellers. But the effect on ordinary engravers was harmful because working from a finished drawing or painting was much more likely to lead to slavishness than working as hitherto from a rough sketch.

Often too their plates were reworked by a hack after they had begun to wear and so any individuality their work may have possessed was lost. This can be seen in the work of the school of engravers whom Rubens trained to reproduce his work. Rubens was of course the great figure in Flemish painting at the outset of the new century as Rembrandt was later, and both of them illustrated books. There the resemblance ends because there is a world of difference between the line-engraved title-pages designed by Rubens and the few etchings which Rembrandt did for books. Rubens was the greatest baroque painter in the north and his attitude to the title-page is that of the painter, rather than the illustrator [121]. He was friendly with Balthasar Moretus, the grandson of Christopher Plantin, and there is a revealing letter written by Moretus to a customer about Rubens's methods of work. 'I must inform him six months ahead that he may think over the title and design it with complete leisure on Sundays; on weekdays he does not busy himself with work of that kind. Also he would ask 100 florins for a single design.' After 1637 we find him passing over all his title-pages to Quellinus who often signed them with Rubens's name.

Rubens's best work for Moretus however was done much earlier. His first commission was to illustrate the *Breviarium Romanum* which appeared in 1614. A year before it appeared however Moretus used Rubens's engravings together with some others in the *Missale Romanum* of 1613 [122]. And in 1615 he illustrated Seneca's *Opera*, edited by Lipsius. Cornelis Galle who worked on this book was his most skilful interpreter and it was probably he who engraved the plates in the *Missale Romanum*, which is the most interesting book of the three. It represents the Roman Church at its most magnificent and its most worldly. Beautiful as it is and perhaps more apparently reverent than the crude cuts of the previous century, it is hard to comprehend how it could have come from the country which little more than a hundred years before was producing block books in the same genre. Sincerity and crudity do not necessarily go together of course, but the elaboration of the baroque gives to such subjects a slightly theatrical air from which the earlier cutters were saved by the

129. *Hortus Floridus*, 1614. 10″ × 6½″. Illustrated by Crispin de Passe

simplicity which technical difficulties forced on them. A commemorative book like *Pompa introitus Ferdinandi*, published after Rubens's death in 1641, provides the ideal subject matter for this style and Rubens exploited it to the full in engravings of the archways which he himself designed for the procession. Hofer acclaims this great folio as 'perhaps the most splendidly illustrated book of the whole seventeenth century [123].[1]

But the baroque book could achieve simplicity when the subject demanded it, and this is shown in a herbal like *Hortus Floridus* which Crispin de Passe produced in 1614 [129]. These plates impress us with the excellence of engraving for any work which involves meticulous attention to detail, a virtue that can be seen too in the maps and atlases of the period. Here, be it noted, the detail is factual and quite distinct from the over-elaboration which marks baroque ornamentation. And the delicacy of these flower pictures is something that would have been quite unattainable by any other process then in use.

There could hardly be a greater contrast than between this book and Thibault's *Académie de l'Espée* which appeared in 1628 and also contained work by Passe [124]. It is an enormous book measuring about 20 × 15 inches and many other engravers also contributed. Everything about it is on a grand scale. It starts off with eight pages of dedicatory engravings and

[1] It is interesting to note that this is another of the earliest books in which the illustrator's name is given on the title-page (but see page 143*n*). Rubens was of course very famous in his lifetime and it was many years before the ordinary illustrator received this acknowledgement. But ac- tually the anonymity of the artist began to disappear with the coming of engraving because it very soon became customary to add at the foot of each plate the names of both designer and engraver. In this book the author's name Gevartius is also sometimes conjoined.

all the other illustrations are double-spreads. We reproduce one by Passe which shows how an engraver of genius could transform a diagrammatic picture by imaginative touches, particularly in the backgrounds. Such touches distinguish the work of the greater engravers in this volume from the lesser men. It must be admitted however that in a book like this where the engravings are printed separately and then pasted in there is nothing to show that they were planned with the type page in mind. The text in fact is embellished with woodcuts which seem clumsy in comparison with the engravings.

Rubens trained many engravers and one or two of them oddly enough took up wood-cutting also. Sallaert designed illustrations for popular works of devotion and Emblem Books, and Jegher cut many such in wood. *Necessaria ad Salutem Scientia* (1654) is one of the most interesting. At first sight it has the look of a little devotional book of the previous century, a *Book of Hours*, say. But on examination the cuts curiously reveal the influence of engraving not only on the technique of the woodcut but also on its style and very iconography. This book could not belong to any other period but that of the baroque and the counter-Reformation. Jegher also cut in 1651 some good designs by Rubens's understudy, Quellinus, for *Reynard the Fox*, a popular Dutch epic at this time. But Van Dyck was Rubens's most famous pupil and he like Rembrandt forsook line-engraving for etching. Only one etching by Rubens is known and Van Dyck's enthusiasm for the new medium is believed to have been aroused by Callot who visited the Netherlands in 1627 and may have taught him the use of his hard etching varnish. It is certain that Callot's influence is plainly to be seen in the work of all this generation, especially in Rembrandt's. About 1650 Van Dyck published his *Iconography*, a collection of portraits of famous men of the time which are more often found loose than in book form. To this he contributed eighteen etched plates (including one of Peter Bruegel the Younger) which according to Hind were so far ahead of contemporary work that thereafter Van Dyck contented himself with supplying drawings for line-engravings only.

Meanwhile an even greater etcher was at work in Holland, perhaps the greatest there has ever been. And although neither Rembrandt nor Van Dyck did much work for books yet by their demonstration of the true character of etching they paved the way for later illustration. Rembrandt was perhaps the first to make a habit of leaving some ink on the surface of the plate and as he generally printed his own work he could control it from beginning to end; even so there are great differences between the various states of his plates, and his comparative failure as an illustrator is due to the delicacy of his etchings which could not stand up to the quantity required. His most successful illustrations were those for *La Piedra Gloriosa o de la Estatua de Nebuchadnesar* (1655) written in Spanish by Rembrandt's friend Samuel Menasseh Ben Israel, a book which helped to persuade Cromwell to readmit the Jews to England [125]. Only two copies are known with Rembrandt's etchings; the rest have en-graved imitations by Salom Italia. There are also single etchings in *Medea Treurspel* (1670) and in *Der Zee-Vaert Lof* (1634), but as the first book is more often found without the plate and in the second the plate is overshadowed by 17 etchings by W. Basse, it is obvious that Rembrandt, who has recently been called 'the most subtle of all illustrators', was not con-sidered a great one by his contemporaries. That he could have been is proved by his innumerable Biblical etchings which are only excluded from our consideration by the mere accident that they were never made into a book.[1] With their freedom and their depth of characterization they show his incomparable skill in this art.

[1] They have of course often been collected since. A magnificent Bible was produced in Sweden in 1954, wholly illustrated with Rem-brandt reproductions.

Flemish painting had been on the decline since about 1600 and when in 1648 the Dutch broke away and formed their own republic the northern Protestants took the ascendance over the southern Catholics, in art as in many other things. There was however no printer in the north to take the place of the great Plantin. The Elzevir books, once so eagerly collected, were very seldom illustrated, and in any case could hardly compare with Plantin's editions. If the north had possessed a printer of Plantin's calibre we might now have had many more books illustrated by Rembrandt and perhaps some by the great Dutch painters who were his contemporaries. As it was, the latter part of the century was dominated by a most versatile artist who was at once painter, sculptor, scholar and doctor of law. This was Romeyn de Hooghe whose illustrations for de Wicquefort's *Advis Fidèle* of 1673 are almost in the same class as Callot's Miseries of War [126]. An indictment of the French invasion of Holland, they show all the baroque tendency to spoil its case by overstatement. It is impossible to believe that soldiers behaved with quite this degree of ferocity and wanton cruelty. His etchings for de la Vigne's *Miroir de la Bonne Mort* (1673) make that book, as Benesch says, a kind of baroque *Ars Moriendi*. But more important was the fact that he was the first to illustrate La Fontaine's *Contes* in 1685 [127]. These little pictures with their contemporary costumes and their prurience which is more typical of the eighteenth century are a foretaste of the miniature art of that period and are in fact at least as good as anything that was done later for this much illustrated book.

During the seventeenth century there was more technical experimenting in the Netherlands than at any time before since printing was invented. 1642 is the date generally given for the invention by von Siegen of mezzotint, a process by which tone was introduced into copper-engraving.[1] As Hind says it was 'no mere coincidence that it was invented at a time when Rembrandt was beginning to turn to problems of chiaroscuro in etching'—an interesting example of a new process produced, as it nearly always is, by a new artistic need. It was to become very popular in the eighteenth and early nineteenth centuries particularly in England for portraiture and the reproduction of paintings, but until then it was only used spasmodically in books. We have already noted an early instance of its use for a frontispiece in Germany, and Prince Rupert also experimented with it in England, where a plate by him was used in an even earlier book. But, being a tonal process, it seems less suitable for illustration than line-engraving or even etching, though it was often combined with etching or stipple in one plate.

There was also a certain amount of experimenting in the printing of colour, which was still in its infancy. It must be remembered that the chiaroscuro woodcuts of the fifteenth and sixteenth centuries (see page 151) were not examples of true colour-printing because they really used subdued shades to produce the effects of tone. Hercules Seghers was one of the first to print engravings in colour, though he seldom seems to have used more than one colour, the rest being supplied by hand.

FRANCE

The sixteenth and seventeenth centuries were glorious years for France and brought with them a steadily increasing political power which rose to a climax in the reign of Louis XIV. And although they were also times of unrest and of almost continuous warfare yet the arts of the book flourished as never before. Under Louis XIV it was chiefly the grand book that excelled, just as it was in Italy and Germany where conditions were even more adverse. We

[1] See page 220 for technical details.

130. Ronsard's *Oeuvres*, 1609. 13″ × 8¼″.
A title page by Gaultier

131. Pluvinel's *Maneige Royal*, 1623.
12¼″ × 8″. Illustrated by Crispin de Passe

Delle ponderationi dell' huomo nel fermarsi sopra dé suoi piedi.
Cap. CCLXVI.

L'huomo che si ferma sopra li suoi piedi, o si caricherà vgualmente sopra essi piedi, o si caricherà con pesi ineguali. Se si caricherà con peso naturale misto con peso accidentale, o si caricherà con semplice peso naturale. Se si caricherà con peso naturale misto con peso accidentale, all' hora gl' estremi oppositi de' membri non sono egualmente distanti dalli poli delle giunture de' piedi: mà se si caricherà con peso naturale semplice, all' hora tali estremi di membri oppositi saranno egualmente distanti dalle giunture de' piedi: e così di questa ponderatione si farà vn libro particolare.

Del moto locale più o meno veloce. Cap. CCLXVII.

Il moto locale fatto dall' huomo, o da alcun altro animale, sarà di tanto maggior o minor velocità, quanto il centro della loro grauità sarà più remoto o propinquo al centro del piede doue si sostengono.

De gl' animali di quattro piedi, & come si muouono. Cap. CCLXVIII.

La somma altezza de gl' animali di quattro piedi si varia più ne gl' animali che caminano, che in quelli che stanno saldi: e tanto più o meno, quanto essi animali son di maggiore o minor grandezza: e questo è causato dall' obliquità delle gambe che toccano terra, ch' inalzano la figura d' esso animale quando tal gambe disfanno la loro obliquità, e quando si pongono perpendicolari sopra la terra.

K iij

132. De Gombauld: *L'Endimion*, 1624. $7'' \times 4\frac{3}{4}''$.
Illustrated by Crispin de Passe

133. Leonardo da Vinci: *Treatise on Painting*, 1651.
$16'' \times 11\frac{1}{4}''$. An engraving after Poussin

134. Humbert's *Combat à la Barrière*, 1627. $8'' \times 5\frac{3}{4}''$. Illustrated by Callot

Ad fextam Verfus.

Eus in adiutorium meũ intende.
Ŗ. Domine ad adiuuandũ me fe
ftina. Gloria patri, & filio,& fpi
ritui fancto. Sicut erat in princi
pio,& nunc,& femper, & in fecu
la feculorum. Amen. Alleluia.   Hymnus.

135. *Book of Hours* with engravings
by Tory, 1525. 8″ × 5¼″

have already noted how extraordinarily independent the fine book is of mundane affairs. Even in the Middle Ages the monasteries continued to produce them when all outside was chaotic; in France during the Second World War the *édition-de-luxe* flourished in the same way.

At the beginning of this period the armies of Louis XII and François I invaded and conquered Italy but Italy took a peaceful revenge. The change that came over the face of the book about 1520 is even more marked in France than elsewhere and it was due almost entirely to Italy. Before that date illustration was still medieval, and illuminated manuscripts were still being produced. In that year appeared a French edition of *In Praise of Folly* with little vignettes filling up the blank spaces at the ends of short lines in the style of some early manuscripts. Only five years later appeared Tory's first *Book of Hours* and the Gothic spell was broken. The French Renaissance style had arrived and with it the pre-eminence of Paris among the publishing centres of Europe. Of the three great men who were chiefly responsible—Geoffrey Tory, Robert Estienne, and Claude Garamond—the one who had the greatest influence on illustration was the first. Garamond was of course a type designer. Estienne, scholar as he was, concerned himself especially with the purity of his texts and although his books are always well designed and ornamented they are almost never illustrated.[1] One always feels that he had something of the distrust of the Italian scholar of the previous generation for pictures in his books.

[1] In 1547 he produced *The Lives of the Twelve Dukes of Milan*, a printed version of an illustrated manuscript presented to King Henry II by the author Jovius, in which the paintings of the original are reproduced by woodcuts.

I

Tory too has been called a reactionary. He modelled his woodcuts in style on the *Poliphilo*, in pure outline without any form of shading. As a draughtsman, says Johnson, he was very much inferior to contemporary German artists. As a theorizer—and his *Champfleury* of 1529 was one of the first theories of typography—he goes right back to the schoolmen of the middle ages, for instance in the way he makes the letters of the alphabet stand for moral qualities. Yet he revolutionized the design of the French book and set it on the path that it was to follow for many years; what is more, his work had its effect on the books of every country in Western Europe.

It cannot be denied that this effect was happier for decoration than for illustration. In a classical era decoration usually flourishes because it profits by order and regularity. To appreciate this one has only to compare the borders used in Tory's *Hours* with those in similar books by contemporary printers [135]. The border is a formal thing and stiffness does not matter. Type too, being by its nature formal, requires impersonal handling in a book; and Tory's substitution of roman for gothic was all to the good. But illustration is a different matter and it is apt to wilt if it is forced into a typographical pattern. Tory's illustrations for Petrarch, the *Roman de la Rose* or for Marot's *Poems* appeal to us at first glance by their regularity and clarity which contrast very favourably with the somewhat chaotic pages of contemporary books. But when we examine the cuts themselves they often seem cold and empty. This is no indictment of the *Poliphilo* illustrations on which Tory modelled his style; Aldus's unknown draughtsman simply had the touch of genius which Tory lacked, for all his skill in organizing the page.

It would be hard to exaggerate the influence of the *Poliphilo* at this juncture. In 1546 Kerver produced a French edition called the *Discours du Songe de Poliphile* in which the cuts are very closely modelled on the originals, but yet with a difference that makes this book a work of art in its own right. If Figs. 89 and 136 are compared the differences may be seen. The French cuts are slightly blacker and thicker (perhaps they are a little better printed); they are also technically more accomplished with their increased use of shading. But although they stick closer to the text they have lost some of the mystery of the earlier work. The typographical self-consciousness of the French Renaissance is seen in the elaboration of the geometrical shapes in which the text of the original edition was set, in the better designed initials and also in the elaborate title page with a highly ornate border which takes the place of Aldus's very modest opening. Only three years later, in 1549, appeared one of the very earliest commemorative volumes of the sort that was to become so popular in the next century. This was the *Entrée d'Henri II* which celebrated the triumphal entry of the King into Paris and it was illustrated by the famous sculptor Jean Goujon. It was the beginning of a steady flow of similar books and of others on architecture, travel, science, anatomy, etc., nearly all with interesting illustrations. Indeed one of the features of this period is the imaginative treatment of what today would be merely a diagram or a photograph. Jean Cousin's famous *Livre de perspective* (1560) and Goujon's own *Vitruvius* of 1574 are humbling examples.

Paris was not the only centre of book production in France. We have already seen how the Trechsels printed Holbein's two books at Lyons in 1538, and later on some of the finest illustrated books of the century were produced there by de Tournes. Before him Sébastien Gryphius had the distinction of being the first printer of Rabelais. His *Pantagruel* of 1532 is still in the old Gothic style with cuts that have never heard of Tory but are all the more vigorous for that. Curiously, though, the title-page has colonnades on either side and foreshadows the architectural title-page of later date. Gryphius anticipated later development

137. *L'Apocalypse figurée*, 1561. $15\frac{1}{4}'' \times 10\frac{1}{2}''$. Engravings by Duvet

LIVRE PREMIER DE

foient des iubilations tumultueufes, accompagnees du fon de plufieurs inftrumens : & alloiét trois fois a l'entour du temple, pour appaifer les trois Deeffes fatales, afauoir Nona, Decima, Morta. & en rentrant dedans le fanctuaire, pédoiét leurs rameaux de Cypres en diuers lieux, ou les laiffoient fichez en la muraille, & la eftoient gardez iufques a l'annee enfuiuante, que les preftres en faifoiét le feu du facrifice. Quand tout eftoit accomply en la maniere qui eft dicte, & les funerailles celebrees, voire fimy le feruice des mortz, auec les prieres & reccommandaces accouftumees, & tous mauuais efperitz chaffez, le grand preftre proferoit les dernieres paroles, difant, llicet: qui vault autant a dire côme, Chacun f'en peult, quã d'l vouldra, retourner en fa maifon. Sur le poinct que Polia paracheuoit ainfi fon compte de ces couftumes anciennes, & ceremonies deuotes, nous arriuames fur le bord de la mer, ou eftoit le temple deftruict.

Línous

136. *Discours du Songe de Poliphile*, 1546. $13\frac{1}{2}'' \times 8\frac{1}{4}''$. Kerver's imitation of the Italian *Poliphilo*

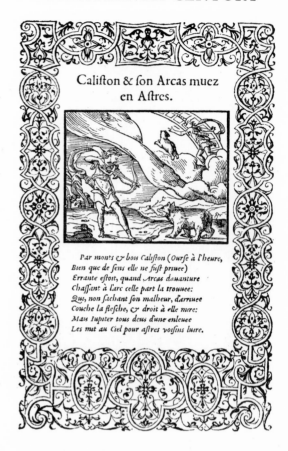

Califton & fon Arcas muez
en Aftres.

Par monts & bois Califton (Ourfe à l'heure,
Bien que de fens elle ne fuft priuee)
Errante eftoit, quand Arcas dauanture
Chaffant à l'arc celle part la trouuee:
Qui, non fachant fon malheur, d'arriuee
Couche la flefche, & droit à elle mire:
Mais Iupiter tous deus d'une enleuee
Les mit au Ciel pour aftres voifins luire.

138. *Métamorphose d'Ovide figurée,*
1557. 6¼″ × 4¼″. Illustrated by Salomon

too in his production at this time of many small books, though here he was merely following the Aldine classics.

Jean de Tournes who was trained by Gryphius was the greatest of all the Lyonese printers though his fame rests more on his typography than on his use of illustration. For him the famous Bernard Salomon worked as a woodcut designer and was responsible for illustrating several fine books of which the best known are the Alciati *Emblems* of 1560 and the *Métamorphose d'Ovide figurée* of 1557 [138]. Here the verses, italic set within very wide borders together with the vignettes, contribute to the florid effect and set us wondering why de Tournes, whose typography was so very chaste, should have produced such highly decorated books.

Salomon himself belonged to the Franco-Italian School of Fontainebleau, which owed its inspiration to the King. Although his work for de Tournes was cut in wood he shows in the smallness and the detail of his designs a talent that would perhaps have been better served by copper-engraving. That technique was in fact coming to the fore in Lyons at this time. It had already been used in *Epitome des rois*, printed there in 1546 by Arnoullet and believed to be the first French book with engraved vignettes. A much finer book followed in 1561 from the office of Jean de Tournes himself, *L'Apocalypse figurée* with engravings by Jean Duvet, the king's jeweller. It is a reminder of the original connexion between the goldsmith's art and the engraver's, and the illustrations are indeed jewel-like in their quality and brilliance [137]. Their rich pattern covers the whole page, leaving hardly any white space showing and enhancing the beauty and simplicity of the facing pages of text. Duvet has been called one of

QVINTI HORATII FLACCI OPERA.
PARISIIS   MDCXLII
E TYPOGRAPHIA REGIA

139. Horace: *Opera*, 1642. 15″ × 10″. A title page by Poussin

140. Marolles: *Tableaux du Temple des Muses*, 1655. 14¼″ × 9¼″. An engraving after Brebiette

LES DELICES DE L'ESPRIT, DIALOGVES.

VNZIESME IOVRNEE.
La Conversion de Philedon.

EVSEBE. PHILEDON.

EVSEBE.

ON Dieu, que voy-ie? Philedon à genoux, & en pleurs, & deuant la Croix?

PHILEDON.

I'iray à ce coup, Eusebe : i'y marcheray auec toy, & tu n'auras plus la peine de m'y traiſner, ny de m'y porter.

Evs. Ah! que ie t'embraſſe, puis que tu embraſſes Ieſus-Chriſt. C'eſt Ieſus-Chriſt, c'eſt Ieſus-Chriſt luy-meſme qui te porte ; & tu n'auras pas grande peine à marcher, pour entrer dans la porte de la foy. Quoy? voila ton lit au meſme eſtat qu'il eſtoit hier. Ie craignois que tu n'euſſes quelque indiſpoſition, ayant ſceû que tu n'auois point voulu ſouper, & que tu t'eſtois renfermé. Il y a peu de iours que tu ne pouuois paſſer trois heures ſans manger & ſans boire ; & tu as pû paſſer vn ſoir & vne nuit entiere, & ſans manger, & ſans boire, & ſans dormir, & à genoux, & en pleurs,

PHIL. Ah! Euſebe, que les heures ſont douces que l'on paſſe auec Ieſus-Chriſt, & qu'il eſt doux auſſi de pleurer auec luy!

EVS. Quoy? Philedon, tu as donc deja gouſté Ieſus-Chriſt, & tu n'as pas

---

METAMORPHOSES

POUR avoir frapé deux Serpens Tireſias fut changé en femme, & au bout de ſept ans ayant reveû, & touché les meſmes Serpens, il reprit ſon premier ſexe.

Corpora serpentum baculi violaverat ictu.

---

141. Desmaret: *Les Délices de l'esprit*, 1658. 12¾″ × 8″. Illustrated by Chauveau

142. Ovid's *Metamorphoses*, 1676. 10½″ × 7″. Illustrated by Leclerc

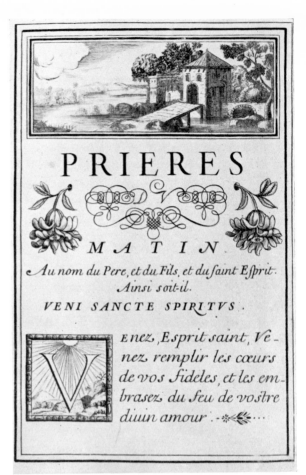

143. *Heures Nouvelles, c.* 1670. $10\frac{1}{2}'' \times 7''$.
Illustrated by Senault

144. Perrault's *Labyrinthe de Versailles*, 1677.
$7\frac{3}{4}'' \times 5''$. Illustrated by Leclerc

44   LABYRINTE

FABLE XXII.

LE MILAN

ET

LES OISEAUX.

L E Milan vne fois voulut payer
sa feste.

Tous les petits Oiseaux par luy furent
priez;

Et comme à bien disner l'assistance
estoit preste,

Il ne fit qu'vn repas de tous les Con-
viez.

DE VERSAILLES.   45

the first of modern illustrators because he interpreted his text and was not content only to translate it into images.

The History of Jason (1563) is another well-printed book with interesting engravings by Woeriot, in which the pictures already show the path that engraved illustration is going to take for the next hundred years. They are quite dwarfed by the elaborate borders in which all sorts of things are going on to steal our attention. We are reminded of the *drolleries* of the early manuscripts.

Le Ballet Comique de la Reyne fait aux Noces de Monsieur le Duc de Joyeuse (1582) with its curious etchings was another book made for a royal occasion. The text was written by Beau-joyeux, valet de chambre to Henri III, and it was a forerunner of many similar volumes which were to be produced at the court of Louis XIV. But this is a comparatively modest volume, not very well printed and showing little promise of the glories to come.

As we leave the century we cannot help feeling that it was an age of decoration rather than of illustration and this is especially noticeable as engraving begins to oust wood. The title-page borders, in which flamboyant elaboration is permissible are often more pleasing than the illustrations proper, where it is not. Occasionally the wording of the title-page itself was engraved and this gave a unity that would otherwise have been lacking. For typographical title-pages Robert Granjon, who was Salomon's son-in-law and a celebrated type designer, showed how printer's flowers could be combined with borders and head-pieces. Delaune and Ducerceau, the former a line-engraver and the latter an etcher (as well as an architect) were both masters of engraved ornament, although they were not strictly speaking illustrators of books.

The religious wars at the end of the century drove many Protestant printers to Geneva whither Robert Estienne had led the way long before. Their place was taken by craftsmen from the Netherlands where engraving was now enjoying an immense vogue and these had their effect on the work of the seventeenth century. For the next 200 years many French books were to be issued from the Dutch and Flemish publishing houses and this was due not only to the prestige of such men as Plantin, nor to religious intolerance and the censorship that went with it; it was at least as much the result of printing monopolies and self imposed restrictions. The former gave privileges to a few printers and fostered incompetence; the latter forbad printers to produce engravings and engravers to produce anything more than books of plates with a short explanatory text. All this made the production of the illustrated book very difficult in France and the wonder is that so many good ones appeared. During the first few years of the new century there was little of note and most of the engraving was done by two foreigners, Thomas de Leu and Leonard Gaultier, who continued the Plantin tradition. Their most famous work was *Les Images ou Tableaux de Platte Peintre des Deux Philostrates* (1617) which they engraved after drawings by Caron. Gaultier, the more skilful of the two, had a passion for architectural title-pages. His best known is that for Ronsard's *Oeuvres* (1609) in which the soldier and the unclad lady are so tactfully unaware of each other's proximity [130].

Another famous book that owes its illustrations to a Flemish engraver is Pluvinel's *Maneige Royal* (1623), a treatise on horsemanship that contains pictures of Louis XIII being instructed in the art, many of them with delightful backgrounds of contemporary Paris [131]. Here the engravings are by Crispin de Passe who had already made his reputation in his own country. This is a ceremonial volume in the same tradition as the *Ballet Comique* of 1582 but very much more accomplished. With its many double-spread plates (among which the text though lengthy plays a minor part) it is at the opposite pole from the books with only an engraved title-page. These two extremes are in fact the rule at this time, and the averagely illustrated book of the previous century is the exception. But exceptions are found, particularly among the novels which are now beginning to appear and which demand this type of illustration. One of the most popular was de Gombauld's *L'Endimion* (1624) which Passe also illustrated and which Hofer calls one of the finest illustrated books of the period. It is no disparagement of its period to say that it might easily be an eighteenth-century book in its delicacy and elegance, no less than in its subject [132].

All this while woodcuts were gradually losing favour. But they still persisted even into the eighteenth century for decorative head- and tail-pieces which are often found in the same books as engraved plates. The conjunction is not always happy but it is not necessary to condemn it outright as Delen does on theoretic grounds. Where the engravings are small and assimilated with the text in the same way as the cuts, the result is sometimes delightful.

But while woodcutting decreased another technique was coming into favour which threatened to oust line-engraving. This was etching and it was later coming to France than to Germany or Italy. When it did come it owed its popularity to Jacques Callot who learnt it in Italy. He started the practice of a 'second bite', which helped to give a varied tone, and this survives even the graver work with which the early etchers always finished off their plates. Most of Callot's energies were expended on separate prints and he produced several 'carnets' or series of pictures, with explanatory verses, e.g. *Les Misères et les Malheurs de la Guerre*. But he also illustrated a few delightful books, the best known *Combat à la barrière* (1627). This is a commemorative volume which proves that such books do not need to be of enormous size to achieve a splendid effect [134]. Callot's engravings all spread across the pages but his use of white space is such that there is no impression of heaviness. But of more importance to the history of illustration are his two Emblem Books, *Vie de la Mère de Dieu* (1646) and *Lux Claustri* (1646). Here at last etching begins to display its peculiar qualities and the freedom of these little pictures, precursors of the eighteenth-century vignette, is like fresh air after the elaboration and ornamentation of the big contemporary line-engravings. They are all of outdoor subjects too; and the impression of emptiness and space is almost miraculous in so small a compass. We have seen how in the last century wood-cutting imitated engraving; now curiously enough we have engravings with some of the qualities of a woodcut. There is hardly any attempt at tone and it has been possible to reproduce two of them here from line blocks [145 and 146].

Abraham Bosse also combined etching with graver work but in his case the result was usually indistinguishable from line-engraving.[1] Like Callot he specialized in separate prints many of which are noted for their realistic description of the daily life of the time, and he sometimes carried this quality into his illustration. He is not so happy in his more ambitious work such as the engravings (from the designs of others) for Chapelain's *La Pucelle* (1656). This is a sumptuous book which contains a magnificent portrait engraved by Nanteuil; but the big illustrations are disappointing. Far more effective are the engraved head-pieces (not woodcuts this time) and particularly the initials which are altogether delightful. The division between the designer and the engraver which marks the work of the eighteenth century had not yet become absolute and such books as the Virgil *Æneid* which Bosse illustrated in 1648 show how much is to be gained when one man does all the work. Benesch says he treats the *Æneid* like a fairy tale, and his approach is quite different from that of the ultra classical title-pages which Mellan had recently engraved for Virgil and Horace after Poussin.

---

[1] Bosse wrote a treatise on engraving which was afterwards revised by C. N. Cochin, the younger.

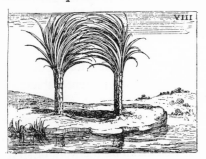

145. *Vie de la Mère de Dieu*, 1646. $7\frac{1}{4}'' \times 5\frac{3}{4}''$ 146. *Lux Claustri*, 1646. $7\frac{1}{4}'' \times 5\frac{1}{2}''$

Two emblem books with etchings by Callot

In 1641 Poussin was visiting Paris and he was persuaded to design two title-pages for the Imprimerie Royale. Both were engraved by Claude Mellan who with Nanteuil was the most prominent portrait engraver of the day, each of them producing mostly separate prints but also some incidental work for books. Mellan is famous for having discarded cross-hatching in favour of shading by parallel lines of varying thicknesses and for doing without outline altogether. The climax of this method was reached, as Hind says, when he shaded a whole face with one continuous spiral line, ending at the tip of the nose for centre. Unlike Callot he was happiest in big books and these Poussin title-pages represent his best work [139]. And although Poussin must have been on unfamiliar ground as an illustrator he produced here two notable designs in the best classical tradition. But perhaps his most interesting works are the illustrations, which are almost certainly his, to Leonardo's *Treatise on Painting* (1651). This is a unique case of one great painter illustrating another [133].

The Imprimerie Royale had been established in the Louvre by Richelieu a year before Poussin's visit to Paris. Its first head was Gabriel Cramoisy, a well-known bookseller, whose elevation shows the beginning of the glorification of the publisher (for that was what he really was) at the expense of the printer. The old days when one man like Tory could design, illustrate, print and sell his own books were gone. We have already seen that the guild regulations separated book printers from illustration printers. The same sort of thing was happening inside the big printing offices which were beginning to wear a familiar departmentalized look. This marks the beginning of a retrograde movement which has ended in the design of books being taken out of the printer's hands altogether; but unfortunately the illustrator seems to have been unable to stake his claim at this early stage and even in the eighteenth century he was seldom, if ever, consulted about the design of his books.

Booksellers increased in numbers as well as in power in the middle of the century because it was a time of great literary activity. It was unfortunate that it was not the great books of the period which got the best illustration. The early editions of Molière, Corneille, Racine and La Fontaine were neglected while the best work was going into the great folios of the *Cabinet du Roy*, produced at the expense of Louis XIV himself. For the King was a great patron of printing and engraving. Not only was he largely responsible for the development of the Imprimerie Royale but he also laid the foundation of the present Cabinet des Estampes in the Bibliothèque Nationale when he bought the collection of Michel de Marolles[1] in 1660. Soon after this he decided to launch the series known as the *Cabinet du Roy* to commemorate the monuments, art treasures, gardens and palaces of France; and although it was never completed it seems to have had the first claim on the work of all the best engravers of the time. These volumes are collections of plates rather than books and they show a predilection for the large engraving (many of them actually fold) which perhaps, by a natural reaction, paved the way for the vignette of the eighteenth century. Louis XIV's patronage of engraving did not stop at commissioning these plates. He also made an edict, at the request of Nanteuil, raising engraving from the status of an 'industrial art' to that of a 'liberal art'.

For Louis were also produced many sumptuous manuscripts. In fact it was due to him that illumination lasted so much longer in France than elsewhere. The splendid manuscripts written for him by Jarry and others are preserved in the Bibliothèque Municipale at Versailles. The *Guirlande de Julie*, a manuscript of flower paintings and madrigals, was the work of a famous calligrapher and painter, Nicolas Robert. Robert's only printed illustration appeared in 1675 in Dodart's *Recueil des Plantes* which was not issued complete until the next century.

François Chauveau and Sébastien Leclerc are the key figures in the second half of the century and in the work of both of them is seen a leaning towards decoration. Chauveau's best book, Desmaret's *Les Délices de l'esprit* (1658) must have been startling when it appeared because of the amazingly elaborate ornamentation above and below the pictures and on the title-pages [141]. This ornamentation is intaglio and contrasts favourably with the rather clumsy woodcut headpieces which were still incongruously appearing in other books with engravings. But Chauveau apparently had no objection to this combination because the woodcut initials which appear in *Les Délices de l'esprit* were probably his also. He was less successful in the first edition of La Fontaine's *Fables* (1668), a book for which perhaps more and better illustrations have since been done than for any other in France. His vignettes here are small without being delicate—but they are not as bad as Hofer would have us believe. They must be compared with Leclerc's vignettes in Ovid's *Metamorphoses* (translated in 1676 by Benserade) which had also the advantage of being impeccably printed at the Imprimerie Royale. It is probable that Chauveau collaborated with Leclerc in this book —he may have designed while Leclerc engraved—but if so the vignettes show a delicacy and lightness of touch which he never achieved elsewhere and which clearly presages the work of the next century [142].

Leclerc was evidently capable of the large elaborate style as well because he did some

---

[1] Marolles was the author of a very fine book called *Tableaux du Temple des Muses* which appeared in 1655. The very large engravings are most of them based on the designs of the Dutchman Diepenbeeck [140].

work for the *Cabinet du Roy*. He was perhaps hampered by having to engrave so often from the stilted designs of the painter Le Brun. But his true genius comes out in a book like his own *Pratique de la géometrie* (1669) where the engravings are a reproach to our modern geometrical diagrams, and in their economy recall the work of Callot. Leclerc is too often thought of as a precursor of the golden age, a link between the seventeenth and eighteenth centuries, and the inventor of the vignette. But as we have seen, Callot was using the vignette long before, though this does not belittle Leclerc's importance. And as we shall see the eighteenth century was by no means as superior to the seventeenth as it is generally supposed to be. Perrault's *Labyrinthe de Versailles* (1677) shows Leclerc as a great illustrator in his own right, and it contains engravings as exquisite as can be seen in any century in any country [144]. The *Books of Hours* with pictures and text engraved about this time by Louis Senault also demonstrate that in calligraphic decoration the earlier period can compete with the later. The *Heures Nouvelles* of about 1670, though perhaps over-ornate, shows a rare combination of calligraphy, decoration and illustration [143].

ENGLAND

Printing in England began by owing much to the Netherlands and so it continued into the sixteenth century. But unfortunately the connexion became progressively weaker as

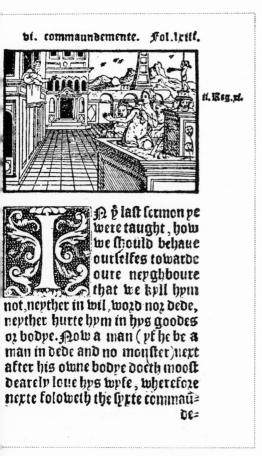

147. Cranmer's *Catechism*, 1548. $5\frac{1}{2}'' \times 3\frac{1}{2}''$

148. Cuningham's *Cosmographicall Glasse*, 1559. $10\frac{3}{4}'' \times 7\frac{1}{4}''$

illustration in the Netherlands improved. A ruling was made in 1523 that apprentices were to be of English birth and though many foreign woodcutters and engravers continued to work here few of them seem to have been of the calibre of those Flemish engravers who offered their services to France.

To begin with, illustration was all of course by woodcut and Pynson's use of Holbein cuts set a fashion. But these cuts were only ready-made decoration as it were and although Holbein himself worked here from 1532 to 1543 it does not appear that he specifically illustrated any English books except for the title-pages of Coverdale's 1535 Bible (which was printed on the Continent), and possibly a cut of Henry VIII in the 1576 edition of Foxe's *Book of Martyrs*. There are also two small Biblical pictures signed by him in Cranmer's *Catechism* of 1548. And it is possible that the other cuts in this delightful little book, which are far ahead of contemporary work, may have been his [147]. It is sad to reflect how great an opportunity was thus missed by English printers of obtaining the services of the man who was potentially the greatest illustrator of his day. Incidentally the very first English Bible was also printed abroad and contained cuts by Beham. The number of service books produced abroad for English consumption suggests that the wealthy and discriminating distrusted the ability of the native printer to satisfy their requirements.

Wynkyn de Worde and Pynson (both of foreign birth) carried on Caxton's work and produced no illustrated books of any great merit. The first book of real distinction was not illustrated with woodcuts at all but with copper-engravings and this was Vesalius's anatomical work *De Humani Corporis Fabrica* (1545). The engravings were made at the command of Henry VIII and were the work of Geminus, a Flemish surgeon. Even though they are based on the woodcuts by Jan Calcar in the Basle edition of 1543 they are still remarkable as a translation from one medium into another and are especially impressive when seen against the uninspiring background of English woodcut illustrations of the time. They are beautifully printed with excellent engraved lettering and matched with a well-set text in roman type [149].

John Day printed the best illustrated books of the century during the second half of which he was at work. His most distinguished productions were, Cuningham's *Cosmographicall Glasse* (1559), Foxe's *Book of Martyrs* (1576) and the *Book of Christian Prayers* (1578), which Pollard calls a sort of Protestant *Horae* [148 and 150]. They all owe much to good typography and presswork. Foxe's great book provided the favourite light reading of our forebears of all ages and the cuts are often reminiscent of those which accompanied the lurid chap-books and broadsheets of the time. But the horror of the proceedings which they picture is somewhat mitigated by the complete unconcern on the faces of the martyrs.

Day used woodcuts for his illustrations, but during this time line-engraving was gathering momentum though comparatively few engraved title-pages are found before the end of the century. But, as Gray says, Holbein's most fruitful influence is found here, especially in portrait engraving which had its vogue in England as elsewhere. And although the earliest engravers like Geminus and the Hogenbergs were foreign, they very soon found ready pupils among the native goldsmiths. One of these, Coxon, illustrated in 1598 the first English edition of *Orlando Furioso* translated by Harington. But he merely imitated Porro's engravings of the Italian edition of 1584 which, as we have seen, imitated in turn Valgrisi's of 1556. The famous portrait of Shakespeare in the first folio of 1623 is by another foreigner, Martin Droeshout, but by then an English style of engraving had begun to emerge. This can be seen in the engravings which Francis Delaram (himself a foreigner) did for Sandys's *Relation of a Journey*, 1615 [151].

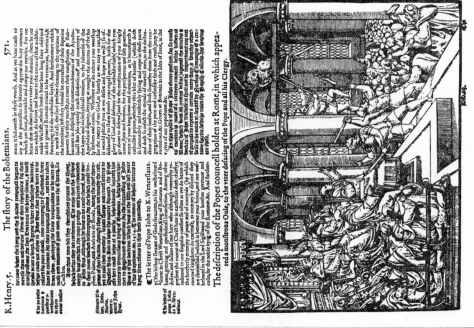

150. Foxe's *Book of Martyrs*, 1576. 12¼″ × 8¾″

149. Vesalius: *De Humani Corporis Fabrica*, 1545. 14¼″ × 10¼″.
Engravings by Geminus

The first half of the seventeenth century was as troubled a time in England as on the Continent, and such popular illustrated books as Quarles's *Emblems* (1635) are not distinguished by good engraving. Even when peace and prosperity came after the Restoration it

151. Sandys: *Relation of a Journey*, 1615. 12½″ × 8″. Illustrated by Delaram

did not bring with it the same output of ceremonial books that we find in other countries.[1] Perhaps the triumph of the middle classes in the Civil Wars had something to do with this. However the century did produce a great illustrator in Francis Barlow; one of the greatest of all times, Benesch calls him. It also produced in William Faithorne a fine portrait engraver worthy to rank with Mellan from whom he derived his style. By now the print-sellers were as active here as in the Netherlands and it was they who supplied the booksellers with illustrations (which had often been published separately already). This sort of thing did not lend itself to good workmanship, and much contemporary illustration was poor and ephemeral as it must be when it is designed for some other purpose and added quite fortuitously to a book. The small-sized portrait engravings which were popularized about this time by the two sons of Crispin de Passe (who came to London in 1616) demonstrate on the other hand that the requirements of the smaller book sometimes dictated the size of the print.

[1] One interesting and excellent early example is worth mention however. This is Stephen Harrison's *The Archs of Triumph* (1603), a very rare book which has a text by Ben Jonson and Thomas Dekker [154]. The designs are by Kip whose name is given on the title-page.

Barlow was usually associated with other designers in his book illustration and though he sometimes etched himself, much of his best work was engraved by Wenzel Hollar. His rhymes and illustrations for *Severall Wayes of Hunting* (1671) for instance were entrusted

152. *Æsop*, 1666. $12'' \times 7\frac{1}{2}''$.
Illustrated by Barlow

to Hollar who etched the book throughout, text and pictures, with great success. But Barlow's best known book was his polyglot *Æsop* which appeared 'illustrated with 110 sculptures' in 1666, one of the very few English productions worthy to stand beside its best foreign contemporaries [152]. There is something typically English in the vigour of his compositions to which however his technique was hardly equal. In Ogilby's *Æsop*, a much bigger book which appeared soon after, some of his illustrations are etched by the indefatigable Hollar and appear in a more polished, though perhaps less vigorous light. Barlow also illustrated one or two lesser known works such as Benlowe's *Theophila* (1652) in which he combined with other artists and which contained also some delicately engraved plates by Hollar [155]. As for Hollar himself there are few books of this period which do not contain some of his work. According to Hind he was responsible for over 2,500 plates, most of them etched, but showing all the qualities of graver work. He is best remembered for his costume book, *Ornatus Muliebris Anglicanis* (1640) which has however no text.

Most of Faithorne's portraits were engraved as separate prints but he did some work for books just as his opposite number Nanteuil did in France. For instance he did a very fine portrait of Thomas Killigrew as a frontispiece for an edition of Killigrew's plays published

153. *The London Bible of 1663*, part of
the Creation Series. 6½″ × 5″

in 1664. But one always feels, as with Nanteuil, that there is no essential difference even in scale between the portrait he engraved for a book and the one he intended for some other use.

The massive *Cambridge Bible* produced in 1660 to celebrate the Restoration was one of the few English books that will compare with the elaborate commemorative volumes coming from the Netherlands or France or Italy. Even so it owes its plates to two of these countries, for some copies are provided with a suite by Visscher, and others with Italian engravings. The engravings nearly all extend over two pages and as the page measures about 17 × 11 inches, they must have involved a prodigious amount of work. It is no wonder that several different artists were employed; but the result is the usual lack of homogeneity which even extends to such elementary inconsistencies as a bearded Adam in one plate followed by a cleanshaven one in the next. This of course does not happen where there is a sequence entirely by one artist such as the wonderfully imaginative series showing the seven days of Creation engraved by Visscher after De Vos, from which we reproduce the first [156]. But the book is found with so many different combinations of plates (sometimes with no plates at all) that it is difficult to establish a standard. The British Museum edition of 1674 has

154. Harrison's *Archs of Triumph*, 1603.
$14\frac{1}{2}'' \times 10''$. A title-page by Kip

155. Benlowe's *Theophila*, 1652.
$10\frac{3}{4}'' \times 7\frac{1}{4}''$. Illustrated by Barlow, Hollar
and others

Lux Deus in tenebris, Lucem tristesq3 tenebras   **I. DIES.**   Separat, atq3 diem primò noctemq3 creavit.

Visscher excudebat.   Gene. Cap.1. Vers 3.

156. *The Cambridge Bible of 1660.*
18¼″ × 12½″. The first day of Creation,
engraved by Visscher after De Vos

157. Milton's *Paradise Lost*, 1688.
14¼″ × 9″. Design by Medina, engraving
by Burgess

158. De la Torre's *Fiestas . . . de Sevilla*, 1671. 12″ × 8″. A large folding plate

159. Yciar's *Libro de letras*, 1555. 7″ × 5″

160. De Gongora's *El Polifemo*, 1629.
7¾″ × 5½″

161. Sadeler's *Theatrum Morum*, 1609.
7″ × 6″. Engravings designed by the author

many additional plates, some of which, like one superb Rubens, can never have been intended for it. Strictly speaking, this puts it into the category of an extra-illustrated book.

In 1663 the King's Printers published a most interesting illustrated Bible which seems to be modelled on the *Cambridge Bible* though it is much smaller. Many engravings are original, others are copied from the *Cambridge Bible*, reduced to about a quarter of their original size. The result is some incredibly fine and delicate work [153]. Many of the original engravings, notably those for the *Apocalypse*, show a high order of imagination.

English engravers of this period show no great aptitude for technical experiment and the appearance here of what is perhaps the first book with a mezzotint plate is the more remarkable. This is John Evelyn's *Sculptura* of 1662 to which Prince Rupert contributed a large portrait in this medium. The book itself is interesting too because it is a description of engraving and of its history. The technique of mezzotint was communicated to the author by Prince Rupert but Evelyn excuses himself from describing it in his book thus: 'I did not think it necessary that an art so curious and (as yet) so little vulgar . . . was to be prostituted.'

The last important book of the century was the first illustrated edition of its greatest classic. This was *Paradise Lost* for which in 1688 John Baptist Medina designed and Burgess engraved the plates. There is nothing else in it quite so impressive as the illustration to Book I which is reproduced here [157]. This has something of the magnificent melodrama of John Martin's mezzotints made for the same poem nearly 200 years later. But the other plates are all somewhat spoiled by the intrusion of that archaic habit of showing successive actions in one picture.

SPAIN AND PORTUGAL

The sixteenth century was a golden age for Spain, both politically and artistically. Throughout the century there were close relations with Italy which were bound to be beneficial to Spanish book design. And there was always the native dignity of the indigenous book on which we have already remarked and which persisted well into the century, even in books printed in Spain by foreigners. Almost until 1550 these books with their gothic type keep their fifteenth-century character and most of the best ones appeared well before that date. These are nearly all religious books. It is indeed strange that Spain and Portugal with their vested interests in voyaging and discovery should have produced so few illustrated books of travel but the fact remains that they cannot compare in this department with the Netherlands.

The best printers of this period were all foreigners—Brocar (who was French), and Coci and the Crombergers (who were German). Brocar printed the magnificent *Complutensian Polyglot Bible* of 1514-17 which though not illustrated was adorned with fine borders. In 1517 he printed *La Cronica del Rey Don Juan II* by Guzman which has some good cuts.

George Coci of Saragossa shows more foreign characteristics than the others and often borrowed or copied blocks from Germany. His *Flos Sanctorum* (c. 1521) by Vega is a remarkable as well as a rare book because it has a title-page printed in five colours and black, a *tour de force* for those days. The use of a second colour is fairly frequent in Spanish books of that period, red being a favourite addition to the title-page. But five workings is rare indeed and we have to go back to the Mainz Psalter of 1457 and to Ratdolt's work at Venice to find anything like it. Besides its title-page *Flos Sanctorum* has several fine cuts imitated from Koberger of Nuremberg and arranged as oblongs across the page [162].

The two Crombergers, father and son, worked at Seville. In 1518 the father produced

Retablo de la Vida de Cristo in which there is a curious page of twenty 'compartment' cuts, small framed pictures of different subjects which fit closely together [163]. The son produced in 1546 the *Libro Llamado Exemplario*, a version of the *Fables of Bidpai* which were almost as popular at this time as those of Æsop. The Cromberger edition has many delightfully humorous cuts of animals; but perhaps the best feature of the work of both father and son is the design of their woodcut initials, white letters on a black background patterned with exquisite effect. It is true of all the Spanish books of this century that the decorative element is stronger and more successful than the illustrative.

The same decorative effect is seen in the text-books on calligraphy and arithmetic which Juan de Yciar produced about the middle of the century. One fascinating book of his called *Libro en el qual hay muchas suertes de letras historiadas con figuras del viejo Testamento* (1555) contains several complete alphabets made up out of initials ornamented with Biblical scenes [159]. A fine example of calligraphic white-line cutting in wood is also to be found in Francisco Lucas's *Arte de escrivir* of 1577; black-line cutting till now had been the usual method of illustrating writing books but although there are a few examples of this in Lucas, it is the white-line cuts that strike us most forcibly by their decorative quality. They quite overshadow the stock woodcuts which are scattered here and there in the text with the express object of decoration.

The reproduction of medals was the occasion in 1587 for a technical advance just as it was in the Netherlands with Goltzius's *Imagines* of 1557. *Dialogos de Medallas*, printed by Mey, has 26 pages of engravings at the end which are far in advance of the average of that time.

Engraving was in fact very late in making its appearance in Spain, and it never seems to have affected book production there in the way it did elsewhere in Western Europe. The making of separate prints was never popular nor did it become so until Goya's time at the end of the eighteenth century. This was bound to handicap the illustrated book, especially the elaborate commemorative one. And as Hofer says there seems to be no particular reason for it. Spain although her political power was on the wane was still wealthy with the riches of the New World, and moreover the seventeenth century was as rich in literature and art

162. Vega: *Flos Sanctorum*, c. 1521. The murder of Becket

163. *Retablo de la Vida de Cristo*, 1518. A page of compartment woodcuts

as the preceding one. But somehow books were neglected by the aristocracy while in every other country it was the aristocracy who fostered the baroque book.

Spain missed a great opportunity with *Don Quixote*. The first properly illustrated edition came in 1657 from Holland, which had also produced for France the first illustrated *Contes* of La Fontaine. It was not in fact until the end of the eighteenth century that a worthy version appeared in the country of its genesis. A similar opportunity had been missed the previous century with the *Amadis de Gaula* which Coci first printed without illustrations in 1508. The Spanish genius does not seem to have lent itself to the illustration of romance. Instead it excelled, as Benesch says, in representations of ecclesiastical ceremonies which it invested with a feeling of mystic jubilation. Such is Leal's wonderful engraving of the interior of Seville Cathedral which is contained in the most noteworthy Spanish book of the century, de la Torre's *Fiestas de la S. Inglesia de Sevilla* (1671). Here, in the engravings of Arteaga, de Herrera, Murillo and others, we have the dying baroque combined with the Gothic, a mixture which is peculiarly Spanish [158]. But apart from this example there is a decided scarcity of interesting books. Luis de Gongora's *El Polifemo* (1629) has a handsome engraved title-page and an extraordinary frontispiece engraved by de Courbes [160]. And Morante's *Nueva Arte de Escrivir* (1636) is a beautiful calligraphic book in the true Spanish tradition. As in earlier books the lettering is shown in white on a black background and wood-cut is used rather than copper-engraving. Such a thing would indeed be almost impossible for the intaglio method and from now on the engraved writing books are generally lettered in black on white.

From 1580 to 1640 Portugal was united to Spain and her books display no national characteristics. Even after she broke away her books have little to distinguish them either relatively or absolutely. Spanish printers in Mexico produced some fine service books during the sixteenth and seventeenth centuries and one or two other presses were started in the cities of Latin America. But no illustrated books of importance were produced and there was no assimilation of the very individual style of the native Mexican book, which will be described later.

OTHER EUROPEAN COUNTRIES

Scandinavia and the countries of Eastern Europe do not have much to show in the period under review. During the sixteenth century printing was in its infancy in Sweden and Denmark and the general style is Germanic. The first Swedish Bible, printed at Upsala in 1541, has many good initials and some excellent cuts [164]. The first Danish Bible, printed by Dietz nine years later, was also well illustrated by Jacob Binck. In the second half of the century several distinguished books were printed at Copenhagen by Lorentz Benedicht, himself a woodcutter of some skill.

During the greater part of the seventeenth century Sweden was at war with Germany, and we find her forsaking the German tradition and seeking inspiration from her ally France. Queen Christina was a great patron of books but her encouragement bore more fruit in France than in Sweden. *Certamen equestre . . . Carolus XI* (1672) is a fine festival book with engravings that might have come from any country in Western Europe; and Dahlberg's *Suecia Antiqua et Hodierna* (1698) is a great volume of views by various hands that presages the topographical books of the early nineteenth century. But like so many of the latter it is less a book than a collection of plates which have not even the homogeneity of uniform size. Many of them fold and some are even printed on paper smaller than the text page. No better example could be found of the disruptive effect of the *hors texte* engraving.

Denmark still remained linked to Germany artistically and it was unfortunate for her that this was such a dull period for German illustration. However, towards the end of the century she produced several fine books. One of the most interesting in Jacobaeus's *Museum Regium* (1696), a description of the contents of King Christian V's collection.

Eastern Europe was an even less fertile field for the arts of the book, although Prague had once been a famous centre for the production of illuminated manuscripts, and although in Matthias Corvinus Hungary had had a king who was a great collector—but chiefly of Italian manuscripts. His attitude to printers was much less friendly however, and Hungary's troubled history was the chief reason why so few books were printed there. Poland in the early

164. *Swedish Bible* of 1541. 11½″ × 7″

165. The first printed illustrated *Haggadah*. 12″ × 8″. Printed in Prague in 1526

166. *Octoechos*. Printed in Cetinje
c. 1495

days had produced many fine manuscripts of her own and her early books were much influenced by this. Her first printers came from Germany and her style of illustration remained Germanic for a long time. Opec's translation of *La Vie du Christ*, which was printed
at Cracow by Vietor in 1522, has full-page cuts by Hans Scheifelin of Augsburg, for instance.
It also has exceptionally fine decorated initials and an astonishing title-page decorated with
pen flourishes. Lam says that more care was taken in Poland over the decoration of the book,
especially of the title-page, than over its illustration. But there are some good cuts to be
found, for instance, in Szarffenberger's *Bible* of 1561 and in the *Kronika Polska* of 1597.

In Prague many Hebrew books were printed, and the 1526 Prague edition of the Haggadah
set the style for the illustrations of this work that was to be followed for a long time throughout Northern Europe [165]. Sadeler's *Theatrum Morum* (Prague 1609) was a collection of
versified fables illustrated by the author, which had a great vogue in Bohemia [161]. Its
extremely skilful engravings have a strong resemblance to those by Gheeraerts for Edward
de Dene's book published in Bruges in 1567; and Barlow must have had some of them in
mind when he illustrated his Æsop of 1666. There is in fact a strong family likeness between
all the books of fables which were appearing so plentifully at this time, irrespective of their
place of origin; and we find a kind of international cycle of Æsop illustrations reminiscent of
the old manuscript cycles. This can be traced via Leclerc and Croxall right down to
Bewick's Æsop of 1818, and later in the numerous illustrated editions of La Fontaine's
Fables.

The Slavonic countries were even less fertile ground for the illustrated book, although presses were at work in most of them from the early part of the sixteenth century. From Cetinje in what is now Jugoslavia came an *Octoechos* in about 1495 from which we reproduce an interesting cut [166].

The history of printing in Russia was very chequered and few books of any sort were produced in the sixteenth century. Although more appeared in the following century there were no illustrated works of note and the same applies to all the Balkan countries.

6

The Eighteenth Century

FRANCE

Any account of illustration in the eighteenth century must begin with France because during this period she easily led the rest of Europe. That is not to say that her work was at a higher level than in the two previous centuries—though it was certainly more prolific. It was simply that there seems to have been a kind of lacuna in other countries which allowed the French style more influence than it would otherwise have had.

The break between the prevailing styles of the two centuries—the seventeenth-century baroque and the eighteenth-century rococo—was sharper than such breaks usually are. Louis XIV died in 1715 and Gillot's vignettes for Houdart de la Motte's *Fables Nouvelles* appeared in 1719. There had of course been vignettes and small delicate engravings in the previous century, notably those by Leclerc; but nevertheless the generalization is as valid as any generalization can be. The difference between the baroque and the rococo book is the difference between the music of Bach and Mozart. The former is not without its lightness nor the latter without solemnity; but they retain their essentially different character which is not merely a matter of style but rather of outlook.

When the rococo arrived (and it came of course in art long before music) it affected almost every aspect of the illustrated book. The size of the page dwindled to suit the style of engraving and it became more intimate. Its subject-matter altered so that now religious, scientific and commemorative books are in the minority; poetry and romance are most favoured by the illustrator. Its style changed to mirror fashions and morals as never before. There is a high degree of realism, for instance in the portrayal of costume, and real people appear in illustration with only a thin disguise. It is easy to regret that so much exquisite workmanship was spent on so much worthless literature (the poetry of Dorat is usually cited) but this is a phenomenon common to all ages. The two forms of inspiration do not always coincide. A glance at the titles of the finest books of the century reveals a high proportion of great literature—Molière, La Fontaine, Racine, not to mention Ovid and Boccaccio. But we have the feeling as with so many limited editions of the present day that the texts have become a vehicle for the illustrations.

It was indeed *Daphnis et Chloé*, so beloved by our modern private presses, that started the ball rolling in 1718. The illustrations were designed by the Regent himself and were not distinguished [167]. But they are a sign of the times and mark the entry of the amateur into our field. Later the Pompadour was to engrave illustrations to Corneille from drawings by Boucher and her book, printed from silver type, was published at Versailles in an edition of twenty copies. Thus illustration became a fashion and a finely printed unillustrated book was almost condemned to failure before it appeared. Sometimes the wealthy bibliophiles themselves took a hand in publishing. One of the great books of the century is the 1762 edition of La Fontaine's *Contes et nouvelles*, paid for by a group of financiers called the *Fermiers Généraux*, who could hardly have hoped to see their money back on such a sumptuous production.

All this activity was concentrated in Paris which became the sole centre for the production of fine books as never before. Printing was hedged about with innumerable regulations and restrictions, but these also had the effect of maintaining a high standard of craftsmanship. The engravings themselves were printed with great skill and care, but the typography of these volumes is sometimes unworthy of their illustrations. It improved wonderfully under the Didots towards the end of the century but at the beginning it compared unfavourably with the typography of the previous century. In the middle years the typefounder Fournier produced much elegant decorative material, some of which is still in use today. It took its cue from the ornamental lettering and flourishes with which engravers were enlivening their title-pages, a symptom this of the illustrator's ascendency. Never before had the printer commanded such a wealth of fleurons and borders. It is all the more strange to see the persistence of the woodcut ornament which still appears in uncomfortable conjunction with the engraving, for instance in Moreau's *Molière* of 1773. By the side of the meticulous engraving which went into the vignettes and *culs de lampe* of this period it appears clumsy indeed.

The eighteenth century in France has often been called the age of the vignette. The Goncourts compared it thus with the preceding century which they called the age of the frontispiece, and there is a good deal of justice in the two labels. But it must not be thought that the vignette was a new invention. The term is a vague one but the engraved vignette of our period did nothing that had not already been done by the woodcuts of the fifteenth and sixteenth centuries and in many books of the seventeenth. It was of Houdart de la Motte's *Fables Nouvelles* (1719) that Bouchot said 'the whole French school of the eighteenth century may have had its origin in this forgotten book', but technically there is little to distinguish it from Benserade's *Ovid* which Leclerc illustrated in 1676. And there is no doubt that the roots of the rococo book go back long before 1719 even if superficially it can be seen as a reaction against the baroque.

Nevertheless Claude Gillot who illustrated the *Fables Nouvelles* is an important figure. He was the master of Watteau[1] and has been called the last pagan of the Renaissance. His vignettes are unusual in that they are pure etchings and Gillot himself executed them. The typical illustration of this period was an etching touched up by the burin and it was executed by a professional from the draughtsman's design. But the employment of several illustrators in the *Fables Nouvelles* is not unusual. Besides Gillot's there are engravings by Coypel and Massé. Coypel's mythologies combine poorly with Gillot's vigorous work and this sort of thing often mars later books as well. In many ways Gillot's delightful animal pictures look back to a book like Barlow's *Æsop* rather than forward [168]. There is nothing about them of the artificiality of the rococo age, little except for their small size and delicacy which can be said to herald it. But if this book is compared with that magnificent swan song of the seventeenth century, the *Médailles sur les principaux évènements du règne de Louis le grand* (1702) the difference will be felt.

Perhaps the chief cause of this change of atmosphere is the rapprochement of painting and illustration. There is no difference in kind between the paintings of Watteau or Boucher,

---

[1] It is possible that some of the anonymous plates in the *Fables Nouvelles* were Watteau's work.

Chloé sauve Daphnis par le son de sa flûte

FABLE TROISIESME.

Le Renard Prédicateur.

LA morale sans doute est l'ame de la Fable;
C'est une fleur qui doit donner son fruit :
Vous voulez seulement lire un conte agreable;
Sans le vouloir, vous allez être instruit.
On badine; il paroît qu'on ne songe qu'à plaire;
Et le jeu se tourne en leçon.
L'homme n'eût point voulu d'un precepte severe;
Pour le prendre, il falloit trouver cet hameçon.
Ainsi

167. Longus: *Daphnis et Chloé*, 1718. 6¼″ × 4″.
With engravings by the Regent

168. Motte: *Fables Nouvelles*, 1719.
10″ × 6½″

169. Boileau's *Oeuvres*, 1718. 14½″ × 9½″.
Illustrated by Picart

170. Boccaccio's *Decameron*, 1757.
7¾″ × 5¼″. A design by Gravelot

202

CONTRE CEUX QUI ONT LE GOUT DIFFICILE . Fable XXIII.

171. La Fontaine's *Fables*, 1733.
$18\frac{1}{2}'' \times 13''$. With designs by Oudry

172. Molière's *Oeuvres*, 1734.
$11'' \times 8\frac{1}{2}''$. With designs by Boucher

L'ÉTOURDI

L'ÉTOURDI,
OU
LES CONTRE-TEMS,
COMEDIE.

ACTE PREMIER.
SCENE PREMIERE.
LELIE.

É bien, Léandre, hé bien, il faudra contester,
Nous verrons de nous deux qui pourra l'emporter;
Qui, dans nos soins communs pour ce jeune miracle,
Aux vœux de son rival portera plus d'obstacle:
Préparez vos efforts, & vous défendez bien,
Sur que de mon côté, je n'épargnerai rien.

A ij

162 *LE DIABLE*

A cela près. On donna telle fomme,
Qu'avec les traits de la jeune Alibech,
Il prit pour bon un Enfer très-fufpect,
Ufant des biens que l'hymen nous envoie.
A tous époux Dieu doint pareille joie!

173. La Fontaine's *Contes*, 1762. $7\frac{3}{4}'' \times 5''$.
A plate by Eisen

174. A tailpiece by Choffard from the same
book

PUBLII OVIDII

NASONIS

METAMORPHOSEON,

LIBER PRIMUS.

INTRODUCTIO.

IN nova fert animus mutatas dicere formas
Corpora. Di coeptis (nam vos mutaftis & illas)
Afpirate meis: primaque ab origine mundi
Ad mea perpetuum deducite tempora carmen.

LES
MÉTAMORPHOSES
D'OVIDE,
LIVRE PREMIER.

AVANT-PROPOS.

J'AI formé le deffein de chanter tous les changemens arrivés
dans la Nature aux corps qui ont été revêtus de nouvelles
figures. Dieux! auteurs de tous ces changemens, favorifez
mon entreprife, & conduifez cet Ouvrage depuis le commen-
cement du Monde jufqu'à préfent.

A ij

175. Ovid's *Metamorphoses*, 1767. $10'' \times 7\frac{3}{4}''$. With designs by Eisen, Boucher, Choffard and
others

176. Marmontel: *Contes moraux*, 1765. $6\frac{1}{2}'' \times 3\frac{3}{4}$. Illustrated by Gravelot

177. Montesquieu: *Le Temple de Gnide*, 1772. $8\frac{3}{4}'' \times 5\frac{3}{4}''$. An illustration by Eisen

Sommeille en paix ma chere Annette ;
Hélas ! c'eſt pour moi ſeul que ſont faits tous les maux .

178. Laborde's *Chansons*, 1773. $9\frac{1}{4}'' \times 5\frac{1}{2}''$.
Engraved throughout by Moreau and others, this
is one of the most exquisite books of the period

C. P. Marillier, inv.   de Longueil, Sculp

CONTE.

LE CHEMIN PERDU

ET RETROUVÉ.

S'EN retournant dans son hameau,
Perrette s'étoit égarée ;
Ruse d'amour ! la fillette éplorée,
Au coin d'un petit bois où gazouille un ruisseau
Bordé de mousse & de son eau ,
Baignant la verdure altérée ,

179. Dorat: *Fables Nouvelles*, 1773. $7\frac{1}{4}'' \times 4\frac{1}{2}''$.
Illustrated by Marillier

180. Restif de la Bretonne:
Les Contemporaines, 1780–5. $6\frac{3}{4}'' \times 4''$.
A curious compendium of trades, crafts
and professions in 42 volumes illustrated
by Binet or his disciples

181. Vadé: *Oeuvres Poissardes*, 1796. $11\frac{1}{2}'' \times 8\frac{1}{2}''$.
Illustrated by Monsiau with stipple engravings
printed in colour

182. La Fontaine's *Contes*, 1795. $11\frac{1}{2}'' \times 8\frac{1}{2}''$.
An illustration by Fragonard

183. Saint-Non: *Voyage pittoresque*, 1781–6.
$20'' \times 13''$. A tail-piece by Fragonard

184. Rowe's *Shakespeare* of 1709.
$7\frac{1}{2}'' \times 4\frac{1}{2}''$

185. *Select Fables of Esop*, 1761. $6\frac{1}{2}'' \times 4\frac{1}{4}''$.
Printed by Baskerville

186. Pine's *Horace*, 1733. $9'' \times 5\frac{1}{2}''$

187. Ariosto: *Orlando Furioso*, 1773. $9\frac{1}{4}'' \times 5\frac{3}{4}''$.
Illustrated for Baskerville by Moreau, Eisen,
Cochin and others

188. Gray's *Poems*, 1753. $14\frac{1}{2}'' \times 10''$. A design by Bentley, engraved by Grignon

and the engravings of innumerable lesser known artists; and the connexion is made closer by the new fashion of issuing volumes of reproductions of paintings, such as was done by Watteau in 1734, and Claude in 1777.[1] For the first thirty years or so of the century illustrations were more often than not a set of plates bound up with the text, their style reminiscent of paintings, their relevance not immediately apparent. Later many painters of the time, among them Boucher and Fragonard, dabbled in etching in imitation of the Pompadour, and even illustrated some books. On the other hand the professional illustrator need no longer be a craftsman for by now the division between draughtsman and engraver is complete—the former supplied the design and then apparently washed his hands of it, taking little interest in what the latter did with it. (Gillot, Cochin and one or two others who engraved their own designs are exceptions.) It may seem strange that this should be so when etching, which is essentially an autographic technique, was used for so many illustrations of the period. But the retouching with the burin which took place after etching changed the whole character of the plate and gave it the precision which we associate with the line-engraving.

It cannot be denied that the best French etcher-engravers did their work supremely well. Men like Le Mire, Delaunay and de Longueil though their names are overshadowed by those of the great draughtsmen from whose designs they worked made their contribution to the glories of the century. It is to be hoped that the designers themselves realized how much they owed to them. Several of them usually combined their work in one book but more often than not there was only one draughtsman to give a unity to the whole. (Several exceptions to this will be mentioned later.) Standing slightly apart from both draughtsmen and engravers were the decorators like Cochin and Choffard who designed the borders, title-pages and head-pieces that add their characteristic flavour to the eighteenth-century book. These people usually did their own engraving because their decoration, unlike the main illustrations, was conceived in terms of the graver. All this work, whether etched, engraved or both, was essentially in line. The tonal techniques like mezzotint, stipple or crayon that were so widely used in England during the century for reproductive work, never became popular in France. Woodcutting however persisted as we have said for ornament, its chief practitioner and apologist being Papillon whose *Traité . . . de la gravure sur bois* (1766) is in spite of its inaccuracies a book of great interest. His cuts however show little appreciation of the peculiar qualities of wood.

The year 1719, though convenient as a starting point, was no deadline. Bernard Picart was a contemporary of Gillot and went on illustrating books all through the first half of the century, but most of his work is reminiscent of Chauveau. He is important too because he trained a whole school of good engravers. Ovid's *Metamorphoses* which he illustrated in 1732 is a large folio and might have been published a hundred years earlier. His *Boileau's Works* of 1718 on the other hand contains vignettes that compete with Gillot's of the following year as the first in the new style [169]. The book is interesting too as containing one of the earliest lists of illustration—in this case with elaborate explanations of the engravings and of the artist's intentions.

With Oudry and Boucher we reach the first famous illustrators of our period, both of them painters. La Fontaine's *Fables* which Oudry illustrated in 1733 was not published until 1755–9, but its large size dates it as belonging to the earlier part of the century [171].

---

[1] Claude's *Liber Veritatis* inspired Turner's *Liber Studiorum* in the next century. As Hind points out Claude's idea was to safeguard himself against copyists by making a record of his pictures whereas Turner produced an original work.

It is a magnificent work in four volumes, beautifully printed and far from being, as Pollard calls it, a collection of plates. The pictures are linked too closely to the text for that. Their large size does not demand such meticulous work as a smaller picture would, and consequently they retain more of an etched than an engraved quality. Their chief fault is a certain ponderousness and lack of the humour which the text demands. Several engravers worked on the book, the best known being Nicolas Cochin; and sometimes we are given the names on the plate itself of the etcher and of the engraver who worked over the etching with his burin. Between them they altered Oudry's work almost out of recognition.

Boucher's pencil sketches were treated more respectfully by his engraver, Laurent Cars, and his Molière of 1734, in six quarto volumes, is a *tour de force* with its fine head and tail-pieces [172]. It is difficult to say how much such a book as this owes to the artist and how much to the engraver, although the former usually gets the credit. But there is no doubt that the fame of the French eighteenth-century book is due largely to the skill of the professional engravers who were able to subdue their personalities and attain homogeneity, yet keep the originality of each artist. A few illustrators, Cochin, Moreau and Eisen, engraved their own designs and in spite of that achieved a remarkably large output. Cochin, as we have seen, often engraved the designs of others as well and Cohen credits him with 143 books, more than any contemporary of his. He was a courtier and a protégé of the Pompadour yet he was always ready to undertake the most ephemeral work such as menus and invitations. His title-pages for the publisher Prault set a fashion for the whole century with their ornamental border, their vignette and their open lettering in two colours. His best illustration proper is to Boileau's *Le Lutrin* of 1740, in which may clearly be seen the neo-classicism which informs nearly all his work and which competed with the rococo all through the century, only to triumph at the end. Bouchot distinguishes two separate strains which persisted throughout the century. One he associates with Boucher and his large mythological subjects; the other with Watteau, smaller in scale, more contemporary, more feminine. The first makes us think of the baroque, the second of the rococo, but they both exist side by side throughout the period and sometimes co-exist in the same book.

Choffard, though he did not himself engrave, was even more of a decorator; in fact he seems to have illustrated very few books by himself, but in spite of this he enjoyed an enormous reputation. To him, more than to any other, the prevalence of the vignette in the second half of the century is due. He carried the elaboration of borders and foliage to extreme lengths yet without loss of elegance or lightness. He seems to delight in making difficulties for himself in order to show his skill in solving them, and much of his work is so minute that it is hard to believe it was done before the days of mechanical reduction. It is all of a piece with the jewellery and interior decoration in which the century excelled.

Choffard was called in to decorate one of the most sumptuous and costly books of the period, the *Fermiers Généraux* edition of La Fontaine's *Contes* (1762) in collaboration with Eisen who undertook the plates [173]. It is significant that such a book should be issued in octavo size, and if we compare it with the larger books such as Oudry's La Fontaine we notice how Eisen's engravings are adapted to make their effect in a smaller space. He no longer aims at a complete picture but contents himself with indicating the background rather sketchily. To Choffard of course the limitation was no hardship and he surpasses himself (and often Eisen too) in the microscopic figures which make up his tail-pieces. Eisen who seems to have had a keener sense of typographic harmony than most of his contemporaries, also triumphed over the difficulties and between them they produced one of the monuments of the period. The indelicacy of which Eisen is often accused is not so much lubricity as grossness—the grossness that is so strange an accompaniment of eighteenth-century elegance in every country. There is less scope for it in a book of poems like Dorat's *Baisers* which he illustrated in 1770. Here the sham rusticity of the indifferent verse has evoked some wholly delightful mythological head- and tail-pieces, which, as they are decorative rather than illustrative, no one could call objectionable. This book is a lesson in the avoidance of the sterile classicism that overtook illustration at the end of the century, and is already visible in such a book as the Ovid of 1767. The text is printed in two colours but the engravings which are printed on the same pages as the type are in black, not in red as they are in Vizetelly's egregious 'facsimile' of 1890. In fact, though engravings could easily have been printed in a different colour from the accompanying type they very seldom are in the eighteenth century;[1] and it is difficult to believe that black could have been improved on. The last book of Eisen that we must notice is Montesquieu's *Le Temple de Gnide* (1772) which had already been illustrated by Cochin père et fils in 1742. Eisen's version is particularly interesting because it is engraved throughout, text and illustrations; and it is significant of the importance attached to the illustrations that the author's name is not mentioned at all on the title-page—only Eisen and Le Mire [177].

Gravelot's early work we shall meet when we come to deal with English books. Bouchot has pointed out how thoroughly French were his illustrations of English books and yet how, when he returned to France, his work showed English traits which seem to have been borrowed from Hogarth. These may be characterized as a certain straightforwardness of approach and a liking for the domestic scene—both of them unusual for the time in France. He was not as good a draughtsman as Eisen though he was more discreet in his choice of subjects which his authors generally seem to have been content to leave to him. He illustrated a Racine in 1768 and a Voltaire in 1769, but his best book was his *Contes moraux* of Marmontel of 1765 in which he instituted a formula which Moreau carried to a conclusion [176]. He also contributed many plates to an even more famous work, the *Decameron* of 1757–61, which contained engravings by Boucher, Cochin and Eisen as well. This book is a landmark because it is the first important octavo and henceforth the small book dominates the illustration of the century. Typographically too it is delightful; its vignettes are printed on the same pages as the type and the plates are on the text paper, framed uniformly, irrespective of their designer. Thus, in spite of so many different contributors the book has a homogeneity which marks it as one of the very best in a wonderful period [170].

Another composite book containing the work of an even more brilliant galaxy of artists is Ovid's *Metamorphoses* (1767–71) to which Eisen, Boucher, Moreau, Le Prince, Monnet and Choffard all contributed.[2] This however lacks the extraordinary unity of the *Decameron* and also its typographical felicity. The paper used for the plates is too thick and there are wood-cut fleurons which look clumsy beside Choffard's exquisite head-pieces [175]. But perhaps the chief stumbling-block was the subject-matter which enforced a neo-classical approach whereas the *Decameron* lent itself to contemporary treatment.

It was in fact neo-classicism that killed French rococo illustration at the end of the century and Moreau le Jeune is the link between the two styles as well as the representative figure of the second half of the century. He is a type of the specialist in illustration who first appeared during this period. A friend of the painter, David, he worked on well into the

---

[1] One or two Italian books provide a not very successful exception.

[2] The title-page however has 'gravées sur les dessins des meilleurs peintres français' by Le Mire and Basan which seems to set a higher value on the engraver's work than one would have expected.

nineteenth century and his work falls into two distinct halves. In his later neo-classical style he repeated with deplorable effect books which he had illustrated earlier, e.g. the Ovid of 1804, the Molière of 1806 and the Rousseau of 1808. In these books and in the complete La Fontaine of 1814 nothing survives of his earlier grace and it is almost impossible to believe that they are illustrated by the same man. It is sad to record that his adaptability did him little good for he died in want.

He will always be remembered however for his earlier work and for one magnificent book in particular to which he contributed, Laborde's *Choix de Chansons* of 1773 [178]. Song-books are a fruitful source of illustration in the eighteenth century and not only in France. They lent themselves to decorative treatment and their title-pages are often of great beauty. Laborde which has one of the most exquisite title-pages of them all is engraved throughout, text and music and illustrations, and it contains decorated lettering of a high order. It also possesses a unity which for a book with music could not have been attained by any other method in those days. It is a unity emphasised by the relevance of the ornament to the text which it often subtly echoes. There are four volumes, and all Moreau's work appears in the first. The other three are illustrated by Le Barbier and St. Quentin; and it is typical of the period that two of its lesser lights were able to match their style so cleverly to Moreau's. Moreau's chief delight was in the contemporary scene and he turned this talent to good effect in his *Monument du costume* of 1777, a sort of social history of Louis XVI's reign in pictures. The use of such large engravings is contrary to contemporary practice and the result is a portfolio rather than a book. The same plates however appear on a small scale in Restif de la Bretonne's *Tableaux de la Bonne Compagnie* (1787) engraved with incredible minuteness, and losing much of their effect in the process. Moreau's Molière of 1773 and his Rousseau contain much delightful work. The latter appeared in three different editions and sizes between 1774 and 1801, each with a newly engraved set of illustrations.

Marillier who collaborated with Eisen in Dorat's *Baisers* is less well known but some of his books are worthy to be ranked with Moreau's. His *Fables Nouvelles* of Dorat (1773) is altogether charming with its head and tail-pieces that seem to hark back to the previous century [179]. There is a strongly decorative element here in the varying frames[1] which are provided for the vignettes; and the unusual sympathy we find in his book between typography and illustration is undoubtedly helped by the fact that he usually engraved his own designs. It is interesting to note that he illustrated the French editions of *Sir Charles Grandison* and *Pamela*. Like Gravelot he was less at his ease in serious subjects, and his illustrated Bible was not a success. The Age of Reason was not a period of great Biblical illustration.

So we come to Fragonard, perhaps the greatest of them all, although he was no professional illustrator. It may well be that his work is all the fresher for being subordinated to his painting and all the better for being so scarce. The output of men like Moreau is so immense that we cannot wonder they grew stale sometimes. But Fragonard only illustrated two or three books that were published, though he made drawings for others which never appeared. It was unfortunate that his work appeared at the very end of the century when the standard of engravings had fallen off and when the Revolution had temporarily killed the demand for fine books and destroyed the art by which he had lived. Nevertheless there is no concession to neo-classicism in his chief book, La Fontaine's *Contes*, published by Didot in 1795 [182].

---

[1] Oddly enough illustrations during this century were distinguished from prints by imitation picture-frames; and Singer has pointed out how as time went on these frames became more and more linear.

It is true that his drawings were made over a period of about twenty years, the earliest in Italy in 1773. But the last which were completed in 1790 show little difference from the first. These superb ink and wash drawings are now in the Louvre, bound up with a calligraphic manuscript of the text. 'In these illustrations', says Benesch, 'everything is dissolved into movement, blinding light, a play of reflections, an almost unsubstantial spiritedness.' But the printed version which was to have had eighty plates was a failure, partly because of the inauspicious moment and partly because Fragonard was poorly served by his engravers. Only two parts were issued, the second without plates. In the first volume, sixteen engravings are by Fragonard, the other four by hacks working in the neo-classical style. The failure of this book seems to have confirmed Didot in his preference for the latter.

The *Voyage pittoresque de Naples et de Sicile* (1781–6) in which Fragonard collaborated is an early example of the topographical book which was soon to be so popular in England. It was written and sponsored by Fragonard's friend, the Abbé Saint-Non, and appeared in four enormous volumes. Fragonard's part was confined to reproductions of pictures and a few decorations, of which, as this is a rare form of his art, we reproduce one here [183]. Another work produced in collaboration with Saint-Non was the *Fragments choisis dans les peintures . . . des Églises de l'Italie* (1770–3), but as this has no text it hardly ranks as a book. It is especially interesting however because of the wonderful freedom of the engravings which are done *à la manière du lavis* (wash), and make a sort of free transcription of the pictures which they reproduce. But Fragonard's best illustrations were done for books which never appeared. The manuscript of La Fontaine's *Contes* we have already mentioned and his wonderful drawings for Ariosto's *Orlando Furioso* have been made the subject of a special study by Elizabeth Mongan and others.[1] There are nearly 150 of them in crayon and wash, and they show clearly how difficult Fragonard's work must have been for the engraver to translate. Then he made also some drawings for La Fontaine's *Fables* and for *Don Quixote* which were never used. It is one of the minor tragedies of the eighteenth century that this artist with all the gifts that make a great illustrator never found the right publisher, nor except in the *Fragments choisis* the right technique for the reproduction of his dynamic style.

The influence on the book of the painter David and what he represented is generally supposed to have been bad. The effect on Moreau was indeed deplorable but the Didots, whose typography was shaped in the prevailing classical atmosphere, performed an inestimable service to French printing, comparable to Baskerville in England and Bodoni in Italy. Apart from their typography they were great innovators and the printing-press, the stereotype and paper were all brought one stage nearer perfection by their efforts. Their Virgil (1798), Horace (1799) and Racine (1801) are magnificent books and show a return to the larger page which suited the neo-classical illustrators, Gérard, Girodet, Chaudet, etc., just as the duodecimos suited their predecessors. It is a pity that the illustration of these Didot volumes is never up to their typography.

Until the arrival of the Didots the eighteenth century in France had seen very few technical innovations. Nearly all the engravings which illustrated books were etched and finished with the burin. The tone processess like mezzotint, stipple and aquatint, which were so popular at this time in England were seldom used in France. The one exception was what is called the 'crayon manner' which seems to have been the invention of a Frenchman, J. C. François. He used it for the portraits which illustrate Savérien's *Histoire des Philosophes modernes* (1760–9) and obtained with it an almost lithographic effect [189]. Incidentally François wrote a note which appears at the end of Volume I about his method. Other

[1] *Fragonard Drawings for Ariosto* (New York, 1945).

Allégorie d'Abbadie

189. Savérien: *Histoire des Philosophes modernes*, 1760–9. $6\frac{1}{2}'' \times 3\frac{3}{4}''$. An illustration in the crayon manner

interesting experiments had already been made earlier in printing colour from wood-blocks in combination with an engraved plate. The *Cabinet Crozat* was produced in this way in 1729, a collection of engravings by various hands which reproduced paintings. But woodcutting proper was of course of little importance during the period as compared with copper engraving in spite of Papillon's jealousy for his craft. Curiously enough, Papillon in his book mentions disapprovingly the use of the graver on wood, a technique which in the hands of Bewick was to exalt wood over copper during the next century.

About the time of the Revolution a few remarkable and little-known books appeared with coloured illustrations produced by stipple-engravings.[1] Monsiau and Schall were the designers of most of them. The colour and the register are a *tour de force* for their date but the designs are not remarkable. The best of these books are Vadé's *Oeuvres Poissardes* (1796), illustrated by Monsiau [181], and *Paradise Lost* which Schall illustrated in 1792. It was a pity that this delightful technique with its pure and clean colours was never used by a really first-class artist.

This account of the eighteenth century in France would not be complete without a mention of two widely contrasting types of book—the learned productions and the almanacs. The latter with their microscopic format and their frivolous engravings are typical enough but one hardly associates the former with this era. Nevertheless books like Buffon's *Histoire naturelle* (which was published in 44 well-illustrated volumes between 1749 and 1804) and Prévost's *Histoire Générale des Voyages* (1745–70) continued to appear all the time. Two botanical books used unusual processes for their illustrations. Gautier d'Agoty's *Collection des Plantes* (1767) has plates printed by the Le Blond method, forerunner of our trichromatic

[1] See page 221 for a description of this technique.

process; and *Fleurs dessinées d'après Nature* (1801) by G. von Spaëndonck (who was Redouté's teacher) has stipple-engravings printed in colour. Here the technique is applied to far finer pictures than Monsiau's or Schall's. The almanacs are of more interest to us however because they depended entirely on their appearance for their effect. Measuring about 4×2 inches, they comprise not only a calendar but also verses and engravings, the last sometimes by famous artists like Gravelot or Eisen but more often by lesser lights like Binet or Queverdo [180].

ENGLAND

Hitherto the great majority of prints had been produced for book illustration but quite early in the new century they began to be used for reproducing paintings. We have already seen examples of this in France and the Netherlands but it was done on a much larger scale in England and Hogarth was the man chiefly responsible. It is said that the engravings of the *Harlot's Progress* brought him in much more money than the paintings upon which they were based and it is easy to see how such a use was bound to degrade the medium. Illustration necessarily suffered although reproductions of paintings were seldom used in books; for it was difficult for engravers to alter techniques which were adapted to simulate tone. When Choffard superciliously said of his English contemporaries, 'Supported by some foreign talent, they are trying to create it among themselves; but they are not able to kindle the flame that illuminates all art in France', he was partly right. Most of the best engravers and etchers of the sixteenth century and of the first half of the seventeenth were indeed foreigners. Choffard's colleague Gravelot, whom perhaps he had in mind, worked over here for many years without having much effect on the native style. But Choffard was wrong in assuming that the French and English genius must necessarily be of the same sort. He was not the man to appreciate the vigour of Barlow or the satire of Hogarth, for both of whom engraving technique was of secondary importance.

This period in England then has nothing to show like the spate of luxury books which appeared in France. There was to all intents and purposes no native baroque art in England. Social conditions here were very different from France and money was not concentrated to the same degree in the pockets of the few. Nevertheless we find some of the same types of illustrated book recurring in both countries, in particular topographical works, poems and novels. As in France the first type was represented to begin with by series of large uninspired volumes such as *Britannia Illustrata* which appeared between 1707 and 1726 with its rather dull engravings by Kip; but by the end of the century the English coloured topographical book is something peculiar to this country and superior to anything France can show. Then there were the classical texts, of which Tonson published a fine folio and quarto series beginning with Dryden's translation of Virgil in 1697 illustrated by Hollar, Faithorne and Lombart down to Ovid's *Metamorphoses* of 1717 on which M. van der Gucht worked.

For some reason or other drama has never been illustrated as successfully in England as in France. All through this century when magnificent editions of Molière and Racine were coming from France we were producing illustrations for our greatest dramatist from Rowe's Shakespeare of 1709 to Boydell's extravagant venture in the 1790s [184 and 190]. Very few were worthy of their subject.[1] Gravelot in fact was responsible for two sets, those which he

[1] Perhaps the best were those by E. Edwards for Bell's Shakespeare of 1773–5. Typographically this is a delightful edition too.

designed for Theobald's Shakespeare in 1740 and a later set which he engraved after Hayman for an Oxford edition in 1744; but they are not as good as the plates for Racine which he did in France in 1768. In Croxall's Æsop of 1722 and Pine's Horace of 1733 however we have two books which challenge comparison with any of the numerous illustrated versions of these works preceding them from whatever country. The Æsop is especially interesting because its vignettes are not engraved at all, they are cut in relief [195]. It is not certain whether they are metal or woodcuts and they are not well printed but their quality still asserts itself. They are the precursors of Bewick's wood-engravings but they also look back to Barlow in their vigour which overcomes the limitations of their small size and of their uniform system of oval framing.

Pine's Horace is an even more important book. Pine, a pupil of Picart, was our best native engraver during the first half of the century and he had already provided a frontispiece for the first edition of *Robinson Crusoe* in 1719. His Horace is engraved throughout, text and illustrations, and possesses the delightful unity that such books always have. Its lettering with its strong contrasts between thick and thin strokes may well have influenced Baskerville and Bodoni in their type design.[1] Its vignettes make it one of the few English books that can be compared with French work of the time for delicacy and finish [186]. Another book that was engraved throughout was Sturt's *Prayer Book* of 1717 but this comes nowhere near Pine's work. About fifty years later Sturt produced a Bible with hundreds of engravings from 'designs of the greatest masters' but he managed to reduce them all to the same standard of dullness. Robert Furber's *Twelve Months of Flowers* (1730) is really a catalogue of that nurseryman's stock but it contains engravings after flower-paintings by Casteels. It is not very important but it represents, Blunt says, the first attempt to convert the Dutch flower-piece into illustration.

Hogarth is the most considerable figure of this period, less by virtue of his actual books than of his famous series of prints. These were later issued with texts, so that even technically they are illustrations; and of course artistically they could be nothing else. Their importance for us lies in the new social attitude which they embody and in their genius for characterization. In the next century this came to fruition in the work of the great English and French caricaturists which usually appeared in an ephemeral form; but to begin with the talent of Hogarth and of Rowlandson after him was partly directed into book illustration. Lamb's comment gives a hint of what he could have done if he had expended more of his energies on books. 'His graphic representations are indeed books; they have the teeming fruitful suggestive meaning of words. Other pictures we look at—his prints we read.' And Hogarth himself said: 'I have endeavoured to treat my subject as a dramatic writer.'

He was trained as a silversmith's engraver but he was never an expert one. Etching gave him more of the freedom he needed but he practised it comparatively seldom; and never for books. In the *Analysis of Beauty* which he wrote in 1753 however the reader may discover in spite of its naive aesthetic a real appreciation of line unusual in a painter. His earliest illustration appears in such works as Aubry de la Mottraye's *Travels* of 1723 and Briscoe's *Apuleius* of 1724 but his first characteristic work is for Butler's *Hudibras* of 1726 [194]. Although these designs are based on an anonymous set from the 1709 edition they are yet recognizably Hogarthian. They have little finesse; they might almost as well have been cut in wood. The fact that most of them are folding plates divorces them even more completely

---

[1] Caslon's first specimen sheet which put England typographically upon the map appeared the year after Pine's Horace in 1734.

MIDSUMMER-NIGHT'S DREAM.
Act v. Scene i.
A Wood. Puck.

190. Boydell's *Shakespeare*, 1791–1804. $16\frac{1}{2}'' \times 12''$. An engraving after Fuseli for *A Midsummer Night's Dream*

191. Thomson's *Seasons*,1797. $18\frac{1}{4}'' \times 12\frac{1}{2}''$. Stipple engravings by Bartolozzi after Hamilton

192. Stubbs: *Anatomy of the Horse*, 1766. 22″ × 17½″. Engravings by the author

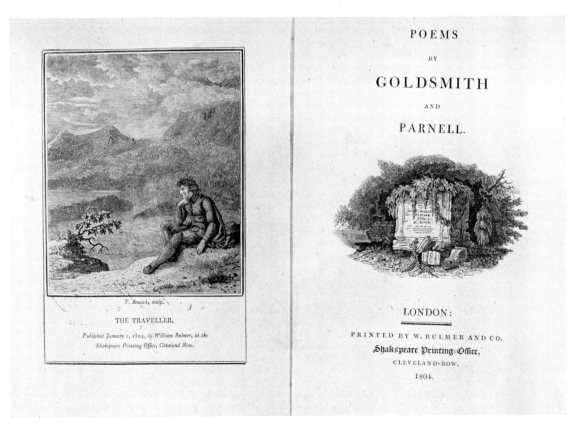

193. Goldsmith's and Parnell's *Poems*, 1795. Illustrated by the Bewick brothers and the Johnson brothers. The frontispiece shows how much tone can be extracted from the wood-engraving

194. Butler's *Hudibras*, 1726. 6″ × 3½″. One of the folding plates

from the text than engravings need be. Yet they are a landmark in English illustration and emphasize its divergence from an international style. Of them Horace Walpole said that they were the first of Hogarth's works that 'marked him as a man above the common'. The native manner which we have already noticed in Barlow is growing to maturity, and nothing could be more different from French work of the time, with its appeal to the connoisseur. Hogarth aims at the common man; where the French illustrator is salacious, he is coarse; where the French illustrator chooses a classical or aristocratic subject he prefers a contemporary plebeian one; and he is moral when the Frenchman is amoral. It is ironical that Gravelot should have illustrated (not very successfully) so many of our great eighteenth-century novels including *Tom Jones* which leaps to the mind as the perfect subject for Hogarth. As it was Hogarth did a few lively designs for *Tristram Shandy*, which is in its way as typically English as Fielding's novel; but there are only enough plates to whet our appetite for more.

Besides his Shakespeare illustrations Gravelot's best English books are Gay's *Fables* of 1738 and Richardson's *Pamela* of 1742. His engravers, who were seldom English, gave to his designs more of an etched quality than we find in his later French work. Its chief importance lies in its beneficial effect on English engraving, for it demanded a new standard of delicacy and Gravelot himself trained craftsmen for this work. One of them was Charles Grignion who engraved Bentley's designs for his famous edition of Gray's *Poems* (1753). This exciting book is quite different from any of its contemporaries and it contains perhaps the first hint in book illustration of the Gothic revival [188]. Its title too gives remarkable prominence to the name of the illustrator, for it is called *Designs by Mr. R. Bentley for Six Poems by Mr. T. Gray*. One can imagine the effect on readers used to the pedestrian and stereotyped work of Hayman or Wale of the big engravings surrounded by curious borders reminiscent of the 'scatter-borders' in fifteenth-century manuscripts. The curious use of mythological figures must have seemed extremely piquant too. It is not surprising to learn that Rex Whistler found some of his inspiration in these plates.

The Gothic revival which was about to revolutionize architecture had less effect on book illustration at this time than one would expect. The average book is still illustrated in the eighteenth-century style but the neo-classical infusion that was so pronounced in France affects the typography rather than the pictures; and to see how uninspired that style can be in the hands of a mediocre designer served by an indifferent engraver one has only to look at Stothard's *Vicar of Wakefield* (1792) or Wale's work for the *Complete Angler* of 1760 esteemed one of the best books of its day. It is pleasant and competent but no more.[1] Hayman who in 1755 illustrated Smollett's *Don Quixote* is in the same category though his work for the Baskerville edition of Congreve in 1761 seems to have been improved by his engraver Grignion. But Baskerville's edition of *Orlando Furioso* (1773), the illustrations for which were designed by Moreau, Eisen, Cochin and others and engraved by de Launay and de Longueil displays a refreshing degree of Gallic lightness and polish [187], enhanced by the impeccable typography of the best English printer of the century. This is a book that compares with anything France can show and perhaps its only fault is that it might easily be French. Baskerville's *Select Fables of Esop* (1761) is peculiarly his own, however. One of the many articles of belief in which the famous printer differed from his times was the possibility of achieving a fine book by typography alone. Illustration for him took a secondary place. In his *Esop* he surmounts the difficulties of printing one engraving for each fable (which would mean one on nearly every page) by grouping twelve little pictures in one plate which was then pasted in [185]. Each picture is only about one inch square and each is a miracle of compression.

There is no economy about the egregious Boydell *Shakespeare* which was launched in 1786. In that year Alderman Boydell approached most of the well-known painters of the day—Reynolds, West, Fuseli, Romney, etc.—and invited them to paint scenes from the plays which could be first exhibited in his gallery and afterwards engraved to illustrate a monumental edition of Shakespeare. Even a Vollard could not have carried through a scheme like this and Boydell had none of Vollard's integrity. The result was that neither the pictures themselves nor the engravings were successful and the former were in fact sold eventually by means of a lottery. The nine volumes, in spite of fine typography and superb printing by Bulmer, are an object lesson in the unsuitability of reproductions of large paintings for book illustration [190]. The processes include almost every known engraving technique of the day, and the styles range from the neo-classicism of Fuseli to the foretaste of Victorian sentimentality which we can savour in the work of W. Peters. Even Boydell's contemporaries, whose artistic consciences were not as tender as ours in such matters, threw scorn on this project. Gillray's famous cartoon of 1791, *Alderman Boydell or a Peep into the Shakespeare Gallery*, testifies to this.

Many of the paintings in this edition were reproduced by mezzotint which was a favourite method of reproducing this type of original because of its range of tone. We have already noted its invention in Holland and its appearance in a book in 1662. It was however used

---

[1] Perhaps one of the reasons for this low standard was the poor repute in which the engraver was held. His status was slightly improved by the Act of 1734 for the Encouragement of the Arts of Designing, Engraving and Etching Historical and other Prints which led to the dating of prints and was known as Hogarth's Act. But when the Royal Academy was founded in 1768 membership was denied to engravers or etchers.

very seldom in books thereafter but it became popular in England during the eighteenth century and was known abroad as the *manière anglaise*. Some of the plates made after Reynold's paintings are masterpieces, however perverse, in their translation of colour into monochrome. The process differs from other forms of metal engraving in that its user works from black to white. He roughens the plate all over to begin with and by smoothing it where necessary can produce tones of varying depth. The rich quality of the print depends on the 'burr' raised by the rocker but this burr is worn away after a very few impressions. Later prints are therefore much inferior to the first to be taken from the plate and this made the process unsuitable for books though it was not such an obstacle to its employment for the reproduction of paintings. During the nineteenth century steel was used instead of copper for mezzotinting and this resulted in a larger number of impressions.

Stipple was another engraving technique very popular in England during this century, though its practitioners were generally foreigners like Bartolozzi and Schiavonetti. Engraved lines were replaced by dots and the result is something like a coarse half-tone print of today. Apart from its use in France, which has already been noted, for colour plates by Monsiau and Schall, it was seldom used for illustration since collections like Bartolozzi's *Imitations of Original Drawings by Hans Holbein* can hardly be called books. It appeared however in one splendid book, Bensley's 1797 edition of Thomson's *Seasons* which has stipples by Bartolozzi after pictures painted by W. Hamilton R.A. [191]. Six copies were printed in colour. The work is remarkable for its printing rather than for its indifferent neo-classical pictures—which yet manage to impress by reason of their presentation.

Aquatint was the latest of the engraving techniques to be discovered and it was not until the turn of the century that it came into vogue. It was then used most extensively for books, especially for the topographical works which became so popular. Along with etching it is the engraving technique most favoured by painters from Goya onwards and to it we owe many handsome books. It relies on a grained ground produced by powdered resin and the result is a faintly dotted texture much less insistent than stipple and much more successful in producing tone. Aquatint plates were often touched up or coloured by hand, and the cold clear washes used by Rowlandson will always be associated with this process. Although he produced many separate prints and caricatures before 1800 most of Rowlandson's book illustration falls in the nineteenth century and will be dealt with in the next chapter. Gillray was another great caricaturist who used aquatint, stipple and etching but he did no work for books.

It is noteworthy that few English illustrators confined themselves wholly to a single method of engraving. It was quite usual to mix several techniques in one plate whereas the French procedure of completing an etching with the burin was much more rigid. Pure line-engraving was mostly reserved for scientific illustration and the monument in this class was Stubbs's *Anatomy of the Horse* (1766), a magnificent book in the direct line of descent from Geminus's *Vesalius* of 1545. In spite of their large size these engravings are of incredible fineness and delicacy [192].

Coloured engravings occasionally appear in English books though there is nothing apart from *The Seasons* like the coloured stipples which France produced at the end of the century. Elisha Kirkall illustrated Martyn's *Historia Plantarum Rariorum* (1728) with large plates after Jacob van Huysum which are printed in several colours and touched up by hand afterwards. The few engravings that are printed only in green make one wonder why, since the printing of engravings had to be done separately from the text in any case, we find so few books of this period with the illustrations in a second colour. Then there was *Plantæ et Papiliones Rariores* (1748–59) written and engraved by the famous flower-painter, Ehret.

Here the colour is applied by hand and the result is exquisite. There were two methods of applying colour. In the first there was only one plate and this was painted selectively with a dabber. In the second, the only true printing method, a separate plate was made for each colour. In 1723 a remarkable book was published in London foreshadowing the trichromatic process which is the most used method of colour-printing today. This was *Coloritto* by Le Blon and it contained what are probably the first progressive prints ever to be seen. The book was however intended more for painters than for engravers or printers.

The woodcut has been left to the end of this brief survey of processes, because it was so little used throughout the greater part of the eighteenth century. Apart from the occasional decoration which assorted so awkwardly with engraved illustration it was reserved for the chap-books which had been appearing ever since the middle of the seventeenth century. These, the equivalent of the illustrated magazines of today, often contained pictures of a vigour and crudity that carry us back to the incunabula. It was on such work that Thomas Bewick started his career and despite his skill and his great reputation it is to this class that his work really belongs. He was a craftsman rather than an artist and it was never his ambition to produce fine books, but rather 'to administer instruction to youth'. And several of the innovations with which he is generally credited were not his at all, nor were they claimed by him. There are white-line woodcuts (from now on properly called wood-engravings) in certain eighteenth-century Armenian books for which the graver has evidently been used and they are probably cut on the end grain of boxwood. But to Bewick belongs the far greater credit of having rescued the woodcut from oblivion and made it a suitable method of illustrating the mass-produced book, just when the Industrial Revolution was making mass production possible.

Bewick was apprenticed to an engraver in Newcastle so he knew from first-hand experience how unsuitable the copper plate was for illustrating books in quantity. His own pictures, though they partake of the delicacy of the line-engraving do not imitate it. But they show possibilities in wood that were hitherto unsuspected; for instance the production of a grey by lowering the block. Yet they never exploit the wood as the reproductive engravers of the later nineteenth century were to do. Bewick was unusual too in the immense care he took not only in engraving his designs but in proving and printing them. The great French draughtsmen of this period, once they had passed their designs over to the engravers seem

195. Croxall's *Æsop* of 1722. 7¾″ × 4½″. Illustrated with metal cuts

196. Gay's *Fables*, 1779. 6¼ × 4″. Illustrated by Bewick

(as far as we can tell) not to have troubled themselves with them any more. And the engravers once they had passed their plates over to the printer probably dissociated themselves from the final printing. But Bewick initiated and supervised the whole process himself for he had a great distrust of 'ignorant rude pressmen', a distrust which was justified in the case of his Æsop.

Bewick's earliest work is little different from that of the chap-books which were issued in such quantities from his own town of Newcastle. Some of his first cuts appeared in the *New Lottery Book of birds and beasts for children* (1771), an illustrated alphabet in which the cuts, in spite of poor printing, already give a hint of his later skill in the representation of the more familiar animals. This is the first real children's book we have noticed since Comenius in the previous chapter but that is not to say that there were none produced in the intervening years. Comenius was imitated all over Europe but these books were all educational and didactic, none was produced simply to delight the child. Even Newbery and his predecessor Boreman, both pioneers in England of juvenile publishing, made the outsides of their little books attractive merely in order to gild the pill of moral instruction. It was not until 1807 when *The Butterfly's Ball* by Roscoe appeared that we find a book whose aim is pure entertainment. And it is worth noting in passing that whereas the illustrations in the earlier books are crude cuts by anonymous hacks, in *The Butterfly's Ball* they are engravings after Mulready.

There is no doubt that children often regaled themselves on the ballads and chap-books which were not really intended for them and which usually contained material that we should consider most unsuitable. Bewick was a man of his age in this matter and in his tail-pieces he shows his affinities not only with the chap-book illustrators but also with the artists responsible for the drolleries of the *Luttrell Psalter*. Yet he considered his work moral too. 'As instruction is of little avail without constant cheerfulness and occasional amusement,' he says, 'I interspersed the more serious studies with tale-pieces (sic) of gaiety and humour; yet even in these seldom without an endeavour to illustrate some truth or point some moral.' And if some of the scenes are not what we would call improving they probably delighted the young reader all the more.

No one who reads Bewick's fascinating *Memoir* can doubt that his work was aimed as much *ad majorem gloriam Dei* as that of the medieval illuminators. Of his *Quadrupeds* and *Birds* he said: 'My writings were chiefly intended for youth; and the more readily to allure their pliable though discursive attention to the great Truths of Creation, I illustrated them by figures delineated with all the fidelity and animation I was able to impart to mere woodcuts without colour.' He had much admiration for Croxall's Æsop which he thought had 'led hundreds of young men into the paths of wisdom and rectitude', and he imitated Croxall's cuts in Gay's *Fables* of 1779 [196] and the *Select Fables* of 1784. The first book is rather better printed and the head-pieces are delightful in their oval frames borrowed from Croxall but decorated with agricultural implements in the corners. As early as this there are instances where parts of the blocks have been lowered to make the backgrounds recede. The tail-pieces are 'vignetted' in the true Bewick style but these are roughly oval in shape too. The horizontal oval is a shape Bewick made peculiarly his own and it fits particularly well into the printed page. It is especially suitable for the head-piece, the constricted shape of which always poses such a problem for the illustrator.

Bewick is generally said to have had little feeling for typography[1] and only one of the

---

[1] Walter Crane went so far as to say that he had 'no regard whatever to the design of the page as a whole'.

197. Bewick's *History of British Birds*, 1797. 9″ × 5½″. One of the main illustrations. The tailpiece on page 227 is from the same book

books he illustrated is exceptional in this respect, yet his engravings always fit well into the page and the general design of the two books with which he was most closely concerned, the *History of Quadrupeds* (1790) and *British Birds* (1797) is reasonably good. But unfortunately many of his books, with these exceptions, suffer from bad printing. Perhaps he was partly to blame for producing work that required presswork beyond the capacity of the average printer of the day. The cuts in *Robin Hood* (1795) and the *Holy Bible in Miniature* (1810) are almost impossible to judge because of this. Later printings from the original blocks, made for collectors when his work was more appreciated, show it to better advantage.

The one exceptional book is Bulmer's edition of Goldsmith's and Parnell's *Poems* (1795) which is beautifully designed and printed [193]. Bewick here joined forces with his brother John and with Robert and John Johnson. The superb presswork shows up the detail and virtuosity of the engravings in a way that is seldom to be seen elsewhere; but Bewick's efforts to match the elegance of the ensemble robbed his work of its accustomed vigour and charm. His Æsop published in 1818 when his powers were flagging suffers from a different disability. Here there were of necessity many subjects which could not be observed at first hand; and, as in the *Select Fables*, many of the engravings are modelled on Croxall; furthermore there is a certain amount of work by pupils and it is doubtful how much of it is exclusively Bewick's. When imperfect presswork is added it will be seen that this book in spite of many good cuts and perhaps too great a virtuosity is something of a disappointment for us as it was for Bewick.

The *Quadrupeds* and *Birds* remain the books upon which his reputation will rest [197]. Bewick's engravings for both volumes of *British Birds* show more use of tone, or 'colour' as he called it, than those for the *Quadrupeds*. As Reynolds Stone says of this work 'The black parts of the block begin to have no more, indeed rather less importance than the white incisions of his graver upon them'. The plumage of the birds themselves was of course an admirable subject for the employment of varying textures and it was this quality that caught the public's eye and helped to build up Bewick's immense reputation. It was this quality also that anticipated photography and in the end led to the downfall of wood-engraving. But nothing had been seen quite like it before, and it is easy to understand why Bewick's name always occupied a prominent position on the title-pages of the books he illustrated and why the engravings of these two books were issued separately in 1800. It is not surprising either

198. Decker's *Gothic Architecture*, 1759. 8½″ × 11″. An English edition of a famous German work

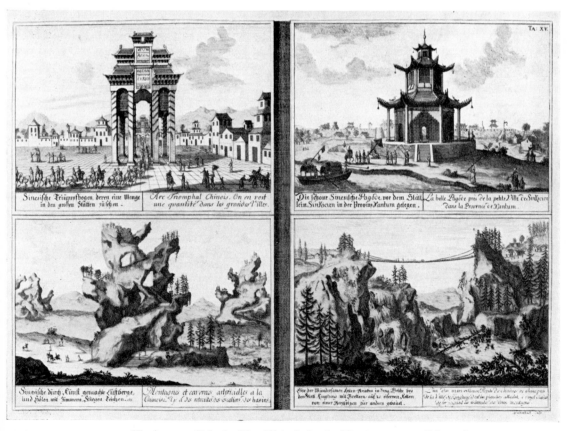

199. Fischer von Erlach: *Eine Historische Architectur*, 1721. 16½″ × 24″

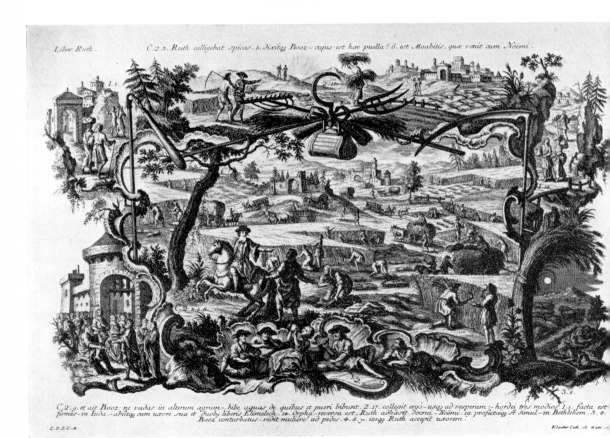

200. Fénélon's *Telemachus*, 1727.
$12\frac{1}{2}'' \times 8\frac{1}{2}''$. An engraving by Sperling
after Leclerc

201. Klauber: *Historiae biblicae veteris et
novi Testamenti*, 1748. $8\frac{1}{2}'' \times 13''$

that so many books on natural history that appeared during the first half of the nineteenth century were modelled on the *Quadrupeds* and *Birds* of Bewick.

It may seem that an inordinate amount of space has been devoted to Bewick when the admission has already been made that he was not a great original artist. But he was a forerunner of the Romantic movement and as John Piper says 'he had that rarest of qualities—normal, unhampered, unclouded vision'; vision which expressed itself naturally in the wood-engraving rather than in his drawing for the wood-engraving. And the change that his influence brought to book illustration in the nineteenth century, not only in England but all over Western Europe, draws all our attention to its originator. That influence was technical rather than artistic, it was rather his way of engraving wood than of seeing things. Yet wood-engraving had to come back and would have done so had Bewick never lived. A method had to be rediscovered of printing pictures with text and of printing them in quantity. It is significant that Bewick once computed that one of his blocks had given 900,000 impressions without wearing out.

His work was often copied quite flagrantly. Alexander Anderson copied the *Quadrupeds* in America and so introduced his methods there. But it was his pupils, Clennell, Harvey and Landells, who were his true successors and the next chapter will attempt to show how from them sprang the great reproductive engravers of the Victorian age.

GERMANY, SWITZERLAND AND THE NETHERLANDS

The change from a feudal to a bourgeois society that came so suddenly to France with the Revolution took place more gradually in Central Europe where bourgeois society had long existed. It was in such a society that the German arts—poetry, philosophy and music in particular—flourished. Consequently illustration was a less aristocratic affair than in France although it took its cue from that country. Towards the end of the century we find the cult of the Gothic just as we do in England but it affected literature more than illustration. Goethe had to wait until 1823 for his ideal illustrator and then he was a Frenchman, Delacroix.

Although Germany has little to show during this period comparable with France or even England she produced several noteworthy books on architecture. One of the first was Paul Decker's *Furstlicher Baumeister* (1711-16) an oblong book packed with magnificent engravings which had a great effect on the course of eighteenth-century architecture. Other books by Decker on Chinese and Gothic architecture (both published in England in 1759) had an even wider significance than the purely architectural one. Decker's delineation of the Gothic must have helped to start the ball of the Gothic revival rolling in England [198].

Fischer von Erlach's *Entwurff einer historischen Architectur*, published in Vienna in 1721, is another wonderfully illustrated book, of interest because it is the first pictorial history of world architecture. It is well printed with a text in German and French and with calligraphic half-titles [199]. Although intended as an architectural text-book it ranks as a finely illustrated volume by any standards, its pictures far more than diagrams in their imaginative and decorative treatment. It is a lesson for the modern makers of text-books.

Paul Decker's book was published in Augsburg and it was from Augsburg that the most outstanding and original productions of the first half of the century came. The small page sizes which, as in France, were later to gain favour had not yet curbed the exuberance of the baroque. *Der spanische Successionskrieg* (1714) is a magnificent collection of plates by Decker and others. J. B. Klauber's engravings for *Historiae biblicae veteris et novi Testamenti* (1748) have the old system of numbered references to the details of the picture; the convolutions of its baroque ornament accommodate delectably the subsidiary scenes [201].

Neukirch's translation of Fénélon's *Telemachus*, published in Ansbach in 1727, is illustrated in the French style and is much more ordinary. It is a handsome folio set in blackletter which contains several engravings after Leclerc and some (one of which is reproduced here) by Sperling [200]. G. F. Schmidt decorated *Oeuvres du philosphe de Sans-Souci* by Frederick the Great with excellent vignettes in the French style (1750–2). French influence is also apparent in the work of the brothers Meil of Berlin, and J. H. Meil's work in Gellert's *Fabeln* of 1768 is quite outstanding. Kniphof's *Botanica in Originali* (1747) is probably the first book to employ nature printing, which had earlier been described by Leonardo and which we shall meet again from time to time in herbals. In this process the impression is taken from the actual plant by means of a sort of stereotype; but the result is interesting rather than beautiful.

The most famous illustrator of the century and perhaps the only one who was widely known outside his own country was Daniel Chodowiecki, the Berlin apothecary's son, who began by decorating his father's boxes of pills. He did more than anyone to popularize the French style in Germany and yet his plates are distinctly un-French. They have the bourgeois air which we have already mentioned and succeed only where they show the people and scenes that Chodowiecki was familiar with. Add to this that like all of his work they are wholly etched without the touch of the graver that gave French engravings their characteristic precision.

Chodowiecki's best work appeared in the little almanacs that abounded in Berlin as in Paris and in which much new literature appeared. Hind compares him with Hollar as having an eye for small things and his best work is in small volumes. Among his books are Goethe's *Werther*, Gessner's *Idylls* (1773) and Gellert's *Fables* (1775). His best known book is Lessing's *Minna von Barnhelm* (1770). That he was much in demand is evidenced by the fact that he was commissioned by a Swiss publisher to illustrate a French translation of the English novel *Clarissa* in 1785. He also illustrated *Tristram Shandy* in 1764 [202] and did suites of plates for *Hamlet* and *Macbeth*.

Das römische Carneval by Goethe (1789) is a rare and interesting book with handsome typography in the Didot manner and a collection of amusing hand-coloured plates by J. G. Schutz [204]. Here at last is something quite different from French illustration though perhaps it is none the better for that.

Switzerland had produced no distinctive illustration since the days of Holbein. The baroque book never flourished there and her art seemed to pass straight to the rococo stage. Rousseau's ideas of nature, says Benesch, which were so explosive in France, produced in

LETTRE SUR LE PAYSAGE.

Vous pensez donc, Monsieur, que je pourrais inte-
resser, peut-être même devenir utile, en indiquant la
route que j'ai suivie pour parvenir à pratiquer les arts
du deffein dans un âge peu favorable aux grands succès.
Il seroit à desirer sans doute que les artistes célébres eus-
sent exécuté un semblable projet. Quel avantage ne tire-
rait-on pas de l'histoire des peintres, si elle contenait
avec les événemens de leur vie le récit des progrès de
leurs talens ? nous y verrions les differentes routes qui

X   peuvent

272 D. QUIXOTE DE LA MANCHA,

qual Don Quixote, dixo entre sì: bien parè-
ce que estos no han visto à mi Dulcinèa del
Tobòso, que si la huvièran visto, ellos se fuè-
ran à la mano en las alabànças desta su Quite-
ria. De alli à poco començàron à entràr por
diversas partes de la enramada muchas y dife-
rentes danças, entre las quales venìa una de
espadas hasta de veynte y quatro zagales de
gallardo parecèr, y brio, todos vestidos de
delgàdo, y blanquissimo lienço, con sus pa-
ños de tocàr labrados de varias colores de fina
seda; y al que los guiàva (que era un ligèro
mancebo) preguntò uno de los de las yeguas,
si se avìa herido alguno de los dançantes? Por
zora, bendito sea Dios, respondiò el mancebo, no se ha herido nadie; todos vàmos sa-
nos; y luego començò à enredàrse con los
demas compañeros con tantas bueltas, y con
tanta destreza, que aunque Don Quixote esta-
va hecho à vèr semejàntes danças, ninguna
le avìa parecido tan bien como aquella. Tam-
bien le pareciò bien otra, que entrò de don-
zèllas hermosissimas, tan moças, que al parecèr ninguna baxàva de catorze, ni llegava à
diez y ocho años, vestidas todas de palmilla
verde, los cabellos parte trençàdos, y parte
suèltos, pero todos tan rubios, que con los
del sol podian tenèr competencia, sobre los
quales traian guirnaldas de jazmines, rosas,
amaranto, y madreselva compuèstas. Guià-
valas un venerable viejo, y una anciàna ma-
trona, pero mas ligèros, y suèltos que sus
años prometìan. Hazìales el son una gaita
zamorana, y ellas llevando en los rostros, y
en

Entrada de Donzellas, a las Bodas de Camacho.

Tom. III. pag. 272.

J. Folkema Sculp.

205. Cervantes: *Don Quixote*, 1744.
$6\frac{1}{4}'' \times 3\frac{3}{4}''$. Engravings by Fokke after
Coypel

206. Cervantes: *Don Quixote*, 1780.
$12'' \times 8\frac{1}{2}''$. Ibarra's edition illustrated by
Castillo, Carnicero, Selma and others

207. Holberg's *Peder Paars*, 1772. $9\frac{1}{4}'' \times 6\frac{1}{2}''$. The frontis-piece

208. *Fables*, 1744. $11'' \times 8''$. The engravings by Fossati are printed in different colours

209. Tasso: *La Gerusalemme Liberata*, 1745. $17\frac{3}{4}'' \times 12''$. A tail-piece engraving after Piazzetta

210. *Componimenti poetici per l'ingresso ... di Ludovico Manin*, 1764. $14\frac{1}{2}'' \times 10''$

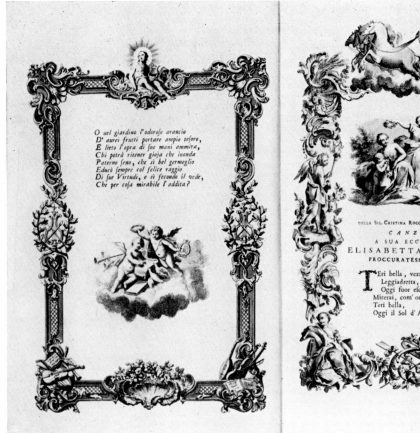

Switzerland the mildly pastoral *Contes Moraux* of Gessner (1773) which the poet himself illustrated with etchings of landscapes [203]. The pleasant designs were handled better by Sparrow in the English edition than by the artist himself. But still they show that landscape *per se* was becoming a subject of illustration in Switzerland as in England.

The Netherlands which under Plantin had led the rest of Europe in the book arts were sadly eclipsed during this period. It is true that many of the best French books appeared under an Amsterdam imprint but this was only a matter of convenience and was no indication of their origin. However two editions of *Don Quixote* appeared in The Hague which, although they were illustrated by Frenchmen it may be legitimate to regard as Dutch. The first with engravings by the Dutchman Fokke after Coypel's paintings was published in 1744 and it contains engravings of great delicacy [205]. The second, dated two years later, is a grander book on the French scale of elaboration with plates after Boucher, Cochin, Coypel and others. One of the earliest French editions of *Robinson Crusoe* was published in Amsterdam in 1720 and was well illustrated by Bernard Picart.

It was not in competition with France that the Dutch printers distinguished themselves during this period, but rather in the production of serious works and in technical innovations. Right at the outset for instance we have Commelin's great herbal (1697–1701) with its engraved, hand-coloured plates; and there is that curious and delightful work, *Metamorphosis Insectorum Surinamensium*, written and illustrated by Maria Merian (1705) with magnificent pictures of tropical insects and flowers. At the end we have Ploos van Amstel's wonderful colour reproductions of paintings made in Haarlem from 1770 onwards by various processes. These were not however collected in book form until Josi did it in his *Imitation de Dessins* (1821–8) which is one of the most important English colour-plate books of the next century.

SPAIN

We had little to record of Spain in the seventeenth century and in the eighteenth there is not much more. The best books were published by Ibarra during the last thirty years and nothing of much note preceded them. An illustrated *Don Quixote* appeared in 1738 with engravings after Vanderbank and Hogarth, but although it was printed in Spanish it was published in England and hardly counts as a Spanish book. Ibarra produced in 1780 the best edition that had yet appeared [206]. This is a large beautifully printed book with plates by various draughtsmen—Castillo, Carnicero, etc.—and various engravers—Selma, Fabregat, etc. Selma did some good vignettes for this work and also for Ibarra's *Sallust*, another fine book which appeared eight years earlier and which Updike has called the most perfect Spanish book. But it has very few illustrations.

Right at the end of this period Goya produced his wonderful series of plates, using etching combined with aquatint. But although his *Caprichos* for instance were bound up together they had no text and cannot therefore qualify as a book. It was ironical that the interest thus aroused in the Spanish print, so lacking up to now, should have come just when wood was about to oust copper.

SCANDINAVIA

The Scandinavian countries with the exception of Denmark do not seem to have produced any interesting work during this period. In all of them illustration followed the French model, generally without the skill of the French designer and engraver. In Denmark however we find some vigorous genre work notably in Holberg's *Peder Paars* (1772) from which we reproduce the frontispiece [207]. This work reminds us more of Hogarth than of the French illustrators and there is also a similar technical crudity about it. An earlier book however, F. L. Norden's *Voyage d'Egypte et de Nubie* (1755) is wholly French in its polish and competence.

ITALY

Italian illustrated books of this period are not very well known and yet from Venice came some of the most beautifully decorated books of the century. They are decorated rather than illustrated, Italy's special discovery being the engraved border made up of vignettes. This development owed nothing to France and in fact it needed a larger page to show it off properly than French books generally employed. There are many Italian books of course which follow the French fashions but Italian painting was still too vigorous not to imprint its own character on illustration. Canaletto, Tiepolo and Guardi were all working in Venice and it is significant that the first two both issued series of etchings though only Tiepolo is known to have illustrated any books.[1] In this climate it would have been surprising if Italy had not produced something noteworthy.

Many of these books were ephemeral productions, made for some special occasion, like the very handsome *Componimenti poetici per l'Ingresso di . . . Ludovico Manin* (1764) with its vignetted border [210], but there were also works of a more lasting nature. Albrizzi's 1745 edition of *Gerusalemme Liberata* exemplifies a decorative treatment of the full-page plate that was typical of Venice. Each plate was surrounded by a floral border, producing an effect of over-elaboration. But the big tail-pieces are delightful with their cut-out edges and their characteristic scrolls at the bottom [209], and so are the head-pieces which are modelled round the engraved words of the argument for each canto. Goldoni's *Comedies* (1761) are illustrated in the French style by Novelli, a prolific designer of the day. And the illustrations for the *Fables* of 1744 which were designed and engraved by the architect Fossati are a curiosity because they are in different colours thus making a virtue of the necessity of separate printing. They are not very striking designs but the effect of the grey, green, sanguine and purple pictures is delightful [208]. Zatta's edition of *Orlando Furioso* (1772) is a fine book, beautifully printed, though it gives the impression here and there of over-ornamentation. We have already noted how Ariosto's earlier illustrators combined several episodes in one picture. The process is here carried a step further by combining them in the border where, as they become separate vignettes, the effect is happier [211]. There is, however, an *embarras de richesse* when the border is put round one of Novelli's large engravings. Each border is repeated from time to time but not too often. It takes up more of the margins than is usual with engraved work and reminds us of the medieval manuscript border, the intention of which was to fill the margins. This conception was later revived by William Morris, but nothing is further from the average eighteenth-century book with its insistence on plenty of white paper.

Wide margins were also a characteristic of Bodoni's work, which appeared towards the end of the century. Bodoni was a typographer of genius, worthy to rank with Baskerville in England and Didot in France, all of whose books have a family likeness. Bodoni's unfor-

---

[1] Piranesi also produced many series of architectural etchings in Rome, for instance his *Roman Antiquities* of 1784–7; but these are hardly books although they were bound up with title-pages and tables of contents.

CANTO I

211. Ariosto: *Orlando Furioso*, 1772. $14\frac{1}{2}'' \times 9\frac{1}{2}''$. The large engravings are by Novelli

212. *Bunrei Gasen,* 1779. 10″ × 6½″

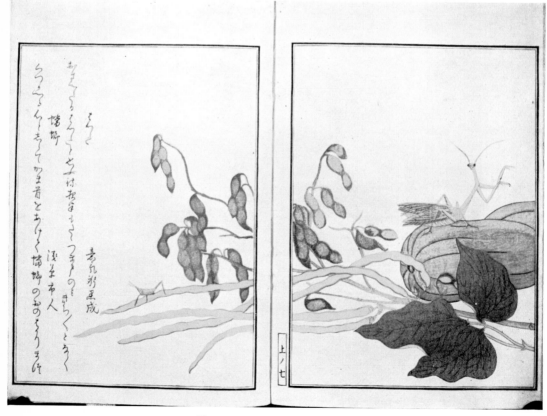

213. *Utamaro:* Insect Book, 1788. 10½″ × 7″

36

214. De Rossi: *Scherzi poetici e pittorici*, 1795. $5\frac{3}{4}'' \times 3\frac{3}{4}''$. A Bodoni book

tunately were sometimes of small literary value and their texts were often inaccurate. He worked for the Dukes of Parma and his attitude to books was essentially aristocratic: 'Je ne veux que du magnifique et je ne travaille pas pour le vulgaire.' None of them had anything exceptional in the way of illustration but they atoned for this by the elegance of their typography. The 1775 edition of *Epithalamia* with engravings by Cagnoni and Volpato is a fine book. De Rossi's *Scherzi poetici e pittorici* of 1795 is unusual in having all its engravings collected at the end. They are interesting designs by Francesco Rosaspina in thin outline, rather reminiscent of the *Poliphilo* cuts [214].

JAPAN

Early in the seventeenth century Japan entered upon a period of peace, and as in the Netherlands, a wealthy middle class appeared with its own bourgeois art. This was known as Ukiyoye, a school of genre painting which found its most characteristic expression in the colour woodcut. And although most of this work took the form of separate prints, designed as wall decorations, yet much also found its way into books. Unlike Europe, there seems to have been no interchange between the two uses; the book illustrations were generally inferior to the prints and made use of poorer paper. But unlike Europe again they often made generous and brilliant use of colour.

Moronobu, the first Ukiyoye artist to use the woodcut extensively, illustrated more than 150 books, and the Yehon or picture book began with him. Most of his work is black and white but sometimes his cuts are hand-coloured with delightful effect and they are often designed for this treatment. The figures in his illustrations are generally large, the backgrounds are rudimentary or non-existent and everything is flat with no tone at all. The text usually occupies the top quarter of the page which has very small margins, and a double rule border surrounds text and picture. Yet working within these limitations and using his white

215. *Onna Shorei Shu*, 1660. 12″ × 10″. Illustrated by Moronobu

space as an asset he produced many wonderful designs. His *Onna Shorei Shu* (1660), a book of etiquette for women, has several pages of beautifully patterned dresses which no colours could make more exquisite [215]. Shunboku was one of the first artists to use colour-printing and his *Mincho Seido Gwayen* (1746) contains many exquisitely printed colour plates of flowers imitated from Chinese work. It was left to Harunobu, however, to exploit the colour-print some twenty years later.

We saw in Chapter 3 how colour-printing flourished in China about a hundred years before. There is little doubt that Japan owed her excellence to her neighbour, and we know that early Japanese prints used flat colours which later, in imitation of China, became gradated. This was achieved partly by brush-work, partly by wiping the block after the colour had been laid on. Japanese work differed however in being generally printed on thicker paper and in using black outlines inside which the colours registered with unerring accuracy. But beyond that is the basic distinction which Binyon makes between the methods of Chinese and Japanese designing. He points out that no Chinese artist of note designed expressly for the wood. But in Japan the best of the designers were 'masters of the first rank. They did not merely reproduce their drawings by means of the colour-print, they conceived their designs in terms of woodcut line and colour block'.

Both Chinese and Japanese used cherry-wood for their blocks, since this is specially suitable for water-colours which they applied by brush. But the Japanese used the colour-print more for book illustration proper although they produced many unsewn albums of prints as well. In order to obtain the maximum size of picture they nearly always spread it across two pages; and their margins were the opposite to what we expect in the West, wider at the top and inside of the page than at the bottom and outside. The paper is printed on one side only but is folded so that no blank pages appear.

Harunobu's work was all done between 1762 and 1770 and it includes several books which are little known in comparison with his prints. Because his genius tended naturally towards smallness and delicacy it found no constraint in the book page. He often used six or more blocks and the result is astonishingly rich without being in the slightest degree laboured. His books are more like albums of pictures and the text is often little more than captions. White space plays a less important part than with Moronobu but backgrounds are still unimportant. *Yehon Serio Bijin Awase* (1770) is a beautiful book, its cuts being printed in a limited range of brown, green, grey and red with the effect of a far richer colour scheme. Like all the great artists of this school Harunobu did not cut his designs himself but left them to be prepared for printing by an intermediary which accounts for his enormous output. All the Ukiyoye artists in fact owed a great deal to their engravers and especially their printers who, as so often in the history of the graphic arts, rose nobly to the unprecedented demands of this new movement. The soft colours and delicate tones which in the West perhaps only modern lithography can produce were obtained with the crudest of tools.

In 1776 appeared the *Mirror of Fair Women of the Yoshiwara* illustrated by Shunsho and Shigemasa, one of the most gorgeous of all the Ukiyoye books with coloured illustrations [216]. Here the colour work is of extraordinary intricacy and gradation of tone is fully exploited. Like so many of these books it contains many double-spread pictures with a break in the middle caused by the gutter. This break however did not seem to disconcert the illustrators nor did they try to disguise it in any way. In the same way they did not hesitate to incorporate captions or text into the framework of their pictures. It is this combination of text and illustration on the same page that distinguishes the *kibyoshi* or yellow-covered novelette from the *yehon* or picture-book. The former which were appearing in enormous numbers at this time were written and designed for the middle and lower classes; the *yehon* for the rich. *Kibyoshi* were the especial preserve of the Ukiyoye artists most of whom started as illustrators of these little books. The *yehon*, which is much older in its origins, was the favourite format of the impressionists.

Two other beautiful coloured books similar to *The Mirror of Fair Women* appeared about this time, both illustrated by Kitao Masanobu, the *Seiro Meikun Jihitsu Shu* (? 1782) and *Yoshiwara shin Bwin Awase* (1784). Both these books, as well as *The Mirror of Fair Women*, deal with the Yoshiwara or courtesans' quarter, a favourite place of Ukiyoye inspiration.

The Mirror of Fair Women was sponsored by Jusaburo, perhaps the greatest of the Ukiyoye publishers and the discoverer and protector of Utamaro. Between 1788 and 1791 Utamaro designed for him besides numerous separate prints an exquisite series of colour-books of which the best known are the *Insect Book* of 1788, the book about shells and seaweed of 1790 and the *Bird Book* of 1791 [213]. These are sometimes called natural history books but their texts are not at all scientific. The *Bird Book* consists of humorous songs; but its pictures which invite comparison with Bewick (he was working exactly at this time) are scientific in their observation of detail. Perhaps they score over Bewick's in the matter of texture since they are aided by colour. The *Insect Book* which is the earliest, makes good use of white space in its backgrounds. In all of them, especially the second, there is an abundance of metallic printing, gold, silver and mica, which adds greatly to their splendour. Besides these three books Utamaro illustrated several erotic works and some volumes of verses by Kyoka poets, in monochrome and in colour; in many of them the landscapes are at least as important as the figures. In the *Kyogetsubo* of 1789 there are several pure landscapes in varying tones of grey. The result is again reminiscent of lithography and it is difficult to realize that the medium is the wood-cut.

216. *The Mirror of Fair Women of the Yoshiwara*, 1776. 11″ × 7″. Illustrated by Shunsho and Shigemasa

Although the Ukiyoye books today enjoy a greater reputation than any others, it was the work of the impressionist schools of Shijo and Maruyama which had the greater contemporary fame. These books, most of them albums (*yehon*) or sketchbooks (*gafu*) were aimed at a more aristocratic market and were generally better printed on paper superior to that used in Ukiyoye books. Their makers reacted against the finished technique of the academic painters in exactly the same way as the French Impressionists about a century later. It has been suggested in fact that the French owed something to these books.

The style itself owed much to Toba Sojo whose eleventh-century rolls we have already noted. One would expect that drawings of such freedom would defy the woodcutters but the skill with which they are translated makes it hard to believe that this is the same medium that Bewick was just then reviving in the West. It is illuminating to compare a cut from *Bunrei Gasen* (1779) with a Bewick engraving [212].

Maruyama Okyo, the most famous artist working in this style, established his school at Kyoto which thenceforward became the centre of the movement just as Yedo was the centre of Ukiyoye. Okyo and his followers were primarily painters and caricaturists who worked for reproduction, and they did not produce many true illustrated books. *Haikai Sansorok-Kasen* (1799) is an anthology by different poets, each of whom is portrayed in a very free cut next to his contribution; and *Shunkyo* (c. 1804), poems illustrated by Bumpo and others, represents a cooperative effort.

Landscape was a favourite subject of the impressionists, but it was Hokusai, a Ukiyoye artist most of whose work falls into the nineteenth century and the next chapter, that really exploited the landscape; and it was Hokusai whose illustrations startled the West in 1862 and caused a revolution in artistic fashion. But he and his successor Hiroshige came at the very end of the Ukiyoye period and their work shows signs of decadence and of contamination by the West.

7

The Nineteenth Century

ENGLAND

Blake's output was divided between the eighteenth and nineteenth centuries but he cannot be fitted into any category. Although he was a technical innovator his books look back to the illuminated manuscript, and the printing of text and illustrations together in relief which he practised was a principle of the block book. As an illustrator he left no disciples. As a craftsman who engraved his own designs he was unique in his time. As a writer and an artist he could hardly have had a smaller public.

He began as an apprentice to an engraver and in his early days he engraved many illustrations after the prolific Stothard. In 1789 appeared his *Songs of Innocence*, the first of his books in which is found that unique combination of a text composed, inscribed and illustrated all by himself. The technique of relief-etching is peculiar too. Blake claimed that it was revealed to him in a vision by his dead brother Robert and 'he immediately followed his advice, by writing his poetry and drawing his marginal subjects of embellishments in outline upon the copper plate with an impervious liquid, and then eating the plain parts or lights away with aqua fortis considerably below them so that the outlines were left as a stereotype. The plates in this state were then printed in any tint that we wished, to enable him or Mrs. Blake to colour the marginal figures up by hand in imitation of drawings.' This book and its successors are sometimes found with their colour printed instead of applied by hand, the method being to paint the pigments on a card which was then pressed on to the page. The result as may be imagined is often crude and the hand-coloured versions are nearly always preferable.

There could be no closer unity than that of text and illustration in these books. There were of course many eighteenth-century books which were engraved throughout, pictures and text together; but in these the engraver always imitated printer's type. Blake's calligraphy embraces the whole page—borders, figures and words without distinction. The verse flows into the borders and the figures encroach on the verse. In this Blake goes back to the very earliest manuscripts of the Middle Ages before there was a division between scribe and illuminator and before the attempt was made to add a third dimension to the page. Consequently his figures are linear and incorporeal. It is useless to criticize Blake's anatomy; his children, his angels, his prophets, God Himself, must conform to the design and any distortion is permissible. This is not the subordination of illustration to text, still less of text to illustration; it is the subordination of both to the page.

Songs of Innocence was followed within six years by a whole series of illuminated books in relief etching, of which only *Ahania* and *The Book of Los* were intaglio etched in the conventional way. But Blake did not altogether forsake the technique to which he had been trained.

THE DANCE

217. Goldsmith: *The Vicar of Wakefield*, 1817. $9\frac{1}{2}'' \times 6''$. A coloured aquatint after Rowlandson

218. Boys: *Picturesque Architecture in Paris, Ghent, Antwerp, Rouen*, 1839. $21'' \times 14\frac{1}{2}''$. A lithograph by Boys

Near Combmartin on the coast of North Devon

COMO.

I LOVE to sail along the LARIAN Lake
Under the shore—though not to visit PLINY,
To catch him musing in his plane-tree walk,
Or angling from his window: * and, in truth,
Could I recall the ages past, and play
The fool with Time, I should perhaps reserve
My leisure for CATULLUS on *his* Lake,

   * Epist. l. 3. ix. 7.

219. Ayton: *A Voyage round Great Britain*,
1814–25. 10″ × 14½″. With hand-coloured
aquatints by Daniell

220. Rogers: *Italy*, 1830. 7½″ × 5″. With steel
engravings after Turner and Stothard

221. Thornton's *Virgil*, 1821. 7" × 4¼". Two wood-engravings by Blake (actual size) from a book which also contains work by Thurston, Cruikshank and others

In 1793 appeared his first original book in line-engraving, a collection of emblems for children called *The Gates of Paradise* in which his characteristic style makes no concession to the young reader. Soon after he executed a large number of water-colour illustrations for Young's *Night Thoughts* some of which were engraved and published in 1797. He did not return to line-engraving for illustration until the end of his life apart from minor works. His middle years were taken up with the production of his two major works in relief etching, *Milton* (1808) and *Jerusalem* (1818). *Jerusalem* is his masterpiece in this medium [222]. Only one coloured copy survives which suggests that Blake himself did not consider colour essential. Also he evidently put in a fair amount of graver work on the plates which has benefited them. Gray calls this Blake's 'grandest effort for imaginative art in England and in every way the biggest of the beautiful books'.

In 1821 Blake made a sudden and magic excursion into wood-engraving which was just then on the way to becoming the most popular mode of illustrating books. He cut seventeen blocks for a school-book, Thornton's *Virgil*, all of them minor masterpieces and quite different from the sharp detailed engravings that Bewick had popularized. They are dark and evocative, showing an unsuspected possibility of mystery in wood which was not exploited until the present century. But their delightful pastoral quality had an immediate and potent influence on Calvert and Palmer, the latter calling them 'visions of little cells, and nooks and corners of Paradise; models of the exquisitest pitch of intense poetry'.

There remain two series of line-engravings which never became books. *The Illustrations of the Book of Job* consists of 22 plates published in 1825; and for Dante's *Inferno* he was only able to complete seven plates before he died. The Job illustrations are distinguished from his other work by the use of wide regular borders, in some of which he engraved lines of text. The Dante plates have no text at all.

Blake has been called the first Englishman to make the print the vehicle of universal themes. This is true but the question is whether the page of a book with all its limitations of size and technique is able to take the enormous force of his imaginative genius. As we turn over the leaves of a book like *Jerusalem* the mind reels before the energy of the posturing figures and in the end they fail to make their impact. It was well that Blake was born to show what could happen to the book in the hands of a genius. But he is right outside the main stream of development and it is difficult to see how even he could have travelled farther along that road. It is significant that he had no followers in book illustration.

Apart from his wood-engravings for Thornton's *Virgil* Blake showed little interest in landscape. Yet the first forty years of the new century were the greatest years in the whole history of English landscape painting and they were also the heyday of the topographical books. These are associated particularly with the publisher Ackermann, but before that the

By Satans Watch-fiends tho they search numbering every grain
Of sand on Earth every night. they never find this Gate.
It is the Gate of Los. Withoutside is the Mill. intricate. dreadful
And filld with cruel tortures: but no mortal man can find the Mill
Of Satan. in his mortal pilgrimage of seventy years.
For Human beauty knows it not. nor can Mercy find it! But
In the Fourth region of Humanity. Urthona namd
Mortality begins to roll the billows of Eternal Death
Before the Gate of Los. Urthona here is named Los.
And here begins the System of Moral Virtue. named Rahab.
Albion fled thro' the Gate of Los. and he stood in the Gate.

Los was the friend of Albion who most lovd him. In Cambridgeshire
His eternal station. he is the twenty-eighth. & is four-fold
Seeing Albion had turnd his back against the Divine Vision
Los said to Albion. Whither fleest thou? Albion replyd

I die! I go to Eternal Death! the shades of death
Hover within me & beneath and spreading themselves outside
Like rocky clouds. build me a gloomy monument of woe
Will none accompany me in my Death? or be a Ransom for me
In that dark Valley? I have girded round my cloke. and on my feet
Bound these black shoes of death & on my hands deaths iron gloves
God hath forsaken me & my friends are become a burden
A weariness to me & the human footstep is a terror to me.

Los answerd. troubled. and his soul was rent in twain.
Must the Wise die for an Atonement? does Mercy endure Atonement
No! It is Moral Severity. & destroys Mercy in its Victim.
So speaking. not yet infected with the Error & Illusion

222. Blake's *Jerusalem*, 1818. A relief etching (actual size)

Rev. William Gilpin had already been at work on his guide-books with their aquatint illustrations, which exploited the picturesque and purported to show all the right views to admire. He was easy game for Combe and Rowlandson with their *Tours of Dr. Syntax* but nevertheless his books are important because they exemplify a new attitude to nature which is also to be found in Bewick's work—an attitude which for want of a better word we call Romantic.

Romantic painting was chiefly concerned with the landscape but in spite of Gilpin's guide-books and Ackermann's great topographical works the landscape has never been a suitable subject for illustration. It made the books in which it found itself—*The History of the Thames* for instance which Farington illustrated in 1794—into hybrids where the text is merely an excuse for the plates and was generally written after them. One of their drawbacks is that landscape plates always have to be inserted sideways which means turning the book to look at them. The alternative is an oblong format which smacks rather of an album than a book. When the plates were hand-coloured, as most of the topographical engravings were, we begin to see the ancestry of the coloured wall-print that Baxter exploited later and made an essential for every Victorian home.

The romantic landscape, however, was not confined to the topographical book. Sometimes it formed the background for botany[1] as in Thornton's *Temple of Flora* (1797–1807) in which it often contrives to steal the footlights from the subject of the picture. The plates here are a mixture of mezzotint and aquatint printed in basic colours and worked over by hand; but the typical landscape illustration of the period is a pure aquatint, hand-coloured in imitation of the water-colour painting from which it was usually reproduced. Weitenkampf points out that it suggested distance by a series of flat planes painted in colours which had little gradation and the effect is rather like old-fashioned stage scenery. But this had the advantage of preventing too great a disparity between the illustration and the two-dimensional type page [223].

It was not by accident that the aquatint became associated with the landscape and the water-colour. Mezzotint, we have already seen, was the process *par excellence* for the reproduction of oil-paintings. But Paul Sandby, the water-colourist, who popularized aquatint in England in about 1775 with his *Views in South Wales* must have realized its suitability not only for reproducing water-colours but also as a basis for hand-colouring in water-colour. Line played an important part in the landscape painting of that date, for painters were still draughtsmen too, and they added colour to their drawings in the form of flat tints. Aquatint was the perfect process to reproduce this sort of picture. Illustration in its turn made its mark on contemporary water-colour painting, for it must not be forgotten that both Turner and Girtin worked at colouring prints in their youth.

Ackermann's Repository of Arts in the Strand was, in effect, a factory for the production of coloured illustrations and prints. Much of the colouring was done by children and a very high degree of skill was attained. The engravers—Stadler, Bluck, Havell, and others—printed two or three neutral tones by selective inking from the one plate before it was hand-coloured. Rowlandson usually etched his design on the plate, leaving the aquatinting to be done by another but he set the style for the colouring himself. Apart from the Syntax series already mentioned he illustrated many books when, in the early years of the century, he

---

[1] Several important botanical works date from this period, the best including some illustrated by the brothers Bauer. Of these the first volume of Lambert's *Genus Pinus* (1803–24) is especially noteworthy. The *Beauties of Flora* (1820) by S. Curtis is less well known than the *Temple of Flora* but it is in many ways superior.

223. J. E. Smith: *A Tour to Hafod*, 1810. $26\frac{1}{4}'' \times 18\frac{1}{4}''$. With hand-coloured aquatints by the author, engraved by Stadler

224. Potter: *The Tale of Benjamin Bunny*, 1904; *The Tale of Timmy Tiptoes*, 1911. With water-colours by the author. *Frederick Warne*

turned his attention away from caricature. But the faces in his illustrations still remain caricatures and he goes a step further in the method of characterization which was initiated by Hogarth and consummated by Cruikshank. *The Microcosm of London* (1808–10), in which he collaborated with Pugin, was his most famous work but his *Vicar of Wakefield* (1817) with its fine crowd scenes is in many ways more endearing [217].

In William Daniell's books we meet the best of the topographical aquatints. His *Voyage Round Great Britain* (1814–25) contains in its eight volumes many superb examples of this delicate art. The aquatinting is so good that it depends very little on colour although this was always skilfully applied [219].

In 1819 Boydell published under the title of *English Scenery* a book of Gainsborough landscapes reproduced by soft ground etchings. Turner, Constable, Cotman and Cox also published books containing reproductions of their work, some by etching, some by mezzotint and some by steel engraving. Amstel and Josi's *Imitations de Dessins* (1821) contained a collection of coloured reproductions of paintings by various hands.[1] The painter was becoming very much aware of the value of the print in bringing his work before a wide public. It was a public too that was better informed than ever before since so many of them were amateur painters themselves; and it was to these that the drawing books such as David Cox's *Treatise on Landscape Painting* (1814) were addressed. Turner's incomplete *Liber Studiorum* (1807–1819) with its mezzotint reproductions was in this class. The 71 plates were etched in outline by Turner and finished in mezzotint by others.

Turner also did a good deal of proper book illustration. He was keenly interested in the reproduction of his work and supervised closely the processes which he did not undertake himself. As Gray says he obviously considered engraving not so much a reproductive as a multiplying process. And when steel-engraving arrived in about 1823 he welcomed it and used it to the full. He used steel for the mezzotints in his *Rivers of England* (1824–30) and for the line-engravings in the *Rivers of France* (1833–5), both superb examples of the topographical book of this period. But it is the small line-engravings and vignettes for such books as Rogers's *Italy*[2] (1830) and his *Poems* (1834) that claim our attention here because in this work the illustration is assimilated so perfectly with the text [220]. The fact that a method was now being used of printing engravings on over-sized paper and then trimming off the plate marks meant that these vignettes belong more to the page and their backgrounds often melt into it imperceptibly. Thus an astonishing amount of tone is achieved by what is really a line technique. The same applies to the vignettes Turner did later for the poems of Byron, Scott, Milton and Campbell. Here the crispness of the steel (which kept its pristine quality much longer than copper) proved that the intaglio could still score over the relief method in this respect despite the astonishing technical skill of Bewick's pupils who just now were extracting all that was possible from the wood-engraving. These books are a world away from the great volumes of topographical plates with a text that no one was expected to read. And it is unlikely that any book illustrated by steel-engravings was issued coloured, though we often find colour has been added later.

The attitude of Turner and many of his contemporaries to what we should call graphic art marks a division between the eighteenth and the nineteenth centuries and presages the advent of the machine age. Later in the century the distrust of the machine reappears with William Morris, and of reproductive engraving with Haden and his Society of Painter-

---

[1] See page 233.
[2] *Italy* also contains figure designs by Stothard, sometimes superimposed on Turner's landscapes.

Etchers, but for the moment we have the rare spectacle of a painter like Turner, then at the height of his fame, producing designs for almanacks and keepsakes. Cotman, though by no means as famous, produced innumerable etchings for the antiquarian books of Dawson Turner, which, as Piper says, have ever since had a strong influence on guide-book illustrators.

Turner's steel-engravings were usually small because steel is an intractable metal to work. The mechanical output of later engravers that was soon to discredit this medium may have been partly the result of this intractability but it cannot be denied that in a small plate steel can give an atmosphere that is quite different from copper. Another new process that was just the opposite in its requirements was at this moment making its appearance. Lithography gives broad effects and it is at its best on a large page. It is as alien from letterpress printing as intaglio engraving but like engraving it can be used for printing the text as well as the illustrations of a book. Unlike engraving it lends itself to freedom of line and it may therefore have contributed to the formlessness of mid-Victorian typography. But autolithography is one of the few processes by which the illustrator's work can be presented direct to the reader without any intermediary save the printing machine, and its peculiar properties therefore presented a welcome alternative to wood and copper-engraving—which interposed a special technique between the artist and the printed result of his work and which were in any case being used generally in a reproductive way at that time.

The story of how Senefelder's discovery was based on the simple fact that oil and water do not mix needs no repetition. It is the only major process to which we can confidently assign a date and an inventor. And its autographic possibilities were first exploited in England. *Specimens of Poly-autography* was a collection of lithographs by various hands published in 1803 by Senefelder's partner, André. It was a portfolio rather than a book but it served to bring the new process to the attention of the painters of the day. Even Blake contributed his only known lithograph.

The first lithograph to be used as a book illustration was probably in J. T. Smith's *Antiquities of Westminster* (1807); and in 1813 appeared *Rustic Figures* by Thomas Barker which was more of an album than a book. Thereafter lithography was taken up very quickly and in the twenties and thirties we find innumerable topographical and drawing books being printed by this method, some of them very charmingly. Gould's famous bird books in which the lithographs are hand-coloured are among the best-known examples. With the advent of the railways many books appeared describing a railway journey and the scenery along the route; for the pictures lithography was a favourite process. Bourne and Britten's *London-Birmingham Railway* (1839) for instance has magnificent hand-coloured lithographs. Because of the ease of execution the process was a great favourite with amateurs especially later in the century when the introduction of transfer paper made it unnecessary to draw directly on the stone. Unfortunately this ease led very early to a facile manner which partly explains the greater popularity of wood-engraving for illustration throughout the century. It was unfortunate too that very few first-rate artists took it up as they did in France where they found in it a method by which their originals could reach a wide public. In England there seems to have been a prejudice against it. 'Let no lithographic work come into the house' Ruskin wrote in 1857 (although he had had his own designs for *The Stones of Venice* lithographed six years before). It was not until the seventies that Thomas Way tried to revive autolithography and persuaded Whistler to turn his hand to it. But book illustration profited only indirectly.

In the early books colour was often applied by hand; it was seldom printed until about 1840. The forerunner of the chromo-lithograph was the lithotint which was popularized by

Hullmandel, though Senefelder himself in printing from two stones had shown the way. One of the stones was simply used for printing a flat tint on which the high lights were scraped out; and Hullmandel in addition used a resin solution which produced an effect akin to the aquatint. One of the best lithotinted books is *Original Views of London as it is* (1842), lithographed by Thomas Shotter Boys and printed by Hullmandel. Here the full beauty of the process is displayed in a great range of tone but the general effect is decidedly monochrome in spite of the striving after the effect of water-colour washes. However in an earlier book, *Picturesque Architecture in Paris, Ghent, Antwerp, Rouen* (1839) Boys and Hullmandel had produced colour plates that were wholly printed [218]. This magnificent collection of pictures (for it has hardly any text) is dedicated to Hullmandel by Boys. 'Every touch', says the preamble, 'is the work of the Artist, and every impression the product of the press.' That the true nature of lithography was still not realized in England as it was in France is shown by the frank avowal that some of the pictures are meant to imitate crayon sketches, some water-colours and some oil-paintings.

Chromo-lithography did not come into its own however until 1851 with Digby Wyatt's *Industrial Arts of the Nineteenth Century*, 'a series of illustrations of the choicest specimens produced by every nation' for the Great Exhibition. Here is a technique quite distinct from the lithotint and much nearer to the trichromatic process, though the colours are separated by eye. As Gray says 'the attempt to imitate water-colours—which still subsists in Boys's work and is the bane of the whole English colour-print in the nineteenth century—is here entirely absent'. The charm of the earlier topographical work has evaporated but in its place is something new and vigorous, though perhaps less sympathetic to us. The title-page which is here reproduced [231] demonstrates the astonishing change that so abruptly led in the Victorian era. Nothing farther from Bulmer's chaste openings can be imagined. Yet if one looks at these great richly coloured pictures of objects from the Great Exhibition of 1851 one forgets the hideousness of much that is displayed in admiration of the craftsmanship that went to reproduce it so splendidly. So much gold had not been seen on the page since the days of the medieval manuscript.

It was Noel Humphreys and Owen Jones who made chromo-lithography an integral part of the book. They were both of them more concerned with the relationship of illustration to text than any of their contemporaries and their work foreshadows that of William Morris, though they had none of Morris's distrust of the machine. Like Morris they looked, especially Humphreys, to medieval illumination for inspiration. It was Humphreys whose *Illuminated Books of the Middle Ages* (1844) contains some of the earliest reproductions of pictures in colour yet attempted. But looking through this book, brilliant as it is, one is struck by the emphasis on ornament. It is a study of illuminated borders and decoration; miniatures are practically ignored and this is significant because Humphreys' own work like Morris's later is so much stronger in ornament than in illustration. And while his illuminated books, such as *The Parables of Our Lord* (1847) and *The Book of Ruth* (1850) show a care for the decoration of the page that had not been seen since Blake it is all second hand decoration, borrowed mostly from Flemish manuscripts. There are broad bands of decoration running down the outer edge of each page and the type is Gothic. The result is of course pastiche, produced by a man who seems to feel that mechanical methods can outdo illumination by hand. It is of course absurd to compare these books with Blake's works of art. They came at the nadir of Victorian art and Humphreys was by no means an outstanding designer of even his day. But they give us a brief glimpse of illustration by lithography before wood-engraving swept all before it.

Owen Jones was more restrained in his use of colour than Humphreys and more sensitive in his handling of type. He is chiefly remembered for his *Victoria Psalter* (1861) where lithography is used for the printing of decoration and initials. But his *Grammar of Ornament* (1856) is also a remarkable book though in it he shows the same preoccupation as Humphreys not only with ornament (which is his subject) but also with technique. And his technique with its rich colour and impeccable register is indeed wonderful.

In none of these books however is lithography used as an autographic process. Redrawing by the lithographer was always interposed between the artist and the printed result. This did not matter much when the purpose of the illustration was merely to reproduce an existing work of art, as it was in most of the books with which Humphreys and Jones were concerned. But in 1846 appeared a landmark in the history of the lithographic book, Edward Lear's *Book of Nonsense*. Here the process was used for text as well as illustration, and the drawings are admirably reproduced although they were conceived as wood-engravings and had in fact already been cut in wood. It is not so strange that later editions were all printed by letterpress as that this first edition was lithographed.

Lithography was much used at this time for botanical works to which it is ideally suited. James Bateman's *Orchidaceae of Mexico and Guatemala* (1837–41) has good lithographs after various artists and also some vignettes by Cruikshank. W. H. Fitch illustrated several similar works in this way, the best of which is H. J. Elwes's *Monograph of the Genus Lilium* (1877–1880) called by Sitwell 'one of the culminating monuments of the Victorian age'. Another botanical book, though it is more of a curiosity, is Thomas Moore's *The Ferns of Great Britain and Ireland* (1855) in which nature printing reappears. The book contains acknowledgements to the experiments in Vienna on the process but the results are not really much better than Kniphof's book of 1747.

The famous German children's book, *Struwwelpeter*, which was published in English in 1848, was the beginning of a spate of cheap chromo-lithographed toy-books which brought the process into disrepute. Kate Greenaway's first efforts in the medium later on did nothing to retrieve its reputation. After 1850 monochrome lithography, like steel and copper-

225. Fouqué: *Peter Schlemihl*, 1824. $7\frac{1}{2}'' \times 4\frac{1}{2}''$. With etchings by Cruikshank

engraving, was used less and less for books. Both processes are however occasionally found together in the keepsakes and almanacs that were produced in such quantities between 1830 and 1850. These of course depended more on their pictures than on their very trivial text which was generally written after and round the plates. The best known was *The Keepsake* which appeared regularly between 1829 and 1857 and was occasionally honoured by a contribution from Turner. Many of Cruikshank's etchings appeared in the *Comic Almanack* which gave him more scope than his books for fantasy and horseplay. But most of these ephemera favoured steel-engraving, which continued to be used here long after it had been replaced by wood in ordinary books. The other intaglio techniques like mezzotint and etching were also gradually disappearing, though etching had a brief revival later in the century. Mezzotint in the hands of John Martin who designed direct on the steel became an autographic process and his startling illustrations for *Paradise Lost* (1824) and for the *Bible* (1831–5) anticipate surrealism in their lurid melodrama and vast perspectives. Etching during this period is indissolubly linked with the name of George Cruikshank who was at work for more than half a century. Yet he started with aquatint and most of his later work was cut in wood. But it is his etchings for Dickens, for *Peter Schlemihl*, and for Grimm's Tales (*German Popular Stories*) in 1824 that represent his best work [225]. There is something of the liveliness and movement that we have last seen in Rowlandson and which needed a spontaneous process like etching to transfer them to paper. The grotesque element that is never far absent from his work is admirably suited to all three authors and there is a Gothic flavour about the Grimm illustrations that is delightfully in keeping with their origin. Dickens was never as well served by his regular illustrators like Phiz (Hablot K. Browne) who perhaps were readier than Cruikshank to take instructions from their author.

Browne was one of a group who illustrated sporting books at this time mainly by etching. He himself undertook some of the Jorrocks series by Surtees, and Alken and Leech did the same though separate prints represent the greater part of their output. Leech's illustrations for *Mr. Sponge's Sporting Tour* (1853) and *Handley Cross* (1854), both by Surtees, are perhaps the best in this genre; and it is interesting to note that Surtees was not popular until Leech illustrated his books. Etching survived well into the sixties for this type of work and for caricature. Its more serious use was kept alive by bodies of amateurs like the Etching Club which produced *The Deserted Village* in 1841, Gray's *Elegy* in 1847 and *L'Allegro* in 1849; or the Junior Etching Club whose *Passages from Modern English Poets* (1862) contained two etchings by Whistler. Most of them are very dull books as one would perhaps expect of amateur co-operative efforts, though they contain occasional good plates. Their example helped to inspire the 'painter-etcher' movement which, under Whistler, came some twenty years later. And it was Whistler who divorced etching from the book and at the same time raised its financial status so that it became associated almost exclusively with the single print.[1] But almost at the end of the century appeared two books with etchings which seem like ghosts from the past. They are Virgil's *Eclogues* (1883) and Milton's *Minor Poems* (1888), both illustrated by Samuel Palmer, the friend of Blake. Palmer lived until 1881 and both books were produced posthumously by his son who supplemented Palmer's own etchings with others made after his drawings. In many of them, except for those in which the photomechanical process intervenes too obviously, there is still a touch of the old enchantment [233].

[1] There were however a few books with etched illustrations by Legros and Strang but they have no great merit.

Cruikshank and Dickens were both thorough townsmen and children of the Industrial Revolution. Cruikshank's art like that of John Leech, 'Dicky' Doyle and Keene was the art of social satire, though it was more bitter, less kindly than theirs. It resembled rather that of Daumier and Gavarni in France yet it was less witty. All of them did much more work for the new magazines than for books, and from now on books become more and more dependent on the magazine illustrators. The decade between 1832 and 1842 saw the beginning of Knight's *Penny Magazine*, *Punch*, and the *Illustrated London News* which catered for the tastes of the new middle class. The type of illustration required and the speed at which it had to be produced led to a general lowering of quality but an even more important feature was the reinstatement of wood-engraving, now to remain the most used process of reproduction almost until the end of the century. Its great advantage was that unlike engraving and lithography it enabled text and illustration to be printed together, which was even more important for a magazine than for a book.

But it would be wrong to give the impression that wood-engraving had ever been eclipsed by these other processes. Since the days of Thomas Bewick it had been developing steadily on the lines laid down by that master. The direction of that development is clearly indicated by a revealing remark about William Harvey, one of Bewick's most promising pupils. Of him it was said that 'he declined engraving, having determined to step into the upper walks of art'. Thus Bewick's technique, without the freshness of his imaginative handling, was soon pressed into the service of reproduction (under the title of facsimile engraving) and became lifeless. It was not so regarded however by contemporaries, even by so gifted a connoisseur as Ackermann. In his preface to Somerville's *Hobbinol* (1831) he compares the engravings by Nesbit and Thurston with those of Bewick in *The Chase*. 'Mr. Bewick in his manner of engraving the blocks studiously endeavoured to introduce that determined breadth of light and shade which wood so eminently possesses over copper-plate engraving. That ingenious man completely effected what he undertook to produce; and his merit is fully

30   CANTO I HOBBINOL v. 321—324

Those to relieve their faint expiring friend,
With gratulations these: hands, tongues and caps
Outrageous joy proclaim, shrill fiddles squeak,
Hoarse bag-pipes roar, and Ganderetta smiles.

226. Somerville: *Hobbinol*, 1831. $11\frac{3}{4}'' \times 9''$. Wood-engravings by Nesbit and Thurston

acknowledged: but at the same time, it is presumed, that he never could have equalled by his mode of engraving what Nesbit and Thurston have done in this volume' [226].

Nevertheless Harvey and his associates produced a fine book in Northcote's *Fables* (1828) even if the result is something quite unlike Bewick. Here the designs generally are by Northcote, but Harvey prepared them for the various engravers whose names are indexed at the end of the book—an interesting example of a practice that was to become common during the nineteenth century of interposing a 'translator' between designer and engraver. The work throughout is extremely fine and delicate, more like copper than wood, and in the initials which were wholly designed by Harvey we can discern the beginning of Victorian baroque which was such a world away from Bewick's romanticism.

But if wood-engraving was to compete with lithography it must find a method of producing colour-prints. Savage's *Hints on Decorative Printing* (1822–3) which has some elaborate examples of these demonstrated the importance of the author's discovery of how to make printing inks without oil; and George Baxter exploited Savage's methods commercially. Baxter's prints however were based on an aquatint or mezzotint foundation, over which he printed colours from as many as ten or twenty wood blocks. His original aim was to reproduce oil-paintings and to bring 'taste of a refined and intellectual nature to the working people'. Book illustration therefore took a second place to the production of separate prints and was soon abandoned altogether.[1] Baxter's relevance to our subject is therefore chiefly technical but his process was used under licence for books in the fifties by such cheap publishers as Kronheim. Baxter also undoubtedly had an influence on the work of Edmund Evans who later became a famous printer of children's coloured books.

Another printer who had a great technical influence at this time was Whittingham who with his publisher Pickering started the revival of 'period printing'. This had nothing in common with the medievalism of Noel Humphreys for it was merely a reaction against the neo-classicism of Bodoni. But Whittingham was an innovator too because he was interested in the technique of printing from wood-engravings; and he is said to have been the first to develop overlay, a method of varying the weight of impression obtained from the block by varying the thickness of the packing behind the sheet to be printed. In 1840 he printed a book on Elizabethan architecture which was one of the earliest to be illustrated by colour wood-engravings but it was his Home Treasury books for children that really exploited this process in books for the first time. This was a series of fairy-tales printed in gay colours,[2] written and designed, under the pseudonym of Felix Summerly, by Henry Cole, who was later to be concerned with the organization of the Great Exhibition and the foundation of the Victoria and Albert Museum. Cole took great pride in the appearance of these little books and had them illustrated by the best academic artists of the day—Mulready, Cope, Webster and others—who were however referred to in the books by their initials rather than their full names. If the result is disappointing to us the fault is that of the period which was not productive of great illustrators. But another ten years was to usher in the sixties when the deficiency was amply redressed. That famous decade however was a period of monochrome illustration and it was not until it was over that colour wood-engravings came into their own in the children's books of Caldecott, Crane and Kate Greenaway.

One neglected illustrator of children's books however must be mentioned here because he anticipated their use of colour and often handled it in a more original way than they did.

---

[1] But not until he had produced some interesting wood-engravings to illustrate missionary books. We reproduce one from W. Ellis's *The Missionary* (1833) which shows an astonishing control of tone [232].

[2] They were sold plain as well as coloured.

227. Lear: *More Nonsense, Pictures, Rhymes, Botany, etc.*, 1872. 7¾″ × 6½″.
Wood-engravings after Lear

Charles Bennett's *The Fables of Æsop Translated in Human Nature*, which appeared in 1857, is a good book which shows Grandville's influence in the way the animals are made to behave like humans. Bennett illustrated many other children's books. In his *Quarles Emblems* of 1861 it is fascinating to see how a Victorian treated themes which we always associate with the seventeenth century.

Edward Lear's work was all black-and-white from the *Book of Nonsense* which as already mentioned was printed by lithography in 1846 to *Laughable Lyrics* in 1877. His work must have been revolutionary when it first appeared, for nothing like it had ever been seen before, and it was just as revolutionary at the end although it had not developed at all. It provides an almost unique example of the perfectly matched text and picture, by no means the inevitable result of an author illustrating his own writings. But then Lear's verse was as new as his drawings and the one is unthinkable without the other. And if his style of drawing had little influence on contemporary illustration, his attitude to children had an effect which can hardly be exaggerated. Though his fantasy was inimitable it was due to him that entertainment bulked larger than instruction in the late Victorian children's book [227].

His drawings, however artless at first sight, betray a practised hand on closer acquaintance and remind us that Lear was a professional illustrator, and produced over a period of twenty-nine years a steady flow of travel books, besides illustrating many ornithological works such as Gould's. The books like *Journal of a Landscape Painter in Southern Calabria* (1852) which he illustrated in the lithotint style are far more successful than the later Journals like the Corsican one (1870) which have wood-engravings, most of them cut by French craftsmen.

The reproductive wood-engravers of the sixties however were most of them English or Scottish: E. J. Sullivan, writing at the end of the century says 'The art of the sixties has been the most British—even the most English—expression yet found since Hogarth'. It is hard to exaggerate the influence of the Dalziels during this period and nearly every illustrated book of any merit seems to bear their imprint; and there were plenty of meritorious books between 1855 and 1875 which are the limits usually imposed on the period. The

Dalziels not only engraved, they printed and they published as well; also they acted as art-editors for other publishers and commissioned illustrations for their books and magazines. We almost seem to be back in the days of the great printer-publishers of the sixteenth century but with one difference—the Dalziels and their contemporaries had no feeling for the printed page.

It is at first difficult to understand how such a high level of craftsmanship could go with such a low level of typography. But it must always be remembered that many of the great illustrated books of the sixties were a by-product of the magazines, and the engravings were made to stand on their own. If they are accompanied by any text it was often written afterwards. That is why so many of them are squared up and so few are vignettes; and why it is possible to say that they generally appear to advantage away from the books they were designed to illustrate and in the collections that were sometimes made of them afterwards.

Forrest Reid in his exhaustive *Illustrators of the Sixties* calls this sudden flowering of graphic art 'a movement'. But it is hard to see where it led. True there is a lowest common denominator of style (partly imposed by the engravers) which gives a superficial uniformity; but on closer examination a gulf appears between the Pre-Raphaelites like Millais, Rossetti and Hughes and the traditionalists like Gilbert and Birket Foster. Gray however sees it as a movement (which failed) to bring art to the masses. The pictures in *Once a Week*, *Good Words* and the other illustrated magazines were folk-art and they remained so when they appeared also in books. The failure in his view occurred when the Pre-Raphaelites, bored by the technical difficulties or tempted by the greater freedom of paint, ceased to illustrate.

The truth perhaps is that the failure began when illustrators began to lose sight of the unity of the page. Bewick's vignettes which contributed so wonderfully to that unity were forgotten but his brilliant technique, first exploited by his pupils, was imitated for the purpose of reproducing drawings that were not only unworthy of it but were also basically unsuitable for cutting in wood. Sir John Gilbert was one of the illustrators most responsible. He was an historical painter and he evidently saw no real difference between painting in oils and designing for wood. He certainly never tried to make things easier for his engravers. He is remembered chiefly for his Shakespeare (1856–8) but he did besides innumerable drawings on wood for the *Illustrated London News* and *Punch*. Similarly the illustrations of his contemporary, Birket Foster, charming as they often are, do not differ basically from his landscape paintings.

There is a sharp distinction between these men and the illustrators of the sixties, not only in style but also in technique. There were many professional painters also among the latter but their illustrations are quite different from their paintings. Their custom of drawing their designs direct on to the wood was one of the chief causes. This had occasionally been done before but with the coming of the illustrated newspaper and magazine it became a common time-saving practice. The result was not so much interpretative as facsimile engraving in the style of Menzel whose work seems to have made a great impression on the Dalziels. When the engraver had an actual drawing on the block to cut (even though Rossetti for instance used wash in his drawing) he had to follow it more accurately than when he was given a painting to translate.

The first important book of the sixties appeared actually in 1855. It was Allingham's small book of verse *The Music Master*, and it contained eight engravings by Arthur Hughes, one by Rossetti and one by Millais, all engraved by the Dalziels. Hughes, whose designs are less impressive than those by the other two, nevertheless shows more care for the look of the

page, and several of his engravings are vignetted. Allingham who speaks in the preface of
'those excellent painters who on my behalf have submitted their genius to the risks of wood
engraving' thus stands revealed as one of the architects of the sixties for it is unlikely that
Routledge, Moxon and the other publishers of the time would ever have dreamed of com-

THE LADY OF SHALOTT.

Died the sound of royal cheer;
And they cross'd themselves for fear,
          All the knights at Camelot:
But Lancelot mused a little space;
He said, "She has a lovely face;
God in his mercy lend her grace,
          The Lady of Shalott."

228. Moxon's *Tennyson*, 1857.
$8\frac{1}{2}'' \times 6''$. A wood-engraving after
Rossetti for *The Lady of Shalott*

missioning illustrations from the Pre-Raphaelites otherwise, or the Pre-Raphaelites of
offering them.

As it was these publishers showed little imagination in their use of illustration. The next
important book, Moxon's Tennyson of 1857, shows an extraordinary mixture of new and
old. Rossetti, Millais and Hunt are represented there but also Mulready, Maclise and Creswick. Sometimes a poem has a head-piece by one and a tail-piece by the other. It is significant that, generally speaking, the work of the old school sits better on the page; this is particularly true of Creswick whose rural vignettes in the Bewick manner are pleasant enough.
In fact the whole volume, although it is often condemned as an inept piece of book-making,
is in its unpretentious way at least as good typographically as anything else of the period and
much better than most—better by far than Millais's famous *Parables*.[1]

---

[1] Moxon's Tennyson was reissued in 1901 with
an introduction by Holman Hunt and a preface
by Joseph Pennell. It contained only the Pre-
Raphaelite illustrations and some of them were
faced by photographs of the original drawings.

Apart from the technical interest of this comparison the new edition is important because it shows
that the illustration of the sixties had already become a legend by the end of the century.

229. *Parables of Our Lord*, 1863. 9¾″ × 7¾″. A wood-engraving after Millais
for the Parable of the Lost Coin

Of course it is Rossetti's designs that make it memorable [228]. There are only four of them and they gave a great deal of trouble to the Dalziels as well as causing some ill-feeling between them and the artist. But they show a wholly new conception of illustration which emerges too from a remark of Rossetti's in a letter to Allingham: 'I . . . fancy I shall try the *Vision of Sin* and *Palace of Art*, etc.—those where one can allegorize on one's own hook on the subject of the poem, without killing for oneself and everyone a distinct idea of the poet's. This, I fancy, is *always* the upshot of illustrated editions . . . unless where the poetry is so absolutely narrative as in the old ballads for instance.' Blake is perhaps the only artist till now in whom we have met this idea of a personal interpretation and his designs are after all an integral and inseparable part of his poetry since he was his own illustrator. But Rossetti was illustrating another man's poetry (it is interesting that in the quotation above he is thinking only of poetry) and the result in this case seems to be something far from Tennyson's intention.

Millais and Holman Hunt followed their texts more closely. Millais although a successful Victorian painter (perhaps because of that) was also a born illustrator and the most prominent figure of the sixties. He was much more at home with his medium than Rossetti and was not above working for the magazines or illustrating Trollope's novels when they appeared in monthly parts. But his best book was *The Parables of Our Lord* (1863) where his magnificent engravings sparkle against a background of pretentious typography and an unfortunate framework of red rules [229]. The illustrations for Trollope's *Orley Farm*, *Framley Parsonage* and other novels are good too and pleased the author immensely. 'As a good artist,' says Trollope in his Autobiography, 'it was open to him simply to make a pretty picture or to study the work of the authors from whose writing he was bound to take his subject. I have too often found that the former alternative has been thought to be the better, as it certainly is the easier method. An artist will frequently dislike to subordinate his ideas to those of an author and will sometimes be too idle to find out what those ideas are. But this artist was neither proud nor idle. In every figure he drew it was his object to promote the views of the writer whose work he had undertaken to illustrate, and he never spared himself any pains in studying that work, so as to enable himself to do so.' High praise indeed from an author!

Arthur Hughes lived on well into the present century and much of his best work was done after the sixties. Forrest Reid compares his vision of childhood with Blake's in the *Songs of Innocence* and it is his work for children's books by which he is chiefly remembered. But the difference between his vision and Blake's is the difference between two centuries. And how narrowly Hughes avoids sentimentality in his treatment of children. He illustrated *Tom Brown's Schooldays* in 1869 but more typical are the engravings for George MacDonald's stories which first appeared as serials in the sixties—*At the Back of the North Wind* (1871)

Fly away, fly away over the sea,
　Sun-loving swallow, for summer is done:
Come again, come again, come back to me,
　Bringing the summer and bringing the sun

230. Christina Rossetti: *Sing-Song*, 1872. $7\frac{1}{4}'' \times 5\frac{1}{4}''$. A wood-engraving after Arthur Hughes

81　　11

231. Wyatt's *Industrial Arts of the Nineteenth Century*, 1851. 19½″ × 12½″

232. Ellis: *The Missionary*, 1833. 6″ × 3¾″. With wood-engravings by Baxter

Engraved on Wood by G. Baxter.

THE MOSQUE OF AURUNGZEBE.

233. Virgil's *Eclogues*, 1883. $10\frac{1}{2}'' \times 14\frac{1}{2}''$. An etching by Samuel Palmer

234. Allingham: *In Fairyland*, 1870. $10\frac{1}{2}'' \times 15''$. Coloured illustrations by Doyle

and others. He liked working in small spaces and sometimes his figures seem too large for the picture, giving a slightly uncomfortable cramped feeling. But the technical short-comings are more than compensated by the remarkable sympathy between author and illus-trator. Christina Rossetti's book of nursery rhymes *Sing-Song* (1872) was another delightful book [230], and as late as 1904 he illustrated an anthology called *Babies' Classics* with numer-ous head-pieces, tail-pieces and decorated initials.

With Houghton, Pinwell and Fred Walker, all of whom died prematurely in 1875, we leave the Pre-Raphaelite group for men who although they all painted in oil and water-colour were really professional illustrators. Arthur Boyd Houghton was perhaps better equipped technically than any we have yet mentioned and his engravings for Dalziel's *Illustrated Arabian Nights* (1863) compare favourably with those of Millais, Tenniel and Pinwell which are also included [235]. It will be seen that the fashion of combining several illustrators in one book which was set at the beginning of the period by *The Music Master* and Moxton's Tennyson persisted in spite of its drawbacks. The reason in the case of such books as the *Arabian Nights*, which appeared in parts, was presumably the impossibility of one man's doing all the necessary work in the given time. Unfortunately the *Arabian Nights* is marred by poor paper and printing (not to mention a poor translation) as well as unnecessary bor-ders round the blocks. But it is still a better book than Houghton's *Don Quixote* of 1866 although the latter did not suffer from the same handicaps.

Another volume to which Houghton, Walker and Pinwell all contributed but which was more carefully presented was *A Round of Days* (1866), a verse anthology. Here a yellowish tint was printed under the engravings (a variation that was very seldom practised at this time) and paper and presswork were good. In the illustrations we even escape here and there from the everlasting rectangle. Pinwell and Walker's engravings here are mostly of country scenes and their work is classified by Reid as 'idyllic'. The epithet applies less to Walker than to Pinwell 'who was endowed with one of the most delicate and poetic talents of his generation'. Unfortunately his technique was not equal to it. His best work is Dalziel's *Illustrated Goldsmith* (1865) in which *The Vicar of Wakefield*, which always seems to lend itself so remarkably to illustration, comes off best. Pinwell also contributed to Jean Ingelow's *Poems* of 1865 with Houghton, North and others and here his work is more mannered. Fred Walker is remembered chiefly as a protégé of Thackeray. He was engaged to translate Thackeray's own drawings for *Philip* into designs for engraving and finished by making his own designs for this book and also for *Denis Duval* when they appeared in serial form. He also contributed with Pinwell, who surpassed himself, and North to *Wayside Posies* (1867), an anthology similar to *A Round of Days* [236].

So many magnificent engravings were made for the ephemeral magazines at this time that it would have been strange if the Dalziels had not sometimes collected them in book form. They were usually so tenuously attached to the accompanying verses that no great violence was done. And we are given the opportunity of seeing these designs properly printed on good paper.[1] Thornbury's *Legendary Ballads* (1876) also gives an opportunity of mentioning Frederick Sandys, who is here represented by nine engravings, nearly half his total output. Sandys never did any book illustration proper and the fact that these engravings are married, often unhappily, to Thornbury's doggerel hardly puts them into that category. But he is important because he was probably the only artist of this period who gave the engraver a perfectly translatable drawing—he drew straight on the wood with a brush and Indian ink—

---

[1] *Dalziel's Bible Gallery* of 1881 was a luxurious portfolio of hitherto unpublished engravings, many of which were executed in the sixties. But it has no text.

235. Dalziel's *Illustrated Arabian Nights*, 1863. $10\frac{1}{2}'' \times 7''$. A wood-engraving after Houghton

236. Buchanan: *Wayside Posies*, 1867. $9\frac{1}{2}'' \times 7\frac{1}{2}''$. A wood-engraving after Pinwell
Nicholson reproduced by lithography

and he also seems to be the only one who acknowledged a debt to the first great wood-engraver Dürer. A sense of continuity with the past (as distinct from pastiche) is a rarity in Victorian illustration and Sandys's signature, which was modelled on Dürer's monogram, is as graceful a compliment as his superb technique.

Another artist who was represented in *Legendary Ballads* and yet can hardly be counted as an illustrator was Whistler. The two etchings that he contributed to a book in 1862 have already been noted[1] and in the same year he also designed four wood-engravings for magazines. 'The Morning Before the Massacre of St. Bartholomew' which we reproduce here besides being a work of art shows how skilfully the engraver translated his impressionistic etched style so different from anything else that was being done in wood at that time [237].

Keene was another superb draughtsman who also etched and whose name is usually connected with *Punch* and other magazines. Yet he produced much illustration, some of it for novels in serial form like Meredith's *Evan Harrington* (1860) and some for books like *Mrs. Caudle's Curtain Lectures* (1866) which is printed on pale green paper [238]. Here we find initials embedded in small vignettes (quite distinct from decorated initials) a fashion that seems to have spread from France.

Tenniel is treated by Forrest Reid as a precursor of the sixties, yet the two books for which he is most famous, *Alice in Wonderland* (1865) and *Through the Looking Glass* (1871) both fall within this period. He illustrated many books besides, the best being *The Gordian Knot* by Brooks (1860, steel etchings) and Thomas Moore's *Lalla Rookh* (1861). The etchings in the first are hardly any different from his wood-engravings in technique. And the second book showed what depths of sentimentality he could descend to when his text gave him no scope for humour. In the *Ingoldsby Legends* of 1864 he collaborated with Cruikshank and Leech to produce a fine book. The three illustrators combine well and the result is a volume that might have appeared thirty years earlier. But Reid says that apart from this last and the two Alice books he 'never got a text that suited him'. There is something Teutonic about his

---

[1] He also illustrated a *Catalogue of Blue and White Nankin Porcelain* (1878).

237. Thornbury: *Historical and Legendary Ballads*, 1876. $9\frac{1}{2}'' \times 7\frac{1}{4}''$. This wood-engraving by Whistler first appeared in the magazine *Once a Week* under the title *The Morning before the Massacre of St. Bartholomew*. It here appears (without explanation) to illustrate a poem by Thornbury called *Lady Mabel's Lovers*.

style and he was happiest in farce, as no one can doubt who examines his Punch drawings. It was this that fitted him so admirably as an illustrator for Carroll; and so spontaneous does his work appear that it is difficult to believe how detailed were Carroll's instructions and criticisms—criticisms that Tenniel sometimes countered with suggestions of his own concerning the text.

The illustrations by F. J. Shields for Defoe's *History of the Plague of London* (1863) display quite a different aspect of the work of this period but one that was almost as much in evidence. No one who looks through the magazines of the sixties can fail to be struck by the

THE TWENTY-SECOND LECTURE. 111

enjoy a walk ; and, as I say, do a little bit of shopping. Oh yes, Mr. Caudle, I do think of the people that are kept in the shops just

as much as you ; but that's nothing at all to do with it. I know what you'd have. You'd have all those young men let away early from the counter to improve what you please to call their minds. Pretty notions you pick up among a set of free-thinkers, and I don't know what ! When I was a girl, people never talked of minds—

238. Jerrold: *Mrs Caudle's Curtain Lectures,* 1866. 8″ × 6¼″. Illustrated by Keene

number of deathbed scenes, nearly always of young girls. But there is a grimmer, more realistic counterpart to this sentimental morbidity which is to be seen in Sandys's famous *Amor Mundi* and many other engravings, more akin to the *Dance of Death* in the incunabula. Shields's designs are almost worthy to be compared with Daumier's in the same medium and on the same subject for *Némésis Médicale* in 1840. In our assessment of Victorian art we are apt to overlook this curious streak.

With William Small we reach the decadence of the sixties. He and others like him began to use wash on the block, leaving the wretched engraver to make an attempt at tone as best he could. The example had been set by Doré who was just then enjoying immense popularity in France and who was to come to England very soon.[1] Rossetti of course had done the same thing earlier but with Small we find a new attitude as well. Reid says 'the old ideal has disappeared: art is turning to journalism, beauty to prettiness, sentiment to sentimentality, the work is planned from the beginning to appeal to a larger and less cultured public'. For it must be remembered that nearly all the great books of the sixties were expensive, many of them in the *édition-de-luxe* class and few, with the exception of the magazine serials, could be called popular. Nevertheless popular illustrated books were appearing all this time and some of them were illustrated by the new class of commercial designer which was now growing up. Most of those whose work has been described were painters first and illustrators afterwards, but a man like John Leighton designed bank-notes, playing-cards, book-bindings

---

[1] His *London* was published in 1872.

and magazine covers as well as engravings. In 1855 he printed George Barnard's *Theory and Practice of Landscape Painting*, a triumph of colour-work which could hardly be bettered today. His *Lyra Germanica* of 1861 seems to have been not only illustrated but designed throughout by him; and the result is as consistent a piece of Victorian ecclesiastical-Gothic as can be seen anywhere. Some of the initials are as intricate and as hideous as those in the *Book of Kells*; the Oxford borders add the final touch of over-elaboration. Nevertheless Leighton shows a real understanding of wood and Gray goes so far as to call him the only artist between Bewick and Blair Hughes-Stanton who really explored its technical possibilities. It is a pity that he had nothing better to say with his technique.

Colour wood-engraving did not really come into its own until after the sixties were over. Until then, as we have seen, chromo-lithography was the most favoured process and Kate Greenaway's earliest illustrations were lithographed. With the triumph of wood for monochrome work however its use for colour could not long be delayed and the two men most responsible, Benjamin Fawcett and Edmund Evans were both of them printers. It is a symptom of the growing complexity of printing that during the nineteenth century innovations of this sort were generally to come from printers rather than artists, and it is hard to exaggerate the influence of Edmund Evans for instance on children's illustration at the end of our period.

Benjamin Fawcett was a little known printer who worked at Driffield in Yorkshire and specialized in books on natural history. A. F. Lydon is the illustrator whose name is most closely associated with him but pleasant as Lydon's designs usually are no one can doubt that most of the credit for these books should go to the printer for his perceptive use of colour. *Picturesque Views of Seats of Noblemen and Gentlemen* (1866–80) contains many delightful pictures printed in numerous colours perfectly registered and touched up afterwards by hand. Contemporary chromo-lithography can show nothing like them and Fawcett was able too to avoid the unpleasant gloss that is caused in so much Victorian work by overprinting colours.

Edmund Evans was a more influential figure though by no means a better craftsman. He had been apprenticed to Landells, one of Bewick's pupils, and he began with colourprinting in the Baxter tradition. His 1860 edition of Goldsmith's *Poems* with coloured woodengravings by Birket Foster is a superb example of colour-printing even though the pictures are paintings rather than illustrations. But his first Walter Crane toy-book *Sing a Song of Sixpence* (1866) marks a new departure with its use of flat colours. Crane's decorative technique was well suited to flat colours and like Leighton he used to design the whole of his book, outside and inside. His concern for the double-page spread anticipated Morris and was unique at that date. The result is something completely different from any predecessor and at its best quite charming. *The Yellow Dwarf* and *The Three Bears* for instance have all the exuberant delight in colour that we associate with the Victorians together with a strong feeling for the large page. *The Baby's Opera* and *The Baby's Bouquet* show great ingenuity in the assimilation of music, borders and pictures, always a difficult combination. Crane was not so happy with black-and-white work. His illustrations for Mrs. Molesworth's stories are ordinary and so is his Grimm of 1882.[1] But he must be given the credit for the rediscovery of the border—not the ubiquitous Oxford border that the Victorian designer so readily clapped round an engraving irrespective of its suitability, but a border which was designed *for* the engraving. Crane was fond of dividing his borders up into compartments, each of which contained something for the eye, lettering or perhaps a symbol. He often

---

[1] His Kelmscott book, *The Story of the Glittering Plain* (1894), will be discussed later.

239. *The Sing a Song of Sixpence Toybook*, 1866. $9\frac{1}{2}'' \times 7''$. A toy-book illustrated with coloured wood-engravings by Crane

incorporated a legend for instance at the foot of the picture using archaic lettering. But he is at his best with colour on a large page and it is there that we can discern the effect on his work of the Japanese print that was beginning to be popular at this time [239].

Edmund Evans is always recognized as the link between the three great children's illustrators of this period because he was able to start Crane and Caldecott and Kate Greenaway on their careers. But he printed toy-books by the old school as well and one of these, Doyle's *In Fairyland* (with a poem by William Allingham, 1870) contains illustrations more exquisite in colour and design than anything the others could do [234]. Doyle of course had made his name in black-and-white work, but Crane, Caldecott and Kate Greenaway all stand or fall by their coloured illustration. They designed plenty of monochrome engravings (most of them not very good), but their work suffers from the lack of discipline that Doyle's long apprenticeship to the magazines brought.

Randolph Caldecott whom Evans chose to succeed Walter Crane in 1878, is the most virile of the three as his work for the *Graphic* testifies. But unfortunately he found it necessary to cast all his pictures for children in an archaic setting. Kate Greenaway followed the same convention, if it was a convention, but whereas her children seem to belong to no period at all, Caldecott's may be vaguely assigned to the late eighteenth century. His colour too is reminiscent of the aquatint washes that one associated with Rowlandson, more subdued than Crane's and reacting perhaps against the garishness of the mid-Victorian chromolithograph. *John Gilpin*, *The House that Jack Built* and *The Farmer's Boy* are among his most successful toy-books.

Kate Greenaway was even more of a protégée of Edmund Evans than the other two. Her earliest work had been reproduced by lithography but when Evans took her in hand in 1877 he soon had her designing in a way to suit his methods (which involved the photographing of the design on to the wood). The first book he printed for her, *Under the Window* (1878), was no different from the last, for no development is discernible in her work. And indeed all her books were so enormously successful that there was little incentive to change. She must have been one of the very few illustrators to have made a fortune purely from illustration.

It is difficult for us to understand the fascination of these books in their day and one suspects that it was exercised over the parents rather than the children. Kate Greenaway, like Caldecott, used subdued colours, but not so much in flat areas as for shading. She had a certain feeling for the page and like Crane designed the whole book herself. She had however none of Crane's *horror vacui* but on the contrary liked plenty of white space round her pictures and verses. The vignettes which she often placed in the margins or at the foot of the page were so small that they never detracted from the emptiness of the page. Of the verses, which she herself wrote to go with her pictures, the less said the better. But her illustrations for the writings of others, her ambitious *Pied Piper* of 1889 for instance, are never as successful as for her own.

In about 1851 an engraver named Langton discovered how to photograph drawings on to wood and although this did not become general practice for some twenty years, the discovery marks an epoch. Not only did it foreshadow the advent of photo-engraving, it also led more immediately to a mechanical manner of engraving. Drawings need no longer be made the exact size in which they were to be cut on the wood, but they could first be enlarged or reduced photographically. Mechanical ruling which was now widely used helped to discourage the artist from designing specially for wood and to make the professional engraver into a hack. Other devices, like Graphotype, though not photographic, were designed to replace wood. In Graphotype the artist drew on a block of compressed chalk with a special

240. Beardsley: *Under the Hill*, 1903. $10\frac{3}{4}'' \times 8\frac{1}{2}''$. An illustration for his own romance designed in terms of the photo-engraved line block

ink which held the block together, allowing the chalk to be brushed out in the parts which were not drawn on. H. Fitzcook produced some good graphotype borders for Watt's *Divine and Moral Songs* (1867), a book which was wholly illustrated by this method. By the time photo-engraving had taken a firm hold in the eighties, wood-engraving was in a sorry state.

The earliest photographers made exalted claims for their craft. Fox Talbot wrote a book called *The Pencil of Nature* (1844) which was illustrated with pasted-in photographs, glorified under the title of 'photographic drawing'. Mrs. Cameron produced a famous series of photographs to illustrate Tennyson's *Idylls of the King*. In 1857 appeared John Pouncy's *Dorsetshire Photographically Illustrated*, the first English book in which photography was applied to lithography. The Woodburytype process (which virtually consists of pasting photographic prints on to the page) was patented in 1864 and was frequently used for book illustration from 1875 onwards. The principle of collotype was discovered in 1855, of the line block at about the same time, of photogravure in 1879, and the half-tone was perfected in the eighties. All these new processes became available to the book printer during the last twenty years of the century and the effect on illustration was bound to be far reaching.

In actual fact the immediate effect on style was surprisingly small. English pen-drawing now lagged far behind French and American. And photo-engraving in England, according to Pennell, was bad to begin with and was only used for cheapness. 'Bad cheap process',[1] says this admittedly prejudiced writer, 'has been responsible in this country for more vile work than in all the rest of the world put together.' For a long time before this artists had not needed to modify their drawings for the wood-engraver but had relied on his skill (and his mechanical devices) to translate them. As we have seen, large drawings could be photo-graphically reduced before being cut in wood and process engraving did the same—though the line block was not limited by the craftsman's ability to engrave fine lines. Most of the early users of the line block, like Hugh Thomson, drew for considerable reduction which gave their pictures a somewhat meretricious fineness; but there was nothing else about them to distinguish them from the work of the preceding decade. Not until Aubrey Beardsley's arrival on the scene in the nineties do we find a really original artist using the line block, with some comprehension of its capabilities and of its essential difference from the wood-engraving. This skill came to him gradually. His designs for the *Morte d'Arthur* done in 1893 in his Pre-Raphaelite period seem to ape the woodcut to which indeed the line block is more closely allied than to the wood-engraving. The heavy borders and the generally archaic atmosphere challenge an immediate comparison with the contemporary Kelmscott books. The little vignettes at the beginning of each chapter by the side of the initials are more original. But what is most significant about a not very convincing book is the develop-ment in machining that made it possible to print these very heavy blocks along with the type not in the Morris style by a hand-press on damped paper, but as an ordinary commercial product. In fact the production of these heavy blocks was soon to raise its own problems of design as we shall later see; but in the meantime they had the fascination of novelty.

Beardsley soon relinquished this style however and his illustrations for Wilde's *Salome* (1894), produced under the influence of the Japanese print, show an appreciation of the value of space. There is still no attempt at tone and the black solids are still there but they are better balanced by white and by the spidery line. Yet when due allowance has been made for their technical skill these pictures are as repellant as most of Beardsley's work.

[1] 'Process' is another term for photo-engraving.

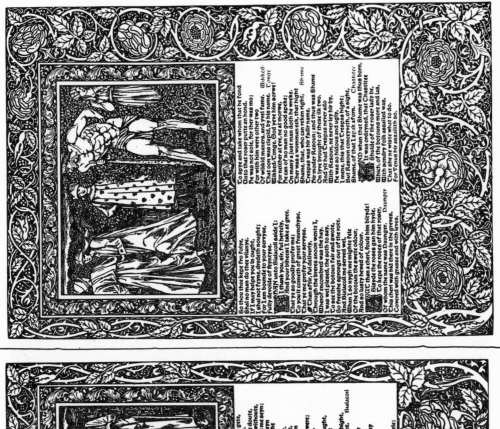

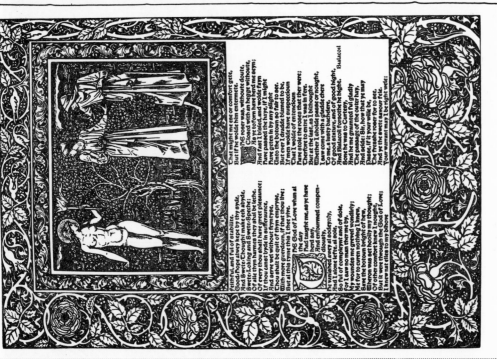

241. Chaucer: *The Canterbury Tales*, 1896. 16¾″ × 11½″. The Kelmscott edition with wood-engraved illustrations after Burne-Jones and borders after Morris. The Franklin's Tale

Oscar Wilde felt this when he said 'They are cruel and evil and so like dear Aubrey who has a face like a silver hatchet with grass-green hair'; and again, 'They are too Japanese while my play is Byzantine.'

In his last phase Beardsley looked back to the eighteenth century and his best illustrations in this manner are for Pope's *Rape of the Lock* (1896) and his own romance *Under the Hill* (1903). Here is the perfection of his line-block method. The blacks are more subdued and a grey is achieved as well. But it is the dotted patterns which are the original feature [240]. This sort of thing was almost impossible for the wood-engraving but is a triumphant possibility for the line block and is of course the basis of the 'mechanical tints' which are used so much today. But Beardsley was using them for pattern rather than tone, and the result is something quite unlike the eighteenth century but no less delightful.

No greater contrast to Beardsley could be imagined than William Morris. His book production was all done in the *fin de siècle* period but shows no trace of Beardsley's decadence. Beardsley played with the eighteenth-century manner but Morris when he was designing his books lived in the fifteenth century. Just when wood had been finally ousted by photo-engraving he brought it back in its most primitive form, the woodcut. Yet in spite of his salutary insistence on good materials and proportions few of the Kelmscott books are notable for their illustrations. The Chaucer of 1896 with Burne-Jones's designs is a remarkable book [241], but in too many of the others he employed mediocre artists. Crane was an exception, but *The Story of the Glittering Plain* which he illustrated in 1894 with congested engravings is not one of his best efforts. Bruce Rogers, the distinguished American typographer, was

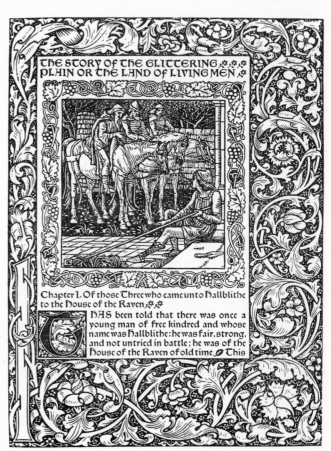

242. Morris: *The Story of the Glittering Plain*, 1894.
$11\frac{1}{2}'' \times 8\frac{1}{4}''$

right when he said that Morris's books 'are some of them very beautiful but they are rather curiosities of book-making than real books' [242].

How is it then that his influence even in his own day was so great that it spread to Germany and America and so much greater immediately after his death? Perhaps the answer is that Morris was only one apostle of an idea that was very much in the air and that we have already met in Owen Jones and Noel Humphreys. Joseph Pennell, writing in 1889 says 'Here [in England] within the last thirty years people have been continuously taught to believe that book decoration, like all other art work, to be artistic must have a spiritual, moral, social, political, literary or sixteenth century value, while beauty of line and perfection of execution have been subordinated to these qualities'. It is hard to believe that these words were written before the appearance of any Kelmscott books.

What was peculiar to Morris and helps also to explain his influence was a refusal to compromise, not so much with the machine as with the shoddiness of the machine product of his day. Everything in his books had to be good—paper, ink, printing and binding. That was a startling lesson for the printers of his day to begin with. And it was the workmanship rather than the design of the Kelmscott books that had the most salutary effect.

Good materials do not necessarily involve good design however. Morris labelled himself a decorator rather than an illustrator when he went back to the fifteenth century for his inspiration. He himself defines illustration as decoration first of all and then story-telling; and his choice of the woodcut technique with its lack of realism and of depth makes his sympathies sufficiently obvious. His own cuts for borders, initials or title-pages are unsurpassed because ornament in the flat shows little development through the centuries. But when the technique is applied to book illustration the result is nearly always a failure because as Burne-Jones himself said 'we cannot paint with the same innocency that once was possible'; and with the best intentions the modern eye is disconcerted by this limitation. Even if we accept the lack of depth the crowded appearance of the Kelmscott page, heavy type, heavy border and heavy cut all in the same plane run counter to our notion of what the book page should be.

Archaism was in the air. For some years Tuer had been issuing his chap-books with cuts by Joseph Crawhall which were coloured by hand. And right at the end of the century, all in one year, 1898, came William Nicholson's illustrations for Henley's *London Types*, Kipling's *The Almanac of Twelve Sports* and *An Alphabet* [243] which owe something to Crawhall but more to Toulouse-Lautrec. And there was something French too in his submission to the discipline of cutting his own designs in wood, and colouring them by hand. This is a rarity in nineteenth-century English books. We seldom find it before William Morris and even Morris's illustrators often used reproductive engravers. But in France the painter had long been used to the task of preparing his own printing surfaces and did not feel that it was below his dignity.

Nicholson's are picture-books and are advertised as his, the contributors of the text, even when they were as distinguished as Kipling, taking a second place. The hand-coloured copies are limited; the ordinary editions were printed by lithography. Nicholson liked a big square page and with his heavy black he aimed at broad effects. He used subdued colours rather in the lithotint style with an occasional flash of bright red or yellow. The result often resembles a linocut but it has little in common with the Japanese print, although it was often so compared at the time.

In 1889, before the appearance of any Kelmscott books, Ricketts and Shannon started *The Dial*; and soon after the Vale and Eragny Presses were established. Their work, which

243. Henley's *London Types*, 1898. 13″ × 11¼″. With hand-coloured woodcuts by
Nicholson, reproduced by lithography

will be discussed more fully in the next chapter, has often been lumped together with Morris's as that of private presses, but it was in reality quite different. For one thing it looked back to Italian originals rather than German; for another it led to a revival of original lithography (though not unfortunately in books) whereas Morris pinned all his faith on the woodcut.

FRANCE

After the uniformity of the eighteenth century in France the nineteenth presents a picture of the utmost variety. There is variety of style and variety of the processes that went to form that style. There is variety too of typography though typography does not always echo the manner of the accompanying illustration. The sudden appearance of Romanticism in art and literature towards the end of the second decade is not enough to account for all the changes that took place, for besides the obvious classifications of classical or romantic it is possible also to divide later French books into such categories as realist and impressionist. The cause of all this variety lies in the break with tradition and the resulting instability, of which the Revolution and the Romantic movement alike were symptoms, and which affected the whole of Western Europe in a greater or lesser degree.

It was curious that the immediate effect of the Revolution was to enforce a tradition much more rigid than anything that had preceded it. If we trace the general evolution of illustration between 1800 and 1870 in the successive editions of a key book like La Fontaine's *Fables* we see how abruptly that rigidity was replaced by the opposite extreme. The Didot edition of 1802 is a large book with woodcuts after Percier in the Davidesque style, combining several subjects within the same framework. Percier was the Emperor's architect and the decorative quality of these cuts enhances the fine structure of the Didot page. Then in 1814 Moreau, a ghost from the eighteenth century, showed not very convincingly what he could do in the same vein but using copper. Moreau may also have been the designer of an interesting edition which had appeared three years earlier embodying an experiment by Duplat. The very small designs were cut in stone (a method already tried by Senefelder) and moulds were then made from which relief blocks were cast. The result is rather coarse and not very impressive.

Engelmann's edition of 1818 broke new ground by using lithography to reproduce the designs of the brothers Vernet and a growing freedom makes itself apparent. The edition of 1826 which Devéria illustrated was one of the very first to employ wood-engraving just then reviving under English influence. With Goujet's engravings for the edition of 1833, however, true Romanticism appears together with all its worst faults. Grandville's La Fontaine of 1839 is the first of the century in which the touch of true genius makes itself felt [244]. Here is a complete break with the past, not only with the classical typography of the Didots (the initials, shadow types and incredibly elaborate typographical ornaments have to be seen to be believed) but also with the old 'Æsop cycle' which goes back at least as far as Gheeraerts's engravings of 1567, if not farther. Like Bewick, Grandville had really observed

244. La Fontaine's *Fables*, 1839. $8\frac{3}{4}'' \times 5\frac{3}{4}''$. Illustrated by Grandville, actual size

animals but unlike Bewick he was fascinated by their similarities to human beings—whom he had observed just as closely. He lacks the occasional cruelty of Bewick and his predecessors but there is something of Bewick in his sudden intensities of vision; Bewick's intensities however were caused by looking simply at the object itself, Grandville's by seeing something behind the object; hence his curious resemblance to the artists of the Emblem Books.

The La Fontaine of 1839, illustrated with wood-engravings by Johannot, Adam and others, is a more typical book of the period. The typography is similar to Grandville, and the illustrations are perhaps more skilfully executed; but they are on the old lines and though the humans are cleverly satirised the animals are stock figures.

In Doré's handsome quarto of 1868 we find a more restrained typography which is belied by the baroque exaggeration of the large engravings. There is no feeling for animals at all, only a determination to extract the last drop of melodrama from every situation. Nevertheless the pictures are unforgettable as so often with Doré. The small vignettes have a freer etched quality which is denied to the large engravings with their mechanical ruling; and they seem to presage the coming of the line block which was so soon to supplant wood.

We see then a clear break between the classical and romantic styles which occurs about 1825 and coincides almost exactly with the reintroduction of wood-engraving (the 1802 La Fontaine was an exception and its illustrations were cuts, not engravings). The classical style of the Didots suited typography better than illustration but they used illustration more than their opposite numbers in England and Italy, Baskerville and Bodoni. They produced many notable books besides the three-volume Racine of 1801 for which they are chiefly famous. In this book the engravings of Gerard and Girodet give an air of lifelessness. P. J. Bernard's *Oeuvres* (1797) and *Daphnis et Chloé* (1800), both illustrated by Prud'hon, are perhaps more friendly.[1] But the book of theirs which undoubtedly had more influence than any other both on literature and illustration was Bernardin de Saint-Pierre's *Paul et Virginie*. It had first been illustrated by Moreau in 1789 and it was to be issued again by Curmer in 1838 with remarkable wood-engravings in the Romantic style. But Didot's edition of 1806 was typographically the most perfect and that remarkable etching of *Les Tombeaux* after Isabey with its premonition not so much of Romanticism as of Impressionism is an eye-opener for all who would divide art into water-tight compartments [245].

The vignettes of Alexandre Desenne are another confutation of this attitude. The early nineteenth century is supposed to be a period of full-page engraved illustration; but all the time Desenne was designing woodcut vignettes as well for his books which if he had been better served by his cutters would have been almost worthy to rank with Bewick. His best work appears in the *Hermite* series by de Jouy between 1813 and 1825 [248]. It is curious to see how the illustrations become less mythological as the series progresses and how awkwardly the woodcuts lend themselves to neo-classical designs. Wood is used mainly for tail-pieces and among them are a few which were engraved by Charles Thompson, a pupil of Bewick. Bouchot belittles Bewick's influence in France at this juncture and claims on doubtful grounds that Brévière forestalled many of his innovations. But there is no doubt that English engravers played a large part in reintroducing wood into France.

In the *Hermite* books there are line engravings (in circular medallions) as well as woodcuts. This mixture of wood and copper was often found, of course, in books of the previous century, though Desenne's woodcuts are usually more illustrative than the decorations by

[1] Prud'hon was less infected by neo-classicism than most of his contemporaries but as a result he seems to have been disliked by David who chose most of the Didot illustrators from among his own followers.

245. Saint-Pierre: *Paul et Virginie*, 1806. $12\frac{1}{2}'' \times 9\frac{1}{2}''$.
An etching after Isabey in the Didot edition

246. Thory: *Les Roses*, octavo edition, 1828–9. Illustrated by Redouté

GALLICA AURELIANENSIS   DUCHESSE D'ORLÉANS

247. Goethe's *Faust*, 1828. 16¾″ × 11″. A lithograph by Delacroix

Je pars demain pour continuer mon voyage dans le département des Basses-Pyrénées; mais avant de quitter ce doux pays, je dirai quelques mots d'Ustaritz, véritable capitale du pays basque, où tout voyageur qui n'a pas de patrie doit être tenté de s'en choisir une.

248. De Jouy: *L'Hermite en Provence*, 1818. 6¾″ × 4″. A vignette by Desenne

Papillon and others. Desenne is therefore a link between the eighteenth century and the revival of wood-engraving in the 1830's. Redouté, however, is simply a relic of a bygone age, delightful though his books are. Without aristocratic patronage they could not have been produced and fortunately for him that patronage was supplied before the Revolution by Marie Antoinette and after it by the Empress Joséphine. His most famous work *Les Roses* (1817–24) was produced for the latter. It consists of three volumes of stipple-engravings in colour after his own paintings with a text by C. A. Thory [246]. Redouté had studied stipple-engraving in England where he learnt to print several colours from one plate and to retouch by hand. After 1835 he used lithography for reproducing his paintings but was never happy with it.

Lithography had 'arrived' in France with Delacroix's *Faust* in 1828, one of the very greatest of all illustrated books [247]. The process seems to have made a slower start in France than in England and was less used for book illustration than for separate prints. In this department, however, because of its freedom and spontaneity which so obviously suited the Romantic temperament, it enjoyed much greater popularity than in England. From the beginning the French saw its possibilities as a means of multiplying (rather than reproducing) original drawings. Besides the *Faust* and the La Fontaine of 1818 already mentioned, there are one or two interesting books which contain lithographic plates. *Voyages pittoresques et romantiques dans l'ancienne France* (1820–78) by Taylor and Nodier is in the same tradition as the English topographical books, and the lithographs (by Fragonard, Bonington and Boys among others) have the same tenuous connexion with the text. But it is a landmark in the development of lithography. Its publication covered some 58 years and Nodier predicted in his preface to the first volume that the journeys recorded were also to be a record of the progress of lithography. 'And he was so far right', says Pennell, 'that in the series you can trace the development of the art from the first pale colourless drawings . . . to the elaborate designs, the difficult lithotints, the perfectly managed colour of the succeeding volumes; from the timid separate print to the amazingly bad and elaborate page decoration, flamboyant borders with pictures set in them, that filled the sections on Languedoc and Picardy beginning in the year 1833 when medievalism was the order of the day.' But the introduction of photo-lithography in 1863 killed the originality of the work though good draughtsmen still contributed to it.

Lami's and Monnier's *Voyage en Angleterre* (1829–30) in which the lithographs are cleverly planned for hand-colouring suggests even more forcibly the comparison with the English topographical book because of its subject matter. Béranger's *Chansons* of 1828 has hand-coloured lithographs (some of the very earliest examples to be found in a book) by Henri Monnier accompanied by wood-engravings by Devéria. And in the same year Monnier collaborated with Bonington to produce *Les Contes du Gay Sçavoir* in which lithography is set the unusual task of reproducing vignettes in what must surely have been one of the first pieces of nineteenth-century medievalism. But all these pale beside Delacroix's *Faust* which made history not only as one of the earliest books in France to be illustrated lithographically but also as the true beginning of Romantic illustration.

It marks too the beginning of the great French tradition of the painter-lithographer, soon to be matched by that of the painter-etcher. True, many great painters illustrated books in the eighteenth century but they never prepared their own printing surfaces. Ever since Delacroix, but more particularly in the present century, France has never lacked great painters who were ready to turn their hand to lithography, engraving, etching, aquatinting or wood-engraving in order to illustrate books. There is no contempt for the processes of reproduction nor even an attitude of condescension such as we often find among the painters of other nations. On the contrary, there is often a surprising virtuosity and an ability to extract more from those processes than the professionals were able to do. Delacroix was no exception. He instinctively understood the peculiar qualities of lithography and many of his effects, his dense velvety blacks for instance, could have been obtained by no other medium. It is these that give such an exciting quality to the night scenes in which *Faust* abounds. And considered as documents of the Romantic movement these pictures with their excitement and intensity are unsurpassed. 'I admit', said Goethe himself rather ambiguously, 'that M. Delacroix has surpassed my own idea of scenes I made myself.' By 1834 when Delacroix started a set of lithographs for *Hamlet* (which were never issued as a book) the effervescence had partly subsided.

The *Faust* lithographs were of course printed separately and were therefore *hors-texte*. They had no influence on the typography of the book nor were they influenced by it. W. J. Strachan has suggested that in this way lithography helped to break the dominance of the vignette and gave the painter-lithographer the freedom he needed. Whether this has benefited the book is a different matter. No illustrations could be more completely divorced from their text than those of the contemporary French *édition-de-luxe*; and physical separation inevitably leads to spiritual separation of course. It is not surprising that in spite of Delacroix's success lithography was used much more for caricatures and separate prints than for book illustration during the remainder of the century. In the hands of an artist like Daumier it was the perfect process for such work. We can only regret that Daumier has left us but one book from which to judge his mastery of the process, *Les Cent et un Robert-Macaire* (1839–40) and even this is more a collection of caricatures than a book, in spite of a substantial text by Alhoy and Huart [249]. Daumier, unlike Gavarni, seems to have been interested more in the freedom that lithography gives than in its tones. He uses chalk textures but these are obscured in the coloured versions of the plates which are found in some (less successful) copies. This is a good example of what we may call 'caricaturist's illustration', a type that was very common in France at this period and whose other great exponent was Gavarni. Its characteristic is that each picture is self-contained and almost self-explanatory. In *Robert-*

249. Alhoy and Huart: *Les Cent et un Robert-Macaire*, 1839–40. $10\frac{3}{4}'' \times 8\frac{1}{4}''$. Lithographs by Daumier

250. Lesage's *Gil Blas*, 1835. $10'' \times 6''$. Wood-engravings after Gigoux

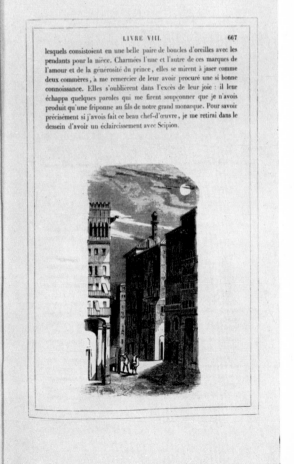

251. *Chants et Chansons populaires de la France*, 1843. 10½″ × 6¾″. Steel engravings after Daubigny, Meissonier and others

Macaire a long and elaborate legend is built into the picture, but the attitude and above all the face of the chief actor carry so much weight of meaning that the legend is almost superfluous. A much later book of Gavarni's carries the method even farther. This is Dumas's *La Dame aux Camélias* (1858) which is illustrated with full-page wood-engravings, one for each character in the story. The solitary figure is shown without background, almost without gesture, again expressing everything in the pose and the facial expression. It is a technical triumph but the effect is curiously static.

After about 1840 lithography was used seldom in books until the end of the century, though it was often used for collections of prints in book form. Philip James has said that its history in France as distinct from other countries 'is remarkable for the fact that at no time did it become submerged in commercial vulgarity'; and it is a fact that France escaped the oily horrors of the chromo-lithograph in which England and Germany were revelling at the mid-century. We find it used reproductively in occasional works like *L'Imitation de Jésus-Christ* (1858) published by Curmer who also produced many of the best wood-engraved books. *L'Imitation*, like the *Contes du Gay Sçavoir* and the similarly lithographed work of Noel Humphreys and Owen Jones in England, goes back for inspiration to the illuminated manuscripts. Unfortunately, it is a mixture of many manuscripts, 'Les plus belles pages de toutes les époques' says the publisher; and this includes oriental work! The result is violent indigestion for the reader, though taken singly there are many fine pages. Curmer's little *Livres de Mariage* which Meissonier illustrated also have something of the medieval quality but price imposed restraint here.

It was not until the very end of the century with Lautrec, Fantin-Latour and Redon that lithographic illustration revived. Its chief competitor was wood-engraving which came back triumphantly in the thirties. Far from divorcing illustration from the text, as lithography tended to do, wood-engraving married them ever more closely. Blocks are embedded in the type and one is overwhelmed by the sheer quantity of them, so that it sometimes seems as if each word is being illustrated. (This is literally the case in some parts of *La Chaumière indienne*.) It was from England that the impetus came. Charles Thompson, Bewick's pupil, was invited to Paris in 1817 by Didot and he soon trained a school of native craftsmen, chief among whom were Porret and Best. He was followed too by other English engravers so that by 1830 there were almost enough highly skilled engravers to satisfy the enormous demand—a demand which as in England came from the newly founded magazines as well as from book publishers.

The coincidence of this revival with the Romantic revolution in literature was not wholly a matter of chance. The reaction against classicism seems to have been particularly violent and it extended to the classical methods of illustration such as line-engraving. Medievalism was the rage and woodcuts were of course used during the Middle Ages—or as near to the Middle Ages as made no matter. We find this same 'Gothic' setting in the horrific novels of Mrs. Radcliffe and others which were now appearing in England; but there is a world of difference between English and French Romantic illustration. In England there was more pre-occupation with landscape and less with medievalism. True, men like Noel Humphreys made a serious study of the Middle Ages but that was a very different thing from the somewhat bogus use of medieval motifs for decoration, just as absurd in its way as David's neo-classicism which it reacted against.

Another effect of the Romantic movement was to democratize books.[1] One would have

---

[1] Three thousand copies of Curmer's *Paul et Virginie* were printed, a very large edition for those days.

12   HISTOIRE

amis de ma jeunesse. A vingt-cinq ans, je n'avois jamais recherché d'autre conversation que la sienne, et quelle conversation!

L'homme le plus mince, le plus géométri strait dans tou sions—le plus de latin, d'éty nomatopées— diathèses, d'h métathèses— syncopes et d' tête qui conti plus long, le plus étroit, le quement ab- tes ses dimen- frotté de gree, mologies, d'o- -de thèses, de ypothèses, de de tropes, de apocopes—la ent le plus de mots contre une idée, de sophismes contre un raisonnement, de paradoxes contre une opinion — de noms, de prénoms, de surnoms — de titres oubliés et de dates inutiles — de niaiseries biologiques, de balivernes bibliologiques, de billevesées philologiques — la table vivante des matières du *Mithridate* d'Adelung et de l'*Onomasticon* de Saxins!...

Le second, créature bizarre et capricieuse —

252. Nodier: *Histoire du roi de Bohème*, 1830. 9″ × 5″. Wood engravings after Tony Johannot

expected this to happen in the political revolutions which occurred some forty years earlier but it did not. The harbinger of this change, as in England, was the illustrated magazine. The *Magasin pittoresque* was founded in 1833, three years after the appearance of Nodier's *Histoire du roi de Bohème* in which were some of the earliest wood-engravings of Tony Johannot. This is probably the first book of the period in which the vignettes were set within the text; previously they had always been head or tail-pieces [248]. The new fashion, which henceforth became the rule, permitted an intimate contact between text and illustration, and prompted the excesses which we have already noted. We even find in this book a few cases of type running round the block on all sides [252] a development that was later to be used in the picture initial. But it was not until 1835 that the typical Romantic illustrated book appeared. This was Lesage's *Gil Blas* which Gigoux adorned with nearly 600 wood-engravings [250]. Their profusion is as typical as their style. The book appeared in parts and as it progressed more and more engravings were included by public demand.

Contemporary witnesses say that books at this time were bought for their vignettes rather than their text, and these were criticized in detail by reviewers. Books began to have a snob value among the bourgeoisie to whom their literary worth was of minor importance. Thus the feebler works were often the best served, even though the period was prolific in novels like those of Hugo, Balzac or Dumas which lend themselves notably to illustration. The comparatively small band of illustrators must have been greatly overworked and we find new engravings being eked out with stock blocks from a *recueil d'illustrations typographiques*. Keepsakes are as popular as elsewhere until about 1842 and we often find the same steel-engravings in French and English volumes. A new kind of literature peculiar to France is the *physiologie*, a facetious little book, usually in a yellow cover, devoted to the description of one particular human type. Bouchot has said that it did for the nineteenth century what the Emblem Book did for the sixteenth. Daumier illustrated one or two, such as the *Physiologie du Rentier* (1840) but the classic in this field (which may in fact have started the craze off) was a larger book, the very successful *Les Français peints par eux-mêmes* (1840), the chief illustrator of which was Gavarni.

The period between 1835 and 1845 in France is comparable with the sixties in England and is in fact more fruitful in books because not so much illustration went into magazines. In France too the Romantic idea gave a stronger impetus and a sense of unity which was lacking in England. Typographically there was little to choose between the two periods. *Gil Blas* has the double-rule borders beloved of English printers and, especially towards the end of the period, we meet in books many of those monstrously decorated types which French founders were copying so avidly from their English neighbours.

Victor Hugo's first illustrated edition of *Notre Dame de Paris* which appeared a year after *Gil Blas* was an equally influential book but not because of its illustrations. These were the work of Tony Johannot and his brother, the former one of the most prolific illustrators of our period. He had already illustrated a Molière and a *Don Quixote*, both of them books which exemplify the Romantic virtues—liveliness, evocation and fun—and the Romantic vices—slovenliness, facility and inaccuracy. *Notre Dame* was reactionary in the technique of its illustrations, which were steel-engraved. Steel had followed wood from England but it did not find much favour in France though it was used for a few notable books, like Balzac's *Peau de Chagrin* of 1838, the first and only volume of a projected series of illustrated Balzacs. Unlike *Notre Dame* which has only full-page plates, *Peau de Chagrin* has vignettes in the text. *The Contes de Perrault* (1843) goes one step farther for it is steel-engraved throughout, both text and illustrations. Another book with steel-engravings, *Chants et Chansons Populaires de la France* (1842-3), in which a large number of artists were represented, is one of the very finest books of the whole period [251]. The illustrations of Daubigny, Meissonier and many others have here a distinct air of the eighteenth century and the way the pictures form a border to the verses remind one of the best Venetian books of that period. Exuberant though the engravings are, the fact that they are engraved seems to impose a discipline that would have benefited many other Romantic books.

Steel-engraving was not the only intaglio method to survive. Etching was used by Celestin Nanteuil for many frontispieces to Victor Hugo's works, each with its pseudo-Gothic border in the true Romantic manner, and crude childlike letters which may have been a reaction against the precision of line-engraved words. Thus, as Michel says, 'for a conventional antiquity was substituted a no less imaginary Middle Ages, which had however the redeeming merit of being more lively and entertaining. For while the antique of 1810 had been chill to the point of being depressing, the Middle Ages of 1830 were staggering and exciting and alas! boisterously hilarious even on the bloodiest occasions.' Apart from a few later productions of Tony Johannot, etching thereafter disappeared unmourned from the book until its revival in *Sonnets et Eaux-fortes* in 1869.

The edition of *Robinson Crusoe* published in 1836 is a real document of Romanticism which yet manages to exude a slightly eighteenth-century air. Translated by Petrus Borel, one of the leading litterateurs of the charnel-house school, it contains about 250 wood-engravings designed by Devéria, Boulanger and Nanteuil. The same elaborate border is used for the full-page pictures throughout the first volume and another throughout the second [253].

There is nothing of the eighteenth century except the text about Curmer's famous 1838

253. Defoe, translated Borel:
Robinson Crusoe, 1836.
$8\frac{1}{2}'' \times 5''$. A wood-engraving
after Devéria

edition of *Paul et Virginie*, probably the finest book of the whole period. A host of different designers and engravers were employed, their names conveniently displayed in an index. Many of the engravers were English[1] and they worked from designs by Meissonier, Vernet, Français, and of course Johannot. Although the book has been so greatly praised for its typography it is less successful in design than as a piece of printing. The presswork is superb, but the text is too much broken up by engravings, especially in *La Chaumière indienne* [254]. The gradual eclipse of the full-page picture, so typical of this period, can almost be seen in progress and it is balanced by the emergence of the initial-picture. We are reminded of the historiated initial of medieval manuscripts; but the difference is this: the illuminated initial was designed round the shape of the letter whereas these printed initials have no influence at all on the design and are in fact quite insignificant—an excuse only for a picture, by which they are quite overpowered.

The most exciting and unexpected illustrator of this period is Grandville, a sort of nine-teenth-century Bosch, whose work is often quite unlike any of his contemporaries'. In the

[1] There seems to have been a shortage of good French wood-engravers until quite a late date. Curmer wrote in the preface of a book published just before *Paul et Virginie* 'We were compelled to have recourse to England to complete our work....' And in Janin's *L'Été à Paris* (1843) Lami's wood-engraved vignettes and also the steel-engravings were produced in England [255]. Facsimile wood-engraving is generally held to have started in England with Bewick's pupils, to have been developed in France first, then Germany (by Menzel) and finally to have been reintroduced to England by the Dalziels.

present century we find echoes of it in surrealism, and the surrealists have done his reputation a disservice by claiming him as a forbear; but in Grandville the shock is tempered by humour and sometimes by sentimentality. He was much more successful with animals than with humans, and in black-and-white than in colour. His edition of La Fontaine's *Fables* (1839) has already been mentioned [244]. His *Robinson Crusoe* of 1840 and his *Scènes de la vie privée et publique des animaux* (1842) are delightful and so is the strange *Un Autre Monde* (1844) with its exotic typography [256]. *Les Fleurs animées* (1847) is a little too pretty for it gives less scope to his curious humour. His *Don Quixote* of 1848 with steel as well as wood-engravings is rather ordinary.

The typical book of this period contains work by several illustrators and Grandville himself sometimes collaborated with others in this way. Often, too, its text was by different authors who combined to produce a sort of miscellany such as *Les Français peints par eux-mêmes*, already mentioned. Although this particular book was widely imitated abroad the type remains peculiarly French. *Le Diable à Paris* (1845) which also contains much work by Gavarni is even more of a hotch-potch for it lacks the unifying idea of the former book. But *Journal de l'Expédition des Portes de Fer* (1844) is more homogeneous [257]. Raffet who had already illustrated Paul de Kock's *Oeuvres* (1830–5) with small copper-engravings was the chief illustrator and he was helped by the excellent printing of the Imprimerie Royale and the toned paper (imitative of rice paper) on which the cuts are printed. The full-page illustrations of that grisly book, Janin's *L'Ane Mort* (1842), are also printed on a yellowish background which distinguished them from the vignettes. This latter is a well-printed book with many excellent wood-engravings by Johannot.

Wood-engravings printed in colour were never as popular in France as in England. But there is one interesting experiment by Gavarni, though this was itself printed in England. *Gavarni in London* (1849) has wood-engravings printed in two colours giving an effect reminiscent of the sixteenth-century chiaroscuro woodcuts or of the lithotint [258]. But unfortunately this experiment was not followed up.

Doré is often called the last of the Romantics and his work, dominating the empty years between 1850 and 1880, does in fact link the disparate beginning and end of the century. His output was enormous and, like his opposite numbers in England, he worked also for the magazines, particularly *Le Monde illustré*. He used reproductive engravers of course but he knew how to enable them to get the utmost from the wood-block on which his designs were directly drawn. Later however he tended to treat the wood almost as if it were copper and gave his engravers wash drawings to work from. Thus there is a steady progression in his work from line to tone but it is hardly a progression in quality. In his own day his fame rested upon the great folios but we find the earlier books more to our taste.

The Rabelais of 1854 is not very successful but in the same year he produced the *Histoire pittoresque, dramatique et caricaturale de la Sainte Russie*, a brilliant comic strip sequence based on the Swiss Toepfer's 'Album de Caricatures'. Then in 1855 came the *Contes drolatiques* of Balzac [260], which is one of his very best books with its numerous small engravings embedded in the text. Between 1861 and 1866 appeared his Dante. 'My idea', he says, 'was . . . to produce in a uniform style an edition of all the masterpieces in literature of the best authors, epic, comic and tragic.' But to begin with no publisher would back this project and he brought out the *Inferno* at his own expense in 1861. Here and in his *Don Quixote* of 1863 there is as much tone as line and the illustrations begin to assume the appearance of paintings. In spite of his enormous success—at this period he was illustrating several books simultaneously—Doré longed to be a painter. But Paris had no use for his huge canvases. His

Bible[1] of 1866 made him so famous in England however that his religious paintings found a ready sale there at the Doré Gallery in Bond Street. His stay in England resulted in two other famous books, *Idylls of the King* (1868–9) and Jerrold's *London* (1872). The former is illustrated not by wood but by steel-engravings based on separate wash drawings, and this departure from his usual methods is not very successful.

Doré worked generally from black to white and in these great folios (which are always well printed) the illustrations take on the quality of mezzotints with their rich blacks so suitable for the dark and menacing scenes in which he delighted so much. He has a certain affinity with John Martin in the gloom and horror of many of his scenes, also in the impression of size which he managed to produce in quite a small picture. There is a strongly vertical feeling about many of his illustrations which gives them on occasion an almost vertiginous quality. But this ability to extract so much from a small space is unfortunately counter-balanced by his habit of accumulating too much detail whenever he had more space at his disposal. Nevertheless he is unsurpassed in what Lehmann-Haupt calls his 'agreeable terror' which probably had a formative influence on the Surrealists just as it undoubtedly derived partly from Grandville.

Doré's effect on French illustration was far from being an unmixed blessing. He has been accused of killing the vignette and it is a fact that although we still find vignettes in for instance *Les Contes Rémois* which Meissonier illustrated in 1858 (a book which Pennell calls the finest ever produced in France) they are painter's rather than wood-engraver's designs. Paris in the Second Empire was the most exciting place in Europe and it had in Constantin Guys and others of his contemporaries a band of artists who were unsurpassed in their presentation of the social scene. It is a mystery why books should have profited so little by their activity, and it seems likely that Doré's inflated reputation had something to do with it.

After Doré the use of tone in wood-engraving fell into disfavour (perhaps the advent of photo-engraving, in which the line block was perfected before the half-tone, had something to do with this), and the best wood-engravings of the nineties such as those of Lepère were linear. But in the meantime countless children's books and adventure stories, those of Jules Verne for instance, were being competently illustrated with drawings that could equally well be reproduced on wood or by line block. The most original book illustration of the sixties and seventies came from the etchers. We last saw etched illustration in the frontis-pieces of Nanteuil in the thirties. After this it disappeared from the book, just when it was being taken up by the painters of the Barbizon school. It soon became a craze not only in the form of 'painter-etching' but also for reproductive work, and in 1868 Henriquel-Dupont originated the *Société française de Gravure* to save line-engraving from a similar fate.[2] Etching in fact was taking the place of lithography in the affections of the amateur just as it had already done in England. In 1862 Baudelaire pointed out the affinity of etching to the art of the poet; and in the same year appeared Delvau's *Histoire anecdotique des cafés* with etchings by Rops and Courbet. These designs though unsuccessful because they show little regard for the requirements of the book are important because they mark the transition from romantic to contemporary etching. In 1869 *Sonnets et Eaux-fortes* was published. The forty-two etchers and poets who co-operated to produce this book belonged to the Parnassian

---

[1] In this great Bible with its pictures which occur at regular intervals of four or eight pages Doré solves the difficulty of illustrating the prophets and the epistles by simply producing extra engravings for the more readily illustrated books and letting them appear out of their context.

[2] He supervised the 1865 edition of Musset's *Poems* with steel engravings by Bida. This work although indifferent in quality helped to break down the barrier between the reproductive engravers and the vignettists whom they considered their inferiors.

puis chez les Maronites du mont Liban,

les moines du mont Carmel;

de là à Sana, en Arabie;

PARIS CHEZ
L. CURMER.

254. Saint Pierre: *La Chaumière indienne*, 1838. 10″ × 6½″. Wood-engravings after Johannot, and others, many of them cut by English craftsmen

255. Janin: *L'Été à Paris*, 1843. 10½″ × 7″. Steel-engraving after Lami

94 UNE ÉCLIPSE CONJUGALE.

qui n'est, à vrai dire, qu'une représaille de la morale.

C'est grande fête aujourd'hui dans le ciel. Si vous n'avez pas la vue courte, vous devez certainement voir les Signes

156 CONSTANTINE.

un caractère chevaleresque qui charme et qui étonne à la fois. Un jeune militaire français, Mustapha Bonnemain, se distingue entre tous par son adresse dans ces brillants exercices.

Le prince rentre à Constantine. Les marchands répandent des parfums sur ses pas; la foule l'en-

256. Grandville: *Un Autre Monde*, 1844. 10½″ × 7¼″. Wood-engravings after Grandville

257. Nodier: *Journal de l'Expédition des Portes de Fer*, 1844. 10¾″ × 7″. Wood-engravings after Raffet and others

258. Ed. Albert Smith: *Gavarni in London*, 1849. 10″ × 7¼″. Wood-engraving after Gavarni in two colours

259. *Sonnets et Eaux-fortes*, 1869. 14″ × 10¼″ Etching by Manet to illustrate *Fleur exotique*

Ores, elle, ne disoyt mot, resgnardoyt le ciel, qui se coeffoyt de nuict, les estoiles et tout pour son plaisir. Voilà qui va bien.

resvasseur, ne saichant plus à quoy se prendre. La croisée grongna soubdain et l'interrompit dans ses phantaisies. Ores, cuydant que sa dame alloyt le huchier, il dressa de rechief le nez, et sans l'appuy de la dessus dicte croisée, qui le préserva en fasson de couvre-chief, il eust recipé fort amplement de l'eaue froide, plus le contenant du tout, veu que l'anse resta aux mains de la personne en train d'estuver l'amoureux. Iacques de Beaune, trez-heureux de ce, ne perdit point l'esteuf et se geta en bas du mur, criant :

« Ie meurs ! » d'une voix trez-estaincte. Puis, se roydit dans les tessons et demoura mort, attendant le reste. Véey les serviteurs en grant remue-mesnaige, qui , en crainte de la dame à laquelle ils advouèrent leur faulte, ouvrent l'huys, se chargent du navré, lequel faillit à rire alors que il feut ainsy convoyé par les degrez.

— Il est froid, disoyt le paige.

— Il ha bien du sang, disoyt le maistre d'hostel, lequel en le tastant se conchioyt les mains dedans l'eaue.

— S'il en revient, ie fonde une messe à Sainct-Gatien ! s'escria le coupable en pleurs.

— Madame tient de son deffunct père, et, si elle fault à te faire pendre, le moindre loyer de ta poine sera d'estre bouté hors de sa maison et de son service, repartit ung aultre. Oui, certes, il est bien mort, il poise trop.

— Ah ! ie suis chez une bien grant dame, pensa Iacques.

— Las ! sent-il le mort ! demanda le gentilhomme autheur du meschief.

Lors, en laissant à grant poine le Tourangeau le long de la vis, le pourpoinct d'icelluy s'accrocha dans une tarasque de la rampe, et le mort dit : Ha ! mon pourpoinct !

— Il ha geint ? dit le coupable, sospirant de ioye.

Les serviteurs de la Regente, car ce estoyt le logiz de la fille du feu Roy Loys le unziesme , de vertueuse mémoire, les serviteurs donecques entrerent Iacques de Beaune en la salle, et le laisserent royde sur une table, ne cuydant point qu'il se saulfvast.

— Allez querir ung maistre myre, feit madame de Beaune, allez cy, allez là...

23

260. Balzac: *Contes drolatiques*, 1855. 8″ × 4¾″. Wood-engravings after Doré

261. Clemenceau: *Au pied du Sinai*, 1898. 10″ × 7½″. With lithographs by Toulouse-Lautrec

— 14 —

II

Le septième jour, nous abordâmes devant une plage sablonneuse remuée de dunes arides. Cabilor, Agloval, Paride et Morgain descen-

dirent; nous les attendîmes vingt heures; ils nous avaient quittés vers

262. Gide: *Voyage d'Urien*, 1893. $7\frac{1}{4}'' \times 7\frac{1}{2}''$. With colour lithographs by Denis

263. Prévost: *Manon Lescaut*, 1889. $9\frac{1}{2}'' \times 6\frac{1}{4}''$. Illustrated by Leloir

gement, je lui dis qu'il fallait en instruire M. Lescaut, afin que nos mesures se prissent de concert. Il en murmura d'abord; mais les quatre ou cinq livres d'argent comptant le firent entrer gaiement dans nos vues. Il fut donc réglé que nous nous trouverions tous à souper avec M. de G... M... et cela pour deux raisons : l'une pour nous donner le plaisir d'une scène agréable, en me faisant passer pour un écolier, frère de Manon; l'autre pour empêcher ce vieux libertin de s'émanciper trop avec ma maîtresse, par le droit qu'il croirait s'être acquis en payant si libéralement d'avance. Nous devions nous retirer, Lescaut et moi, lorsqu'il monterait à la chambre où il comptait de passer la nuit; et Manon, au lieu de le suivre, nous promit de sortir, et de la venir passer avec moi. Lescaut se chargea du soin d'avoir exactement un carrosse à la porte.

L'heure du souper étant venue, M. de G... M... ne se fit pas attendre longtemps. Lescaut était avec sa sœur dans la salle. Le premier compliment du vieillard fut d'offrir à sa belle un collier, des bracelets et des pendants de perles, qui valaient au moins mille écus. Il lui compta ensuite, en beaux louis d'or, la somme de deux mille quatre cents livres, qui faisaient la moitié de la pension. Il assaisonna son présent de quantité de douceurs dans le goût de la vieille cour. Manon ne put lui refuser quelques baisers; c'était autant de droits qu'elle acquérait sur l'argent qu'il lui mettait entre les mains. J'étais à la porte où je prêtais l'oreille en attendant que Lescaut m'avertît d'entrer.

Il vint me prendre par la main, lorsque Manon eut serré l'argent et les bijoux; et me conduisant vers M. de G... M...

CHEZ MONSIEUR DE G... M...

CROQUIS PARISIENS

PAR

J. K. HUYSMANS

H VATON,

EDITEUR.

264. Huysmans: *Croquis parisiens*, 1880. 8½″ × 6″. The frontispiece etched by Forain

school whose object was to protest against the excesses of Romanticism. Among them was Doré who contributed one of his earliest etchings, and Manet who is represented by the remarkable Goya-like 'Fleur exotique' [259].

During the last twenty-five years of the century there were few good books with etched illustrations, probably as a result of the coming of the photo-processes which drove etching from the book publisher to the print-seller. There are two books of Huysmans, however, for which Forain did some outstanding etchings. *Marthe* (1879) has only a frontispiece and in the *Croquis Parisiens* (1880) he shared the illustrations with Raffaelli; but we can see enough to regret that he was not invited to produce many more designs for this strange author [264].

It was at about the time of the publication of *Sonnets et Eaux-fortes* that Manet threw in his lot with the Impressionists and we are reminded of the excitement of this moment in French painting. But Impressionism seems to have had little immediate effect on illustration. It relied on colour to represent light and colour was virtually denied to the illustrator of the mid-nineteenth century. Of all the Impressionists however Manet was the one most able to adapt himself to black-and-white[1] and his lithographs for Poe's *The Raven* (1875) show an

[1] A colour lithograph of his dating from 1874 is said to have led to the renewal of original colour lithography as practised by Lautrec at the end of the century. But the posters of Jules Cheret, which were enjoying a vogue in the 70's, are likely to have had more effect than a single print by Manet.

instinctive grasp not only of the capabilities of lithography but also of imaginative illustration [265]. It is interesting to compare them with Doré's sentimental wood-engravings for the same poem published eight years later in the year of his death. By means of transfer paper which was just coming into wider use Manet was able to draw with the brush and the resulting lithographs have a distinctly painterly quality, which Doré for all his efforts at tone never achieved. As Felix Man says, Manet was the first painter of standing since Delacroix to concern himself with the stone, but it is going too far to add that 'he must be regarded as the father of modern lithography and book illustration'. His work in books is woefully small. Apart from the two contributions already mentioned he also illustrated with etchings a poem by Charles Cros called *Le Fleuve* in 1874 and provided a wood-engraving for Mallarmé's *Après midi d'un faune* in 1876. He is however the first of the modern French painter-illustrators and of his graphic work Roger-Marx says 'An ally of the impressionists, Manet in his etchings ... is the first to give a foretaste of that complete disorganization of form by light which ends in suppressing the contour'. It was however to lithography that his successors naturally turned as the printing process most nearly related to painting and the most diverse from the time-honoured technique of engraving. The fact that his work was commissioned at all shows that the traditionalist French publisher was beginning to change his attitude to the unpopular Impressionists; and in the closing years of the century the *avant-garde* painters were actually being sought after as illustrators.

The illustrations of Fantin-Latour are a warning of the dangers that lithography holds for a painter. The freedom conferred by it seems to have been an invitation to the type of 'imaginative illustration' that even now sometimes bedevils our books. He illustrated works by Jullien on Wagner (1886) and Berlioz (1888) with lithographs bearing such titles as 'Wagner and his muse'. It is not until we reach the few books illustrated by Toulouse-Lautrec right at the end of the century that we find again the work of a master.[1] Lautrec's posters had already shown his skill in the medium. His illustrations for Clemenceau's *Au pied du Sinai* (1898) and Jules Renard's *Histoires naturelles* (1899) are enchanting [261]. The freedom of lithography which Fantin abused is here exploited to the full and with triumphant effect. Lautrec was fortunate in having texts which suited him, the cynicism of Clemenceau and the humour of Renard.[2]

Lautrec's debt to Japan is obvious; but it was on the French Impressionists that the Japanese colour-print made its first European impact in the sixties. The influence on these painters of its colour simplification is well known, but its effect on the development of the colour lithograph at the end of the century was even more potent. To begin with, this development was confined to posters and to the various series of prints which Vollard launched in the nineties. Then there are albums like Henri Rivière's *Les Trente-six Vues de la Tour Eiffel* (1888–1902) which is obviously inspired by Hokusai's *Thirty-six Views of Fujiyama* and which helped to revive printing in water-colours from the wood-block. But it is not until the next century that at the hands of Bonnard and others the book begins to benefit, and then the results are truly spectacular. There was however one book which appeared in 1893 and which gave promise of new developments in colour lithography. This was André Gide's *Voyage d'Urien*, probably the first book illustrated by Maurice Denis. Denis, most of whose

---

[1] Odilon Redon produced in 1896 some excellently macabre lithographs to illustrate Lytton's *La Maison Hantée* but they were never made into a book.

[2] In 1931, long after Lautrec's death, appeared E. de Goncourt's *La Fille Elisa*, a facsimile of a copy of this book which Lautrec had illustrated very freely in water-colour.

265. Poe: *The Raven*. 1875. 21¼″ × 13″
With lithographs by Manet

work falls in the next chapter, was already famous enough to have his name hyphened to the author's on the title-page and had recently issued a manifesto calling for a revival of ornate pages like those of the medieval manuscript. It is the more surprising to find these exciting lithographs printed in two colours one of which is a background tint which changes throughout the book and is sometimes scraped away to make a high light [262]. Nothing could be less like an illuminated manuscript or indeed less like Denis's later work.

The photo-mechanical processes, when they arrived, resulted in the same lowering of standards as in England. Between 1873 and 1897 four new bibliophile societies came into being where there had only been one before; and these were ostensibly founded to enable fine books to be produced. But many of their members became obsessed with the fetish of the limited edition and the result of their efforts was a flow of pretentious books like *Les Quatre Fils Aymon* which Eugene Grasset illustrated in 1883. This is one of the earliest books in which colour was printed by Gillot's new process but the result, though excellent technically, is hardly reassuring. The illustrations are nearly all marginal but they often take up the greater part of the page and sometimes they exude splashes of colour which run across the page under the type. The colours are dingy and generally flat but here and there a certain amount of tone is introduced. Where the borders are plain they generally follow Celtic patterns but these are unmercifully distorted to suit the artist's whim. Altogether it is a ghastly example of what can happen when the decoration assumes more importance than the book itself.

It is however important because it is the first book in what the French call 'modern style' and the English (perversely) 'art nouveau'. Its colour scheme as well as its decoration set a new fashion and we shall find both in many books which come after. Two of the most popular illustrators in this style were, like Grasset, foreigners, Carloz Schwabe and Alphonse Mucha. Lucien Pissarro was French but he worked mostly in England. In Schwabe's illustrations for Zola's *Le Rêve* (1892) we can discern Japanese influences [266]. Whatever we may think about the overcrowded pages of this school (caused by a *horror vacui* such as we find in Walter Crane and the Kelmscott products), most of these books at least had the merit of being designed all of a piece.

One particular fetish of the bibliophile societies was the eighteenth-century pastiche for which the enthusiasm of the Goncourts was partly responsible. This extended to the texts chosen for illustration and it is indeed strange that this period, which was so rich in great poetry, should not have provided illustrations to match. The professionals of the time simply were not interested and it was not until the twentieth century that the symbolist poets found worthy collaborators in the *peintres-graveurs* and a new style of illustration in keeping with their own originality. In the meantime we find the engravings of Eisen, Fragonard and their fellows served up again and again, particularly by Jouaust, the publisher for the Bibliophiles. He had a penchant for the eighteenth century but oddly enough he often reproduced this work by photo-engraving, a habit which caused some protest among the more purist of his members.

One illustrator however showed some skill and imagination in handling one of the new processes. Daniel Vierge's drawings for *Pablo de Segovia* (1882) are reproduced by means of gillotypes, the forerunners of the modern line blocks. These had already appeared three years earlier in one of Doré's last books, his *Ariosto*, but their use had not altered Doré's accustomed style. Vierge however relied on the photo-mechanical method to reduce the size of his drawings and so to tighten them up considerably. The result is some very fine line-work that must often have been difficult to print, but which was also quite different

from anything that had hitherto been produced by wood [267]. Pennell who wrote an introduction to the English edition of 1892, and in it compares Vierge with Dürer and Holbein,
says rather ambiguously that Vierge reckoned on this reduction though the appearance of
his work was changed by it. The illustrations in the English edition are more impressive
than the French just because they are not reduced so much.

Vierge also illustrated Victor Hugo and Poe (who was enjoying a vogue at this time among
French artists). But he did nothing better than *Pablo de Segovia* nor did any of his contemporaries. One of them, de Neuville, who had worked under Meissonier, illustrated *A Coups
de fusil* (1876) by Quatrelles with drawings that were among the first illustrations to be
reproduced by gravure. But they are not otherwise remarkable. Then there is a curious
series of little books in the eighties with their illustrations reproduced by the Guillaume
half-tone process. *Tartarin de Tarascon* with its curiously photographic illustrations by
Myrbach and Rossi is one of the better examples. Maurice Leloir illustrated a few books
in colour by the new processes, both in France and England. His *Manon Lescaut* of 1889
is one of the best of these, the colour plates curiously reminiscent of stipple-engravings.
There are small black-and-white wood-engravings at the top of each page [263]. Louis
Morin, himself a writer and illustrator of decorative children's books, compiled in 1893
a pretentious volume called *French Illustrators*, which gives a deplorable picture of illustration at this time. The demand seems to have been for books illustrated with reproductions of paintings; and by the side of these pictures Victorian academism has nothing to be
ashamed of.

266. Zola: *Le Rêve*, 1892.
$10\frac{1}{2}'' \times 7\frac{1}{4}''$. Illustrated by
Schwabe

267. Queverdo y Villegas:
Pablo de Segovia, 1882.
$8'' \times 5\frac{1}{4}''$. Pen drawings
by Vierge reproduced by
gillotype, an early form
of line block

Fortunately however there were still a few wood-engravers[1] like Auguste Lepère and at least one publisher, Pelletan, with some notion of how a book should be designed. Although in his early work he imitated Doré's tonal effects, Lepère understood wood far better than Doré, and usually engraved his own designs. He also understood the menace to it of photography which he castigated in the following words: 'Formerly when an engraver had a work to reproduce it was absolutely necessary for him to see it. . . . His art was that of transposition. . . . Photography has come to change all that. It has facilitated the task of the engraver who for the most part has not even seen the work he reproduces . . . a photograph forms a perfect gamut in which nothing can be changed without losing everything. . . . Photography is a reproduction; it becomes a betrayal.' Most of Lepère's best work, his remarkable illustrations to Huysmans, for instance, falls in the next chapter, but his career as an illustrator began in the nineties with a series of books which he illustrated and supervised for the famous bibliophile, Henri Beraldi.

In the nineties, too, occurred a revival of interest in woodcutting (as distinct from wood-engraving). Gauguin[2] claimed to have started this but it seems to have begun quite spontaneously. It was promoted by the magazine *L'Ymagier* which was founded at this time by Remy de Gourmont and Alfred Jarry and which was itself illustrated in this fashion. *L'Ymagier* also sponsored a few curious books like Gourmont's *Phocas* which are quite unlike anything else produced at this time. Jarry's *Ubu Roi* (1896) containing two primitive cuts by the author, was published by another magazine, *Mercure de France*, which was run by Gourmont.

[1] They had their apologist in Félix Bracquemond whose *Étude sur la Gravure sur Bois* was published in 1897.

[2] Gauguin did no work for books and his own illustrated manuscript *Noa Noa* was only published in part as magazine articles in 1897. It was not until 1926 that a facsimile edition appeared in Germany.

Edouard Pelletan, the publisher, was also devoted to the use of wood at the beginning of his career though he recanted later. It was unfortunate that his entry into publishing in 1899 came too late to save the end of the century from being perhaps the poorest period in the whole history of French illustration. His precepts were better than his practice for few of his books are distinguished.[1] He believed in suiting the type-face to the spirit of the text and he thought that illustration should be as closely integrated too. This led him to favour the wood-engraving and later on he came to think the line-engraving preferable to etching for the same reason. 'To illustrate a book', he said, 'is to interpret a text and to decorate a page.' Such dicta, banal though they may sound to us, were among the first formularies of the aesthetic of book illustration and they had a considerable effect on Pelletan's contemporaries. Just as important was his conception of the *beau livre démocratique* in opposition to the limited edition of the bibliophile, though this idea has never really found favour in France.

Nothing has yet been said about the technical works of this century though it was of course a period rich in books with documentary illustrations. But the coming of photo-engraving while it perhaps added to accuracy deprived these illustrations of all their aesthetic importance. There are a few works however like G. Thuret's *Études Phycologiques* (1878) which still use the old methods. This book has exquisite engravings of algae after the designs of A. Riocreux.

AMERICA

American illustration of the nineteenth century derived wholly from Europe. It shows no Mexican or Spanish influences and not until comparatively recently has it struck out in its own direction. It has often been distinguished however by brilliant or novel techniques, from the days of the early steel-engravers of bank-notes down to the amazing reproductive wood-engravings of Timothy Cole after the paintings of the Old Masters. And right at the end of the century we have a last example of nature printing in Denton's wonderful book of 1900 on moths and butterflies.

There is little to record before the nineteenth century. Several books appeared in the previous century with engraved illustrations but none of much distinction. Crude woodcuts adorned the broadsides which appeared frequently throughout the eighteenth century and also the almanacs which began with Benjamin Franklin's *Poor Richard's Almanac* in 1733 and culminated in the Davy Crockett series of 1830–50. *Philip Astley's Modern Riding Master* (1776) is one of the earliest books with illustrations of any promise. In the 1790's two illustrated Bibles appeared but they are of little interest. In the early years of the new century however there was a great deal of line-engraving after English originals for reprints, such as Hayley's *Triumphs of Temper* (?1809) which has plates by Joseph Seymour.

The Birds of America by J. J. Audubon was published in London between 1827 and 1838. It is not therefore strictly an American book but it may be convenient to mention it here because Audubon was an American painter. Sacheverell Sitwell says of this work that it is 'all in all one of the American achievements in the world of art'. The illustrations were aquatinted by the Havells in the best tradition of the English colour-plate book and then hand-coloured, but the American edition which was published in a smaller size in 1860 was

---

[1] Some account of them, particularly of those illustrated by Steinlen will be found in the next chapter.

FLIGHT OF HAGAR.

deep sleep fell upon Abram; and lo, a horror of great darkness fell upon him.

13 And he said unto Abram, Know of a surety ʷthat thy seed shall be a stranger in a land *that is* not theirs, and shall serve them; and ˣthey shall afflict them four hundred years;

14 And also that nation whom they shall serve, ˣwill I judge: and afterward ʸshall they come out with great substance.

15 And ᶻthou shalt go ᵃto thy fathers in peace; ᵇthou shalt be buried in a good old age.

16 But ᶜin the fourth generation they shall come hither again: for the iniquity ᵈof the Amorites ᵉ*is* not yet full.

17 And it came to pass, that ʷhen the sun went down, and it was dark, behold a smoking furnace, and †a burning lamp that ᶠpassed between those pieces.

18 In that same day the Lord ᵍmade a covenant with Abram, saying, ʰUnto thy seed have I given this land, from the river of Egypt unto the great river, the river Euphrates:

19 The Kenites, and the Kenizzites, and the Kadmonites,

20 And the Hittites, and the Perizzites, and the Rephaims,

16

21 And the Amorites, and the Canaanites, and the Girgashites, and the Jebusites.

CHAPTER XVI.

1 Sarai, being barren, giveth Hagar to Abram. 4 Hagar, being afflicted for despising her mistress, runneth away. 7 An angel sendeth her back to submit herself, 11 and telleth her of her child. 15 Ishmael is born.

NOW Sarai, Abram's wife, ᵃbare him no children: and she had a handmaid, ᵇan Egyptian, whose name *was* ᶜHagar.

2 ᵈAnd Sarai said unto Abram, Behold now, the Lord ᵉhath restrained me from bearing: I pray thee ᶠgo in unto my maid; it may be that I may †obtain children by her. And Abram ᵍhearkened to the voice of Sarai.

3 And Sarai, Abram's wife, took Hagar her maid the Egyptian, after Abram ʰhad dwelt ten years in the land of Canaan, and gave her to her husband Abram to be his wife.

4 ¶ And he went in unto Hagar, and she conceived: and when she saw that she had conceived, her mistress was ⁱdespised in her eyes.

5 And Sarai said unto Abram, My wrong *be* upon thee: I have given my maid into thy bosom; and when she saw that she had conceived, I was despised in her eyes: ᵏthe Lord judge between me and thee.

6 ᶦBut Abram said unto Sarai, ᵐBehold, thy maid *is* in thy hand; do to her †as it pleaseth

268. *The Harper Illuminated Bible*, 1846. 13″ × 9″. Wood-engravings by Adams after Chapman

Had been to us companionship,
And, in our lonely life, had grown
To have an almost human tone.
As night drew on, and, from the crest
Of wooded knolls that ridged the west,
The sun, a snow-blown traveller, sank
From sight beneath the smothering bank,
We piled, with care, our nightly stack
Of wood against the chimney-back,—

269. Irving: *Knickerbocker's History of New York*, 1850. 8½″ × 6″. Wood-engravings, after Darley

270. Whittier's *Snow-bound*, 1868. 8½″ × 5¾″. Wood-engravings by Anthony after Fenn

271. Bryant's edition of *Shakespeare*, 1888. 12″ × 9″. An illustration to *Hamlet* after a painting by Darley

lithographed. As in Thornton's *Temple of Flora* the backgrounds of these paintings make them into something much more than mere documentary illustration.

It was however in steel-engraving that America made her most original contribution during the early years of the century. In 1810 Jacob Perkins substituted steel for copper in the engraving of bank-notes and the use of the new material soon spread to Europe. The various devices used by the early engravers of bank-notes were bound to lead to a mechanical manner unlikely to benefit book illustration but nevertheless there were a few interesting books by men like A. B. Durand who were active in both fields. W. C. Bryant's *The American Landscape* (1830) has steel-engravings by Durand, sometimes after his own designs, sometimes after others. It paved the way for a later more famous book by the same author, *Picturesque America* (1872–4), which contains steel and wood-engravings, many of them by English craftsmen. This is a much more accomplished affair and it exemplifies too the delight of the American in his own landscape, just as the earlier topographical works do in England.

Steel-engraving seemed to persist later in America than in Europe and the keepsakes with which it is always associated persisted too. As in England we find the mixed methods of intaglio engraving (scraper, burin, roulette, ruling machine and stipple) which always seem to be associated with a decadent style. But it was in wood-engraving that the real future of American illustration lay and it was a wood-engraver, Alexander Anderson, who can most properly be called its father. We have already met Anderson as an imitator of Bewick. His copy of Bewick's *Quadrupeds* was published in 1802 and it was followed by many imitations of contemporary English work. He also engraved occasionally on type-metal, a practice not uncommon in America at that time. Though there was little that was original in Anderson's enormous output he opened up the way for the facsimile engravings of Felix Darley that enlivened the middle years of the century. But before Darley came the first really ambitious American book, the Harper *Illuminated Bible* of 1846 with 1,600 engravings most of them from designs by J. G. Chapman [268]. This would have been a considerable undertaking anywhere but for a country where book production had not long been in progress it is quite remarkable. The influence of steel-engraving can be discerned in the sharpness of the engraving, all of it in the facsimile style, most of it undertaken by J. A. Adams. Adams also supervised and took part in the printing of his own cuts, and his work marks the beginning of a great improvement in wood-engraving generally. This is one of the few Bibles that is generously and consistently illustrated throughout. Literally every opening has a half-page block, a tiny vignette or a decorated initial, often all three; and the illustration of the Psalms or the Epistles, usually left severely alone, presents no obstacles. The result is however a technical rather than an aesthetic *tour de force*, remarkable in its time and place and expertly printed but with all the limitations of the age. The same applies to the *American Drawing Book* of 1847 which contains wood-engravings by various hands after J. G. Chapman. 'The very perfection of mechanism' says W. J. Linton of this book, but he adds, 'I know no other book like this, so good so perfect in all it undertakes.'

Although his best work was done in wood Darley worked for several other processes. He used lithography for *Scenes in Indian Life* (1843) and steel-engraving in the Household edition of Dickens' works (1861–76); his illustrations for *Rip Van Winkle* (1848) are etchings. But his main fame rests on the Irving books, *Knickerbocker's History of New York* (1850) and the *Irving Sketch Book* of 1848 in which he collaborated with others. Both books contain wood-engravings of incredible fineness and they suggest a mixture of Doré and Cruikshank in their vigour and atmosphere [269]. It was a pity that so much of his work was wasted on ephemeral literature even though his talent was so well suited to the adventure stories in which he specialized. Often he collaborated with others as for instance in Tennyson's *Enoch Arden* (1866), a book in which some of John La Farge's designs appear. The mixture of styles in this book cannot disguise the fact that American illustration has already acquired a flavour of its own, quite distinct from that of England in the sixties. Darley's last important work was in steel-engraving for the Stratford edition of Shakespeare (1886), which he shared with Chappell.

In a few books of this time we find pictures printed from wood-blocks in two colours. Along with the black design a tint was printed from which the high lights had been cut out to give an effect rather like the lithotint. We have already seen this method used in *Gavarni in London* and now we find Darley using it in *A Selection of War Lyrics* (1866). But full colour such as the Baxter process was producing from wood is not to be found at this period in the United States—and perhaps it was no great loss when we reflect on the Victorian taste in colour.

The fifties saw the starting of many illustrated magazines like Harper's, which both helped and hindered book illustration. They increased the demand for wood-engraving and this led to the training of new craftsmen; but they also claimed much good work that would otherwise have gone into books. Ever since then the American illustrated magazine, so far ahead of magazines in most other parts of the world, has usurped some of the functions of the American illustrated book.

The arrival of photo-engraving in the late seventies coincided just as it did in England with a craze for tone among wood-engravers, especially those working for the magazines and newspapers. Perhaps they felt they had to compete with the new processes on their own ground—and in fact engravers like Timothy Cole with his astonishing technique did just this. These men introduced a method of redrawing photographs in line for translation into wood (quite distinct from photographing a specially made design on to wood) which certainly made the best of both worlds. W. J. Linton, a wood-engraver of the old school and the author of *A History of Wood-Engraving in America* protested strongly against the new fashion. He condemned photography on wood because it made the engraver 'forget form and attend only to colour'. And in another interesting passage he says: 'The continual reproduction and imitation of current English books . . . could not but affect the character of American art. . . . When the emasculated style of engraving became popular in England, its popularity was repeated here. I can find no fitter word to characterize a style whose users forgetting that the graver is a tool with which *to draw*, lose all their vigour as artists, content with effects to be obtained by smooth and delicate tones and multiplication of weak because meaningless lines.'

But Linton exempted from his strictures a book called *Insects injurious to Vegetation* (1862) which contained detailed engravings by Henry Marsh. In such work, he thought, fineness was justified. His own work upheld his theories, good honest illustration designed and engraved by himself, undistinguished perhaps and a little sentimental. Some of it may be seen in a book of poems by W. C. Bryant called *The Flood of Years* (1878). Another craftsman approved by Linton was Anthony who himself supervised the production of many of the books in which his work appeared. His little engravings after drawings by Fenn for Whittier's *Snow-bound* (1868) are charming [270].

Linton's protests seem to have been quite unavailing, for Cole and his fellows were greatly admired not only in America but also in Europe. In 1876 was held the Centennial, the first international exhibition, and this marks a turning point in American illustration. American artists could here see what was being done abroad and the results during the last quarter of the century were most noticeable. The influence of Vierge is obvious for instance in the work of Blum and Brennan. But in spite of a more international outlook a national style of engraving now emerged; and it is interesting to compare the American engravings for Doré's last book, *The Raven* (1884), with the illustrations for his previous works cut by French craftsmen. The use of photo-engraving in books could not long be delayed however, and we find illustrators like Howard Pyle who started with line work reproduced by wood (e.g. *The Merry Adventures of Robin Hood*, 1883) going over to painted illustration which had to be reproduced by half-tone or photogravure in such books as *The Autocrat of the Breakfast Table* (1893). This last book has an odd mixture of vignettes which hover between line and tone, and full-page illustrations from paintings to which the gravure process has given a curiously photographic and documentary air [274]. Pyle exerted great influence through his schools for American illustrators, and like so many of his contemporaries in America and Europe he had a penchant for eighteenth-century subjects—in his case eighteenth-century America. He was more unusual in being the author of so many of the books which he illustrated, of which the *Book of Pirates* is well known. But *The Wonder Clock* (1888) with its wood-engravings from his earlier period modelled on Dürer is more distinguished and its use of black letter for the legends gives it a pleasant decorative flavour [272]. His colour work falls into the next chapter.

Pyle's later habit of painting his illustrations was not uncommon during the last decade of the century when many painters turned illustrators [273]. Elihu Vedder in his *Omar Khayyam* of 1884 made an attempt at integration by inscribing the text in panels surrounded by his Pre-Raphaelitish drawings. But unfortunately he had no gift for calligraphy. Bryant's edition of Shakespeare (1888) has gravures after the veteran Darley but he seems to have lost his touch in his old age [271]. It may have been this sort of thing that Linton foresaw when he wrote in 1882 of his contemporaries: 'I find not only an appearance of too great desire to be yet finer than the last scratchiness but the continually increasing subservience of the engraver to, not the knowledge but the ignorance or the capriciousness of the draughtsman.' However he concludes that all this was forced on the engravers by evil reviewers, photographers and painters.

Linton would not have approved of Edwin Abbey either, because of the fineness of his line. Yet Pennell called Abbey 'the greatest living illustrator' while in the same breath he says that his drawings 'have become so refined that no engraving can reproduce every line in them'. Abbey is the chief figure in the American discovery of pen-drawing. Pennell goes so far as to say that 'until 1880 pen-drawing did not begin to flourish as an art in itself'. But when he assigns its beginnings to Menzel in Germany and Fortuny in Spain he is really equating it with the use of facsimile wood-engraving which allowed the pen line to be seen. Hence its success in America where facsimile engraving had reached such a pitch of perfection and where process engraving was shortly to give even more perfect reproduction.

Abbey was born in the same year as Pyle and like him worked mainly for Harpers. In fact he was employed by them for the greater part of his working life and it was they who sent him to England to collect material for an illustrated *Selections from the Poetry of Robert Herrick* which they published in 1882 [275]. This is an elegant book with plenty of white space round the illustrations. The drawings themselves are worthy of their subject-matter but it is a pity that on many of them the poem or part of it is poorly inscribed. In *Old Songs* (1888) Abbey joined forces with Alfred Parsons who provided the small decorations. Like Pyle Abbey had a flair for the seventeenth and eighteenth centuries, but he lacked the force to illustrate Shakespeare effectively. His *Comedies of William Shakespeare* (1896) is pleasant

272. Pyle: *The Wonder Clock*, 1888. $9\frac{3}{4}'' \times 7''$. With wood-engravings by the author

but undistinguished and his pen-drawings are here mixed up with a few paintings. His talent is better suited by *She Stoops to Conquer* (1901), but here the effect of his drawing is spoilt by the use of squared up half-tones surrounded by a thin line. In this series of books produced between 1882 and 1901 we can trace the steady advance of the photo-processes and their effect on the artist's work. The Herrick is wood-engraved most expertly; the illustrations of *Old Songs* are printed from line blocks, well made but lacking something of the the quality of the wood; in the Shakespeare the drawings are reproduced by photogravure,[1] and here paintings begin to intrude; lastly we have the Goldsmith, all printed on coated paper because of its half-tones, with little left to suggest pen-drawing. The speed of this evolution is one of the most remarkable things in the history of printing and it is not surprising that it left its indelible mark on the style of illustration.

America seems to have taken to the photo-mechanical processes much more quickly than any European country and with much less constraint. American illustrators exploited more fully the freedom thus offered, not only in magazines where their advantages are obvious but also in book-art which is notoriously conservative. The comic artist Fougasse has suggested one reason which he applies particularly to pictorial humour, but which holds good for all illustration. Wood-engraving demands a static treatment, and in England this style had taken so firm a hold that it persisted for a long time after the arrival of the new processes. In

[1] At this time photogravure seems to have been much preferred to lithography as a means of reproduction.

America however the wood-engraving tradition had never established itself to the same extent (Linton, it must be remembered, was an Englishman) and the freedom offered by photography was more readily welcomed. Pennell was able to say in 1895 that illustration was more advanced in the United States than elsewhere—but he was not referring specifically to book illustration and the advance of which he spoke was technical rather than artistic.

In the work of Joseph Pennell we find yet another process used, the almost forgotten one of lithography. Although he was an American, Pennell lived and worked for a long time in England and it is by his lithographs for the *Highways and Byways* series of English guidebooks that he is chiefly remembered. Yet these were reproduced in reduced size by photoprocess in the ordinary editions and only in the limited editions were they printed lithographically. Pennell was very versatile but his favourite illustrative medium was pen and ink. He was also one of the few illustrators to write at length about his craft. *Pen-Drawing and Pen-Draughtsmen, Lithographers and Lithography, Etchers and Etchings* are all books of his which in spite of a certain argumentative and dogmatic strain are filled with sound sense. He had none of Linton's distrust of new methods. In fact he said, 'The development of process has made pen-drawing into a distinct art, equal in importance to etching,' and again, 'The draughtsman of today who is most in sympathy with Dürer is he who adapts his work to the methods of Theodore de Vinne in New York or the Guillaume Frères in Paris.' Yet he could see the value of wood-engraving and foretold its survival. 'It has survived the backing of Mr. Linton which at one time threatened to kill it entirely.' (Pennell, it will be seen, was a great admirer of Timothy Cole.) He had too a European outlook (commoner among Americans of that date than amongst Englishmen, oddly enough) which enabled him to discern the influence of Menzel on the wood-engravers of the sixties. On the other hand he was inclined to rate his contemporaries, especially Abbey, too high, and to attach too much importance to technique.

His own technique was beyond reproach and yet most of his work is raportage. Van Rensselaer's *English Cathedrals* (1892) contains good examples of his architectural drawing, some of it in line some in tone. Irving's *The Alhambra* (1896) offers another example of lithographs reproduced by process blocks. And Henry James's *Italian Hours* (1909) contains colour plates printed by the trichromatic process, the first we have met so far. Here there is an attempt to link the colour plates to the monochromes by the use of a dark brown background. But nothing can make the trichromatic plate at home in a book when it is used for original illustration.

Like Pennell Charles Dana Gibson worked on well into the present century but it may be as well to mention him here because the Gibson Girl whom he invented was a vogue of the nineties. He also found his natural expression with pen and ink but he was more of a magazine artist than a book illustrator. The illustrations he produced for the novels of R. H. Davis and Anthony Hope are more like fashion plates than anything we have encountered hitherto, with their impossibly handsome young men and women. The art paper on which they are printed (for they are usually and unnecessarily reproduced by half-tone) completes the illusion. Nevertheless Gibson enjoyed a great reputation and his influence is one of the most potent of the nineties. Another less potent was that of William Morris which worked against the photo-processes and all that Gibson stood for. But Morris revolutionized printing rather than illustration, and his opposite numbers in America were printers like Updike and De Vinne. We find a few books like De Vinne's *Book of Common Prayer* of 1893 and Updike's *Altar Book* of 1896 in the design of which Goodhue played an important part; but the average American publisher with all the new reproductive methods at his disposal saw no need to turn back to the distant past for his inspiration. Another English influence which may be detected at this time was that of Beardsley, a distinct reflection of which may be seen in the early work of W. H. Bradley. But Bradley was more truly a poster-artist than a book illustrator.

One scientific book must be mentioned here on account of its wonderful illustrations. This is S. F. Denton's *Moths and Butterflies of the United States* (1898–1900) in which nature printing makes one of its last appearances. The process gives a curious actuality to the colour plates so that the scales of the insects may almost be felt. The amount of work involved must have been prodigious, for the author mentions that over 50,000 transfers were used; and in addition colour has been applied by hand.

Latin America produced few good illustrated books during this century but a good *Don Quixote* came from Mexico in 1842. This has lithographs by Heredia in the authentic Spanish style—which Spain herself had so strangely failed to bring to the illustration of her greatest book.

GERMANY

The nineteenth century was hardly a great period of German illustration, though it seems to have enjoyed an immense prestige abroad. Illustrators whose names are hardly remembered today like Retzsch, Hoffmann, Schnorr von Carolsfeld and Overbeck (not to mention Menzel) were household names in France and England, their works appearing often in polyglot editions. At the very outset a German invented lithography, but apart from children's books it was hardly exploited at all in Germany for book illustration. There was one illustrator of genius however, and it is especially in the work of Menzel that one can discern what may be called the characteristic feature of German nineteenth-century illustration—a growing nationalism and even militarism. Menzel was born in the same year as Bismarck and it was no accident that he was called upon to illustrate the works of Frederick the Great. However keen his eye for the foibles of the Prussian officer, the Prussian officer still remains the central figure in his major works.

Dürer's *Prayer Book of Maximilian* was lithographed by Strixner in 1808 and was printed in Munich under the supervision of Senefelder himself. It was probably the first use of lithography for reproduction in a book and it 'may be said to have fixed the general character of lithography in Germany, that is as a reproductive not an original art'. Senefelder's own book, *A Complete Course in Lithography*, which was first published in Munich and Vienna in 1818 makes it clear that to begin with the author thought of his invention only as a cheap method of multiplication. German lithographers thereafter seem to have been obsessed with the reproduction of their national works of art. Senefelder's brothers reproduced in 1817 a fourteenth-century manuscript from the Royal Library in Munich which they coloured by hand. A little later Senefelder's successors von Mannlich and Zeller produced a book of Cranach's drawings with printed colour. From then on wherever there was a famous collection of pictures a portfolio of reproductions was almost sure to appear, very finished and elaborate most of them, by expert craftsmen like Piloty, Strixner and Hanfstangl. But none of this skill seems to have gone into original illustration, and very little went into books at all. In *Randzeichnungen zu Goethes Balladen und Romanzen* (1829) we find marginal drawings by Eugen Neureuther reproduced by lithography very much in the style of *Maximilian's Prayer Book* [276]. They are printed in different colours and exhibit a strong calligraphic quality in the flourishes which connect drawing to type. Many of them are charming and they met with Goethe's approval, but they show little appreciation of the possibilities of the medium.

In chromo-lithography for children's books however Germany was soon to set a fashion which pervaded the whole of Western Europe. Senefelder had forecast chromo-lithography and had experimented with it himself but it was J. A. Barth of Breslau who produced in 1816 the first book to be successfully printed by this method, *Pacis Monumentum*, a work which celebrated the peace of 1815. Theodor Hosemann used hand-coloured lithography for his children's books. Ebeling's *Fantaska* (1870) has a distinct charm as have also his Cruikshank-like lithotints for E. T. A. Hoffmann's *Gesammelte Schriften* (1857) [282]. But it was Heinrich Hoffmann, a physician of Frankfurt, whose *Struwwelpeter* popularized true chromo-lithography for children's books. The original title of this book was *Lustige Geschichten und drollige Bilder* and it appeared in 1845. Hoffmann himself drew the pictures and insisted on the lithographer copying them exactly 'to ensure that my amateurish style was not artistically improved and idealized'. Within a few years a Leipzig publisher had produced editions in many foreign languages, some of which are still in print.

Engraved illustration at the beginning of the century was predominantly neo-classical, but neo-classical in the English style of Flaxman rather than the French style of David. It is seen in the outline engravings of Genelli for Homer and Dante (albums of illustrations rather than books because they have no text) and in the etchings of Retzsch for Goethe, Schiller and Shakespeare. Retzsch's *Outlines to Shakespeare* (1828) is appropriately named. It is a sort of polyglot anthology, the oblong plates being printed sideways on an upright page and the text (in three columns, one for each language) also sideways on the facing page. Alfred Rethel who was to produce a much more vigorous manner in his wood engravings for his *Dance of Death* (1848) used the same outline style in his drawings for *The Rhenish Minstrel* by A. von Stolterfoth (1835) but here the medium of reproduction is lithography. Whether it be Genelli's engravings, Retzsch's etchings or Rethel's lithographs the result is equally insipid and devoid of any of the true characteristics of the medium. It is possible that the American Darley's illustrations in outline were inspired by this tenuous style, which seems to have appeared in many countries about this time. Its typical manifestation is in a sort of album of pictures (often a large oblong quarto) based on scenes from a famous play or epic poem. At the beginning of the book is a list of the scenes together with a brief description, but the plates themselves are usually quite separate and are designed to be 'read' more or less consecutively. In this way the illustrator becomes an anthologist and may be said to trespass on the domain of the author.

Menzel has been called (with so many others) the founder of modern illustration and he did in fact wield an immense influence far beyond the borders of Germany. To him has often been attributed the beginning of facsimile wood-engraving and there is no doubt that by his insistence on accurate copying he raised the technical standard everywhere. But he was tied to no particular medium: he started as a professional lithographer, returning to lithography later in life; and he lived long enough to see his drawings reproduced by photo-engraving. He was also a history painter of great reputation. He called himself a disciple of Chodowiecki, but Pennell whose admiration was unbounded ('future generations will look back to him as the Michelangelo of illustration') thinks that Meissonier had a greater influence on his work.

Nevertheless his early work, done during the period when Frederick admired the French, was decidedly of the eighteenth century. By degrees, as the unification of Germany proceeded under Bismarck we can see romanticism being replaced in his work by something quite different, something which has been called rationalism and realism and which is peculiarly modern and German in feeling, although it drew almost exclusively on the past. As Singer has said there was little encouragement for the arts in Germany at that time except in so far as they glorified the past. It was not so much that Menzel traded on this as that he belonged to the intellectual climate that produced this outlook and he accepted it without question.

In 1834 he produced a series of auto-lithographs (he was really the first auto-lithographer in Germany) called *Denkwürdigkeiten aus der Brandenburgisch—Preussischen Geschichte* which shows the trend of his evolution. But his first important book illustrations were for Kugler's *Life of Frederick the Great* (1840) and these wood-engravings were executed in Paris. This suggests that he knew and admired the French illustration of the time; but it seems that he was dissatisfied with the results because he set about training his own school of engravers, Bentworth, Unzelmann, the Vogels and others. These men reached an astonishing degree of proficiency in meeting his requirements which were exacting in the extreme. He insisted on having his lines exactly followed and he frequently used cross-hatching, straining their technique to the utmost. His great work was the thirty-volume edition of the *Life and Works of Frederick the Great* published between 1843–56 by the Berlin Academy of Sciences at the command of Frederick William IV. All the illustrations had to be of a certain specified size, usually in the exacting form of head or tail-pieces. It is Menzel's triumphant acceptance of these limits as well as his sympathy with his author that is the measure of his success. He could not hope in the space allowed him to illustrate his author in the accepted sense but these engravings are far more than decorations. He solved the problem sometimes by a simple symbolism, reminiscent of the Emblem Books and fulfilling the functions both of illustration and decoration [278], sometimes by a simple vignette generally of a battle-scene. The engravings are so closely bound up with the text that it was a mistake to reissue them by themselves as was later done.

This work occupied Menzel for six years but he seems to have found time while it was in progress to illustrate by lithography a three-volume work on the *Uniforms of the Army of Frederick the Great* (1851–7). The lithographs are hand-coloured and the text, also lithographed, was written by hand. The same figures appear again and again in slightly different uniforms and one can only marvel at the life and vitality with which they are endowed by Menzel's art and which just prevents their being monotonous. Another less ambitious book, Lange's *Soldiers of Frederick the Great* (1853) contains hand-coloured wood-engravings, and being less documentary it gave Menzel greater scope for his humorous observation. The attitudes of the soldiers show that he had a keen eye for the absurd side of German militarism.

In later life Menzel did less work for reproduction although he still continued to produce separate lithographs. It seems however as if his pioneer work in perfecting facsimile wood-engraving killed auto-lithography in Germany for the rest of the century. In 1877 he illustrated Kleist's *Der Zerbrochene Krug* in a new style which did not depend on facsimile reproduction. The book contains numerous wood-engraved vignettes based on wash drawings [277] and a few full-page illustrations reproduced by photographs of the original drawings. These show what material the interpretative engraver of the day had to work from; but the combination is not happy and the French edition of this book published in 1884 is a great improvement because all the illustrations are wood-engraved.

One of the major subjects of German nineteenth-century illustration was, as it had been in the earliest days, the Bible; and in the work of Schnorr von Carolsfeld there is something

273. *Omar Khayyam*, 1884. 15½″ × 12½″. Illustrated by Elihu Vedder

274. Holmes: *The Autocrat of the Breakfast Table*, 1893. 8″ × 4¾″. A painted illustration by Pyle

275. *Selections from the Poetry of Robert Herrick*, 1882. 11½″ × 9″. Illustrated by Abbey

276. *Randzeichnungen zu Goethes Balla-
den and Romanzen*, 1829. $16\frac{1}{2}'' \times 10\frac{3}{4}''$.
Lithographs by Neureuther

277. Kleist: *Der Zerbrochene Krug*, 1877.
$15'' \times 11\frac{1}{4}''$. A wood-engraving after Menzel from the French edition of 1884

inconsidéré, qui avait entrepris au delà de ses forces : le succès le fit
regarder comme heureux. Réellement ce n'est que la fortune qui
décide de la réputation : celui qu'elle favorise est applaudi; celui
qu'elle dédaigne est blâmé.

Après l'échange des ratifications,[a] le Roi retira ses troupes de la
Bohême. Une partie passa par la Saxe pour rentrer dans ses pays
héréditaires; l'autre partie marcha en Silésie, et fut destinée à garder
cette nouvelle conquête.

a Il eut lieu à Berlin, le 28 juillet.

278. *Oeuvres de Frédéric le Grand*, 1843–56. 13½″ × 10″. A wood-engraved tail-piece after
Menzel

reminiscent of the German incunabula. *Die Bibel in Bildern* (1853–60) contains over 200
large wood-engravings competently cut[1] and immensely dignified which is more than can be
said for the engravings of Overbeck in *Darstellungen aus den Evangelien* (1846–52). In this
latter book perhaps is the beginning of the sentimental religious picture which is still with
us and which many people today would regard as the norm of Biblical illustration. How different from the miniatures and cuts that came from the Ages of Faith. The illustrations both
of Schnorr and Overbeck had an enormous vogue abroad but Overbeck's influence was
greater.

Schnorr also illustrated, with Neureuther, *Der Nibelungen Noth* (1843) in wood-engravings
which are a sort of graphic counterpart to Wagner's music, and which reflect the same preoccupation with the racial mythology. Here is a romantic medievalism which corresponds to
the French brand of the same date yet with a subtle difference. French medievalism was
frivolous without thought of historical accuracy; the German variety is serious and pains-
taking. Nevertheless these engravings have much to commend them and they are often skilfully combined with borders [283].

With the passing of the halfway mark of the century, the sentimentality which we have
already noted in England becomes ever more intrusive. It is especially noticeable in the
children's books of Ludwig Richter. In Hebel's *Allemanische Gedichte* (1851) for instance
there are enough cherubic children, angels and deathbeds to delight the Victorian heart;
and even Andersen's *Tales* (1870) provided food for sentimentality. In *Hymnen für Kinder*
Richter is competing with Overbeck on his own ground.

1 Some of the them were reproduced as photo-   England this sort of art became the preserve of the
graphs in Keble's *Christian Year* (1875). In   Tractarians.

Wilhelm Busch although he is generally considered a children's illustrator was different in every respect from Richter. He is more commonly compared with Edward Lear. He is often given credit for originating the comic strip, the series of pictures which tells a story without words; but as we shall see this distinction really belongs to the Swiss Rodolphe Toepfer; and most of Busch's books in any case have a short text made up of doggerel composed by himself, although this is not necessary to an understanding of the pictures. His work is as typical of German humour as Lear's is of English. *Max und Moritz, Die fromme Helena* (1872), *Fipps der Asse* (1879) and the rest are delightful in their way and must have appeared very funny after the books of Richter and his contemporaries but they lack the fantasy, the complete craziness of Lear. The drawings are very free and the freedom of the earlier ones is wonderfully preserved by the wood-engraver (the later ones are somewhat spoilt in process reproduction); but their subject-matter, the slapstick and the characteristic *schadenfreude*, palls rather quickly [279].

To Paul Konewka belongs the distinction of popularizing a completely new form of illustration based on the silhouette. The cutting of silhouettes for the purpose of portraiture was of course an old art but the method has seldom been adapted for book illustration although as Lotte Reiniger's scissor cuts have shown more recently it can be extraordinarily effective. It has however strict limitations and the suggestion of background is a great problem. Hence

279. Busch: *Die fromme Helena*, 1872. Wood-engravings after the author's pen-drawings. A reproduction from a later edition of 1892 which shows six drawings to the page instead of two

Kind und Kätzchen.

Es sitzt auf seinem Plätzchen
Ein kleines Mädchen hier
Und lockt zu sich das Kätzchen:
„Komm, Kätzchen, komm zu mir!

Von meiner Milch ein Tröpfchen
Gönn' ich dir gern — auch zwei.
So leck' doch an dem Näpfchen
Und sei doch nicht so scheu!

Du hast ein tüchtig Schlücklein
Getrunken — ei, man sieht's.
Hätt'st wohl auch gern ein Stücklein
Zu essen, gute Mies?

Die Köchin schilt: Die Mäuse,
Die gehn uns über'n Speck.
Geh leise, Kätzchen, leise
Und fang' ein Mäuschen weg.

Doch iß die Maus nicht ganz auf,
Sonst machst du dich noch krank.
Heb' dir den Mäuseschwanz auf,
Den stell dir in den Schrank.

Das wär' wohl eine Freude,
Käm ich zu dir zum Schmaus!
Milch trinken wir alle beide,
Ich aber eß' nicht Maus."

280. Konewka: *Der schwarze Peter*, 1870. 10″ × 7¾″. Silhouettes by the author

it is best used in a decorative fashion and Konewka's books for children such as *Der schwarze Peter* (1870) where the silhouettes serve as head-pieces [280] are better than his more ambitious volumes of extracts from *Faust* and Shakespeare. Nevertheless Konewka is able to make his silhouettes with their calligraphic appendages carry a surprising amount of expression.

The chief German comic paper of this period was *Fliegende Blätter* whose staff Busch joined in 1859; and it was in this paper that much of the best graphic work appeared. Many young artists whose illustrations were to appear in the books of the eighties and nineties started here after studying at the Munich Academy—which also trained several American illustrators of the time. Artists like Schlittgen, who illustrated many of Hackländer's books, produced much competent work which is yet distinctively by magazine illustrators. Simultaneously we meet what Pennell calls 'a school of mystical decorators' influenced by Böcklin and the English Pre-Raphaelites and 'unequalled, unappreciated and curiously unknown outside of their own country'. If they were unequalled it is a sad reflection on the art of the time. The outstanding figure was Max Klinger who is chiefly remembered as a sculptor, but who also produced many etchings and sequences of prints. In the *Amor and Psyche* of Apuleius which he illustrated in 1880 the etchings are pasted within ornamental borders which, as Weitenkampf says, at once removes them somewhat from an organic connection with the book. The *Brahms-Phantasie* of 1894 is an even stranger piece of book-making, for the place of text is taken by passages of music. These are accompanied by copper-engravings and lithographs, the latter somewhat in the manner of Fantin-Latour, showing naked figures in attitudes of despair. Brahms seems to have admired these pictures but it is difficult to see why.

At the very end of the century we find in Germany the two opposing strains that we have already noted in contemporary England and that are associated with William Morris and Aubrey Beardsley. Morris's work was to have an immense effect later on German printing, but in the meantime there is a certain antiquarianism which like Morris's medievalism is a product of the *Zeitgeist*, rather than a derivative of Morris. We can study this best in the work of Joseph Sattler, particularly in the *Geschichte der rheinischen Städtekultur* by Boos (1897–1901), the whole of which he designed. Sattler's illustrations, which are nearly all circular in shape have the same simplicity (not to say crudity) of design as Morris's but they are really much nearer to the drawings of the American Howard Pyle.

The other *fin de siècle* strain is exemplified in *Rolands Knappen* by J. K. A. Musaeus (1898) illustrated by H. Lefler and Josef Urban. This book is as exuberant and over-decorated as Sattler's is restrained. There are borders which not only run round but run into the type and the pages have an appearance of disorganization and mess [281]. Lefler also illustrated Hans Andersen's tale *Die Prinzessin und der Schweinehirt* in 1897 in colour. The text is inscribed and the margins are enormous. The general effect of the flat colours is luxurious if a little decadent.

ausgeathmet. Die Saracenen aber freuten fich ihres Sieges und legten ihrem Heerführer den Ehrennamen Malek al Naffer oder des fiegreichen Königs bei.

In dem Getümmel der Schlacht waren die Schildknappen und Waffenträger des tapferen Roland, indem er fich mitten in die feindlichen Gefchwader warf, von ihrem Herrn getrennt worden und hatten ihn aus den Augen verloren. Da nun der Held fiel und das muthlofe Heer der Franken fein Heil in der Flucht fuchte, wurden die mehrften von ihnen in die Pfanne gehauen. Nur Dreien gelang es aus dem Haufen, durch die Leichtigkeit ihrer Füfse dem Tode oder den Sclavenfeffeln zu entrinnen. Die drei Unglückskameraden flüchteten tief in's Gebirge in unbetretene wüfte Gegenden und fchauten nicht rückwärts auf ihrer ·Flucht; denn fie meinten, der Tod trabe mit rafchen Schritten hinter ihnen her. Von Durft und Sonnenbrand ermattet, lagerten fie fich unter eine fchattige Eiche,

um da zu raften, und nachdem fie ein Wenig verfchnoben hatten, rathfchlagten fie zufammen, was fie nun beginnen wollten. Andiol, der Schwertträger, brach zuerft das pythagorifche Stillfchweigen, welches ihnen die Eile der Flucht und die Furcht vor den Saracenen auferlegt hatte.

›Was Raths, Brüder‹, frug er, ›wie gelangen wir zum Heere, ohne den Ungläubigen in die Hände zu fallen, und welche Strafse follen wir ziehen? Lafst uns einen Verfuch machen, durch diefe wilden Gebirge zu dringen; jenfeits derfelben, meine ich‚ haufen die Franken, die uns ficher in's Lager geleiten werden.‹

›Dein Anfchlag wäre gut, Kumpan‹, verfetzte Amarin, der Schildhalter, ›wenn Du uns Adlerfittiche gäbeft, uns damit über den Wall der fchroffen Felfen zu fchwingen; aber mit diefen gelähmten Knochen, aus welchen Mangel

3

281. Musaeus: *Rolands Knappen*, 1898. 14″ × 19″. Illustrated by Lefler and Urban

282. Hoffmann: *Gesammelte Schriften*, 1857. 6½″ × 4½″. Lithotints after Hosemann

283. *Der Nibelungen Noth*, 1843. 11¼″ × 8¼″. Wood-engravings after Schnorr

318

— Chi mi compra Ranocchino! Chi mi compra Ranocchino! (pag. 40)

284. Holberg's *Comedies*, 1884–8. $11\frac{3}{4}'' \times 9''$. Illustrated by Tegner

285. Capuana: *C'Era Una Volta*, 1883. $10'' \times 6''$. Line blocks after designs by Montalti

OTHER EUROPEAN COUNTRIES

It is surprising how few outstanding books came from countries other than those already mentioned. Their best artists seem to have migrated to Paris and to have practised there. Italy with her great tradition is particularly disappointing. Spain on the other hand exerted an influence on illustration quite disproportionate to her books through two painters who never themselves illustrated a book—Goya and Fortuny. The former used many reproductive processes including aquatint and lithography. The latter is generally held to have started the fashion of pen-drawing which led to facsimile engraving.

Lithography began in Spain under official patronage. Ferdinand VII set up the Royal Printing Establishment in Madrid quite early in the century, and beginning in 1826 it produced the famous *Colleccion Lithographica* of reproductions of Prado pictures. One other great book with lithographic illustrations appeared in Madrid and that was the 1853 edition of *Don Quixote* which may be counted as a Spanish book though it was illustrated by the Frenchman Nanteuil [286]. Here Nanteuil, whom we have already seen as an arch-romantic, had a subject that suited him perfectly and how magnificently he rose to his opportunity. The soft colouring of his lithographs is wholly delightful and the way the background tints run off the page must provide one of the earliest instances of 'bleeding'. No greater contrast could be imagined than the 1898 Barcelona *Don Quixote* with its sticky chromo-lithographs, so gaudy and empty.

For the rest of the century Spain was content to follow the example of France, and her best illustrator Vierge worked in France all his life as we have seen. *Los Españoles pintados por si mismos* (1843–4) is a pale reflection of *Les Français peints par eux-mêmes*. Several other editions of *Don Quixote* appeared, illustrated by processes other than lithography. But Spain's greatest classic has never fared well in the hands of native illustrators. The 1883 edition from Barcelona is well printed but the wood-engravings are mechanical. The 1892 edition printed by Gorchs is the most interesting apart from Nanteuil's because the text is set in 'bastarda' type. But the plates are gravure reproductions of the engravings which appeared in the Ibarra edition of 1780. Their eighteenth-century elegance, fitting as it must have appeared in its period, looks jejune after Nanteuil's lithographs.

The century ended with several examples of the large topographical books so common at this time in all countries, the pictures reproduced by process from paintings or wash drawings. Typical of such books is *La Tierra de Maria Santisima* (1891) which Garcia y Ramos illustrated and Pennell admired. But nothing could be more pretentious and uninspiring to our taste.

Denmark is worth mentioning for one book, Holberg's *Comedies* (1884–8) which Hans Tegner illustrated. During the production of this work a change was made halfway through from facsimile wood-engraving to process engraving; but in spite of this and in spite of too much decoration Tegner's work is quite outstanding. Much of it is of the antiquarian type that we have already met in Abbey and others, but the coloured designs that appear behind the part titles are more original [284]. Tegner seems to have been one of those rare illustrators more expert at creating an atmosphere than at particularizing a scene. Yet most of his work falls into the latter category.

Although Denmark was the birthplace of one of the world's most frequently illustrated books, Hans Andersen's *Tales*, no good illustrated editions were published there until

...que yo procurare no apartarme de estos contornos, dijo D. Quijote.

286. Cervantes: *Don Quixote*, 1853. 9¼″ × 6″. A Spanish edition with lithographs by Nanteuil

Tegner's of 1900. Andersen's first illustrator was Pedersen whose work was not remarkable. But the Tegner edition is a fine piece of typography for its date. Perhaps it is too ponderous for Andersen however; the pictures certainly are.

Martin Disteli was a Swiss illustrator and caricaturist who worked during the early years of the century. He was a contemporary of Grandville and his etchings for A. E. Fröhlich's *Fables* (1829) are in a similar style, although the book preceded most of the French illustrator's. Disteli's etchings for *Münchhausen* of 1840 are among the best illustrations ever done for that much illustrated work. A drawing is here reproduced from the *Heuschrecken Lebenslauf* by Alfred Hartmann (1841) in which Disteli's own special talent will be seen [287].

Rodolphe Toepfer is usually credited with the invention of the comic strip. *Les Amours de M. Vieuxbois, Dr. Festus, Histoire de M. Crépin* and the rest, all produced during the thirties and forties, were called by him *Albums de Caricatures* and they were hardly illustrated books because the text was of no importance by the side of the pictures [288]. But yet they helped to shape the development of the children's book not only during the nineteenth but also in the present century. Wilhelm Busch had obviously looked hard at these books.

At the beginning of the century in Italy Bodoni's influence was still strong and can be seen in a few works like the *Virgil* of 1819 with copper engravings by V. Camuccini or the *Divina Commedia* of 1817–19 illustrated by L. Ademollo and F. Nenci; both of them better examples of typography than of illustration. There were a few large topographical books just as there were at that time in other parts of Western Europe. But the key figure of this period is Bartolomeo Pinelli, a Roman engraver best known for his *Raccolta di Costumi* (1809) which is really only a bound collection of plates. Here we can see that outline style which spread to Germany and later to America. Its association with literary extracts which has already been noted is exemplified by Pinelli's *Orlando Furioso* of 1828–9. By the side of Fragonard's drawings for this book these seem empty indeed.

Manzoni's *I Promessi Sposi* of 1840 has many good wood-engravings after F. Gonin but it is in no way distinguished from French books of the same date. *Pinocchio* which has had such a great influence on children's books, especially in America, and which has been illustrated so often everywhere, gave birth to no outstanding illustrations during this century; the first were by Chiostri but perhaps the best are those of E. Mazzanti in the 1883 edition [289]. After the introduction of photographic processes we find a few books in which an attempt has been made to extract from them something different and characteristic. One of these is Capuana's *C'Era Una Volta* (1883) which A. Montalti illustrated. He used *papier Gillot* and the resulting line blocks have a tonal effect [285]. In the drawings themselves a slightly Oriental flavour is discernible. *La Reginotta* by the same author was illustrated in 1883 by N. Facchinetti who also managed to produce interesting effects from the line block.

The best illustrations in Holland and Belgium appeared right at the end of our period. In Félicien Rops Belgium produced a great etcher but most of his work was done in Paris. *Les Epaves* by Baudelaire (1866) contains some of his best illustrations. Marius Bauer was a Dutch painter who was in love with the East. He ornamented the pages of the Mardrus translation of the *Thousand and One Nights*, once with 3,000 drawings and once with 4,000; but these unfortunately were never reproduced. He also treated two copies of the Bible in this way. His more conventional illustrative work was etched and much of it has a haunting

287. Hartmann: *Heuschrecken Lebenslauf*, 1841. Etchings by Disteli

288. Toepfer: *Histoire de Mr. Jabot*, 1833. $6\frac{1}{2}'' \times 10\frac{3}{4}''$. Lithographs by the author

— 57 —

Povero Merlo, non l'avesse mai detto! Il Gatto spiccando un gran salto, gli si avventò addosso, e senza dargli nemmeno il tempo di dire *ohi*, se lo mangiò in un boccone, con le penne e tutto.

Mangiato che l'ebbe e ripulitosi la bocca, chiuse gli occhi daccapo, e ricominciò a fare il cieco come prima.
— Povero Merlo! — disse Pinocchio al Gatto — perchè l'hai trattato così male?

289. Lorenzini: *Pinocchio*, 1883. $7\frac{1}{2}'' \times 4\frac{3}{4}''$. Illustration by Mazzanti

and numinous quality. It includes Villiers de l'Isle Adam's *Akédysseril* and W. Ritter's *La Jeunesse inaltérable et la vie éternelle* (1897). For Flaubert's *La Légende de Saint Julien l'Hospitalier* he used lithography.

The example of William Morris can be discerned in the decorations of Vondel's *Gysbrecht van Aemstel* (1893–1901) with its heavy borders and its general tendency to over-decoration. It contains however some pleasant plates lithographed in subdued colours by A. J. Derkinderen which redeem the book.

But perhaps the most influential figure of this time was Van Hoytema, an illustrator of children's books, and especially of Hans Andersen. His *Het Leelijke Jonge Eendje* (1893) and his *Twee Hanen* (1898), both by this author, have the alternate pairs of blank pages that always intrigue the child though they result from a perfectly utilitarian technical expedient. These big coloured picture-books remind one of Crane or Caldecott but yet they have a much more modern flavour, and are in fact the forerunners of the twentieth-century revival of autolithography. Not only did Van Hoytema achieve by lithography far more variety of texture than the wood-block could ever give but also he helped to start a minor revolution in the *scale* of illustration, prompted perhaps by the use of the close-up in photography. This will be discussed more fully in the next chapter but the accompanying illustration [290] will help to clarify the point and also to show how this artist forestalled the famous Père Castor series some thirty years later, not only in scale but also in his sympathetic and humorous understanding of the characteristics of animals.

JAPAN AND CHINA

Japan steals the limelight from China during the nineteenth century as indeed she did during the eighteenth. The reason for her greater fame in both periods was of course the

Ukiyoye book and the Ukiyoye colour-print which had such an effect on European art. But, as we have seen, the Shijo and Maruyama schools which were less popular in their appeal also produced fine books, and their best period was from about 1800 to 1820. During these years they produced many delightful albums of impressionistic sketches printed in two or three pale colours. What text there was generally took the form of 'accompanying verses' and was completely subordinate even though it often appeared so close to the drawing that it almost formed part of it. Such a book is *Chikudo Gafu* of 1815 which contains paintings by Ki Chikudo together with verses the author of which is not mentioned [291]. Our reproduction shows how well the impressionists managed the illustration which spread across two pages and how cleverly they contrived the break in the middle. The subject matter was various, flower books and caricatures predominating, and although the colours were flat and rather subdued the effects are astonishingly varied, partly because of the better paper and printing than was enjoyed by Ukiyoye books.

It was the Ukiyoye illustrators and Hokusai in particular who exploited the landscape which Utamaro and the impressionists had brought into the book at the end of the previous century. It was in fact the discovery of the landscape that gave a new life to the waning Ukiyoye movement. Thus in the early years of the nineteenth century Japan had something in common with Western Europe where the topographical book was in great favour. And in spite of the dissimilarities both the Oriental and the Occidental book suffer from the disruptive effect of the scenic illustration. First it demands an oblong area and here the Japanese solution of spreading it across two facing pages is more satisfactory than the European expedient of printing it sideways; secondly and more seriously it tends to turn the book into an album with detachable plates. In Japan however this would hardly have seemed a disadvantage since the *yehon* has always occupied a more honourable position than the illustrated book proper. And in Japan, the double page has always been the basis and the starting point of illustration to a greater extent than in Europe. From which the segregation of the text follows almost inevitably.

Hokusai is one of the chief figures in the whole history of Ukiyoye but his reputation is inflated partly because of his enormous output. His pictures are more widely known than his books but he started as an illustrator [293]. Although he 'matured slowly like Rembrandt' he shows more sophistication than Utamaro even in his early work. He illustrated several books of poems in monochrome such as *Azuma Asobi* (1799) and there are those who think that his best work is in black-and-white. But it is for his work in colour that he is best remembered and this may be seen in the *Mangwa* set of fifteen volumes which appeared between 1817 and 1849, the last five of which are almost entirely his own work. Each volume consists of a preface and a collection of coloured plates and it is in his audacious use of colour that Hokusai broke away from tradition. His followers imitated his style with colouring that became too rich and ornamentation that became too lavish, and so the Ukiyoye decline began. Hokkei was the best known of his disciples and he illustrated many books.

Hiroshige was a later contemporary of Hokusai and shares his reputation as a master of the landscape. But he illustrated books of all types. *Kyoka Hyakunin Isshu* (c. 1815) and *Kyoka Sokon Shu* (c. 1848) are both delightful books of poems, the first a collection of humorous verses. Like Hokusai he sometimes combined several pictures on one page dividing them by thin lines, a practice that can be seen in his *Sohitsu Gafu* (1850) [292]. It is common in Japan to find a caption incorporated in the illustration but Hiroshige sometimes makes his pictures carry a really considerable amount of text. He was a master of the line and wash

Eindelijk barstste het groote ei. „Pie ë piep" zei het jong en kroop er uit. Het is erg groot en leelijk dacht de Moeder, zou het werkelijk een Kalkoen zijn? We zullen het eens gauw proberen.

VII

290. Andersen: *Het Leelijke Jonge Eendje*, 1893. 11″ × 9¼″. Lithographs by Van Hoytema

291. *Chikudo Gafu*, 1815. $13\frac{1}{2}'' \times 11''$. Verses by an unknown author, illustrations after the painter Ki Chikudo

292. Hiroshige: *Sohitsu Gafu*, 1850. $13\frac{1}{2}'' \times 11''$. Woodcuts after Hiroshige

drawing, and it is astonishing to see how much variety his engravers could extract from two simple blocks.

In 1842 there was an edict against popular colour-prints which also affected illustrated books, but it seems not to have interfered with the more elaborate *yehon* or with ceremonial books. A magnificent example of the latter had recently appeared in Osaka, describing a religious festival there, *Konshi-jo-no-Roku* (1831). And Sugakudo's *Sho Utsushi Shijuhachi Taka* (1848) with its colour plates of birds and flowers (quite different from but just as beautiful as any Ukiyoye work) marks a revival of the *yehon*.

When Japan was opened up to foreign influences in 1868 we find many strange stylistic results. China on the other hand had never been closed to the West and it is not uncommon to find Western books illustrated by Chinese artists, who seem to have been able to do this without making any concessions. For instance, there is a delightful Jesuit *Life of Christ* dating from 1637 in which the familiar Biblical pictures have a fascinating Oriental slant. And in the middle of the nineteenth century we meet another missionary venture, *The Pilgrim's Progress*.

But Japan preferred to look at the foreigner through Japanese eyes and the results are often very funny. *Yokohama Kaiko Kenbunshi* (1862–5) is a travel book in which the Westerner will find a fresh view of himself. There is however an interesting edition of La Fontaine's *Fables* published in Tokyo in 1894 under the direction of P. Barboutan and illustrated by 'un groupe des meilleurs artistes de Tokio'. It is quite different from any other La Fontaine but delightful in its way.

Kyosai was the last of the important Ukiyoye artists and his most interesting book was *Kyosai Gwaden* (1884), a history of Japanese art with illustrations in the styles of different artists.

浪裡白跳
張順

293. Hokusai: *Suiko Den*, 1827. 8¼″ × 6″. Woodcuts after Hokusai

8

The Twentieth Century

FRANCE

If any reasons were needed beyond simple convenience for starting each chapter of this history with a new century one can be found in the publication of Verlaine's *Parallèle-ment* by Vollard in 1900. Seldom can the first year of any century have given such a clear indication of what new things were to follow. It is not a question of new techniques. All the processes used in the first half of the present century were used also at the end of the last, and many contemporary French illustrators have gone back to the earlier techniques of etching and engraving. Rather it is a matter of scale. We saw in the last chapter how the Dutchman Van Hoytema in his children's books dared to use the enlarged scale of the close-up [290] rather as if he was reproducing a detail from a picture. Bonnard does the same in *Parallèlement* with infinitely greater artistry. Instead of the whole scene we have the signifi-cant detail from the scene; and these two types of illustration have continued side by side to the present day. It is curious that Bonnard in this case chose the *croquis*, or marginal drawing, a style which always appealed to him. By limiting his space he seems to make the triumph of his method even greater [294].

In their licence as well as in their freedom of drawing these lithographs foreshadowed the development of the French *édition-de-luxe*[1]—though neither quality was new to the printed book. The pink voluptuous lines overflow the margins and trespass on the type, welding the book into more of a unit than it could have been if the illustration had been *hors texte*. But while the illustration is typical of the French twentieth-century book in owing nothing to the past, the typography is no less typical in being wholly traditional. To the magnificent Garamond italic, so well printed by the Imprimerie Nationale, the book owes a great part of its success. But it was only a *succès d'estime*, for the director of the Imprimerie Nationale decided after he had printed it that the subject matter was undignified and he made Vollard return the whole edition (apart from a few copies which had already gone out) so that his imprint might be removed.

Bonnard, a member with Maurice Denis, Vuillard and Maillol of the Nabis, was of all his contemporaries the one man, says Denys Sutton, 'whose feelings for surface decoration and for *mise en page* and whose conception of perspective most approximated to the oriental pattern.' He had already illustrated Nansen's *Marie* (1897) but his drawings were poorly

---

[1] An article in the *Times Literary Supplement* of 20 March 1953 suggests that 50 per cent of all *éditions-de-luxe* depend for sales on their erotic appeal. But 'the illustrations, though frankly erotic, can rarely be said to be openly porno-graphic, though in some cases such tastes are directly catered for by the publication of *éditions-de-tête* with a suite of "rejected plates" in which the artist is allowed a greater licence than is thought appropriate for the integral illustrations themselves'.

De la grâce externe & légère
Et qui me laiſſait plutôt coi
Font de vous un morceau de roi,
O conſtitutionnel, chère!

Toujours eſt-il, regret ou non,
Que je ne sais pourquoi mon âme
Par ces froids penſe à vous, Madame
De qui je ne sais plus le nom.

294. Verlaine's *Parallèlement*, 1900. $11\frac{1}{2}'' \times 9\frac{1}{4}''$. Lithographs by Bonnard

reproduced by line blocks and the quality of the work suffers. But in 1895 Vollard had published a set of separate lithographic prints which revealed Bonnard's brilliance and Vollard's
perspicacity. For it is Vollard who is the key figure in French illustration for the first forty
years of the twentieth century. He was of course a dealer in pictures and prints as well as a
publisher and he had the distinction of arranging the first one-man show of Cézanne's pictures in 1895. It was on the proceeds of his picture sales that he published books, and books
remained his chief love. 'Little by little,' he says in his autobiography, 'the idea of becoming
a publisher, a great publisher of books, took root in my mind.' He brought the same principles to the commissioning of illustrations as he did to that of prints. 'My idea', he said,
'was to obtain engravings from artists who were not engravers by profession.' What was
even more unusual was his partiality for younger, comparatively unknown painters. He was
not well read and his interest lay definitely in illustration. But although he briefed his artists
so carefully and must often have driven them to distraction, it is said that once an artist
started work Vollard never interfered with his interpretation. He was exacting in the choice
of paper and in typography; the printers who worked for him deserve great credit especially
Auguste Clot, the lithographer. But when a book was finished he often had a strange reluctance to publish it, perhaps because of his desire for absolute perfection. Flaubert's *La
Tentation de Saint Antoine*, for instance, which Odilon Redon illustrated with lithographs
and wood-engravings, was not ready until long after the artist's death in 1916 and then only
'exhibition copies' were on show in 1938. As a result of all this more than twenty books were
in preparation at the time of Vollard's death in 1939 and some of them have only recently
been completed. Rouault spoke truly when he wrote in his *Miserere* preface, 'If injustice has
been done to Ambroise Vollard let us remember that he had great taste and a passion for
making beautiful books without haste, taking such time as was needed; but it would have
taken three centuries to have completed the works which he wanted, without considering
our human limitations, to entrust to the artist.'

Parallèlement was followed in 1902 by *Daphnis et Chloé*, also with lithographs by Bonnard.
This time the format is more conventional but the drawings are still distinguished by an
exquisite lightness that only lithography could have rendered. They have, too, a numinous
quality which is lacking in the earlier book and which provides the greatest possible contrast
with Maillol's *Daphnis et Chloé* of 1937. What is perhaps even more remarkable is the fidelity
with which Bonnard sticks to his text. He proved, if proof were needed, that the painter
could meet the professional illustrator on his own ground and often beat him; and this was
demonstrated over and over again by the artists whom Vollard subsequently employed,
among them Redon, Denis, Chagall, Picasso, Rouault, Segonzac and Dufy. Not only were
these men easily able to adapt themselves to the demands of reproduction; they also excelled
in illustrating a text without fear of being thought 'literary' although many of them were at
one time or another abstract painters. Picasso in fact took the bold step of combining in one
book, *Le Chef d'œuvre inconnu*, representational etchings and cubist wood-engravings [307].

Both his Bonnard books being financial failures, Vollard turned from lithography to
wood-engraving in an attempt to interest the bibliophiles of the day. *L'Imitation de Jésus-
Christ* (1903) has wood-engravings by Maurice Denis, *Gaspard de la Nuit* (1904) by Armand
Seguin and *Fleurs du Mal* (1905) by Emile Bernard. In the first of these three Tony Beltrand,
who engraved Denis's designs, produced an effect from the wood that might have passed for
lithography [302], quite different from the meticulous work of the contemporary American
reproductive engravers. More brilliant still are the wood-engravings which Jacques Beltrand
produced after Denis's designs for Verlaine's *Sagesse* in 1911, also published by Vollard.

295. Descaves: *Barabbas*, 1914.
8″ × 6″. Illustrated by Steinlen

In these the engraver is more even than a collaborator. Often Denis gave coloured sketches to his engravers to work from and his best illustrations are coloured wood-engravings such as those for Dante's *Vita Nuova* (1907) or the superb *Fioretti* of St. Francis of Assisi (1913). In a much later book however, Francis Thompson's *Poems* (1936), he used colour lithographs instead, returning to wood for the coloured illustrations in Claudel's *L'Annonce faite à Marie* (1940).

Coloured illustration is of course a natural result of so many painters working for books and it is found in many Vollard books of this period. It is found also in books from other publishers for others were beginning to follow his example in employing painter-illustrators. No one examining the books of this period can fail to be struck by the growing prevalence of the limited *édition-de-luxe* in France. Nearly every illustrated book of any pretensions produced during the century carries a *justification de tirage*, giving the limits of the edition, the type of paper and so on. One of the causes of this was the spread of bibliophile societies, the beginning of which we saw in the last chapter. In the early years of the present century were founded *Le Livre contemporain*, *Les Amis du livre moderne* and others, a phenomenon almost wholly peculiar to France. Between the wars it has been estimated that these societies were responsible for almost half the *éditions-de-luxe* published. Lepère, an illustrator who also appeared in the preceding chapter, worked particularly for the bibliophile societies. His wood-engravings for Huysmans's *La Bièvre* (1901) [303] and for Erasmus's *Éloge de la Folie* (1906), excellent though they are, seem to belong more to the nineteenth than to the twentieth century. Those for the Erasmus are printed in two or three colours on the chiaroscuro principle. It is almost unbelievable that they should have appeared six years after *Parallèlement*; and yet Lepère was a forerunner of the twentieth-century *peintres-graveurs*.

All this time the publisher Edouard Pelletan, who had considerable influence during the first decade of the century, was continuing to produce his conception of *le beau livre démocratique* but even he limited his editions. Books of his were illustrated by Vierge and Grasset but his best illustrator was the Swiss Steinlen, an artist with a distinct feeling for the printed page. For Anatole France's *L'Affaire Crainquebille* (1901) he produced some very fine, detailed wood-engravings. Later his drawings were reproduced by line blocks as in Richepin's *La Chanson des Gueux* (1910) where they were retouched by the burin, or *Barabbas* by L. Descaves (1914). In the latter the chalk texture has been very skilfully preserved [295], making one wonder why so few of the painter-illustrators used process. Perhaps their distrust was founded on the poor printing of the average trade edition of the time. *Barabbas* is not poorly printed but then, in spite of its line blocks, it is not really a trade edition for it too is limited. The impetus given by Gillot and other early process engravers to inexpensive illustration seems to have been lost and the autographic methods now occupy the limelight. Sometimes line blocks are used in a cheap edition to reproduce wood-engravings made for an earlier limited edition; this was done for *L'Enchanteur pourrissant* which Derain illustrated but here, one feels, the mechanical process is only used *faute de mieux*.

In the 1905 edition of *Fleurs du Mal* Emile Bernard returned to the woodcut (as distinct from the wood-engraving) which Gauguin had recently revived. But it was Derain and Dufy who exploited it to the full. The *Fauve* movement was now in full swing and these two were in the middle of it. The *Fauvists* were pre-eminently colourists and it may seem strange that two painters who relied so much on colour should be satisfied with a monochrome technique.

296. Apollinaire:
Le Bestiaire, 1911. Woodcuts by Dufy

But it was the simplification of the woodcut that appealed to Derain and Dufy, a crudity and directness that accorded well with the 'wildness' of the *Fauvists*. In 1909 Derain illustrated *L'Enchanteur pourrissant* and in 1911 Dufy illustrated *Le Bestiaire*, both by Apollinaire [296]. In both these books the pictures have the character almost of the chap-book cut.

Neither Derain nor Dufy however limited themselves to the woodcut (though it has always remained Derain's favourite) for one of the most astonishing things about contemporary French illustrators is their versatility in the matter of techniques, and the way they are able to vary their style to suit the chosen method. Derain chose lithography for his *Fables* of La Fontaine, prepared by Vollard but not published until 1950. He illustrated Oscar Wilde's *Salome* for the Limited Editions Club of America in 1938 with gouache drawings on black paper and these were reproduced in Paris by *pochoir*, also on black paper. This bold experiment was successful and the pictures in spite of their technique have the antique quality of the text [305]. The *Satyricon* of Petronius (1952) had black-and-white etchings. But in his best book, *Pantagruel* (1946), he returned to the woodcut, this time in colour. The colour was however reproduced in a peculiar way, for he used one block only for each picture and painted it with different colours which were then printed simultaneously. The result is reminiscent of the old playing-cards, and the colour-printing has a special texture all its own [304].

Dufy, for his illustrations in the *Madrigaux* of Mallarmé (1920), used lithographs coloured by *pochoir*, a French stencilling technique that here produces the most lovely fresh results unobtainable by any other means. The illustrations of many French books of this century have been coloured by *pochoir* though the method has been used very little elsewhere. It is of course no more a printing process than the hand-colouring used in the English topographical books a hundred years before; but it is a delightful way of reproducing a water-colour if water-colours must be used for illustration. For Montfort's *La Belle Enfant* (1930) Dufy produced a very large number of etchings, their fineness and delicacy as different as possible from the coarseness and strength of his wood-cuts. This was another Vollard book and one of Dufy's best. With the farcical text of Daudet's *Tartarin de Tarascon* which he illustrated in colour lithography in 1936 one feels he has little sympathy but yet he has produced an effective personal interpretation. The *Aphorismes* of Brillat-Savarin, which was published in 1940, has etchings and as in *La Belle Enfant* they often form a border for the type. Seldom can etchings and type (which the purists cannot reconcile) have lived in such calligraphic harmony together. Finally came *Vacances Forcées* by R. Dorgelès published after Dufy's death in 1956. In this remarkable book Dufy's water-colours are reproduced with uncanny skill by Jacques Beltrand as wood-engravings, retaining all their spontaneity of touch and freshness of colour [297].

In 1911 Vollard produced another kind of illustrated book of a type that has since become very popular. This was *Lettres de Vincent van Gogh à Emile Bernard* and it contained reproductions of the artist's paintings and drawings. Similar books followed, written by Vollard himself on Renoir and on Cézanne. Between 1934 and 1936 he made an interesting experiment, using various monotypes of Degas to illustrate three books for which of course they had never been intended. *Mimes des Courtisanes* by Pierre Louys (1935) is the best known and the most successful, the aquatints by Maurice Potin after Degas being quite exquisite. Somewhat similar in its genesis is Mirbeau's *Le Jardin des Supplices* (1902) for which Vollard used drawings by Rodin not originally intended for illustration. The combination of nude drawings and erotic text is one which few French publishers can resist; but books made in this way are seldom aesthetically successful. Rodin also did three series of lithographs

Je souffrais à me mordre les poings devant
cette boîte à cadran emportée de Paris, le jour de
la grande fuite, et qui, de soir en soir, au hasard
des étapes, ne m'avait plus soufflé que des mots
d'épouvante. Une seule fois, je me suis endormi

297. Dorgelès: *Vacances Forcées*, 1956. 13″ × 10″. Wood-engravings by Beltrand after Dufy's
watercolours. Editions Vialetay

before 1900 for Flaubert's *Tentation de Saint Antoine* which were never produced in book form and a remarkable set of marginal drawings for Baudelaire's *Fleurs du Mal* which were later reproduced in facsimile in 1918.[1] The last book in which his illustrations appeared was the posthumous *Élégies amoureuses* of Ovid (1935) where they took the form of wood-engravings.

It has been necessary, in order to trace the history of artists like Dufy and Derain, to trespass into the years after the First World War. In fact Dufy and Derain exemplify excellently the general development which took place and which broadly distinguishes the years after the First World War from those before. During the first twenty years of the century Vollard was the key figure but afterwards, although his importance hardly diminishes, his battle was won and the work of the *peintre-graveur* is more or less taken for granted. Vollard's was not only a battle against prejudice, it was also to some extent the old struggle between illustration and decoration, between the freedom demanded by the painter and the purist ideals of Pelletan.

We return to Bonnard in whose work that freedom is embodied and who, if it can be said of anyone, started all this. After his triumph in *Daphnis et Chloé* he forsook lithography for the humble line block in Renard's *Histoires naturelles* of 1904, and in Mirbeau's *La 628–E8* published in 1908. Neither of these books falls into the *édition-de-luxe* class and although they are less spectacular than his early Vollard books they are none the less successful. In *La 628–E8* as in the earlier *Marie* he used the 'croquis marginal' which had always fascinated him and which had found its most triumphant expression in *Parallèlement*, printed in a second colour. After that however there was nothing of importance until 1924 when he illustrated Mirbeau's *Dingo* for Vollard with etchings.[2] His last book for Vollard was the superb *La Vie de Sainte Monique* of 1930, in which he surpassed himself. It contains etchings, lithographs and wood-engravings but in spite of this mixture it makes a satisfying whole. Finally we have *Le Crépuscule des Nymphes* by Louÿs (1946) in which he returns to lithography.

Maillol, like Rodin, was a sculptor who illustrated books but in a very different manner. He used the woodcut, which, for one used to relying in his work on line rather than colour, was a wise choice. He supervised the printing himself, he even made the paper, but he did not actually cut the blocks which were used in his first book, Virgil's *Eclogues* (1926). This task was undertaken by Eric Gill, the English engraver, who also cut the initials, and the book was printed at the private press of Count Kessler in Weimar. The prospectus for this work reminds one of William Morris's influence in Germany for it lays great stress on 'unity of type, illustrations and paper' such as distinguished the medieval manuscript. We never find such sentiments coming from a French publisher.

Maillol's next book Verhaeren's *Belle Chair* (1931), was less ambitious though it contained lithographs as well as woodcuts, and it was published in France. But the next two came from Lausanne, which was soon to rival Paris as a centre for *éditions-de-luxe*. Ovid's *L'Art d'aimer* (1935) containing lithographs and woodcuts and the *Pastorales* of Longus (1937) containing only woodcuts are 'pure masterpieces', says Guignard, 'which recall by their technique the best work of Renaissance artists under the spell of antique beauty'. These two books were printed by the Gonin brothers by hand and the presswork leaves something to be desired. In 1938 however Vollard commissioned his first Maillol book, *Livret de Folastries*

---

[1] Bonnard also left a wonderful set of marginal drawings for La Fontaine's *Fables* but these have not yet been published.

[2] Two children's books of his are given on p. 356.

LES GÉORGIQUES.

Les vins plus délicats, les victimes plus belles,
Offre des vœux nouveaux pour des moissons nouvelles;
Choisis pour temple un bois, un gazon pour autel,
Pour offrande du vin, et du lait, et du miel.
Trois fois autour des blés on conduit la victime;
Et trois fois, enivré d'une joie unanime,
Un chœur nombreux la suit en invoquant Cérès:
Même, avant que le fer dépouille les guérets,
Tous entonnent un hymne; et couronné de chêne,
Chacun d'un pied pesant frappe gaîment la plaine.

SI ce culte pieux n'obtient pas de beaux jours,
La lune de l'orage annonce au moins le cours;
Et le berger connoît par d'assurés présages
³⁰ Quand il doit éviter les lointains pâturages.
Au premier sifflement des vents tumultueux,
Tantôt, au haut des monts, d'un bruit impétueux
On entend les éclats; tantôt les mers profondes
Soulèvent en grondant et balancent leurs ondes;
Tantôt court sur la plage un long mugissement,
Et les noires forêts murmurent sourdement.
Que je plains les nochers, lorsque aux prochains rivages
Les plongeons effrayés, avec des cris sauvages,
Volent du sein de l'onde; ou quand l'oiseau des mers
Parcourt en se jouant les rivages déserts;
Ou lorsque le héron, les ailes étendues,
De ses marais s'élance et se perd dans les nues!

QUELQUEFOIS, de l'orage avant-coureur brûlant,

64

LIVRE PREMIER.

Cui tu lacte favos et miti dilue Baccho;
Terque novas circum felix eat hostia fruges
Omnis quam chorus et socii comitentur ovantes,
Et Cererem clamore vocent in tecta: neque ante
Falcem maturis quisquam supponat aristis
Quàm Cereri, tortâ redimitus tempora quercu,
Det motus incompositos et carmina dicat.

ATQVE hæc ut certis possemus discere signis,
Æstusque, pluviasque, et agentes frigora ventos,
Ipse Pater statuit, quid menstrua luna moneret,
³⁰ Quo signo caderent austri, quid sæpe videntes

65

298. Virgil: *Les Géorgiques*, 1950. 12¾″ × 9½″. Woodcuts by Maillol. *Gonin*

à Janot parisien and here of course the printing is immaculate. But the illustrations are etchings instead of woodcuts and this seems to run counter to Maillol's genius, as do the lithographs for Lucian's *Dialogue des Courtisans* which appeared in 1948. In his illustrations for Verlaine's *Chansons pour elle*, which he published himself in 1939, Maillol returns to his first love, the woodcut. And at his death in 1945 he had in preparation Virgil's *Les Géorgiques* but this book was not published until 1950, three years after Segonzac's with which it offers an interesting comparison [298].

Marie Laurençin illustrated some charming books in colour during the twenties, using various processes. *La Tentative Amoureuse* by Gide (1921) contains coloured wood-engravings after her water-colour drawings and *L'Adroite Princesse* by L'Héritier de Villandon (1928) coloured lithographs. Dumas' *Camille* was printed in England in 1937 for the Limited Editions Club of America and here her water-colours are reproduced by stencil, giving an effect of richness that could hardly be obtained in any other way. Even more delightful because typographically superior is Katherine Mansfield's *The Garden Party* published in England in 1939 but printed in Italy at the Officina Bodoni [306]. The exquisite pastel colours of the lithographs perfectly suit their subject-matter. But it is in the subject-matter that the limitations of the artist appear, because practically every picture in the book is one of women's heads. At first sight the illustrations (and this applies especially to her black-and-white ones in other books) have a nineteenth-century air. But on closer acquaintance one finds a timelessness in them which reminds one of the poetry of Walter de la Mare.

Vuillard, although he produced one of Vollard's most famous sets of coloured lithographs in 1899, the *Paysages et Interieurs*, seems never to have illustrated until 1935 and then he only contributed six lithographs to Jean Laroche's *Cuisine*. But they are delightful pictures and apart from them the book is worth mentioning because with its different coloured papers

giboyeux. J'aime ses petits ports de pêche, ses grands ports commerciaux, ses villages, ses bourgs et ses villes. Partout, j'y vois couler la vie plus abondante — plus facile qu'ailleurs, me semble-t-il — naissant comme par miracle, presque sans effort, d'une terre

299. Reuillard's *Grasse Normandie*, 1926. $7\frac{1}{2}'' \times 5\frac{1}{2}''$. Line blocks from Vlaminck's lithographs

it is exceptionally well produced and also because it is an experiment in co-operative illustration such as was common in the French books of the two preceding centuries. Besides Vuillard's lithographs there are in *Cuisine* six fine etchings by Segonzac and six less impressive copper-engravings by Villeboeuf.

Vlaminck like Derain and Dufy was a *Fauvist* painter but he started to illustrate books much later than they. He followed their example in beginning with woodcuts—in Vanderpyl's *Voyages* of 1920—but later he went over to lithography, for instance in Duhamel's *Les Hommes abandonnés* of 1927 which is perhaps his best book. But mention must be made of Reuillard's *Grasse Normandie* (1926) because it is one of the very few books described in this section which was first produced in an ordinary trade edition (though a limited edition was published at the same time). In this unpretentious volume line blocks do ample justice to Vlaminck's drawings and the result is the very best sort of guide-book [299].

Matisse was of course the leader of the *Fauve* movement and he remained a great colourist all his life. Yet coming, like Vlaminck, to book illustration comparatively late he became a great graphic artist in black-and-white also. 'Je ne fais pas de différence entre la construction d'un livre et celle d'un tableau,' he said. His first important book was Mallarmé's *Poésies* which Skira published in Lausanne in 1932. Here the etchings, refined to the minimum number of lines, often fill the whole page and the margins as well. The effect of the double-page is more carefully calculated than was usual with the painter-illustrators. 'Je

300. Montherlant's *Pasiphaë*, 1944. 14¼" × 9¾". Linoleum engravings by Matisse. *Fabiani*

compare', says Matisse, 'mes deux feuilles à deux objets choisis par un jongleur.' He is pre-occupied with the balance of black-and-white, of type and drawing in all his books. In the Mallarmé the white is provided by the tenuous etchings but for H. de Montherlant's *Pasiphaë* (1944) he made engravings on linoleum, simple white lines on a black ground, which turn the type page into a white area [300]. Matisse had a great opinion of lino, a material which we have not so far encountered and which even now is disdained by most artists. 'La gravure sur lino', he said, 'est un vrai moyen prédestiné au peintre-illustrateur.' And he warns against its use as a cheap substitute for wood, pointing out that it has quite a different character.

Matisse's concern for the balance of text and illustration appears also in *Jazz* (1947). Here the text is written out in the artist's own hand, its purpose being, as he says, to interrupt the brightly coloured plates which are stencilled reproductions of paper-cuts. The hand-written text is found again in his last book, the *Poèmes de Charles d'Orléans* (1950) where it is accompanied by coloured chalk drawings and calligraphic borders, the whole being litho-graphed. (Matisse seems to have regarded lithography purely as a method of reproducing freehand drawings.) The fashion in hand-written texts has not been an altogether happy one though it has been followed by Picasso himself.

So we come to Picasso who has been called a born illustrator. In addition he is a key figure, because his working life has spanned almost the whole of our period and he has been a leader in nearly all the great twentieth-century movements in French painting, helping to bring them into the book. He has shown great versatility in his use of media, for he has been equally at home with etching, aquatint, lithography, wood-engraving and the humble line block. His output of prints (apart from book illustration) has been enormous, for in spite of his immense reputation he has never hesitated to work for reproduction. But it is interest-ing that most of his graphic work is as Philip James has said 'in a traditional classical style to which he has always reverted from time to time as a curb upon his innate romanticism and the turbulent baroque character of his draughtsmanship'. Much of it too is in black-and-white.

Nearly all his best work, like that of his contemporaries, has appeared in limited editions simply because publishers of *éditions-de-luxe* were the ones to commission him. In his early days he contributed a few etchings to some books of Max Jacob's like *Saint Matorel* (1911), one of the very first to have cubist illustrations; and this was followed by a steady flow mostly with etched illustrations. It was not until 1931 however that he was given a task worthy of his talent for in that year he produced two remarkable books, one for Skira and the other for Vollard. Ovid's *Métamorphoses* has many remarkable etchings and Balzac's *Le Chef d'œuvre inconnu* has etchings *and* wood-engravings. Curiously enough the etchings are classical in style while the wood-engravings (executed by Georges Aubert) are some classical, some cubist and some calligraphic. But the plan of the book is such that there is no clash and its execution under Vollard's care makes this 'one of the world's most beautiful books' [307].

Picasso became interested in lithography in 1919 but he has used it mainly for separate prints until quite recently. Etchings appeared in Aristophanes' *Lysistrata* which he illus-trated in 1934 for the Limited Editions Club of America; and line blocks were used (very successfully) in Eluard's *Les Yeux fertiles* (1936). His sugar aquatints for Buffon's *Histoire naturelle* (1942) however could almost pass as lithographs so varied is the interplay between grey and black obtainable by this technique [308]. It was Roger Lacourière who introduced it to Picasso, showing him how to make two drawings in sugar, one for the grey and a subsequent one for the black. Others have pointed out the subordination of the text in this book which is heralded by the title-page 'Picasso. Eaux-fortes originales pour les textes de Buffon' and how the pretence is only kept up for the first half of the book, the remainder having no text at all, only aquatints. Sabartés in his *Picasso, portraits et souvenirs* says, 'When a book was to be illustrated by him one could always find something among the abundance of his output provided one was not too exacting; his work has so much merit and gives so much value to the book that nothing else wants. The aquatints for the Buffon were done as free designs. Afterwards the publisher sought in the text for what was best suited to each plate. When the book was finished the text seemed to have been written as a commentary on the plates. That is why Picasso's name appeared at the head of the title-page.'

The process is carried a step farther in Reverdy's *Le Chant des Morts* and Gongora's *Vingt Poèmes*, both published in 1948, the first with lithographs and the second with sugar aquatints. In these books the text is still further subordinated by being reproduced in a facsimile of hand-writing, Reverdy's in the first and Picasso's own in the second. In neither case is the writing good or even particularly legible and it is often defaced by erasures. There is nothing specifically lithographic in the blobs of colour that surround Reverdy's page but there is a curious reminiscence of the illuminated manuscript in the way those blobs are sometimes placed to fill up a short line of text. The powerful aquatints in Gongora are a very different matter and in this book again there are calligraphic marginal decorations, this time engraved in drypoint and in quite a different style from the aquatints. Both these books were published in very small editions and some later books have been even more severely limited. Roch Grey's *Chevaux de Minuit* (1956) for instance, to which he has contributed drypoints and line-engravings, was published in an edition of 68 copies. In *Hélène chez*

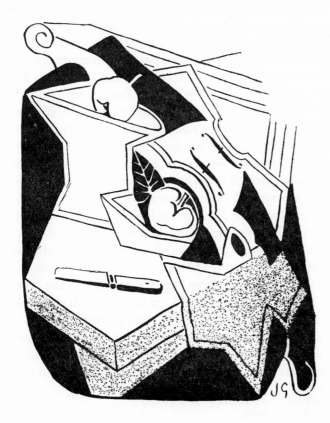

301. Radiguet: *Denise*, 1926.
$10\frac{3}{4}'' \times 7\frac{1}{2}''$. Lithographs by
Gris. *Galerie Simon*

Archimède by Suarès which was not published until 1955 wood-engravings appear which were commissioned from Picasso by Vollard at a much earlier date and cut by Aubert. This is a magnificent book.

Not all the great painters of this period were able to illustrate books with such felicity as Picasso. Fernand Léger's few books are unconvincing, from the wood-engravings for André Malraux's *Lunes en papier* (1921) down to the egregious *Cirque* (1950) with its colour lithographs and its text which, following the prevailing fashion, Léger has composed and written out himself.

It is curious to reflect that although twentieth-century France has seen many diverse artistic movements—Fauvism, Cubism, Dada, Surrealism—few of them have engendered any great illustration. We have noted one or two books into which cubism was introduced by Picasso. There are also one or two illustrated by Braque such as Erik Satie's *Le Piège de Méduse* (1921) with its three-coloured wood-engravings and Reverdy's *Une Aventure Méthodique* (1949). Braque's later work such as the etchings for Hesiod's *La Théogonie* (1955) which was originally commissioned by Vollard is in a different class. It was Juan Gris however who most successfully adapted the cubist formulae to the book, achieving abstract illustration without a hint of decoration in the etchings of Tzara's *Mouchon de Nuages* (1925) and the lithographs of Radiguet's *Denise* (1926) [301]. Dada was even more sterile and it was hardly to be expected that a movement which set out to be anarchic could achieve success in so traditional a form as the book. The few books which appeared under its auspices will be discussed under the heading of Switzerland.

Surrealism on the other hand is illustrative by its nature and one would have expected to find its influence in many contemporary books. Chagall who is sometimes regarded as the father of Surrealism can hardly be regarded as a Surrealist illustrator in the sense that Chirico was in such books as Apollinaire's *Calligrammes* (1930) and Cocteau's *Mythologie* (1934),[1] both with lithographs; and in 1934 Dali did some fearsome Surrealist etchings for Lautréamont's *Les Chants de Maldoror* [309]. Then there are some interesting experiments by Max Ernst and Man Ray. The former illustrated some books with collages, e.g. R. Crevel's *Mr. Knife, Miss Fork* (1931) and the latter used photomontage in Eluard's *Facile* (1935).

The two artists who suffered most from Vollard's habit of procrastination (a habit which became more marked towards the end of his career) were Rouault and Chagall. Their books too are among the greatest that Vollard ever published. Michael Ayrton has said that 'they are both capable of exactly the same force of expression in an illustration between the pages of a book as in an easel picture, and their approach is consistent to both'. Neither is afraid of being labelled 'literary'. Rouault's etchings and wood-engravings for Vollard's own *Les Réincarnations du Père Ubu* (1933) lifted that comic figure to the level of real drama. But in the *Cirque de l'Etoile Filante* (1938) for which he wrote his own text and in André Suarès's *La Passion* (1939) he found worthier subject-matter [310]. Of the *Passion* Vollard himself said 'On n'a jamais fait de tels livres et on n'en fera plus', and this might well have been said of their size as well as their quality. Rouault needs a large page for he relies on the broad effects of the stained-glass window, and for the same reason he is happiest with colour. In most of his books he employs a mixture of processes, generally sugar aquatints printed in colour and wood-engravings; it is said that the wood-engravings needed a specially constructed press to do them justice and this was provided by Vollard. Rouault's great *Miserere* etchings, originally intended to accompany a text by Suarès, were finally published in 1948

[1] This book has a hand-written text (it cannot be called calligraphic) by the author, anticipating a contemporary French habit.

CHAPITRE XXIV.

QU'IL NE FAUT POINT ÈTRE CURIEUX DE LA VIE DES AUTRES.

JÉSUS-CHRIST.

1. Mon fils, gardez-vous bien d'ètre curieux et de vous abandonner à de vaines inquiétudes.

Que vous importe que ceci ou cela se soit fait? suivez-moi.

LA BIÈVRE   13

normes foudres, de formidables coudrets, emplâtrés de chaux, tachés de vert de gris, de cendre bleue, de jaune de tartre et de brun loutre; des piles de tan

soufflent leur parfum acéré
d'écorce, des bannes de cuir

302. *L'Imitation de Jésus-Christ*, 1903. 12″ × 9″.
Wood-engravings after Denis

303. Huysmans: *La Bièvre*, 1901. 11¼″ × 7½″.
Wood-engravings by Lepère

304. Rabelais: *Pantagruel*, 1946. $13\frac{1}{2}'' \times 1$
Coloured woodcuts by Derain. *Skira*

305. Wilde's *Salome*, 1938. $11'' \times 7\frac{3}{4}''$. Illu
trated by Derain. *Limited Editions Club*

to No. 26 she thought of those four flights of stairs. Oh, why four flights! It was really criminal to expect people to live so high up. Every house ought to have

a lift, something simple and inexpensive, or else an electric staircase like the one at Earl's Court—but four flights! When she stood in the hall and saw the first

3

306. Mansfield: *The Garden Party*, 1939. 10″ × 7″. With lithographs by Laurençin. *Cambridge University Press*

307. Balzac: *Le Chef d'oeuvre inconnu*, 1931. 13″ × 10″. A wood-engraving and an etching by Picasso. *Vollard*

Trois mois après la rencontre du Pouſſin et de Porbus, celui-ci vint voir maître Frenhofer. Le vieillard était alors en proie à l'un de ces découragements profonds et ſpontanés dont la cause eſt, s'il faut en croire les mathématiciens de la médecine, dans une digeſtion mauvaiſe, dans le vent, la chaleur ou quelque empâtement des hypochondres ; et, ſuivant les ſpiritualiſtes, dans l'imperfection de notre nature

63

308. Buffon: *Histoire naturelle*, 1942. $14\frac{1}{2}'' \times 11''$. Sugar aquatints by Picasso. *Fabiani*

309. Lautréamont: *Les Chants de Maldoror*, 1934. 13″ × 10″. Etchings by Dali. *Skira*

310. Rouault: *Cirque de l'Etoile Filante*, 1938. 17″ × 12½″. Etchings and wood-engravings by the author. *Vollard*

Entends donc, Tristes Os, mon pote,
Et vois enfin ce qu'ils ont fait
De cette voix humaine, si belle,

films trop sonores peut-être bien, tant de bruits incongrus que le Préfet d'Athènes a prohibés hier sur beau papier blanc — cela nous a coûté quelques deniers, et ces bruits renaissent plus discordants encore. Le Préfet affirme que tout homme de progrès devra s'y habituer; d'autres assurent mettre au point des disques parfaits, admettons-le, à condition que ce soit ma colombe qui roucoule sur mon cœur en mineur et non les aboyeurs de la Bourse de Paris par haut-hurleur. La vie est amère et ce peuple, dont on vantait la bonne humeur, semble triste à crever: ce n'est pas vous, vaillants humoristes, qui lui rendrez la joie avec vos petits croquetons, si amusants qu'ils soient.

91

XXI

Dans ce charnier d'amants qu'a dévorés la Chine,
Où tu glapis ton cœur sur leurs os corrompus,
N'es-tu pas lasse encor d'opium ni de pus,
Hyène jaune, à qui frémit sa haute échine ?

XXII

Ô nuit parmi les nuits de laque et de vermeil,
Es-tu l'aurore, — ou les degrés d'un noir sommeil?

311. Gogol: *Les Ames Mortes*, 1948. $14\frac{3}{4}'' \times 11''$. Etchings by Chagall. *Vollard*

312. Toulet: *Les Contrerimes*, 1939. $8'' \times 5\frac{1}{4}''$. Vignettes by Daragnès printed in blue

313. *The Book of Job*, 1946. 11″ × 8″. Etchings by Goerg

LIVRE QVATRIESME

Je chantois toutes ces chofes fur le labeur des champs & fur le foin des troupeaux & des arbres; tandis que le grand Cefar foudroye par fes armes fur les bords de l'Eufrate, & que les peuples s'eftants volontairement foubmis à fes loix, il fe trace avec fes victoires un chemin au Ciel.

Alors dans l'agreable fejour de Parthenope, Virgile s'occupoit à l'eftude d'un loifir peu glorieux, apres avoir recité des airs pour les bergers, & apres que durant le plus grand feu de fa jeuneffe, il a fait des chanfons de toy, Tytire, qui repofois fous le couvert d'un heftre au fueillage efpais.

314. Virgil's *Les Géorgiques*, 1947. 18″ × 13½″. Etchings by Segonzac

315. Virgil's *Bucolica* (translated by Valéry), 1953. 15″ × 11¼″. Coloured lithographs by Villon. *Scripta et Picta*

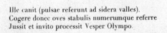

Ille canit (pulsae referunt ad sidera valles).
Cogere donec oves stabulis numerumque referre
Jussit et invito processit Vesper Olympo.

Tout ravi : les échos le redisent aux astres !
Mais il faut à présent rentrer, compter les bêtes
Vesper le veut, qui vient en dépit de l'Olympe.

316. Le Marchand: *L'Odyssée d'Ulysse*, 1947. 12″×9″. Lithographs by François *Guy Le Prat*

317. Lucian's *Dialogues*, 1951. 15½″ × 11½″. Coloured woodcuts by Laurens. *Tériade*

partout où vous irez, je vous suivrai pour vous molester, vous chansonner et rire à vos dépens.
CRÉSUS. N'est-ce pas là de l'insolence?
MÉNIPPE. Non; mais si ce qui était de l'insolence, c'est ce que vous faisiez quand vous prétendiez être adorés, que vous vous jouiez des hommes libres, sans jamais vous souvenir de la mort. Pleurez donc à présent que vous êtes privés de tout cela.
CRÉSUS. Ah oui, de biens nombreux, ô dieux, et considérables.
MIDAS. Et moi, de combien d'or!
SARDANAPALE. Et moi, de quelles délices!
MÉNIPPE. Bravo! continuez. Pour moi, je ne cesserai de vous corner aux oreilles le dicton: « Connais-toi toi-même; » c'est l'accompagnement qui convient à de telles lamentations.

MÉNIPPE, AMPHILOCHOS ET TROPHONIOS

MÉNIPPE. Vous êtes morts tous les deux, Trophônios et Amphilochos. Aussi, je ne comprends pas comment on vous a jugés dignes d'avoir des temples, comment vous passez pour divins et comment les hommes sont assez fous pour s'imaginer que vous êtes des dieux.
AMPHILOCHOS. Hé quoi! est-ce notre faute, si les hommes ignorants se forment de telles opinions sur les morts?
MÉNIPPE. Ils ne se les formeraient pas si vous-mêmes, de votre vivant, vous n'aviez pas, par vos prestiges, fait croire que vous prévoyiez l'avenir et que vous pouviez le prédire à ceux qui vous interrogeaient.
TROPHONIOS. Amphilochos, ici présent, Ménippe, sait ce qu'il doit répondre pour lui-même; mais moi je suis un héros et je prédis l'avenir à ceux qui descendent chez moi. Mais il parait que tu n'es jamais allé à Lébadéia; autrement tu ne serais pas si incrédule.
MÉNIPPE. Que dis-tu? Si je ne suis pas allé à Lébadéia, et si, affublé de tes toiles ridicules et tenant un gâteau dans les mains, je n'ai pas pénétré dans ton antre en rampant par sa basse ouverture, je ne peux

74

Iceulx je suis d'advis que nous poursuyvons, ce pendent que l'heur est pour nous, car l'occasion a tous ses cheveulx au front : quand elle est oultre passée, vous ne la povez plus revocquer ; elle est chauve par le derriere de la teste et jamais plus ne retourne.

— Vrayement, dist Grandgousier, ce ne sera pas à ceste heure, car je veulx vous festoyer pour ce soir, et soyez les tres bien venuz. »

— Ce dict, on apresta le soupper, et de surcroist feurent roustiz : seze beufz, troys genisses, trente et deux veaux, soixante et troys chevreaux moissonniers, quatre vingt quinze moutons, troys cens gourretz de laict à beau moust, unze vingt perdrys, sept cens becasses, quatre

cens chappons de Loudunoys et Cornouaille, six mille poulletz et autant de pigeons, six cens gualinottes, quatorze cens levraulx, troys cens et troys hostardes, et mille sept cens hutaudeaux. De venaison l'on ne peut tant soubdain recouvrir, fors unze sangliers qu'envoya l'abbé de Turpenay, et dix et huict bestes fauves que donna le seigneur de Grandmont, ensemble sept vingt faisans qu'envoya le seigneur des Essars. et quelques douzaines de ramiers, de oiseaux de riviere, de cercelles, buours, courtes, pluviers, francolys, cravans, tyransons, vanereaux, tadournes, pochecullieres, pouacres, hegronneaux, foulques, aigrettes, cigouingnes, cannes petieres, oranges flammans (qui sont phœnicopteres), terrigoles,

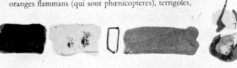

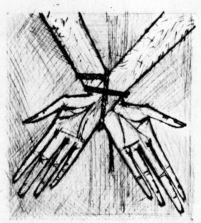

moteurs s'alimentent de rêves, d'illusions personnelles, de désirs égoïstes, de multiples résolutions désespérées prises par chacun dans la solitude de son être. Nous ne voyons que le bouillonnement de la surface. On l'imagine offert aux idées générales directrices de l'armée ; comme les sacrificateurs regardant avec des yeux de prêtres

318. Rabelais: *Gargantua,* 1955. 15″ × 11″. Lithographs by Clavé. *Les Bibliophiles de Provence*

319. Giono: *Recherche de la Pureté.* 1953. 15″ × 10¼″. Engravings by Buffet. *Creuzevault*

without any text apart from captions. They started as drawings in Indian ink, then they became paintings from which the engravings were made photographically for Rouault to work on in various techniques. They were first printed in 1927 but the reproductions were destroyed because they did not come up to Vollard's expectations. The final production, though it can hardly be called a book, is one of the monuments of graphic art.

Chagall's first commission of importance was from Vollard in 1923 for Gogol's novel, *Les Ames Mortes* [311]. But the work was not published until 1948 and in the meantime he illustrated a few other books. *Les Ames Mortes* was of course well suited to an artist of Russian descent and for it Chagall completed ninety-six original engravings, of which L. Venturi says 'One cannot say whether certain scenes belong to the years 1835–40 and to Gogol's imagination, or to the years 1923–4 and to Chagall's fantasy'. His next book was La Fontaine's *Fables* and this did not appear until 1952. The illustrations for both these books were printed three times before Vollard approved them and even then he did not live to see them published. The illustrations for La Fontaine were originally planned as gouaches to be reproduced as colour engravings but eventually they were completed as aquatints. Chagall's last commission from Vollard has not yet been published as a book. This was the *Old Testament*, which Chagall has followed up with the *New Testament*, the whole set of plates having been published in 1956 without a text. In a sense the Jewish Chagall is here complementing the illustrations for *La Passion* and *Miserere* by the Catholic Rouault.

The reader may feel that too much space has been devoted to the books illustrated by the *peintres-graveurs*. These were all expensive limited editions and in many of them admittedly the pictures are not integrated with the text, so that they might be regarded rather as collections of plates than books. What, it will be asked, was happening to the ordinary illustration of the trade book as practised by the professional? The answer is that it was continuing all this time, but it was completely overshadowed. The 1914 war caused the usual lowering of standards and the paper and presswork of the ordinary book were generally deplorable. It was the painters who set the pace; and it has been noted that some of their books already described were re-issued in unlimited editions, their pictures reproduced by line blocks. One of the results of the prestige of the *édition-de-luxe* is that almost every illustrated book however poorly or cheaply produced bears a *justification de tirage*. A surprising number of them contain just three or four plates.

By 1920 the ideals of Pelletan were fast disappearing and the *beau livre démocratique* (if it had ever existed) was a thing of the past. But a glance through the special number of *The Studio* called *The New Book Illustration in France* (1924) reveals that Pelletan's influence still lingered in certain quarters. The author is Léon Pichon, himself a printer and publisher of the twenties and a firm believer in the necessity of illustration by original wood-engraving as well as a disbeliever in the use of colour. Reading his essay one is struck by the almost complete absence of any mention of Vollard; and looking through his examples one is equally struck by the insipidity of this typographical purity so uncongenial to Frenchmen and apparently so unproductive of good illustration.

The notion of well-produced but completely undecorated books is quite alien to France. Pelletan had tried in his *Artistes et Penseurs* series (which sold at 5 francs) to find a middle way by producing well-printed inexpensive books decorated only by vignettes and fleurons. He was followed by René Helleu. Then came La Libraire Crès which published a cheap series of illustrated books called *Les Maîtres du Livre*. And in 1916 was founded *La Société Littéraire de France* which had the same object. Their edition of E. Verhaeren's *Poèmes légendaires de Flandre et de Brabant* (1916) has woodcuts by Dufy but again they are merely floral decorations, not illustrations. Later this society turned to *éditions-de-luxe* like their *King Lear* of 1917 with illustrations by Lebedev, and Salmon's *Le Manuscrit trouvé dans un chapeau* (1919) in which Picasso's drawings are reproduced by line blocks.

Perhaps middlebrow illustration may best be studied in the so-called 'demi-luxe' books such as those produced by *Les Editions Mornay* between 1919–34. These were small squarish books and editions were nearly all limited to 1,000 copies. Most of their illustrators were professionals who, though they might paint as well, made their reputations in the graphic arts, men like Jou, Carlègle, Sauvage, Bofa and Laborde. The first book in this series was Duhamel's *Vie de Martyrs* with woodcuts by the Russian Lebedev and this sold for 25 francs. Most of the early books contained woodcuts or wood-engravings, first in black only, later in colour. As the demand for colour grew we find more and more being illustrated by water-colours reproduced by *pochoir* (a reminder that these are still limited editions from which photo-mechanical colour processes must be banished) and the prices of the books rising correspondingly. If unlimited editions were illustrated (e.g. the *Collection Maîtrise*) it was generally by means of the wood-block.

One wood-engraver who made his reputation during the twenties was Fernand Siméon. He began as an etcher and certain books have etchings by him in addition to woodcut decorations. In Anatole France's *Marguerite* (1920) he handles the rectangular wood-block (cut by himself) with great skill [320] and in his later work he uses colour, still printed from wood with delightful effect. Perhaps his best book in this category is P. Arène's *Jean-les-Figues* (1927). Pichon places him with the minor masters of the eighteenth century, but would not perhaps have approved of his use of colour.

320. France's *Marguerite*, 1920.
10″ × 6½″. Woodcuts by Siméon

Louis Jou was also a wood-engraver, a Spaniard who started life as a compositor and signed himself in the colophons of his books 'l'artisan Jou'. He retained what is called 'a strong feeling for type' but unfortunately this led him into extravagancies which stem from the fitting of blocks into the text. He is a rare instance of an illustrator whose work deteriorated steadily. Anatole France's *Les Opinions de Jérôme Coignard* (1914) is an impressive book with good monochrome wood-cuts. In *De la Servitude volontaire* by Boethius (1922) we find the blocks being distorted into preconceived shapes to fit the decorative plan of the page. And finally in *Thais* by Anatole France (1924) this process is carried to its limit, the triangular cuts forming the corners of the type area and so on. Moreover they are printed in colour—hot unpleasant colours for hot unpleasant designs.

The work of Louis Jou, Charles Guérin and Edy Legrand (all of them working during the twenties) now looks dated beside the books of the *peintres-graveurs*. That of Laboureur, Laborde, Gus Bofa, Sylvain Sauvage and Daragnès is in quite a different category. These too were professionals but their work appeared in limited rather than trade editions chiefly because it was generally engraved and therefore expensive to produce. Laboureur seemed to prefer line-engraving to etching and his work consequently has the precision of the eighteenth century. It can be seen in *Le Diable Amoureux* (French edition 1921, English edition 1925) in which also there are a few decorations cut in wood in the eighteenth-century manner but with a modern twist. Laborde's illustrations are mostly etched and if they seem dated to us now it is because they were topical and dealt with a period (the years immediately after the First World War) that is now as far from us in feeling as the eighteenth century. Laborde was a social satirist and in *Rues et Visages de Paris* (1926) and his similar books on London (1928) and Berlin (1930) he catches something of that strange feverish post-war excitement. Gus Bofa too was a social observer with a distinct bent for comedy. His *Don Quixote* of 1927 with its 400 coloured designs has the distinction of owing nothing to the countless illustrations of that work which had gone before. His *Synthèses littéraires et extra-littéraires* (1923) is equally unconventional for it attempts a literary assessment by means of the illustration, turning the tables on the art critic, who does exactly the opposite. Each picture is labelled with an author's name and into it is distilled the whole of his work.

Jean-Gabriel Daragnès is perhaps the most important of this group and not only on account of his very large output. He showed more interest than most of his contemporaries in the book itself and often undertook the whole design of those in which his illustrations appeared, as well as of some (e.g. *Les Éditions de la Banderole*) which others illustrated. His technique was always brilliant and among artists who have always been notable for their readiness to experiment he stands out by the variety of his media. His interest in the book extended to the study of its past illustration and much of his inspiration was drawn from the seventeenth century (rather than the eighteenth which has generally been more popular among French bibliophiles). One of the consequences of all this is a more highly decorative sense than is usual among his contemporaries. It can be seen in an unostentatious little book which he printed himself and which has sometimes been called his best—*Les Contrerimes* by P.-J. Toulet (1939) with its little vignettes printed in blue on a bluish paper [312]. It can be seen too in his habit of designing decorated initials for books which he illustrated, a practice which is being followed today by Chastel and Clavé.

Like so many others he started with wood and this medium remained a favourite all through his life. In the 1918 edition of *The Ballad of Reading Gaol* the geometric woodcuts are printed *en camaïeu* (i.e. in two tones from the same blocks) and this device was used again later. But the 1945 edition of the same book has mezzotints. For Carco's *Suite Espagnole* (1931) he produced dry-points, for Marcel Schwob's *Mimes* (1933) colour engravings on copper, for Flaubert's *La Tentation de Saint Antoine* (1942) colour engravings on wood, and for Carco's *Les Jours et les Nuits* (1946) colour lithographs.

Dunoyer de Segonzac has used etching in nearly all his books and he is without doubt the greatest etcher in France today. One of his first books was *Les Croix de Bois* (1921) by R. Dorgelès with its dry-points. Then came Philippe's *Bubu de Montparnasse* (1929) with its 67 etchings which made his reputation as an illustrator. Since then his etchings have appeared in many books but sometimes they have been reproduced by process. In 1932 he illustrated Colette's *La Treille Muscate* in which he seems to be preparing for his *chef d'œuvre*, using in fact the same sunlit background of the Midi. Finally in 1947 came the long awaited *Géorgiques* of Virgil, originally commissioned by Vollard but delayed by the war [314]. This is a wonderful book, enhanced by grand typography as dateless as its illustrations, one of the few works of this period that has been praised unstintingly by all bibliophiles, however purist. The etchings are superbly printed by Roger Lacourière who has printed much of Picasso's work. The explanation given by Philip James for the choice of classical texts by the *peintres-graveurs* does not apply here. James believes that a familiar text, giving a 'kind of subconscious running commentary' allowed the picture to take pride of place. But nothing could be more restrained or more deferential to the text than the exquisite quietness of these etchings. Segonzac has in fact lived wholly up to his own precept: 'Il faut faire l'œuvre parallèle à celle de l'auteur.'

One special class of illustration that deserves mention here is that of the children's book. France had nothing to show in the nineteenth century like Crane and Caldecott in England or Van Hoytema in Holland. But in the early years of the present century there are several pleasant books illustrated by Boutet de Monvel in outline and flat colours, such as Anatole France's *Filles et garçons* (1915). Bonnard also illustrated two little-known books by L. Chauveau, *Histoire du poisson-scie et du poisson-marteau* (1923) and *Les histoires du petit Renaud* (1927), one of the few occasions when a *peintre-graveur* worked for the young. Carlègle did several books for children, the best being *Une Histoire qui finit mal*. But France's real addition to this genre came between the wars when she introduced the Russian picture-book to the West. Lebedev, one of the best Russian illustrators, worked in France as we have seen and undoubtedly assimilated many French ideas. The Père Castor series with its big colour lithographs by Rojankovsky was epoch-making in its day, and it must have had far more influence than is generally admitted.

André François has illustrated with subtle humour several delightful books, sometimes providing the text himself. *L'Odyssée d'Ulysse* (1947) by J. Le Marchand is one of the earliest and best [316], and his own *Crocodile Tears* (1955) is a *tour de force*. Etienne Morel is carrying on the work of Rojankovsky with a similar delight in animals and in bright colours. Jean de Brunhoff in his Babar series forestalled the current practice of the École de Paris in providing a hand-written text.

It hardly needs to be said that the years between the two World Wars were the years which marked the triumph of the painter-illustrator. His work no longer struggled for recognition, it was sought after by publishers and book-clubs alike. And if it nearly always appeared in limited editions that meant less in France (where so few unlimited editions were illustrated) than elsewhere. A more significant feature of this period was the increasing number of brilliant professionals, men like Daragnès who could compete with the painters, illustrating in the same idiom and with greater fecundity if not as much originality. It was of course a time of great individuality. The co-operative illustration that had distinguished the French romantic books is hardly ever seen. There were two such efforts in the twenties, the *Tableau de Paris* (1927) in which such painter-illustrators as Bonnard, Segonzac, Matisse and Rouault collaborated, and Perrault's *Contes* (1928) which contains the work of the professional illustrators—Daragnès, Laborde, Laboureur and others. It is significant that neither makes a really satisfactory book.

The Second World War and the German occupation of France seem actually to have stimulated the production of the *édition-de-luxe*. Paper was scarce and publishers' capital was idle. Small editions selling at a high price were therefore the order of the day. They also offered a convenient form of investment for the speculator at a time when there was little else to buy; and this more than compensated for the disappearance of most of the bibliophile societies. Anyone who scans the issues of *Le Portique*, a review devoted to our subject which began in 1945, must be impressed by the enormous lists of elaborate books 'in preparation'. But by 1950, when the review ceased, the list had dwindled to a handful.

The pattern since the war has been much the same as before. The most exciting books have come from the painters backed by those superlative craftsmen like the Mourlot brothers who seem to live only in France. The younger generation of painters have perhaps shown more interest in lithography than their elders and less in wood-engraving. Henri Laurens, the sculptor, is an exception however, because (like Maillol before him) he has preferred the wood-block [317]. In his *Théocrite* (1945), *Odyssey* (1952) and in other books he has used woodcuts printed in flat colours to give a highly individual and powerful effect, quite different from the meticulous use of the coloured woodcut to imitate the water-colour, which is

321. Shakespeare: *The Phoenix and the Turtle*, 1944. 17″ × 13″. Woodcuts by Gischia

322. Green: *Le Visionnaire*, 1950. 9¾″ × 12¾″. Lithographs by Marchand. *Editions du Grenier à Sel*

found in books illustrated by Pierre Bouchet. Leon Gischia has used both the woodcut and the lithograph. In *The Phoenix and the Turtle* (1944) he had shown his skill in the first medium [321] and in de Bèze's *Abraham sacrifiant* (1943) in the second; but there is less difference between the two than one would expect.

Lithography has been used most successfully by Jacques Villon, Edouard Goerg, André Marchand and Antoni Clavé. Villon is a veteran who worked with Lautrec in 1895 but his finest book did not appear until 1953. This is Valéry's translation of Virgil's *Bucolica* which he provided with many fine coloured lithographs and which is notable for the unusual assimilation of illustrations and text [315].

But the most imaginative use of lithography, though perhaps not the most suitable for the book, has been Goerg's in his *Apocalypse* (1946) and *Fleurs du Mal* (1947). There is something of John Martin in his horrific vision and the same temptation to use too much black. His etched illustration in for instance *The Book of Job* (1946) has not the same drawback but neither has it quite the same distinction [313]. André Marchand used lithography in a much more restrained way in Gide's *Les Nourritures Terrestres* (1948) and in *Le Visionnaire* (1950) by Julien Green [322]. He draws direct on the stone, black on white, without very much texture and the result sits more comfortably on the page and fights less with the text than the lithographs in Goerg's huge volumes. Antoni Clavé, a Spaniard working in Paris, uses lithography unconventionally and more in the Picasso manner and he is especially interested in colour lithography. His *Candide* of 1948 contains monochrome lithographs but they are extraordinarily rich in texture. In his greatest book, the *Gargantua* produced in 1955 for a Bibliophile Club to celebrate the four-hundredth anniversary of Rabelais's death, there are some lithographs printed in eight colours. He also designed in wood many initial letters in colour, a welcome return of an old fashion which we have already noted in Daragnès [318].

Je ne pouvais les tenir cachées sans
pécher grandement contre la loi qui nous
oblige à procurer autant qu'il est en nous
le bien général de tous les hommes

323. Descartes: *Discours de la Mé-thode*, 1948. $13\frac{1}{4}'' \times 9\frac{1}{4}''$. Engravings by Vieillard

324. Eluard: *Le Bestiaire*, 1949. $15'' \times 12\frac{1}{4}''$. Engravings by Chastel. *Maeght editeur*

e jour m'étonne et la nuit me fait peur
L'été me hante et l'hiver me poursuit

Un animal sur la neige a posé
Ses pattes sur le sable ou dans la boue
Ses pattes venues de plus loin que mes pas
Sur une piste où la mort
A les empreintes de la vie.

325. Shakespeare: *Hamlet*, 1928. 14″ × 9½″. Woodcuts by Craig. *Cranach Press*

326. Coleridge: *The Ancient Mariner*, 1929. 12½″ × 10″. Copper engravings by David Jones. *Douglas Cleverdon*

Roger Chastel has also designed decorated initials and many of them appear in his most important book to date, Eluard's *Bestiaire* (1949). His illustrations here (printed by himself) are a mixture of etching and aquatint but previously he had used lithography in P.-J. Toulet's *La Jeune Fille Verte*. In the Eluard *Bestiaire* he had, as W. J. Strachan says, to meet the challenge of Dufy's Bestiary and of Picasso's Buffon. He does this successfully by designing quite a different sort of book from either of the others. It is a book which is planned more carefully, the whole basis of the design being the double-spread. Asymmetric folding gives a narrow verso page for the poem against a broader recto for the illustration; and the decorated initials help to tie up the text and the pictures [324].

Bernard Buffet produced some remarkable engravings in 1953 for Giono's *Recherche de la Pureté*. Curiously geometrical without being abstract they are many of them ostentatiously squared up and some cover two pages. They have a peculiar astringent quality which is not often extracted from this medium [319].

French illustrators of this century have not been notable on the whole for an interest in typography and book design. But it is a distinguishing feature of the work of several young artists in France today, and with it goes a taste for decoration as distinct from illustration. In addition Vieillard and Flocon have a strong literary bent and this, strange as it may seem, is an even rarer thing in an illustrator. In Roger Vieillard's case it shows itself in the choice of texts which are not usually held to be suitable for illustration. What at first sight would seem to be less rewarding than Descartes's *Discours de la Méthode* which he illustrated in 1948 [323]? Many of his books, Ovid's *La Fable de Phaëton* (1939), *Homère* (1946), *L'Ecclésiaste* (1950) are classics. And *L'Ecclésiaste* contains line-engravings with a strange decorative border. (Most of Vieillard's work is line-engraved.) What is even more interesting is Vieillard's method here of illustrating what must have seemed an unpromising text by allusions to odd sentences and images, irrespective of their context. Albert Flocon's illustrations for *Perspectives* preceded the poem by Eluard which accompanies them. But like other books which have been born in this unconventional way it is none the worse to look at. In such cases it is usually the literary quality which suffers.

ENGLAND

After the splendour of French illustration, the English product during the early years of this century seems at first sight rather tame. Philip James has pointed out that the revolt of the nineties which in France led to better illustration led in England to better book-design. In England, he says, the whole movement of art begins in literature; in France painting is the source. Consequently the English flair is for the design of the book as a whole, the French for illustration alone. Morris's influence which was non-existent in France was exercised in England on typography rather than on illustration. Perhaps as a result of this the present century has on the whole been a period of black-and-white illustration in England while coloured illustration was at least as common in France.

In England too illustrators have relied on the wood-block and the line block in contrast with the widely varying media used in France. The reason has probably been partly economic; we have had nothing to correspond with the *édition-de-luxe* and consequently we have stuck to the cheaper methods of reproduction. Books from the private presses (which flourished during certain periods of this century) have only their limited editions in common with the French *éditions-de-luxe*; otherwise with their stress on good typography and elegant binding they could hardly be more different. Some of them had no illustration at all; for

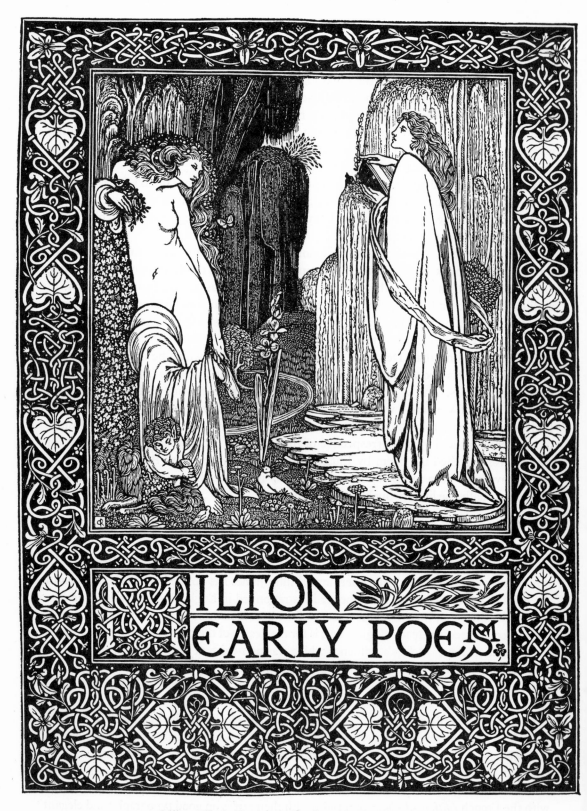

327. Milton: *Early Poems*, 1896. 10″ × 7½″. Woodcuts by Ricketts

328. *The Book of Ruth and the Book of Esther*, 1896. 6¾″ × 3¾″. An Eragny Press book with woodcuts by Pissarro. This one is reproduced actual size

those which had, original wood-engraving was *de rigeur*, whereas French wood-engraved illustration came more often via the reproductive craftsman. The books published by Pichon and others in the twenties which have already been noticed are an exception; but their mediocrity only throws into relief the superiority of the English book so far as general design is concerned.

It is not surprising that, with so little in common, there was hardly any interchange between the two countries. Lucien Pissarro of course came from France, and in the twenties

329. Perrault: *Peau d'Ane*, 902. 8″ × 5″. Woodcuts by Moore

and thirties Laboureur's copper-engraving was popular here. But neither seems to have exercised any real influence. Pissarro's use of the colour wood-engraving has had very few imitations and there have been even fewer intaglio illustrations in England. In both cases cost has probably been the deciding factor for even the private presses could not ask the prices that were charged for French *beaux livres*.[1]

Daphnis and Chloë, published in 1893 by Ricketts and Shannon, and their *Hero and Leander* of the following year, are the first books of the new era with original woodcuts. These two artists were undoubtedly inspired by Morris and were more consistent than Morris in cutting their own designs. Their pages have a welcome lightness and their cuts a wonderful amount of white space after the congested illustrations of the Kelmscott books. But they were not designed in terms of the wood in the way William Nicholson was doing it at this time, and in the way an associate of theirs, Sturge Moore, was able to do it. Moore's cuts for de Guérin's *The Centaur, The Bacchante* (1899) go to the opposite extreme in their use of heavy blacks, raising a problem of balance that was to exercise many illustrators in this medium thereafter.

The Vale Press, whose products Gray too generously calls 'the most perfect examples of the English illustrated book', officially began in 1896. Shannon who had done some fine lithographs for *The Dial* was perhaps barred from using this process in books for purist reasons. Ricketts was the moving spirit and it was he who illustrated most of their books. He thought that 'the illustration ought to give to the book the accompaniment of gesture and decoration, perhaps also an added element of visible poetry'. How he put this into practice may be seen in Milton's *Early Poems* (1896), in Moore's *Danaë* (1903) and in *The Parables* of 1903 [327]. These are pleasant if somewhat precious little books with hardly enough illustration in them to justify Gray's commendation.

Lucien Pissarro, son of Camille Pissarro, studied wood-engraving in France under Lepère. He came to England in 1883 and started the Eragny Press in 1894. From then until 1914 he produced many small books, a large proportion of them French classics, like Laforgue's *Moralités légendaires* (1897) and Ronsard's *Choix de sonnets* (1902). Perrault's *Peau d'Ane* (1902) was illustrated for him by Sturge Moore [329], but the wood-engravings in nearly all the rest were his own or his wife's. Like the Vale Press books Pissarro's have few illustrations (sometimes only a frontispiece) and they depend as much on decoration—borders and initials—as on pictures. The cuts themselves are generally surrounded by a border and even when they are printed in colours they rely for their effect on simplicity. Pissarro sticks much closer to Morris's precepts than Ricketts and no evolution is discernible in the design of the books which he produced over a period of twenty years. The engravings are essentially copies of drawings even though design and cutting were by the same hand. But there is something much more simple and direct in his work than we can find in Morris [328].

In his colour Pissarro did break fresh ground. He usually printed in four or five colours from wood-blocks, the key being often in a dark green. As early as 1894 he published *The Queen of the Fishes* with a few coloured woodcuts; but his most ambitious work was done at the end of his career. The *Livre de Jade* (1911) and *La Charrue d'Erable* (1912), the latter with twelve plates after designs by Camille Pissarro, have, as Balston says, 'a variety of colour and texture which can never have been surpassed on wood.'

[1] It was unfortunate that the hand-made paper always used in these books was far from being an ideal surface for wood-engravings. The *mystique* of the private press demanded a hard rough paper and also a hand-press. As a result most of the engravings, in order to preserve their blackness, were over-inked and so lost detail. The French *édition-de-luxe* was generally printed on far more sympathetic paper and one too which was pleasanter to handle.

330. Milton: *Comus,* 1937. 15¼″ × 10″. Coloured lino-cuts by Farrar. *Nonesuch Press*

331. *The New Testament,* 1927. 12¼″ × 8″. Copper engravings by Gooden. *Nonesuch Press*

332. Bennett: *Elsie and the Child*, 1929. 10″ × 7½″. Stencil-coloured illustrations by Kauffer. *Cassell and Co*.

333. Browne: *Urne Buriall*, 1932. 12″ × 8½″. Stencil-coloured illustrations by Paul Nash. *Cassell and Co*.

112

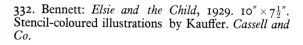

makes the object seen in a perpendicular unto it self, and as farre below the reflectent, as it is from it above; observable in the Sun and Moon beheld in water.

And this is also the law of reflexion in moved bodies and sounds, which though not made by decussation, observe the rule of equality between incidence and reflexion; whereby whispering places are

framed by Ellipticall arches laid side-wise; where the voice being delivered at the *focus* of one extremity, observing an equality unto the angle of incidence, it will reflect unto the *focus* of the other end, and so escape the ears of the standers in the middle.

A like rule is observed in the reflection of the vocall and sonorous line in Ecchoes, which cannot therefore be heard in all stations. But happening in woody plantations, by waters, and able to return some words, if reacht by a pleasant and well-dividing voice, there may be heard the softest notes in nature.

And this not only verified in the way of sence, but in animall and intellectuall receptions. Things entring upon the intellect by a

William Nicholson's wood and lithographic work was described in the last chapter but he continued to illustrate books at long intervals during the present century. He was not connected with any private press and he only used the woodcut when it suited him, not because he was bound to it. For *Characters of Romance* he used colour lithography, for Siegfried Sassoon's *Memoirs of a Foxhunting Man* (1929) process, and colour lithography again for his enchanting but little known children's book, *The Pirate Twins* (1929). His distinctive style is able to make its impact whatever method is used to reproduce it.

Apart from Nicholson there was little experiment with reproductive techniques. Line-engraving and etching, so popular in France, were hardly ever seen in English books, though etching was still popular for its own sake. William Strang, a Scot, produced etched illustrations between 1892 and 1905, notably for *The Pilgrim's Progress* and for Milton. Some of these were actually published without their text and most of them are better as individual designs than as part of a book.

At the outbreak of the First World War trade-book design was at a low ebb. Anthony Gross has attributed the poverty of illustration to a lack of documentation which is at least partly true. 'The great school of Victorian and Edwardian illustrators petered out owing to a decrease in observation and study of the subject, the later illustrators replacing this mainly by clichés.' The special *Studio* number for 1914 entitled *The Art of the Book* shows by its examples how strong the influence of William Morris was then, and how unhealthy too when absorbed at second hand from the private presses. In the nineties the trade books published by the Bodley Head, unpretentious and well designed, using mechanical processes for their illustration, had provided a salutary counterbalance to the Kelmscott extravagancies. But Morris had triumphed, helped, according to A. J. A. Symons, by the discredit brought by the Oscar Wilde scandal.

The ordinary trade book used line and trichromatic blocks for its illustration. Mrs. Marion Spielmann's *Littledom Castle* (1903) even has half-tone reproductions of drawings by Kate Greenaway together with a three-colour frontispiece by Hugh Thomson. Thomson, an indefatigable illustrator of eighteenth-century subjects (like Abbey and Pyle in America), continued industriously during the first years of this century to provide pictures for the *Highways and Byways* series of guide-books and for Jane Austen's novels, all by means of photo-process. Anning Bell using the same method imitated Ricketts in his *Midsummer Night's Dream* (1895) and E. J. Sullivan, by it, produced some vigorous pictures for Carlyle's *Sartor Resartus* (1898). Arthur Rackham's most characteristic and best-known illustrations are for children's books, using three-colour process. One of the few English illustrators of this period popular in America, he produced a steady stream of books from *Rip Van Winkle* in 1905 to *The Wind in the Willows* which he illustrated for the Limited Editions Club in 1939. But most of these are too elaborate to be real books for children, and fall into the gift-book class.

Beatrix Potter's enchanting series, beginning with *The Tale of Peter Rabbit* in 1900 and continuing regularly until 1930, also have their little water-colours reproduced by three-colour process. But these are in quite a different class from Rackham, for they are inexpensive books, meant to be handled and read by children themselves. The stories too, being written by the artist, are integrated with the pictures in a way that is seldom found in any book of this type. Miss Potter herself planned each book with extreme care, even to the extent of deciding exactly what words should go on what page. As for the pictures it is difficult for anyone brought up on Beatrix Potter to see them with a dispassionate eye. They have entered into the national consciousness of more than one generation of children, in America as well as in Britain. Janet Adam Smith has pointed out the difference between these pictures and those of Kate Greenaway or Randolph Caldecott. The latter show a nostalgia for an idealized countryside but Beatrix Potter's are of real places in the Lake District of England. Her animals too are not the disguised humans which we have seen in countless illustrations of Æsop; for 'under the petticoats and aprons there are real pigs and hedgehogs'. Nothing could be farther from the brightly coloured lithographs on which the young of today are reared. They belong, however humbly, to the great period of the English water-colour which early in the nineteenth century was productive of so many finely illustrated books [224].

Almost immediately after the First World War there was a revival of original white-line wood-engraving which seemed sudden but which in fact had its beginnings early in the century. Eric Gill and Noel Rooke, then teacher of book illustration at the Central School of Arts and Crafts, were chiefly responsible, and by 1915 Gill had illustrated *The Devil's Devices* by this method. In 1924 the foremost private press in the country, the Golden Cockerel Press, was taken over by Robert Gibbings, another enthusiastic wood-engraver, and thenceforward there is no dearth of books with this type of illustration. General publishers too began tentatively to commission wood-engravings; Richard Jefferies's *Story of My Heart* (1923) was thus illustrated by Ethelbert White, Johnson's *Rasselas* (1926) by Bliss, and Armstrong's *Desert* by Eric Ravilious in 1926.

This movement is different from the parallel enthusiasm for wood in France because only one of the English practitioners was first and foremost a painter. This was Paul Nash and he in any case illustrated very few books. Gill, it is true, was a sculptor, but it is by his books and type designs he will be remembered. For Gill, more than the others, was concerned with the relationship of the wood-engraving to the text. Many of the others were in fact more interested in producing separate prints, since it was some time before the trade-book publisher (perhaps because he was wedded to photo-engraving and shy of anything new, including new illustration) began to commission wood-engravings on any scale. The publication of Shaw's *Adventure of the Black Girl in her Search for God* in 1932 with illustrations by John Farleigh marked the beginning of the new era.

Gill, whose views on the machine are well known, was of course distrustful of process. 'The photographic line', he said, 'is essentially an inferior article.' But he was less interested than his contemporaries in the wood-engraving as an end in itself. He saw it rather as 'a sort of printer's flower' and the fact that he was also a letterer—the first Englishman for a long time to have combined design of illustration and type[1]—must have accentuated this attitude. In his *Four Gospels* he makes great play with the combination of letters and human figures, something that had not been seen on this scale since the days of the illuminated manuscript. He seems not to have insisted so strongly as some of his fellows on the designer cutting his own wood-block; at all events he himself engraved Maillol's designs for the Cranach edition of Virgil's *Eclogues* as we have seen. His three best books were all done for the Golden Cockerel Press, *Troilus and Criseyde* in 1927, *Canterbury Tales* in 1929 and the *Four Gospels* in 1931. They show a steadily increasing mastery and they helped to gain him an international reputation—which made him unique among English illustrators of his day.

An engraver who sees his work as 'a sort of printer's flower' is of course bound to be a decorator. And it is no denigration of Gill to admit that his decoration is usually stronger than his illustration. He seems to feel the need of a framework for his stark designs, or rather

[1] So also has Berthold Wolpe, a pupil of Rudolf Koch in Offenbach, who is now working in England. His contribution to books like Walter de la Mare's *Collected Rhymes and Verses* (1944) is wholly decorative with a strong affinity to type.

were exceeding sorrowful, and began every one of them to say unto him, Lord, is it I? And he answered and said, He that dippeth his hand with me in the dish, the same shall betray me. The Son of man goeth as it is written of him: but woe unto that man by whom the Son of man is betrayed! it had been good for that man if he had not been born. Then Judas, which betrayed him, answered and said, Master, is it I? He said unto him, Thou hast said.

AND AS THEY WERE EATING, JESUS TOOK BREAD, AND BLESSED IT, AND BRAKE IT, AND GAVE IT TO THE DISCIPLES, AND SAID, TAKE, EAT; THIS IS MY BODY. AND HE TOOK THE CUP, AND GAVE THANKS, AND GAVE IT TO THEM, SAYING, DRINK YE ALL OF IT; FOR THIS IS MY BLOOD OF THE NEW TESTAMENT, WHICH IS SHED FOR MANY FOR THE REMISSION OF SINS. But I say unto you, I will not drink henceforth of this fruit of the vine, until that day when I drink it new with you in my Father's kingdom. ✠ And when they had sung an hymn, they went out into the mount of Olives. ✱ Then saith Jesus unto them, All ye shall be offended because of me this night: for it is written, I will smite the shepherd, and the sheep of the flock shall be scattered abroad. But after I am risen again, I will go before you into Galilee. Peter answered and said unto him, Though all men shall be offended because of thee, yet will I never be offended. Jesus said unto him, Verily I say unto thee, That this night, before the cock crow, thou shalt deny me thrice. Peter said unto him, Though I should die with thee, yet will I not deny thee. Likewise also said all the disciples.

COMETH JESUS WITH THEM UNTO A PLACE CALLED GETHSEMANE, AND SAITH UNTO THE DISCIPLES, SIT YE HERE, WHILE I GO AND PRAY YONDER. AND HE TOOK WITH HIM Peter and the two sons of Zebedee, and began to be sorrowful and very heavy. Then saith he unto them, My soul is exceeding sorrowful, even unto death: tarry ye here, and watch with me. And he went a little farther, and fell on his face, and prayed, saying, O my Father, if it be possible, let this cup pass from me: nevertheless not as I will, but as thou wilt. And he cometh unto the disciples, and findeth them asleep, and saith unto Peter, What, could ye not watch with me one hour? Watch & pray, that ye enter not into temptation: the spirit indeed is willing, but the flesh is weak. He went away again the second time, and prayed, saying, O my

69

334. *The Four Gospels*, 1931. 12½″ × 7½″. Woodcuts by Gill. *Golden Cockerel Press*

of a stem from which they can grow. Sometimes, as in *Troilus* and the *Canterbury Tales* it is foliage, sometimes, as in the *Four Gospels*, letter-forms. The two earlier books have little else but vertical strips of decoration on the outer edge of each page. These designs are repeated from time to time and naturally they do not always fit the context. For although they are decorations they also contain figures which relate them to the text. The borders in the later of the two books are generally more successful because they are more abstract.

In the *Four Gospels*, which is the crown of his achievement, Gill dropped this formula of the border and found a much more successful one in the combination of figures and type [334]. Like the borders this device looks back to the manuscript, but Gill uses whole words as the basis of his design rather than a single initial. The result is monumental yet simple, and it is enhanced by fine printing and by the use of Gill's own Cockerel type. After this great book Gill did little else of note. He produced occasional decorations for his own writings but these writings themselves seem to have occupied most of his attention. The *Aldine Bible* (1935) which was printed in his own type, Joanna, was one of his few ventures into the trade book. For Donne's *Holy Sonnets*, printed by his own firm Hague and Gill in 1938, he produced a new kind of outline engraving which loses all the quality of wood. Lastly in 1939 he illustrated Shakespeare's *Henry VIII* for the Limited Editions Club of America.

Before continuing with the wood-engravers who worked for the private presses mention must be made of two who stand somewhat apart. Laurence Housman's illustrations engraved by his sister have been called the last of the facsimile school; and Gordon Craig's best (which are woodcuts rather than engravings) were done for a German press. Housman began to illustrate in the nineties, e.g. Christina Rossetti's *Goblin Market* (1893), and although most of his life has been lived in the twentieth century he is really a nineteenth-century illustrator. His designs for his own *A Doorway in Fairyland* (1923), engraved by his sister do in fact date from the nineteenth century. Gordon Craig is more of an innovator although he went back to the older style of cutting on wood. His *Hamlet*, printed by Count Kessler at the Cranach Press in Germany in 1928, is original in other ways too [325]. Craig has aimed here at producing a grey as well as a black in one impression by means of lowering the block, an idea quite at variance with current practice which sought to make engravings as black as possible. All the illustrations in this book are planned with the double-spread in mind.

The engravers who favoured black are those whom we have come to think of as most typical of this period. There was Robert Gibbings who ran the Golden Cockerel Press and illustrated many of his own writings for trade publication; there was Agnes Miller-Parker who illustrated *The Fables of Esope* for the Gregynog Press in 1931; there were Gertrude Hermes and Blair Hughes-Stanton whose joint contribution to the 1928 edition of *The Pilgrim's Progress* is one of the landmarks of the period; and there was John Farleigh whose *Black Girl* really opened the eyes of the ordinary publisher to the wide appeal of the woodblock. One new feature was the high proportion of women-engravers; and it seems to have been their work which was most popular with the ordinary reader. Clare Leighton for instance favoured country scenes which for some reason or other have become linked in most people's minds with the wood-engraving. She wrote and illustrated several books for trade publishers like *Farmer's Year* (1933) and *Country Matters* (1937) which reinforced this impression. In 1939 she went to live in America and some of her later work has appeared there. Hughes-Stanton was perhaps the most accomplished technically. His *Revelation of St. John* (1932) and his *Lamentations of Jeremiah* (1933) have engravings so fine that it is hard to believe they are of wood. He and Gertrude Hermes, although their idiom is absolutely modern, look back to the technical virtuosity of the facsimile engravers; and they have revived the use of the multiple tool which engraves several parallel lines at the same time. Seldom have such a variety of textures been extracted from wood [335]. Gwen Raverat was another talented woman engraver but she was less enamoured of black than most and as a result her blocks always go well with type. The *Daphnis and Chloë* which she illustrated for the Ashendene Press in 1933 is a good example of her work. In addition she is one of the few to make colour wood-engravings for a book, and *The Bird Talisman* (1939) is a children's book with four romantic examples.

Few of these artists were tempted to engrave anything but wood. David Jones however was a painter who worked on both wood and copper. His work for the Golden Cockerel Press (*Gulliver's Travels*, 1925, for instance) was in wood-engraving, but his most remarkable book has copper plates. This is *The Ancient Mariner* (1929), an impressive volume with its fine typography and its engravings printed in grey-green ink which were quite unlike anything being done on copper in contemporary France [326]. John Buckland-Wright also worked in both media. Although he started to engrave on wood in 1925 and illustrated several books for continental publishers it was not until 1936 that he did his first for the Golden Cockerel Press, *Love Night* by Powys Mathers. Many followed and after the Second World War he produced a large amount of line-engraved illustration for the Golden Cockerel Press and for the Folio Society, whose books will be discussed later.

Another publishing venture now demands our attention and one which had a greater

335. *The Lamentations of Jeremiah*, 1933. 15″ × 10″. Wood-engravings by Hughes-Stanton. This one is reproduced actual size. *Gregynog Press*

influence on the trade book than any of the private presses. The private press movement in fact, as Lynton Lamb has said, 'tended to drive a wedge between the "prestige" and the popular book-artist where none had been before.' The ordinary book-buyer might never see a limited edition (most of them were sold by subscription) but Nonesuch unlimited editions were to be found in every bookshop. And although the illustrated Nonesuch books were usually limited yet they were not generally expensive. Also they differed radically from the French *édition-de-luxe* in the attention which was paid to textual accuracy, showing a care which has not often distinguished the publishers of illustrated books.

Even more important from our point of view they used a wide variety of media as compared with the inevitable wood-engraving of the private press. There were coloured linocuts by Mildred Farrar in the *Comus* of 1937, line-engravings by Stephen Gooden in the *Anacreon* of 1923, pochoir illustrations in the books of the American McKnight Kauffer, lithographs by Marion Dorn in Beckford's *Vathek* (1929), as well as woodcuts by Paul Nash in the *Genesis* of 1924. The *Comus* is especially interesting not only because the illustrations are delightful [330] but also because they are printed from the neglected linocut which Matisse did not revive in France until 1944. As a matter of fact Edward Bawden had been

336. Power: *How It Happened*, 1930.
9″ × 6¼″. Lino-cuts by Miller-Parker
Cambridge University Press

using the medium for some time and in 1930 Agnes Miller-Parker contributed some fine cuts to Rhoda Power's *How it Happened* which exploit the peculiar quality of linoleum [336]. William Kermode's linocuts for Henry Williamson's *Patriot's Progress* (1930), on the other hand, are far too heavy for the page. Generally speaking the linocut, the effects of which are even broader than the woodcut, needs a large page all to itself, preferably without type.

To return to the Nonesuch Press, one of the most striking features of its books is the literary catholicity of its founder Francis Meynell, and the wide variety of types of illustration. No greater contrast can be imagined than that between Stephen Gooden and McKnight Kauffer. Gooden's line-engravings are modelled on those of the seventeenth century. In his *Anacreon* he revived the engraved title-page with its border embodying small pictures, and emphasis on the border is found in all his subsequent work including the engravings for the great *Nonesuch Bible* of 1926 [331]. Kauffer's work on the other hand is inclined to be amorphous, bearing little relation to the text page as one would perhaps expect of a poster artist. This effect is emphasised by the stencil colouring that was usually applied. It is most noticeable in Melville's *Benito Cereno* (1926) where the very large coloured drawings practically bleed off the page. His illustrations for Burton's *Anatomy of Melancholy* of 1925 are perhaps his most successful as they are certainly his most bookish, most of them being small square column-width pictures. 'Kauffer on Burton' its publisher called this book and the phrase aptly describes the brooding quality of the illustrations. All his work is in the nature of 'non-literal interpretation' and could be criticized as showing us more of the artist than of the author concerned. The *Don Quixote* of 1930 is perhaps less successful but it is interesting in its use of stencilled colour. Here Kauffer uses the black line as a key but by degrees he was to make the black a colour in its own right and dispense altogether with a key. This happened in Arnold Bennett's *Elsie and the Child* (1929) and *Venus Rising from the Sea* by the same author (1931). The former with its bright poster colour is more immediately attractive [332] but the subdued tones of the latter are very subtle. Kauffer in fact was the only illustrator in England to use stencil on anything like the French scale and since 1931 it has hardly been found in any English books.[1] Kauffer went to America in 1941 and the few books he illustrated there will be dealt with later.

In 1931 appeared the *Odyssey* and the *Iliad* decorated with figurines by the German type designer Rudolf Koch and his pupil Fritz Kredel (whom we shall meet again later) which were cast and used as type ornaments. This interesting experiment in 'typographical illustration' or rather decoration was thoroughly successful here.

One of the few Nonesuch books illustrated with woodcuts and one of its most striking is Paul Nash's *Genesis* of 1924. Nash, who is better known as a painter than an illustrator, had been caught up in the revival of wood-engraving in the twenties and had been one of the few to recognize thus early the possibilities of the woodcut. In 1927 he wrote: 'Of all the arts which are crafts it is the most autobiographical. . . . But there is always the dangerous seduction of skilfulness to be taken into account. Hitherto this has been a temptation mainly for the craftsman. Today it is likely to prove the artist's snare. Because . . . I fear such a danger invading the art I practise I have become lately more interested in woodcut patterns than in woodcut pictures. It is always a relief to be rid of the responsibility of representation.' Nash had already, in 1922, used woodcuts in his own book *Places* (on the title-page of which he refers to his text as 'illustrations in prose') and in Ford's *Mr. Bosphorus and the Muses* (1923), but with less success. In the *Genesis* he has a wonderful subject for abstract designs and for the symbolism that was already beginning to engross him. The text set throughout in Koch's Neuland capitals is a fine if rather insistent accompaniment. Martin Armstrong's *Saint Hercules* (1927) had stencil colouring but not until his last venture, Browne's *Urne Buriall* which Cassell published in 1932, did he fully exploit this process, and produce into the bargain his finest book [333]. Herbert Read has called it 'one of the loveliest achievements of contemporary English art'. Here the symbolism which almost makes this a modern Emblem Book is given full scope and seldom has an illustrator found a text which suited him so perfectly.

Paul Nash's brother, John Nash, has also illustrated several books, some of them herbals. One of his earliest was Swift's *Directions to Servants* (1925), a Golden Cockerel book with rather poor typography, but good wood-engravings. Later he drew for line reproduction and White's *Natural History of Selborne* (1951), a text obviously near to his heart, has line blocks that possess some of the quality of wood.

Gilbert White was also the author of one of the most delightful Nonesuch books. *The Writings of Gilbert White of Selborne* illustrated with wood-engravings by Eric Ravilious appeared in 1938. It was the perfect book for an artist whose flair was not only for country subjects but also for small decorations [337]. In addition the book is extremely well printed and his work stands out to advantage. The title-page however with its engraved lettering

---

[1] It was only done commercially by one firm, the Curwen Press, and was not readily available when they gave it up. Harold Curwen and Oliver Simon of this press have had as much influence on jobbing printing in England as Meynell of the Nonesuch Press has had on book design.

compares poorly with Gill's mastery of this skill. Gill in fact was the only wood-engraver of that time who could successfully incorporate good lettering into a design.

Martin Armstrong's *Desert* which Ravilious illustrated in 1926 has already been mentioned as one of the very first commercial books with work by a member of the new school of wood-engravers. His best work however is to be seen in the books he did a little later for the Golden Cockerel Press, Nicholas Breton's *The Twelve Moneths* (1927) and particularly Shakespeare's *Twelfth Night* (1932). The Golden Hours Press edition of Marlowe's *Jew of Malta* (1933) also has a few fine wood-engravings of his. In this mature work his great interest in texture is to be seen, and Robert Harling has pointed out how he obtained his 'rich and often opulent colour by simple contrasts of black-and-white', getting more subtle contrasts by patterned areas based on fifteenth-century prints in the *manière criblée*. This skill in simplification only really bore fruit in the commercial work to which he now turned, and in which he showed his great versatility. Besides work for ephemeral publications and advertisements he also designed decorations for pottery which were applied by lithography. Lithography in

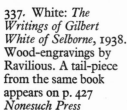

337. White: *The Writings of Gilbert White of Selborne*, 1938. Wood-engravings by Ravilious. A tail-piece from the same book appears on p. 427 *Nonesuch Press*

fact was used for his coloured illustrations of shop fronts in J. M. Richards's *High Street* (1938) one of his last and most attractive books. After the monochrome of his engravings these plates give us a glimpse of Ravilious, the water-colourist.

Lovat Fraser's work, modelled on the chap-book but usually enriched with bright colour, must have come as a bombshell on the sober typographical scene of the early twenties. He was one of the first to rediscover the possibilities of flat colours for children's books reproduced by means of the inexpensive colour-line process. The method can be seen in such a book as his *Nursery Rhymes* of 1919 or in Walter de la Mare's *Peacock Pie* of 1924 [341].

John Austen too used the colour-line process. He started off like Beardsley in his *Hamlet* of 1922, an incredible book which showed what monstrosities publishers could produce in the days before the Nonesuch Press in the name of fine printing. Austen always avowed that he was 'more interested in decoration than character' and his illustrations for Perrault's *Tales of Passed Times* (1922) with their flat, rather crude colours strike a characteristic note. Thereafter we find little change except that in Jane Austen's *Persuasion* (1944) the colours are much softer.

Rex Whistler was another decorative illustrator but of greater stature. If he had lived he might have become one of the greatest of his time in spite of the strict limitations of his style. 'He made himself familiar', says his brother Laurence, 'with the idiom of the High Renaissance, of Baroque and of Rococo as no modern designer has been familiar; but he transmuted the forms he mastered, he threw on them a poetic light unknown to their originators.' The 'scatter borders' of his *Gulliver* have been called an imitation of Bentley's designs for Gray's *Poems* but a far more potent influence than the Gothick has been the eighteenth-century baroque of the Augsburg or the Venetian book. Whistler was also a student of architecture and this in its turn influenced the construction of his borders.

The first books to attract attention were *The New Forget-me-not* (1929) and *The New Keepsake* (1931) both almanacs. His style became fashionable and he had many commissions for ephemera, posters, menus, book jackets and so on. Consequently he illustrated fewer books than he should have done and only one which allowed him to extend himself. This was *Gulliver's Travels*, a magnificent book which appeared in 1930 [340]. Here the big pictures are pen-drawings with colour added by hand, but his favourite method of line and wash has been used for the head and tail-pieces and for the maps which are such a decorative feature. The elaborate borders tend to steal the thunder from the main illustrations; they are so elaborate that there is not much space left for the picture itself though it is delicately and minutely drawn. But this is nevertheless one of the great English books of the present century. After it came several others, notably *The Lord Fish* (1933) and *Desert Islands* (1930) by Walter de la Mare, a writer for whom Whistler had a special affinity, and Hans Andersen's *Fairy Tales* (1935) where he used scraper board to produce an effect similar to wood-engraving. Lastly came the drawings for *Konigsmark*, commissioned by the author A. E. W. Mason in 1940.

Edmund Dulac and Russell Flint can both be described as gift-book illustrators. The gift book is different from the *édition-de-luxe*, and it has now gone out of fashion. It tends to use four-colour reproductions of paintings, printed on art paper and protected with tissues, and aims at a wider if less discriminating public. Its illustrators are often men who have made their reputations as painters. Dulac's work certainly depends a great deal on colour and is often reminiscent of the Persian miniature. Flint's makes even less concession to the book in which it appears.

During the economic depression of the thirties most of the private presses disappeared. They had helped greatly to raise the standard of British book design and much of the wood-engraving already described was done for them. But with the arrival of the Nonesuch Press their *raison d'être* was ended. Thereafter, apart from the Golden Cockerel Press which continued and survived the 1939 War, all the illustrated books came from commercial publishers. These by now had taken their cue from the private presses, and the ordinary book printer had become used to machining wood-engravings (generally from electros). But by no means all of this illustration was wood-engraved. Some of the best book-artists were men who like McKnight Kauffer had made their name in advertising and consequently found themselves as much at home in designing the dust-wrapper as the illustrations. They had little in common with the private press wood-engravers, and although many of them were painters (perhaps because of that) they had no objection to photo-processes and were often expert in designing for them. The modern advertising studio has in fact shown itself to be a good training ground for the book illustrator and vice versa. And the influence of journals like the *Radio Times*, with its demand for decorative vignettes has yet to be assessed.

Barnett Freedman was not ashamed of working for advertisers. A painter and illustrator of true originality, he was also a brilliant lithographer at a time when auto-lithography was almost unknown in England. His earliest work was for Lawrence Binyon's *The Wonder Night* in 1927, a pamphlet in the Ariel Poems series which introduced many new artists.[1] His first book was Siegfried Sassoon's *Memoirs of an Infantry Officer* (1931) where colour was added to his line-drawings lithographically. In 1936 appeared *Lavengro* with true auto-lithographic illustrations in which he displays his characteristic method of portraying the principal characters rather than presenting scenes from the text. In both these books and in most of those which followed the line-block vignette plays an important part, not purely decorative but offering what Mayne calls a 'marginal comment'. The chalk and pen-drawings which Freedman made for these hardly suggest line reproduction but they do in fact reproduce well by this method and have the advantage of blending well with the chalk drawing of the lithographs. Walter de la Mare's anthology *Love* (1943) was illustrated entirely in this way but here the drawings assume the functions of illustration as well as decoration.

The American edition of Tolstoi's *War and Peace* which appeared in 1938 is Freedman's best and most ambitious effort. The colour lithographs here are a development of his penchant for a rather narrow vertical picture which was already to be seen in the Sassoon book. In *War and Peace* he emphasized even more the relationship of illustration to type by bleeding the picture off the top and bottom of the page, leaving broad bands of white on either side. Several other books for the Limited Editions Club or the Heritage Club of America followed, the most successful being another by Tolstoi, *Anna Karenina*, which appeared in 1951 [342].

The Second World War which so tragically cut short the careers of Eric Ravilious and Rex Whistler had a far more deadly effect in England on the publication of illustrated books than in France—where it seemed to stimulate it. British publishers imposed strict economy rules on themselves in order to save paper and these made it difficult to produce any book really well, though not absolutely impossible.[2] Many illustrators were serving in the forces, some as official war artists; consequently the pre-war years and the post-war years are divided by this gap although there is no noticeable difference between their respective styles. Certain illustrators like Freedman with a strongly idiosyncratic manner produced the same sort of work after the war as before. Edward Ardizzone was another such, but unlike Freedman not very much of his output was for advertising. He is much more in the English tradition than Freedman, the tradition of Rowlandson and Cruikshank, and he has been more prolific also, working often in less exacting media than auto-lithography, sometimes for children's books which he writes himself. He started the delightful *Tim* series in 1936 and resumed it after the war. But before that came Le Fanu's *In a Glass Darkly* (1929), his first book and one in which his style already appears fully formed. The little drawings fit perfectly into the text, physically and temperamentally, their lively pen-drawn quality wonderfully retained by line-block reproduction. Then came H. E. Bates's *My Uncle Silas* (1939) in which there are many full-page drawings, coarser and darker, without the delicacy of the first book. In *The Local* by Maurice Gorham published in the same year he used colour lithography which was proving so successful in his children's books.

During the war Ardizzone wrote and illustrated his experiences as a war artist in *Baggage to the Enemy* (1941) and after the war came the *Poems of François Villon* (1946) in which the broadening effect of lithography on his style is apparent. But in *The Pilgrim's Progress* of the following year his pen-drawing reappears in unabated vivacity, catching in a few lines the

---

[1] This series deserves a note although its constituents can hardly be called books. Each poem had a coloured illustration, usually in colour line. Among the artists whose earliest work appeared thus were Eric Ravilious, Edward Bawden, Blair Hughes-Stanton and David Jones.

[2] There was actually a small spate of illustrated reprints immediately after the war, some of them published by Paul Elek and containing distinguished work. But too often they were marred by indifferent printing.

338. Reeves: *The Blackbird in the Lilac*, 1952. $8\frac{3}{4}'' \times 5\frac{1}{2}''$. Line drawings by Ardizzone. *Oxford University Press*

basic human types which were the same in Bunyan's England as in ours. His latest and most ambitious books have been for the Limited Editions Club of America, Thackeray's *The Newcomes* (1954) where colour is applied by stencil, *Ali Baba* (1949) and Dickens's *Great Expectations* in both of which colour lithography is used. But in spite of their splendour, Ardizzone remains a black-and-white illustrator *par excellence*, one who, paradoxically, 'draws like a painter' [338].

Edward Bawden has also done much work for advertising and for ephemeral publications (it is difficult to find a contemporary English illustrator who has not) but he has a natural bent for book illustration. He was a pioneer in the use of the linocut (for the jackets of cookery books by Ambrose Heath) and no one has been better able to exploit the peculiar texture of linoleum when it is not too heavily inked. These same cookery books have delightful title-pages printed from line blocks, and again Bawden has shown himself to be adept at getting the most out of that humble medium. He himself has said that his manner of drawing for reproduction with its shading by parallel lines has been influenced by the Victorian fac-simile wood-engravers. His first book was Paltock's *Peter Wilkins* (1928) where he used flat colours rather in the manner of John Austen. There are also numerous black-and-white drawings; and black-and-white sufficed for *A Gardener's Diary* (1937) and *The Week-End Book* (1939) which contains some of his best work. After this his book illustration relies rather more on colour, in for instance Herring's *Adam and Evelyn at Kew* (1930) and Lloyd Thomas's *Traveller's Verse* (1946) with its auto-lithographs, and in the *Gulliver's Travels* which he illustrated for the Folio Society in 1948. But some of this work tends to a certain coarseness of colour and for many his black-and-white pictures will be preferable. They can be seen at their best in the Limited Editions Club *Herodotus* (1958) from which a drawing is here reproduced [339].

Bawden's debt to Lear has often been pointed out. His humour is just as inconsequential as Lear's and far more so than Ardizzone's. It differs from both in being satirical. In addition he has an architectural sense which Lear lacked and this fits his drawings better for the book. There is, as the Frenchman Saurat has pointed out, something peculiarly English in his fantasies; but there is nothing haphazard about his technique.

John Piper, like Freedman, Ardizzone and Bawden, is a painter-illustrator but since he has also worked for the stage and only very little for advertising he is nearer to the French conception than the other three. What is more he is the only modern English illustrator to have used aquatint though, as we have seen, it has been frequently employed in France. His *Brighton Aquatints* (1939) was also his first book but it had no successors—perhaps because of the difficulty of finding aquatint printers in England. He used auto-lithography in the verse anthology *English, Scottish and Welsh Landscapes* (1944) and photo-lithography was used to reproduce the paintings which illustrate his own *Romney Marsh* (1950). This last is a King Penguin which subtly indicates by its very cheapness the difference between the French and the English painter-illustrator. Finally there is *Wordsworth's Guide to the Lakes* (1952) in which all sorts of curious and subtle textures are evoked from the line block by means of patterned papers and even printed music worked into the design [343]. But in spite of his experiments with technique Piper's illustration strikes us first and foremost as being the work of a painter.

Graham Sutherland is another painter who has very seldom turned his hand to book illustration. His *Henry VI Part One* for the Limited Editions Club Shakespeare series is a very fine book. But the illustrations for David Gascoyne's *Poems 1937–42* which appeared in 1943, though excellent, suffer from unsympathetic reproduction.

The sculptor Epstein has worked very little for books but there is one of his which must be mentioned. This is Baudelaire's *Flowers of Evil* published by the Limited Editions Club

339. *The Histories of Herodotus*, 1958. 9¾″ × 6″. Line drawings by Bawden.
Limited Editions Club

340. Swift: *Gulliver's Travels*, 1930. Hand-coloured pen drawings by Rex Whistler.
Cresset Press

341. De la Mare: *Peacock Pie*, 1924.
$9\frac{3}{4}'' \times 6''$. Coloured line illustrations by
Lovat Fraser. *Constable and Co.*

342. Tolstoy: *Anna Karenina*, 1951.
$8\frac{1}{2}'' \times 5\frac{1}{2}''$ Lithographs by Barnett Freedman. *Limited Editions Club*

Mʳ Alacadacca

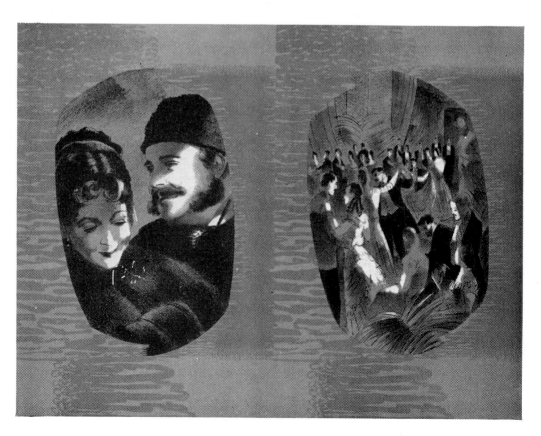

343. Wordsworth: *Guide to the Lakes*, 1952. $7\frac{1}{2}'' \times 5''$. Line drawings by Piper. Actual size. *Hart-Davis*

in 1940. The lithographs, which were printed in France by Mourlot, are powerful and morbid, as befits the subject.

Henry Moore, another great sculptor, has engaged as little in illustration. In 1952 however he illustrated for a French publisher Gide's translation of Goethe's *Promethée*. These are colour lithographs prepared by Mourlot from plastics supplied by Moore. Consequently they have a statuesque quality, are more obviously the work of a sculptor than Epstein's.

Anthony Gross is known chiefly for one work, John Galsworthy's *Forsyte Saga* (1950) which has a fine set of colour lithographs produced by a special transferring method which makes them more or less autographic. They have a characteristic quality which may be partly due to this process, with transparent colours and thin delicate lines which go well with the type [345]. They are accompanied by some delightful black-and-white line drawings, a few of them tail-pieces, the rest full-page designs which like the coloured illustrations bleed off the page. Of the genesis of this work the artist himself wrote: 'I already knew that the only reason for failure in illustration is lack of sufficient documentation—but by this I mean research carried out to the extreme.' He has certainly done all he can to make these pictures historically convincing.

Mervyn Peake is often thought of as an illustrator of children's books perhaps because his first was in this category. *Ride a Cock Horse* appeared in 1940, one of the very few books since 1931 with stencilled colour. It was followed by *Captain Slaughterboard*, Carroll's *The Hunting of the Snark* in 1941 and *Grimm's Household Tales* in 1946 but (apart from a Swedish edition of *Alice in Wonderland* and *Alice through the Looking Glass*) his other books have been for adults. It is in fact questionable how far his subtle satirical drawing appeals to children. Often too it must seem to parents to be too gruesome; and this quality is rightly to the fore in *The Ancient Mariner* of 1943, one of his best books.

The early work of Robin Jacques was somewhat similar as can be seen in his *Arabian Nights* (1946). But later the grotesque element was subdued and his *Forty-Two Stories* by Hans Andersen (1953) is remarkable for its exquisitely delicate and decorative drawings [344].

The work of Lynton Lamb on the other hand is remarkably consistent [348]. He is unusual too in being directly involved like Daragnès in the design and production of books ever since he became associated with the Oxford University Press in 1930. Here his original task was the design of bindings but he is also a wood-engraver, a lithographer, a painter, an

344. Andersen: *Forty-Two Stories*, 1953. $8\frac{1}{2}'' \times 5\frac{1}{2}''$. Line drawings by Jacques. *Faber and Faber*

advertising artist and a writer on illustration. His illustrations for Trollope's *Can You Forgive Her?* (1948) are typical of his nostalgic gift which gravitates naturally to the nineteenth century. What he himself said is true of his own work (as it is not true of Rex Whistler's for instance): 'The best period illustrations frankly impose their own judgement upon the past that they are portraying.' The full-page lithographs here have a characteristic soft, rather blurred quality which Lamb even managed to obtain also from the line blocks, by means of dots and short broken lines. George Eliot's *Silas Marner* which he illustrated for the Limited Editions Club in 1953 is a magnificent book in every way. Here the head-pieces are lithographed in two colours on the text paper.

John Minton illustrated one or two good books before his premature death. Alain-Fournier's *The Wanderer* (1947) has many impressively sombre line-drawings. Alan Ross's *Time was Away* (1948), the record of a journey to Corsica, is the very reverse. Here Minton has extracted the most from the colour-line process, one of the few examples of a really sophisticated use of that neglected medium.

Keith Vaughan produced some powerful and imaginative lithographs for Rimbaud's *A Season in Hell* (1949) but they suffered from inadequate presentation. They have a Gallic quality but no French publisher would have produced them in such an unprepossessing way. English publishing since 1945 has in fact shied too far away from the idea of the *édition-de-luxe*. The War provided an excuse and the enormous increase of the reading public another. A cheap illustrated series like the King Penguins is altogether laudable but while it can present the work of a first-class illustrator it cannot use the format or the techniques or the paper which such work often demands. The decay of the private presses and the disappearance of the Nonesuch Press moreover removed a spur which had made itself felt in the thirties.

The advent of a book club like the Folio Society, confining itself to reprints, is all the more welcome because, although its books may be regarded as somewhat precious by the ordinary publisher, they do set out to sell themselves largely by virtue of their illustration and design. In them the time honoured media of wood and copper-engraving find a place, even though the editions are too large to make intaglio reproduction practicable for the latter.

345. Galsworthy: *The Forsyte Saga.* 1950. 9″×6½″
Lithographs by Anthony Gross
Heinemann & Co.

Foreign illustrators too like Ru van Rossem, Mark Severin and Marcel Vertès have made their distinctive contributions. Several of these books, such as Bawden's *Gulliver*, have already been mentioned. Buckland-Wright we have also met as a wood-engraver for the Golden Cockerel Press. For the Folio Society he illustrated the *Odyssey* in 1948 with copper-engravings and *The Decameron* in 1954–5 with aquatints. Joan Hassall produced some delicate wood-engravings for Jane Austen's *Pride and Prejudice* in 1957. Two other outstanding books contain etchings, by Susan Einzig for Daudet's *Sappho* (1954) and by Vertès for Zola's *Nana* (1956). Van Rossem, a Dutch engraver influenced by Eastern art, produced some good copper-engravings for Flaubert's *Salammbô* in 1940 and some exceptional lithographs for Dostoevsky's *Crime and Punishment* in 1957. Eric Fraser's illustrations for Nievo's *The Castle of Fratta* (1954) are remarkable because they were reproduced by collotype from line and wash drawings on linoleum which was treated as a drawing (not a printing) surface. The result has a texture all its own [349]. Nigel Lambourne's drawings for Defoe's *Moll Flanders* (1954) must be mentioned for their brilliant exploitation of a process as simple as the line block [346]. But this method of reproduction is comparatively rare in Folio Society books which exhibit an unusual variety of processes. A publishing venture that keeps alive so many neglected techniques is to be congratulated.

One or two wood-engravers have continued to work for commercial publishers, notably Reynolds Stone and Joan Hassall. Both excel at the small engraving and the decorative vignette; and Stone, a pupil of Eric Gill, has also made his reputation as a letterer and type designer. His first major work was Guevara's *Praise and Happinesse of the Countrie-Life* which the Gregynog Press published in 1938. Adrian Bell's *The Open Air* (1946) has many delightful vignettes by him, all filled with very fine work [347]. Joan Hassall's engraving, even more meticulous and detailed, can be seen in Mrs. Gaskell's *Cranford* in 1940 and Miss Mitford's *Our Village* in 1946. C. F. Tunnicliffe, also a wood-engraver but now working chiefly on scraper-board, has helped to produce many delightful books on the country. And

346. Defoe: *Moll Flanders*, 1954. 8¾″ × 5½″. Line drawings by Lambourne. *Folio Society*

finally there is a host of competent illustrators mostly working for line reproduction of black-and-white. Since about 1948 much of this work has been confined to books for older children, a class which has always been treated more liberally to illustration than the adults. The drawings of Jack Yeats for *The Turf Cutter's Donkey* (1934) and other books must be mentioned, many of them reproduced in colour. It is a pity that the economical and effective colour-line process is not more generally used.

347. Bell: *The Open Air*, 1946. 7½″ × 5″. Wood-engravings by Stone. *Faber and Faber*

The most original illustration of today both in Britain and America, however, is in the big books for the very young, which rely on pictures rather than text. Here long runs make it possible to print several colours, generally by lithography, in the style which seems to have come to the West from Russia. Significantly it was two Polish artists, Le Witt and Him, who provided the pictures for one of the most popular books in this class, Diana Ross's *The Little Red Engine gets a Name* (1942); and Le Witt has managed to keep ahead of his imitators in his latest book, *The Vegetabull* (1956). Manuel Gasser shrewdly said that to foreigners Le Witt and Him appear as 'the most English of all the English' whereas the English themselves value their work chiefly because it seems continental to them. Certainly Ardizzone's *Tim* series, which has already been mentioned, seems defiantly English by the side of Le Witt and Him. Finally mention must be made of Alan Howard's brilliant lithographs for Prokovief's *The Story of Peter and the Wolf* (1951).

Groping against the wall

348. Collins: *The Woman in White*, 1956. $8\frac{3}{4}'' \times 5\frac{1}{2}''$. Lithographs by Lamb. *Folio Society*

349. Nievo: *The Castle of Fratta*, 1954. $8\frac{3}{4}'' \times 5\frac{1}{2}''$. Drawings on linoleum by Eric Fraser. *Folio Society*

not displease her to be either Angelica followed by Rinaldo, or Marfissa the unstained virgin, or even Alcina who enchanted and ensorcelled the captain of the island. For my part, I chose the role of Rinaldo with resignation enough, and fought fierce battles against rows of poplars which became dragons, or countered the desperate feats of some treacherous magician, bearing my ladylove behind me as if on the crupper of a horse. Sometimes we pretended to be taking long voyages, to the Kingdom of Cathay or the Republic of Samarcand; but we created terrible obstacles to be overcome, some hedge that must be a forest, some dyke that was a mountain, some brook that became a river or torrent. Then we used to comfort one another with brave gestures or took counsel with hushed voices, wary eyes and bated, half-stopped breath. At last we would decide to try our fortunes; down, therefore, at breakneck speed through puddles and ditches, leaping and shouting like two demons. The obstacles were not insuperable, but not seldom the little girl's clothes suffered some damage or she got her feet soaked paddling in the water in her little brown leather shoes. As for me, my jacket was an old familiar of the thorns, and I could have stayed in the water for a hundred years before the damp seeped through the calloused soles of my feet. It was therefore my part to console her, to repair the damage and to dry her when she got a little sulky after such misfortunes; whenever she did not begin to cry, or to start scratching me, I would make her laugh by taking her on my shoulders and leaping with her over ditches and brooks. I was as strong as a young bull and the pleasure I felt when she leant her face against my neck in order to have her hands free to sport with greater ease, would have given me wind enough to have reached, with this precious burden, if not to Cathay or Samarcand, at least to beyond Fossalta.

Wasting in this way the early hours of the afternoon, we began to range further and further from the immediate vicinity of the castle and to become familiar with other roads and paths and more distant retreats. The downland meadows where our first excursions took place sloped westward towards a fine

350. Grahame: *Dream Days*, 1902. 8″ × 6″. An early photomontage illustration by Parrish

351. Melville: *Moby Dick*, 1943. 10″ × 7¼″. Painted illustrations by Boardman Robinson. *Limited Editions Club*

352. Fouqué: *Undine*, 1930. 12½″ × 9½″. A chiaroscuro wood-engraving by Lewis. *Limited Editions Club*

THE BEAUTIFUL BEARDED

353. Shui Hu Chuan: *All Men are Brothers*, 1948. 12¼″ × 9½″. Illustrations in colour by Covarrubias. *Limited Editions Club*

Bruce Rogers, writing in 1912, said that the work of William Morris had 'an enormous influence upon American printing and not, on the whole, a beneficial one except in its effect on sound craftsmanship'. Rogers himself, although he started as an illustrator, had more feeling for type than for illustration and he recognized that the American imitators of Morris, when they were not pure typographers were likely to be decorators. 'The best we have done in the decoration of our books', he continued, 'is to borrow the work of the earlier masters of design and adapt it to our purposes.' This may be a little unfair to the efforts of Updike and De Vinne but it does perhaps help to explain why America did not follow the same course as England during the first quarter of the century. The private presses, which shaped the development of illustration in England, were more interested in typography in America; so were the 'fine' American printers like Updike. The technical standard of the average American book printer was low and this was bound to lower the standard of illustration. Even as late as 1947 Henry Pitz was saying in his excellent *Treasury of American Book Illustration*: 'Our highest standard of printing craftsmanship usually still suffers by comparison with the best of many other countries; in fact there is, if anything, a declining standard of artistry among our engravers and printers.' The illustrators themselves worked primarily for magazines, and books were for them something of a side-line.

Now this was nothing new and we saw in the last chapter that ever since the foundation of Harper's the magazines claimed much work that in other countries has gone into books. A similar state of affairs existed in England in the sixties but it had more or less ended by the time photo-engraving arrived. In America on the other hand the newspapers and magazines were themselves largely instrumental in developing photo-engraving and their illustrators were used to working for process, adapting their style accordingly. This close connexion between magazine and book illustration has been a characteristic of America ever since. It has made for vigorous and varied work, and though the results are not always bookish, they are none the worse for that. It has also helped to produce an extraverted type of illustration which in any case one would expect to be congenial to the American character. Many of the American books described in the last chapter were adventure stories. Many in this chapter, though they must not be demeaned by such a title, are narratives of action.

Process-engraving was exploited by illustrators earlier and more thoroughly in America than elsewhere. Half-tone in particular led to painted (as opposed to drawn) illustration, and we have already noted how this change came over the work of Howard Pyle. The trichromatic process made it possible to reproduce paintings in full colour and Pyle's latest illustration was of this nature. As it is an expensive process it resulted too often in the drastic reduction of the number of illustrations, though most novels of this period *were* illustrated, however poorly. Later when coloured book jackets became an essential we find many books with simply a jacket and a frontispiece as if the presence of 'full colour' made all else unnecessary. Edward Penfield and Maxfield Parrish, both poster and magazine artists, also produced work in this vein, and the former in his own *Holland* (1907) and the latter in his *Arabian Nights* of 1909 have shown how difficult it is to assimilate a colour plate on coated paper with the book. In the case of *Holland* things are made worse by the green mounts on which the plates are pasted. These two books reflect the recent discovery of the coloured picture poster which excited America as much as Europe and in which Penfield and Parrish played an important part. But their black-and-white book illustration was more successful.

In Grahame's *Dream Days* (1902) Parrish experimented with photomontage and used a photographic background for his drawings, often with striking effect [350]. His work had immense popularity. 'His epicene figures and dreamy prophylactic landscapes made him the best-selling artist of modern times,' says Thomas Craven.

Generally speaking however there was little experiment during the first twenty years of our new period and there are few high lights. But with the First World War a change comes over the scene. This cataclysm helped, says Carl Zigrosser, 'to jolt the country out of its provincialism or rather out of its complacent acceptance of a genteel art tradition;' and he puts this down to the fact that for many of the Americans who went to Europe the myth of European superiority was exploded. But he also feels that the international style of illustration, which has always flourished more in France than in Britain, has had its effect in America and this has been particularly noticeable in the years since 1920. Even before this many European artists had come to live in America and soon there was a steady and increasing flow. This reinforced the already diversified racial background of the native-born American which in itself was enough to produce more variety than in Britain. But just as France has put her stamp on the Spanish and Russian artists who went to work there so America has left a faint but detectable impress on her Central European guests.

The nature of this impress is to be found partly in the taste of the American reader. The American appetite for pictures, which has been fostered by the film, the magazine and the advertisement, is well known; but the book which even in America is one of the last strongholds of tradition has been less affected than might be expected. The category that has been most influenced is the one which was able to benefit most, the child's book; and it is here that the best contemporary American work is often to be seen. The requirements are much the same as in the poster or in advertising, a bold self-explanatory picture that catches the attention and is almost independent of its text. The same characteristics are to be found in humorous illustration and here the link with such magazines as *The New Yorker* is even more obvious.

Bookish illustrators have not been wanting in America, however, though they are in a minority. Warren Chappell, himself a talented illustrator, has said that 'Americans are not natural decorators' but there have been notable exceptions. The books which Updike produced at the Merrymount Press and Bruce Rogers at the Riverside Press during the first decade of the century often have drawn (as opposed to typographic) ornament, of very high quality. T. M. Cleland and W. A. Dwiggins are two other exceptions. Both of them have designed type faces and have a flair for the design of the book as well as its illustration. Cleland started as a printer and became interested first in Italian Renaissance ornament and then in the ornament of other periods and countries which he used skilfully in advertising. In this he was happily and far ahead of his time, but in illustration his taste for the eighteenth century has led him to a style which has been revived too often. The very titles of his books —*Tristram Shandy* (1935), *Jonathan Wilde* (1943) and *Tom Jones* (1952)—show where his affections lie. More original are his illustrations for Wentworth and Smith's *High School Mathematics* (1917) in the style of early engraved text-book illustration. Dwiggins was an illustrator with a more personal style which sometimes degenerated into whimsy. His feeling for type was such that even when his ornament is drawn it appears to have been set up. Similarly there was something typographic about his illustrations, about the little drawings which occupy the margins of *The Travels of Marco Polo* (1933) for instance. This book also has elaborate double-spread section titles in colour-line, one of the earliest examples of what has since become common American practice. During the period in which he worked for the

XLI

354. Daudet: *Tartarin of Tarascon*,
1930. $6'' \times 4\frac{1}{2}''$. Line drawings by
Dwiggins. *Limited Editions Club*

publisher Knopf Dwiggins was responsible for many felicitous touches in the books he
planned but also for some rather obtrusive ornament. His coloured illustrations, in for
instance the Limited Editions Club *Gargantua and Pantagruel* (1936), were planned with
transparent stencils which he himself cut. But his best work in black-and-white is to be
found in books like *Tartarin of Tarascon* (1930) from the same publisher [354].

Of Boardman Robinson it has been said: 'He was perhaps the first American illustrator
to believe strongly that any drawing is to be dealt with as a composition just as seriously as a
painting is.' His early work as a pictorial reporter and a cartoonist had an immense effect on
the newspapers and his first book, John Reed's *The War in Eastern Europe* (1916) could be
called newspaper drawing. But it has a vivid graphic quality which makes it the reverse of
ephemeral. His later illustration has been painted rather than drawn—for the *Brothers
Karamazov* (1933) and *The Idiot* (1935) both published by Random House and for *King
Lear* (1939) and *Moby Dick* (1943) published by the Limited Editions Club [351].

In England the period between the wars was a great one for the original wood-engraver.
In America wood-engravings in books were much rarer but nevertheless there were one or
two artists working in this medium, in particular Allen Lewis (who favoured the woodcut
rather than the wood-engraving) and Rudolph Ruzicka. Lewis was an American with an
international style and a wider knowledge of techniques than most. He trained in Paris as an

etcher but soon after his return to America he began to make his reputation with wood-engraved illustrations. *Journeys to Bagdad* (1915) by C. S. Brooks shows his command of the monochrome woodcut; and he has also produced much chiaroscuro illustration, particularly in La Motte Fouqué's *Undine* published by the Limited Editions Club in 1930. Here the cuts are mostly used for elaborate borders, printed in three or four colours. They are very skilful but have an air of *fin de siècle* [352]. Scott's *Ivanhoe* which he illustrated for the same publisher in 1940 contains linocuts.

Ruzicka, a Czech by birth, is more versatile in the matter of techniques. His first book with wood-engravings appeared, like Lewis's, in 1915 but here the illustrations were coloured. The book was the Grolier Club edition of W. P. Eaton's *New York* and it was printed in Paris. Ruzicka has obviously been influenced by the French use of colour wood-engraving and he has produced a large number of separate prints by this technique. But he has by no means confined himself to it. Washington Irving's *Notes and Journal of Travel in Europe* (1921) contains hand-coloured aquatints, in the style of the nineteenth-century English topographical books [363]. La Fontaine's *Fables* (1930) has exquisite little copper-engravings (probably the first modern use in an American book) and Thoreau's *Walden* (1930) has line-drawings. Ruzicka has worked in close conjunction with many printers, notably Updike, and has always been interested in typography. Like several other American illustrators he has designed type, but he is not a typographer first and foremost in the way that Dwiggins was.

Rockwell Kent is also interested in the design of books he illustrates and he too has worked in a variety of media but especially for the line block. He is perhaps the best known of all American illustrators of the older generation and a certain type of line-drawing has become associated with him [355]. He uses a system of shading by means of parallel lines of uniform thickness which becomes peculiarly obtrusive in the sky. It gives to his drawings the some-what mechanical appearance of the nineteenth-century reproductive wood-engravings in which machine ruling was used. It can be seen in the books that Kent wrote himself, e.g. *Salamina* (1936), and it appears to a greater or lesser degree in all his work. It is not his fault that it has been copied *ad nauseam* but the debasement of the style has made it hard to look at his work with an unprejudiced eye.

Voltaire's *Candide* (1928) is one of his better books, for here the tones are produced by dots rather than parallel lines. The drawings take the form of strips at the bottom of the pages. In Melville's *Moby Dick* (1930) we have drawings more typical of Kent but in Shakespeare's *Venus and Adonis* (1931) he uses a very fine line and a second colour. *Beowulf* has lithographs and *The Decameron* illustrations are reproduced from water-colour drawings. In Goethe's *Faust* (1941) all his drawings occupy double-spreads.

VIII. O LIBERTY!

355. Kent: *Salamina*
1936. 8½″ × 5½″. Illustrations by the author.
Faber and Faber

The house that we have come to, with the

356. Shay: *Iron Men and Wooden Ships*, 1924. 12″ × 8¾″. Woodcuts by Wilson. *Doubleday*

Iron Men and Wooden Ships, which Edward Wilson illustrated in 1924, marks, says Norman Kent, a 'milestone in American book illustration quite as important as the advent of Howard Pyle's *Book of Pirates*; and since Wilson had been a student of Pyle, it was Wilson's way of paying tribute to his master.[1] It is a connecting link with the chap-book art of eighteenth-century England when woodcuts were bold without apology and gay with colour, and type consistently "fat". Wilson had taken his place in that small fellowship of blithe spirits: Joseph Crawhall, Lovat Fraser and William Nicholson, who are his artistic brothers' [356]. In his later work Wilson has gradually forsaken his bold and decorative style. The series of books done for the Limited Editions Club, *Robinson Crusoe* (1930), *The Last of the Mohicans* (1932) with its coloured illustrations printed by the Jean Berté water-colour process, *The Man without a Country* (1936), perhaps his best book with its stencilled-coloured lithographs, and Shakespeare's *Tempest* (1940), with illustrations coloured by *pochoir* in France, show his development away from decoration towards illustration proper. His work has also shown a diminishing scale and a growing interest in tone.

[1] Pyle had many other pupils who were prolific illustrators but, as Henry Pitz has said, only Wilson 'creates important illustrations that are an integral part of the books they illustrate'. N. C. Wyeth however was in his day a very popular and prolific illustrator of children's books in four-colour process.

The reader will have noticed how many of the books already described have been published by the Limited Editions Club; and any account of the contemporary American illustrated book must pay tribute to the publisher, the late George Macy, who founded the Club in 1929, and followed it up with its 'unlimited' satellite, the Heritage Club. The *édition-deluxe* is practically unknown in U.S.A. as in England, but these books (all of them reprints and limited to 1,500 copies), are the nearest American equivalent. Macy, an even more eclectic counterpart of Francis Meynell in England, made it his aim to produce a book a month for his members and this ambitious programme inevitably led to a lower standard than that of the Nonesuch Press. But the best American books are as good as anything Europe can show. Macy cast his net wide, using not only foreign illustrators but foreign typographers and printers too. In the thirties he produced several books illustrated by English artists, Austen, Gibbings, Agnes Miller-Parker, and (posthumously) Hugh Thomson, some of which have already been mentioned. He also employed French, Belgian, Swedish and Italian illustrators whose books will be described under their appropriate countries. In his Shakespeare series, designed by Bruce Rogers and published between 1939 and 1940, we find more American illustrators but still a fair number of Englishmen, one of them, Graham Sutherland, producing in *Henry VI Part One* a minor masterpiece. But this is rather an uneven series as far as illustration is concerned and it was perhaps too ambitious a venture. Macy seems to have been somewhat tied in his selection of titles to the preferences of his members as revealed by ballot. Even when he purported to give his illustrators a free choice there was always this to be taken into account.

That being so it is surprising to find one or two books of bibliographical interest, for instance the Æsop of 1933 with cuts taken from Florentine incunabula; and more interesting still, because wholly original, *The Pilgrim's Progress* of 1941 illustrated with a series of watercolours made by William Blake in about 1824 for the purpose but never published. They do not represent Blake at his best (they are supposed to have been retouched by his wife) but they deserved to be rescued from oblivion.

Macy cast his net so wide, tried to appeal to so many tastes and was above all tied so rigidly to his monthly programme that it would have been very surprising if he had not had some failures. Some of these were the result of trying to put too much into a book. The volumes illustrated by Arthur Szyk are an example—*The Book of Job*, *The Book of Ruth*, the *Canterbury Tales*. Szyk is a Polish artist whose work is based on the medieval miniature, a painter rather than an illustrator. *The Arabian Nights* of 1954 contains sixty of these miniatures reproduced by colour-process and the result of so much gaudy colour is frankly indigestible. There is something reminiscent of Noel Humphreys in the work of Arthur Szyk; and he has also a great deal in common with his contemporary from Hungary, Willy Pogany, whose emphasis on decoration now gives his work a very unfashionable air.

Inspired perhaps by Macy's success we find a few new ventures like Doubleday's Limited Editions (among which there is a *Benvenuto Cellini* characteristically illustrated by Salvador Dali), the Folio Club and, more significant because designed to reach a wider public, the Illustrated Modern Library from the firm of Random House. Yet this last venture, (which like the Folio Club was short-lived) made no concessions in its choice of artists and was often bolder than the Limited Editions Club. For instance there was another typical Dali among its books, the *Don Quixote* of 1946 illustrated mainly with double-spread colour plates. There were also volumes illustrated by Edward Wilson, Boardman Robinson and many others whose work has generally appeared in expensive editions. For some artists the small format must have been cramping but the low price was the buyer's compensation. And the hazards of the small page were successfully surmounted by such an artist as Edward Wilson whose *Jane Eyre* (1944) was one of the best volumes in the collection.

Hans Mueller is a German who made his reputation as a teacher of wood-engraving in the State Academy of Graphic Arts in Leipzig. He came to America in 1937 after having illustrated a few books which will be dealt with in the German section. He is a master of the coloured wood-engraving, most of his illustration being designed on the chiaroscuro principle and printed in two colours only. With these ingredients he can produce an effect of great richness and variety as may be seen in the Limited Editions Club *Kidnapped* of 1938 and the Random House *Don Quixote* of 1941. This latter provides an interesting contrast to the Dali *Don Quixote* published by the same firm in 1946. Dali, though he has a much smaller page uses full colour for his double-spread plates. Mueller's little engravings (none of them occupying more than half a page) give a somewhat monochrome effect even though they are hardly ever printed in black and more often than not are in two colours. Nevertheless they belong to the book in a way that Dali's cannot [357].

Fritz Eichenberg is another German from the Leipzig Academy who like Mueller has specialized in wood-engraving—to which he has added great skill in lithography. He came to America in 1933 and illustrated many books for the Limited Editions Club and for other publishers, among them Turgenev's *Fathers and Sons* (1941), and Dostoevsky's *The Brothers Karamazov* (1949), the latter with lithographs. In 1944 he illustrated Poe's *Tales* [358], and in 1954 Goethe's *Reynard the Fox*. The grotesque element in his work is very noticeable and so also is the satisfying balance between his illustrations and the text. Like Wilson's his later work has shown an increasing use of tone.

357. Cervantes: *Don Quixote*, 1941. 10″ × 6¾″. Wood-engravings by Mueller. *Book of the Month Club*

Fritz Kredel, too, came from Germany where he had studied under the famous type designer, Rudolf Koch of Offenbach. His most distinctive work is woodcut rather than wood-engraved and he is an expert at recreating the Italian Renaissance cut. For the Officina Bodoni edition of *Il Ninfale fiesolana* he performed this task in 1940 and he illustrated *The Decameron* for the Heritage Club in the same style in 1940. Several children's books, notably the fairy-tales of Andersen and Grimm, contain his pictures but one of his most distinguished works is *Soldiers of the American Army* (1941) in which he vies with Menzel on his own ground. Like Menzel he contrives to make his pictures much more than mere documents; the very attitudes of the soldiers seem to tell a story. And a very rich effect is achieved by hand-colouring. This is an important book but it is by no means typical of America. More typical, and indicative also of the change in Kredel's style, is the delightful edition of Heine's *Poems* which was published in 1957 [359].

Warren Chappell, though an American, also studied with Koch in Germany and his chief interest is type designing. But like many type designers he is a good illustrator with a vigorous line which has been likened to Cruikshank's. His *Don Quixote* (1939) and *A Connecticut Yankee in King Arthur's Court* (1942) both show this off to advantage [362]. He also illus-

358. Poe: *Tales*, 1944. Wood-engravings by Eichenberg.
Random House

THE HOME-COMING

Und als ich euch meine Schmerzen geklagt

When I told of my sorrows that wounded and tore
You answered with yawns and nothing more.
But now, since I've added a lyrical phrase
And put them in verse, you are lavish with praise!

Ich rief den Teufel und er kam

I called the devil and he came;
And then I saw, with a wondering gaze,
He was not hideous, he was not lame,
But a genial man with charming ways.
A man in the very flush of his prime;
Experienced, suave, and in touch with his time.
As a diplomat, his talent is great,
And he speaks wisely of Church and the State.

113

359. Heine: *Poems*, 1957. $9\frac{1}{2}'' \times 6''$. Line drawings by Kredel. *Limited Editions Club*

360. Dickens: *Dombey and Son*, 1956. $9\frac{3}{4}'' \times 6\frac{1}{2}''$. Line drawings by Pitz. *Limited Editions Club*

trated *The Temptation of Saint Anthony* for the Limited Editions Club in 1943. In his later books line has begun to give way to tone.

Lynd Ward studied under Mueller in Leipzig and he is best known for his wood-engravings, though he is also a skilled lithographer. He made his reputation with *God's Man* which was published in 1929. This is 'a novel in woodcuts', and it tells its story by means only of the pictures without any text. As an experiment it is interesting but it cannot be called a successful art-form because no picture can survive if it is made to carry too much meaning. Moreover the woodcut is not exactly a subtle medium and in order to convey meaning gestures and expressions have to be greatly exaggerated, often with a faintly ridiculous air. Lynd Ward has illustrated many other books in a more conventional way, chief among them being Hugo's *Les Misérables* for the Limited Editions Club in 1938, and *Gargantua and Pantagruel* for the Heritage Club in 1942 [361].

McKnight Kauffer was an American to whose important work in England much space has been devoted. He returned to America in 1941 and illustrated several books there but unfortunately without much success. The drawings he did for the Limited Editions Club *Timon of Athens* were never used because they were too abstract; and his gouaches for W. H. Hudson's *Green Mansions* (1945) suffered too much in reproduction. Only in his *Complete Poe* (1946) does the old touch momentarily reappear.

361. Rabelais: *Gargantua and Pantagruel*, 1942. 8″ × 5½″. Illustrations by Ward.
Heritage Club

Valenti Angelo came from Italy and joined the Grabhorn Press, a noted Californian printing firm. Here he decorated many books with head-pieces in the style of the fifteenth century Italian woodcut. In Voltaire's *Zadig* (1929) for instance they are printed in sanguine. In Sterne's *Sentimental Journey* (1929), however, he uses wash drawings which have an eighteenth-century air. The most ambitious book of this period was a great folio edition of Whitman's *Leaves of Grass* (1930). After 1933 he illustrated a few books for the Limited Editions Club including, in 1936, *The Rubaiyat of Omar Khayyam* which is an example of neo-illumination.

Miguel Covarrubias was a Mexican who worked in the States, one of the few first-class illustrators to come from Latin America. He started as a caricaturist but he achieved fame with his murals. Much of his illustration was painted and displays a rich flamboyant colour sense [353]. In *Mexico South* and *The Island of Bali*, both written by himself, this has full play and the result is splendid. W. H. Hudson's *Green Mansions* too which he illustrated for the Heritage Club in 1936 gave him plenty of scope and although it might be objected that this painted illustration (reproduced by four-colour process) is but tenuously connected with the book it cannot be denied that it adds verve and panache.

With Aldren Watson we reach the later generation of illustrators that started work during or after the Second World War. Watson undertook several books for the Peter Pauper Press, publishers of many excellent inexpensive little books. The most distinguished of this group was Thoreau's *Walden* (1941). Watson also designed and illustrated an edition of Shakespeare's *Sonnets* in 1945 which is very successful. In his work can be traced the steady progression from line to tone which we have already noted in several others and which perhaps reflects the ubiquitous use of the photograph in advertising and magazines. Photography in America has reached such a high pitch of perfection and has obtained such wide currency that it would be strange if it had not powerfully affected the graphic arts. Another factor

362. Cervantes: *Don Quixote*, 1939. 8½″ × 5½″. Line drawings by Chappell.
Knopf

which has to be taken into account is the widespread employment by publishers of the free-lance book-designer, a phenomenon almost entirely American and one which has become general since the War.[1] It may be that eventually these men will stand in the same relationship to the illustrator as the literary editor to the author. In any case they are bound to influence the manner of illustration. Their advocacy of the double-spread title-page, now such a feature of the American book, is a case in point, for the illustrator is usually called in to provide a picture for this purpose.

Humorous illustration occupies a very important position in America today and it is associated of course with magazines (especially *The New Yorker*) rather than with books. But many of the great humorous artists, Arno, Thurber and Bemelmans, have produced books, mostly written by themselves. There is of course no difference in kind between magazine and book illustration; and the masterly control of line by which these artists have made their reputation produces its effect almost as well (allowing for the reduced size) on the book page as in the magazine. But the personality of the artist is such that the drawing tends to overbalance the text—except perhaps in the books of Ludwig Bemelmans, such as *The Blue Danube* (1945) and *Hotel Bemelmans* (1946) [367].

Bemelmans has also written and illustrated a delightful series of children's books. Now children's books as we have already said, are the ones most powerfully affected by advertising art and, being less bound by tradition in format or reproductive technique, stand to gain most. But it was not so at the beginning of the century. Then the scene was dominated by Howard Pyle, 'a giant to his contemporaries—a very much taller man than he is now.' At that time too the American children's book was nearer to the English but 'in the succeeding years came the infusion of many different foreign bloods that has brought about the cosmopolitan books of the present day'. These judgements are by Henry Pitz, himself a prolific illustrator of children's books, mostly in the manner of Pyle, and like Pyle an influential teacher [360]. In his *Treasury of American Book Illustration* he has stressed the contribution of the heads (mostly women) of the children's book departments of the big publishing houses to the renaissance of the illustrated children's book—a contribution comparable to that of the free-lance designer and perhaps more beneficial because more self-effacing.

One of the very first illustrators in the new style was Boris Artzybasheff whose Russian tale *Seven Simeons* (1937) was a landmark [365]. Here is the brightly coloured lithography and the big page that were characteristic of the new children's book in France and England at this time, and again it was a Russian who used them. Feodor Rojankovsky, another Russian, whose pioneer work we have already noticed in France, came to America and produced *The Tall Book of Mother Goose* and *The Tall Book of Nursery Rhymes* with their delightful drawings and unusual formats. His drawings for Hans Andersen's *The Ugly Duckling* (1945) and for Duplaix's *Animal Stories* (1944) are in the same vein, naturalistic but without sentimentalizing the animals which are his subjects. In *Daniel Boone*, which is a 1945 reissue of an earlier book produced in France, animals appear only incidentally, but the same skill is seen in the organization of the page and the use of brilliant colour [364].

Roger Duvoisin is a Swiss who wrote and illustrated an attractive book called *The Three Sneezes* in 1943. Here his drawings are reproduced by line-blocks; but in 1947 he went over to colour lithography for an even better book, *Moustachio* by Douglas Rigby. In this he exploits like Rojankovsky the possibility which lithography offers of marrying the text and the

---

[1] Though perhaps the exhibitions of 'The Fifty Books of the Year' first organized by the American Institute of Graphic Arts in 1923 marked the beginning of this movement.

363. Irving: *Notes and Journal of Travel in Europe*, 1921. 6¾″ × 4¼″. Coloured aquatints by Ruzicka. *Grolier Club*

364. Averill and Stanley: *Daniel Boone*, 1945. 14½″ × 11″. Colour lithographs by Rojankovsky

The Boones were pioneers moving from one frontier to another. When Pennsylvania became too crowded they journeyed down to North Carolina, into the valley of the Yadkin River.

The Indians were growing hostile in the East and England sent an army to aid her Colonies. Boone joined the troops as wagoner and blacksmith.

Trained soldiers knew nothing of Indian warfare. They wore scarlet uniforms and marched in close formation, carrying muskets on their shoulders.

The Redskins smeared their bodies with paint and crept through the woods, one by one, with tomahawk in hand. From behind trees they shot their arrows into the unprotected British ranks. Frontiersmen like Boone could fight in the Indian way.

By the campfire at night he talked with a trader named Finley, who had been into the Wilderness of Kentucky.

Traders were the first to go into new lands. They bartered with the Indians for pelts of the mink, the fox, the deer, the otter and the beaver. Then the hunters went to get these skins themselves. When a trail had been blazed, the settlers followed.

Boone listened to stories of Kentucky where buffaloes roamed in herds of thousands. He dreamed of exploring its forests and hunting in its game fields.

good fellows. But my Generals and my Senators had a thought. If you, second Simeon, can see the world from the top of your tower, you must go up and look. For I am told that somewhere beyond the Great Sea is an island. On this island is a king and the king has a daughter. I am told that this princess is as good-looking as myself."

The second Simeon ran to the tower without delay. From the tower he looked this way and that way, then came down and reported.

"King Douda, your command I have carried out. I looked beyond the Great Sea and I saw Boozan Island. From what I see the king there is very proud and unfriendly. He sits in his palace and talks like this: 'I have a daughter, beautiful Helena, and nowhere in the world is there a king or a prince worthy of her hand. Should one come here to woo her, I would declare war on him! I would chop off his head and burn his kingdom to ashes!' "

"But how big is his army?" asked Douda. "And how far is his kingdom from my kingdom?"

"To make a rough guess, to sail there would take ten years less two days, but should a storm break out it might take a bit longer. I did see the king's army, too. It was training in the field, but there were not many: a hundred thousand lancers, a hundred thousand gunners, and of his horsemen about the same number. The king also has another army in reserve. It never goes any place but is fed and groomed for some emergency."

King Douda thought very long, then exclaimed,

"I do want to marry beautiful Helena!" After he had exclaimed this the Generals and Senators kept silent and only tried to hide behind each other's backs.

"If I may speak, Sir," said the third Simeon, and he coughed a little. "I would say, Sir, but I am only a simple man and have no education, I would say, that although my ship is a crude, home-made thing, it could bring the Princess. While the real ship takes a year to sail, mine is back in an hour; while the real ship takes ten years to sail, mine would be there in a week."

"Now we are getting somewhere!" said Douda. "Hey, my brave Generals and wise Senators, think quickly! Should I, your King Douda, win beautiful Helena by war or shall we first try diplomacy? I now give you my promise that he who brings her to me shall be in my favor. He shall be made the Lord High Keeper of the Kingdom's Treasury and can help himself to it!"

All were silent as before, and there was a shuffling of feet as the Generals and Senators tried to hide behind each other's backs. King Douda frowned and was about to speak an angry word to them when, as if someone had asked for it, the King's Jester jumped forward. The

365. Artzybasheff: *Seven Simeons*, 1937. $11\frac{1}{4}'' \times 8\frac{3}{4}''$. Coloured illustrations by the author. *Cassell and Co.*

366. *The Rainbow Dictionary*, 1947. $11'' \times 8\frac{1}{4}''$. Illustrations in colour by Low. *World Publishing*

building Our store is a **building**. A house is a building. There are many different kinds of **buildings**. Find another building in this picture.

14   Hotel Bemelmans

could see Grandfather being wheeled out, and he would say: "The Zipperl! Aha! It's got you again, Herr Fischer!" and so said the policeman outside, while he made the streetcar wait, and so did all the other people. Everybody in the city knew Grandfather, and since life was without any other excitement, they had time to say: "Have you seen Herr Fischer? The Zipperl has him again!"

3. THE ANIMAL WAITER

THE day was one of the rare ones when Mespoulets and I had a guest at our tables. Most of the time I mugged into a large mirror in back of me. Mespoulets stood next to me and shook his head. Mespoulets was a chef de rang and I was his commis. Our station was on the low rear balcony of the main dining room.

Mespoulets had a passion for his language. "Your accent is good," he said, "your grammar very bad. I shall try to improve your French." He had plenty of time to teach me.

"When I say 'Le chien est utile,' there is one proposition. When I say 'Je crois que le chien est utile,' there are two. When I say 'Je crois que le chien est utile quand il garde la maison,' how many propositions are there?"

"Three."

"Very good."

367. Bemelmans: *Hotel Bemelmans*, 1946. 8½″ × 5½″. Illustrations by the author. *Viking*

illustrations more closely than letterpress printing permits. His *Robinson Crusoe* is mentioned below.

Joseph Low is a young artist of quite unusual promise and also considerable achievement —although the latter includes more advertising work than book illustration. His black-and-white line-drawings for *A Harvest of World Folk Tales* edited by Milton Rugoff (1949) prove that the light-hearted fantastic drawing that is usually reserved for children, if it be a good drawing, is not out of place in a book for adults. But his *Rainbow Dictionary* (1947) with more than a thousand drawings in colour [366] and *Mother Goose Riddle Rhymes* (1953), an amusing collection of picture puzzles, seem to show that his real genius is for the coloured picture-book. Here his skill in lettering, developed perhaps in advertising, has full scope and demonstrates how much commercial art has in common with children's art.

Many other good books of this type have appeared during the last few years, some of them in series like the *Rainbow Classics*, designed by Ernst Reichl. This series, printed by offset lithography sells at a remarkably low price. *Robinson Crusoe*, illustrated by Roger Duvoisin in 1946 is one of its more successful volumes [368]. Then there are the *Golden Books*, produced by the Artists and Writers Guild which owe something to France in their format. Nearly all of them show a freedom not only of technique but also of conception that is somewhat lacking in serious American illustration of the present day. The *Golden Book of the New Testament*, one of the best in the series, is illustrated by the Provensens in a style that is delightfully reminiscent of Byzantine illumination. The Provensens make no concession to the slavish realism that the child is sometimes supposed to demand [369].

The Artists and Writers Guild has produced several of the books already described, and most of its volumes are distinguished by their originality and high standard of design. This is a printer's organization specializing in children's books, the distribution of which is undertaken by a publisher. Such an arrangement marks a welcome return by the printer to the practice of design from which he had previously been excluded by the publisher.

368. Defoe: *Robinson Crusoe*, 1946. $8\frac{1}{4}'' \times 5\frac{1}{4}''$. Illustrations by Duvoisin.
The World Publishing

LATIN AMERICA

South America has hitherto produced few illustrated books of importance but latterly there have been some promising signs. A few bibliophile societies like the Cem Bibliofilos do Brasil have sprung up and a few noteworthy books like Olavo's *O Caçador de esmeraldas* (1949) have been produced by them. This particular volume has line-engravings by Enrico Bianco which, though their printing leaves something to be desired, are interesting. An even more ambitious book also from Brazil is a translation of Kafka's *Metamorfose* which Walter Lewy illustrated in 1956 with some really impressive abstract designs. Luis Seoane is an artist who trained in Spain and now works in Argentina producing books illustrated by a variety of processes—*Libro de Tapas* with linocuts and Varela's *Lonxe* with wood-engravings [370].

GERMANY

At the turn of the century German book-art exhibited various tendencies, some of them conflicting. There were the opposing styles which we associate with Morris and Beardsley in England and there was also the romanticism of such artists as Klinger. This latter continued

69. *The Golden Book of the New Testament.* 1953.
12¼″ × 10″.
Illustrations by the Provensens
Artists and Writers Guild

370. Varela: *Lonxe*. Wood-engraving by Seoane reproduced in actual size

into the new century but it was a waning force. Morris's influence on the other hand was a much more permanent affair and it lasted well into the twenties. In addition there was the *Jugendstil* movement, taking its name from the magazine *Die Jugend* which first appeared in 1896. This was the harbinger of abstract art and its influence can be seen in Paul Klee's early illustrations. But its immediate manifestation was something very like *art nouveau* in England.

Upon this somewhat confused scene appeared three painters, Max Liebermann, Max Slevogt and Lovis Corinth, who are generally described as German Impressionists. But their graphic work owes less than might be expected to French Impressionism except perhaps for Liebermann's, echoes of it appearing in his later illustration such as the lithographs for H. von Kleist's *Kleine Schriften* [373].

Lithography, the most painterly of all the processes, was a medium favoured by all three, especially by Slevogt who rescued it from oblivion as far as Germany was concerned and who made it the favourite German illustrative process during this period. He was the most important and original book illustrator of the three and by far the most prolific. He picked books of action and his pictures are pictures of action, often violent or febrile. Some of them like the *Achill* of 1906 are bound up without text; some like *Sindbad der Seefahrer* (1908) are in proper books, and unlike most lithographed illustrations are printed on the same pages as the text—a practice that became common in Germany at this time [372]. But in spite of this attempt at integration there is no real marriage of text and drawing such as we find for instance in Slevogt's occasional woodcut books which came late in his career, e.g. the *Kinderlieder* and the *Märchenbuch* series (1918–29) [371]. For one thing Slevogt's chalk line is too indefinite by the side of the black-letter type which accompanies it; for another too many of these drawings are just a little wider than the type measure which gives an uncomfortable feeling. Those which have a full page to themselves are happier. Goethe's translation of *Benvenuto Cellini* which Slevogt illustrated in 1913 is even less satisfactory because it has a much smaller page and the wash lithographs (mostly half-page in size or less, many of them surrounded with type) lack air. Lithographed illustration, unlike intaglio engraving, generally needs a large page to show off its broad effects. The pen lithos for Cortez's *Conquest of Mexico* (1919) are stronger. But best of all are the big borders and illustrations he did for his last major work, Goethe's *Faust* of 1927.

In Liebermann's *Holländisches Skizzenbuch* (1911) which has a text by Oscar Bie, the lithographs have a larger page and more air. They are still set into the text here and there, together with a few drawn initials. The effect is fairly homogeneous though Liebermann is not such an original artist as Slevogt. His later work, Kleist's *Kleine Schriften* (1917) which has already been mentioned and T. Fontane's *Effie Briest* (1927) is more impressionistic [373].

Von den Watschelgänschen

Eio popeio, was raffelt im Stroh?
Das find die lieben Gänschen, die haben keine Schuh.
Der Schuster hat Leder, kein' Leisten dazu;
Drum kann er den Gänschen auch machen keine Schuh.

Eio popeio, schlag's Kickelchen tot!
Es legt mir keine Eier und frißt mir mein Brot.
Rupfen wir ihm die Federchen aus
Und machen dem Kindlein ein Bettchen daraus.

Eio popeio, das ist eine Not!
Wer schenkt mir einen Heller zu Zucker und Brot?
Verkauf' ich mein Bettchen und leg' mich aufs Stroh,
So sticht mich keine Feder und beißt mich kein Floh.

Der Butzemann

Es tanzt ein Bi-Ba-Butzemann
In unserm Haus herum di dum,
Es tanzt ein Bi-Ba-Butzemann
In unserm Haus herum.
Er rüttelt sich, er schüttelt sich,
Er wirft sein Säckchen hinter sich.
Es tanzt ein Bi-Ba-Butzemann
In unserm Haus herum.

371. *Zeichnungen zu Kinderliedern, Tierfabeln und Märchen,* 1925. 12¾″ × 9½″. Wood engravings after Slevogt Cassir

den Kapitän und dachten: morgen wird es einem anderen von uns ebenso er-
gehen, und wir werden alle hinsterben, ohne daß jemand etwas von uns wisse.
Wir beschlossen, auf der Insel einen Versteck zu suchen, oder zu entfliehen.
Wir fanden aber keinen sicheren Ort, wir kehrten daher, nachdem wir einige
Pflanzen als Nahrung zu uns genommen, wieder in das Schloß zurück und
setzten uns auf unsern früheren Platz. Kaum saßen wir, so erbebte die Erde,
der Riese erschien, trat auf uns zu, nachdem er ein wenig auf der Bank aus-
geruht hatte, drehte uns einen nach dem andern herum, ergriff dann einen von
uns und verfuhr mit ihm wie mit dem ersten. Nachdem er ihn gebraten und
verzehrt hatte, legte er sich wieder auf die Bank und schnarchte, wie wenn
ein Sturmwind brauste, die ganze Nacht durch, wir aber konnten vor Furcht
nicht schlafen. Als der Tag leuchtete, verließ er uns, wir traten dann zusammen,

27

372. *Sindbad der Seefahrer*, 1908. 14″ × 10¾″. Lithographs by Slevogt. *Cassirer*

der erste Fechter der Welt, alle meine Stöße parierte; auf Finten (was ihm kein Fechter der Welt nachmacht) ging er gar nicht einmal ein: Aug' in Auge, als ob er meine Seele darin lesen könnte, stand er, die Tatze schlagfertig erhoben, und wenn meine Stöße nicht ernsthaft gemeint waren, so rührte er sich nicht.

„Glauben Sie diese Geschichte?"

„Vollkommen!" rief ich, mit freudigem Beifall; „jedwedem Fremden, so wahrscheinlich ist sie: um wie viel mehr Ihnen!"

„Nun, mein vortrefflicher Freund", sagte Herr C . . ., „so sind Sie im Besitz von allem, was nötig ist, um mich zu begreifen. Wir sehen, daß in dem Maße, als, in der organischen Welt, die Reflexion dunkler und schwächer wird, die Grazie darin immer strahlender und herrschender hervortritt. — Doch so, wie sich der Durchschnitt zweier Linien, auf der einen Seite eines Punkts, nach dem Durch-

36

gang durch das Unendliche, plötzlich wieder auf der andern Seite einfindet, oder das Bild des Hohlspiegels, nachdem es sich in das Unendliche entfernt hat, plötzlich wieder dicht vor uns tritt: so findet sich auch, wenn die Erkenntnis gleichsam durch ein Unendliches gegangen ist, die Grazie wieder ein; so, daß sie, zu gleicher Zeit, in demjenigen menschlichen Körperbau am reinsten erscheint, der entweder gar keins, oder ein unendliches Bewußtsein hat, d. h. in dem Gliedermann, oder in dem Gott."

„Mithin", sagte ich ein wenig zerstreut, „müßten wir wieder von dem Baum der Erkenntnis essen, um in den Stand der Unschuld zurückzufallen?"

„Allerdings", antwortete er; „das ist das letzte Kapitel von der Geschichte der Welt." —

37

Ein großer Saal beim Herzog von Friedland.

Dreizehnter Auftritt

Wallenstein (im Harnisch).

Du hast's erreicht, Octavio — Fast bin ich
Jetzt so verlassen wieder, als ich einst
Vom Regenspurger Fürstentage ging.
Da hatt' ich nichts mehr als mich selbst — doch was

230

373. Kleist: *Kleine Schriften,* 1917. 13″ × 9¾″. Lithographs by Liebermann. *Cassirer*

374. Schiller's *Wallenstein,* 1915. 11″ × 7½″. Lithographs by Meid. *Maximilian Gesellschaft*

glücklichen Jünglings, begleitet von dem rohen Geschrei der Soldaten, sich mit den leidenschaftlichen
Seufzern und Liebesgestammel der beiden Glücklichen vermischte, die sich in größter Furcht und
Hast aus ihren Umarmungen lösten. „O Gott," flüsterte die Gräfin, „das ist Savoisy, der für mich
stirbt." „Aber ich werde für Euch leben," antwortete ihr Bois Bourredon, „und glücklich werde ich

19

375. Balzac: *Die Frau Konne-
table*, 1922. $13\frac{1}{2}'' \times 10''$. Lithographs by Corinth. *Cassirer*

Lovis Corinth was the most considerable painter of the three but his best illustration did
not come till much later than theirs. It shows few traces of the baroque style which charac-
terizes his paintings, and an early book like J. Ruederer's *Tragikomödien* (1897) with its line
and half-tone blocks has nothing to distinguish it. But his later work such as Goethe's
Reinecke Fuchs (1921) with its large exciting colour lithographs is much more original. This
is the right way to use lithography and the hand-written text helps to unify the book. It has
a great deal in common with the big lithographed children's books which at this time were
invading Western Europe from Russia. But these latter were essentially cheap books, relying
on mass production to lower their price; whereas *Reinecke Fuchs* is a limited edition. Balzac's
Die Frau Konnetable of 1922 has black-and-white lithographs, equally bold, almost too large
for the page and made with a vigour that contrasts strikingly with Slevogt's feverishness [375].

In about 1903 a group called *Die Brücke* appeared in Dresden. Reacting against the
Impressionists and filled with admiration for the work of the Norwegian Munch who was
then in Germany, its adherents paved the way for Expressionism. This movement was parallel to Fauvism in France, but unlike the Fauvists the Expressionists produced much graphic
work. Their chief figure, Oskar Kokoschka, is a great lithographer as well as a painter and
has illustrated several books in this medium. In *Die Träumenden Knaben* (1908), written
ostensibly for children, there are elements of *art nouveau* and of medievalism too—for the
Expressionists followed the Middle Ages in their fondness for symbols. In 1911 Kokoschka

illustrated Albert Ehrenstein's *Tubutsch* with a set of line-drawings which are much more mature and characteristic [376]; and in 1913 came lithographs for a play by himself called *Der gefesselte Kolumbus*. His *Bachkantate* of 1914 is an example of an art-form which seems to be peculiarly congenial to the German, a combination of music and drawing which dispenses with text. Klinger had already attempted this in his *Brahms-Phantasie*, and Slevogt's *Magic Flute* and Corinth's *Das Hohe Lied* are similar essays. Kokoschka's lithographs for his play *Hiob* (1917) are probably his best known illustrations. They are in two colours and are so free that they seem better suited to be separate prints than book illustrations.

Although lithography was the most favoured medium during the early years of the century, it was not the only one in use. There are plenty of undistinguished books with illustrations printed from line blocks and there are occasional etchings like Alfred Cossmann's for Keller's *Die drei gerechten Kammacher* (1915); but these latter are quite empty with none of the quality of a true etching. Perhaps the best illustrator in line at this time was Alfred Kubin whose career started in 1908 with the illustrations to his own book *Die Andere Seite*. His drawings, sometimes fantastic, sometimes morbid and sinister, are always arresting.[1]

---

[1] An interesting review in *The Times Literary Supplement* of a book on Kubin has this passage: 'At the turn of the present century a counterpart to Kubin could be found in most countries of Europe. The names of Rops, Beardsley, Redon, Ensor, Schiele and Arturo Martini immediately suggest themselves. This phenomenon of a group of successful black-and-white artists, each purveying illustrations whose inspiration is demonic and decadent, surely deserves closer investigation than it has hitherto received.'

376. Ehrenstein:
Tubutsch, 1911.
Line drawings
by Kokoschka

377. Kubin: *Die Andere Seite*, 1908.
8″ × 5″. Line drawings by the author

He was the perfect illustrator for Poe's *Tales*; but in Paul Scheerbart's *Lesabendio* (1913) he reaches greater heights of fantasy. His Andersen's *Tales* of 1922 is more restrained [377].

But already the typographical movement had started which was to produce so many fine books in the twenties, and which was in opposition to all that Expressionism stood for. It was perhaps in the first books of the Maximilian Gesellschaft that it manifested itself. Germany has never been as rich as France in bibliophile societies and the Maximilian Gesellschaft was the first to produce books that aimed at physical perfection. The society like so many in France had a strong antiquarian bias and its magnum opus is the great edition of the *Theuerdank*. One of its best books with contemporary illustration was Schiller's *Wallenstein* (1915) which has lithographs by Hans Meid [374]. Its publishers, whom one would have expected to choose almost any medium but lithography, salved their purist consciences by insisting that the illustrations be printed on the text page; and the result is as successful an integration as can be obtained with letterpress and lithography. A less successful book from this point of view but one with more distinguished illustrations is Kleist's *Prinz Friedrich von Homburg* (1916) with lithographs by Karl Walser. Here the excellent drawings are on the same page as the text but they tend perhaps to be a little too heavy for it [381]. From now on lithography begins to be replaced by the woodcut as the favoured medium.

One of the features of the typographical revival of the twenties was the number of finely printed unillustrated books. The *Hausdruckereien* of the great type foundries like Klingspor

378. Schiller: *Lied an die Freude*, 1927. Woodcuts by Barlach

were responsible for many of the best and naturally they were interested chiefly in typo-graphical experiment. As in Britain and America at this time, we find painters who were also type designers, men like Tiemann and Weiss—but they were decorators rather than illus-trators in such books as they embellished. F. W. Kleukens, on the other hand, started as a typographer but after 1919 the publications of his Ratio Presse were mostly illustrated. Private presses like the Cranach Press of Count Harry Kessler who looked back to William Morris and to Edward Johnston, the English calligrapher, were true to type in preferring the woodcut and wood-engraving. Virgil's *Eclogues* which Maillol illustrated in 1928 and Gordon Craig's *Hamlet* of 1928 have already been mentioned as outstanding Cranach books, neither, be it noted, illustrated by a German.

Craig had already illustrated H. von Hofmannsthal's *Der weisse Fächer* with wood-engravings as long ago as 1907 but we do not find wood much used until the twenties and then not on the scale of its use in England. Kirchner however had been producing original woodcut illustration since 1913. Georg Heym's *Umbra Vitae* which he illustrated in 1924, cutting its text as well as its pictures in wood, is a remarkable document of Expressionism. Ernst Barlach, the sculptor, produced some vigorous woodcuts for his play *Der Findling* (1922) and for Schiller's *Lied an die Freude* (1927) in which the white areas are almost em-bossed by the force of the impression [378]. These cuts are a welcome relief after the refine-ment of the contemporary lithograph. A designer for wood with a more delicate touch was Heinrich Holz who provided Holderlin's *Der Tod des Empedokles* in 1925 with three outstanding illustrations. Ernst Nückel used lead plates instead of wood, producing cuts in his *Schicksal (A Story in Pictures)* which are almost indistinguishable from wood. Lastly we have Hans Mueller, a teacher of wood-engraving at the Academy of Graphic Arts in Leipzig, whose later work we have already encountered in America. In his own book on *Woodcuts and Wood Engravings* he describes the abrupt break with tradition that took place in Germany just after the First World War, leading to the use of the woodcut as opposed to the wood-engraving. His own use of the woodcut is somewhat sophisticated and later he was to use it extensively in America for chiaroscuro prints in two colours. His *Don Quixote* of 1923 and his *Treasure Island* of 1936 are both good books.

In the meantime other processes continued to be used. Hans Meid forsook lithography for etchings (printed by half-tone) in Toller's *Die Rache des verhohnten Liebhabers* (1925) and for line blocks in Schaeffer's *Die Schuldbrüder* (1926). Both processes do justice to his lively sketchy line which still retains a lithographic quality. Kurt Werth's lively colour lithographs decorate Shakespeare's *Troilus and Cressida*, printed at the Leipzig Academy in 1921. These are skilful but rather gaudy pictures in the Slevogt tradition. Hugo Steiner-Prag, like Mueller, taught at the Leipzig Academy of Graphic Arts, an institution which has done a great deal to mould not only German but also American illustration. Goethe's play *Clavigo* which he illustrated with lithographs in 1917 for the Weimar Gesellschaft der Bibliophilen, another influential society, is a book whose typography is more impressive than its illustrations. Although Steiner-Prag did not go to live in America until 1941 he illustrated many books before that for American publishers, such as Molière's *Tartuffe* for the Limited Editions Club in 1930.

The famous Bauhaus at Weimar, whose teachers were such potent figures in the world of architecture and painting, seems to have produced little in the way of illustrated books. Its leaning was towards functionalism in typography and abstraction in art, neither of which is fertile soil for illustration. It is true that Paul Klee, who taught there from 1920 onwards was responsible for two or three remarkable books but his increasing absorption in abstract painting seems to have been incompatible with illustration. His drawings for Voltaire's *Kandide* have echoes of the Jugendstil movement. Made in 1911 though not published until 1920 they show thus early the repudiation of naturalism and give a foretaste of his later abstractions [379]. In 1920 also he illustrated C. Corrinth's *Potsdamer Platz* with photo-lithographs and in 1949 his drawings for *The Novices of Sais* by Novalis were published posthumously in America.

379. Voltaire: *Kandide*, 1920. Line drawings by Klee

Klee's colleague at the Bauhaus was the Russian Kandinsky, a great figure in the history of painting and a true abstract artist as Klee was not. Kandinsky illustrated his own poems, *Klänge*, in 1913 with colour woodcuts. Man Ray, the photographer, also taught there and he, as we have seen, was later to illustrate books in France by photomontage.

Not long after the founding of the Bauhaus another group of illustrators and type designers gathered round Rudolf Koch in Offenbach. Koch himself worked for the Klingspor type foundry and his interests were chiefly typographic and calligraphic. But in collaboration with his pupil Fritz Kredel he produced *Das Blumenbuch* in 1930, a delightful little flower book which has inspired many King Penguin volumes in England. Kredel, before he went to America, illustrated another little Insel book of verse called *Wer will unter die Soldaten* (1934) with coloured pictures. Other pupils of Koch included Berthold Wolpe and the American Warren Chappell, both of whom have found a place elsewhere in this history.

This group like so many others was broken up under the Nazi regime and ever since then the times have not been propitious for German illustration. Richard Seewald who made some fine woodcuts in 1919 for Virgil's *Bucolica* and also illustrated his own travel books before the war in simple line and with extreme economy and effect has produced a few equally good books since. After the war some of the type foundries began again to produce fine books and one of these was Karl Rössing's *Bilder zur Odyssee* (1955). Here is a modern and partly successful attempt to recreate the classical feeling. The wood-engravings are printed on a pale tint which occupies the upper part of the page and shows them off admirably.

Books in Eastern Germany have been handicapped by poor materials but latterly a few interesting ones have appeared, for instance, a translation of Dickens's *Dombey and Son*, illustrated by Josef Hegenbarth in 1955 with good brush-drawings. The same technique is used by Gunter Böhmer in Thomas Mann's *Thamar* published in Western Germany in 1956. Werner Klemke is one of their cleverest and most prolific illustrators, working in a variety of media. His wood-engravings for Christian Reuter's *Schelmuffsky* (1955) are among his very best [380].

In the province of children's books Germany does not seem to have been quite so enamoured of the large lithographed page as some other countries. But one remarkable example must be mentioned which appeared quite early in the century. This was Christian Morgen-

380. Reuter: *Schelmuffsky*, 1955. 8″ × 4¾″.
Wood-engravings by Klemke. *Aufbau Verlag*

So reißt, entsendet aus der Feldredoute,

Ihn schon ein Mordblei, Roß und Reuter, nieder:

67

381. Kleist: *Prinz Friedrich von Homburg*, 1916. 12″ × 9″. Lithographs by Walser. *Cassirer*

382. Morgenstein: *Hasenbuch-Osterbuch*, 1908. 9¼″ × 12″. Stencil-coloured illustrations by von Freyhold. *Cassirer*

Poi, vòlto a me, per farmi un gran favore,
  Disse: «Sta sera ne verrete meco,
  Che sarete alloggiato da signore:

Io ho un vin che fa vergogna al greco;
  Con esso vi darò frutti e confetti,
  Da far veder un morto, andar un cieco;

Fra-tre persone arete quattro letti,
  Grandi, ben fatti, spiumacciati, e voglio
  Che mi diciate poi se saran netti.»

Io che gioir di tal bestie non soglio,
  Lo licenziai, temendo di non dare,
  Come diedi, in mal'ora, in uno scoglio.

«In fe' d'Iddio, diss'egli, io vo' menare
  Alla mia stanza almanco duo di voi:
  Non mi vogliate questo torto fare.»

«Be', rispos'io, messer, parlarem poi;
  Non fate qui per or questo fracasso;
  Forse d'accordo restarem fra noi.

La sera, doppo cena, andammo a spasso;
  Parlando Adamo et io di varie cose,
  Costui faceva a tutti il contrabasso.

Tutto Vergilio et Omero ci espose,
  Disse di voi, parlò del Sannazaro,
  Nelle bilancie tutti dua vi pose.

10

«Non son, diceva, di lettere ignaro;
  Son bene in arte metrica erudito.»
  Et io diceva: «Basta, l'ho ben caro.»

Animal non vid'io mai tanto ardito:
  Non avrebbe a Macrobio et Aristarco,
  Né a Quintilian ceduto un dito.

Era ricciuto, questo prete, e l'arco
  Delle ciglia avea basso, grosso e spesso:
  Un ceffo accomodato a far san Marco.

Non ci si volse mai levar da presso,
  Fin che a Adamo e me diede di piglio,
  E bisognò per forza andar con esso.

11

383. Berni: *Capitola del Prete da Povigliano*, 1951. 10″ × 6½″. Coloured etchings by Sommaruga. *Officina Bodoni*

384. Virgil's *Georgics*, 1952. 12″ × 8½″. Wood-engravings by Bramanti. *Limited Editions Club*

385. Battistini: *Agnolo Morto*, 1947. Pen and wash drawings by Vespigniani

386. Kafka: *Metamorphoses*, 1953. Pen and wash drawings by Gentilini

387. Siemaszko: *The Sparrow Family*. A black and white illustration

388. *Usaty i polosatyi*, 1930. Coloured lithographs by Lebedev

А сама пошла ужинать. Приходит — что такое?

Ни перинки,
Ни простынки,
Ни подушки не видать,
А усатый,
Полосатый
Перебрался под кровать.

Разве так спят? Вот какой глупый котёнок.

Захотела девочка котёнка выкупать.

Принесла кусочек мыла
И мочалку раздобыла
И водицы из котла
В чайной чашке принесла.
Не хотел котёнок мыться —
Убежал он из корытца.

Вот какой глупый котёнок!

stern's *Hasenbuch-Osterbuch* of 1908 with its surprising and fantastic pictures by K. F. von Freyhold. Colour was applied by stencil and the result is as fresh and original as anything that Germany has to show during this century [382].

An unusual edition of *Pinocchio* illustrated by Werner Klemke came from Eastern Germany in 1956. Klemke's designs are the very reverse of what is usually considered suitable for children for they are almost typographic in their conception. Perhaps they would have been better suited to a different sort of book, but they have a certain charm.

ITALY

Italian illustration during the nineteenth century could not free itself from foreign influences, first French, then German, and finally Anglo-Saxon. During the twentieth she has begun to recover her individuality, but she has been somewhat handicapped by the apparent reluctance of Italian publishers to illustrate their ordinary trade editions. The onus has therefore fallen on the small publishers and the private presses of which the Officina Bodoni at Verona, run by Giovanni Mardersteig, is the most notable. Italy has not been as rich in private presses as some countries but the Officina Bodoni has compensated for the lack by its considerable output and by its eclectic use of processes. Mardersteig has always made a point of using a hand-press for his texts and limits himself to editions of about 200 copies, but he also produces machine set and machine-printed books elsewhere. Nor does he follow private-press practice in confining himself to the time-honoured wood-engraving for his illustrations. Lithography seems to be his favourite medium, often hand-coloured, and it may be seen at its best in *I Carmi di Catullo* (1945) illustrated by Filippo de Pisis and in Ovid's *Epistles* (1953) illustrated by Luigi Castiglioni. In Aldo Palazzeschi's *Stampe dell' Ottocento* (1942) Vagnetti's fine lithographs are hand-coloured. Etchings, also hand-coloured, appear in one of Mardersteig's most elegant books, Berni's *Capitola del Prete da Povigliano* (1951), the work of Renzo Sommaruga [383]; and etchings by the sculptor Giacome Manzu adorn Virgil's *Georgics* of 1948. Wood-engraving does sometimes appear however. A most interesting and bold use is made of it in Boccaccio's *Il Ninfale Fiesolano* (1940) where some fifteenth century Florentine cuts have been re-engraved by Fritz Kredel. And Virgil's *Georgics*, printed in 1952 for the Limited Editions Club of America, contains quite exceptional wood-engravings by Bruno Bramanti [384].

All this reads like a list of books published by Vollard except that the illustrators themselves are not as famous as most of Vollard's were. And therein lies the difference. Mardersteig is primarily a printer and for him the text is the most important part of the book. His texts are chosen and edited with greater care than Vollard's were and on the whole he avoids the more hackneyed titles. His books never become portfolios of pictures. But on the other hand, his artists are seldom very adventurous, for it must be admitted that Italian illustrators (and publishers) are conservative to a degree, clinging for the most part to an outworn classical tradition. Another private press, however, that of Piero Fornasetti in Milan, has shown itself more daring. In 1952 it published in a limited edition a book by J. B. Marino entitled *Paris 1615* which contains original lithographs by Fabrizio Clerici in a linear style that has been called 'baroque volutism' [389]. These would be remarkable in any country. Another contemporary illustrator similarly unconcerned with classicism is Franco Gentilini who in 1953 illustrated a limited edition of Kafka's *Metamorphoses* with pen and wash drawings—one of the few artists to tackle this difficult author [386]. Renzo Vespigniani also did some interesting pen and wash drawings in 1947 for Battistini's *Agnolo Morto* [385].

389. Marino: *Paris 1615*, 1952. Lithographs by Clerici

SWITZERLAND

It was in Zurich that the Dada movement had its headquarters and one or two curious books were produced there. The first was Hugo Ball's *Cabaret Voltaire* of 1916 which contains some collages by Hans Arp. Arp also illustrated with woodcuts Tzara's *Vingt-cinq poèmes* (1918) and, with Picabia and others, the *Anthologie Dada* of 1919. All these books suffer from appallingly bad presswork and strange typographical tricks which prevent one from taking them seriously.

Latterly there has been in Switzerland an enormous increase of interest in the graphic arts of which the fine magazine *Graphis* is one manifestation. The very high quality of Swiss reproduction and printing has also helped, and several illustrators have experimented with unusual techniques. Imre Reiner has worked generally in wood from which he has been able to extract some strange and interesting textures not usually associated with that material. These are to be seen in his *Don Quixote* of 1941 and in Voltaire's *La Princesse de Babilone* [391] which he illustrated in 1942. He has a great feeling for the period of his books (few of them are contemporary) and his work has been called 'an attempt to bring the writing of past ages near to the modern reader'. Max Hunziker is even more of an innovator for he used hand-etchings on zinc (in relief) in Grimmelshausen's *Simplizissimus* (1945). This technique which has never been seriously used since Blake produces an autographic line block on which certain effects impossible for the photo-engraver may be achieved.

Of recent years we can see in Swiss illustration the same phenomenon which has already been noted in British and American, the entry of the advertising artist, whose approach to book illustration is no different in kind from his approach to his usual work. This can be studied in the work of Hans Fischer and Hans Erni. Fischer, a lover of fairy-tales who had already illustrated Grimm, produced in 1949 some exquisite lithographs in pure calligraphic line for La Fontaine's *Fables* [390]. In the same year Erni who had already made his reputation as a painter of murals, illustrated the *Oedipus* and the *Antigone* of Sophocles with some exciting etchings. He followed these in 1954 with some good lithographs for that perennial favourite Buffon's *Histoire Naturelle*.

Alois Carigiet is a skilful illustrator of children's books by Selina Chonz, a *Bell for Ursli* (1951), *Florina and the Wild Bird* (1952) and others. These are in the tradition of the big

390. La Fontaine: *Fables*, 1949.
Lithographs by Fischer

391. Voltaire: *La Princesse de Babilone*, 1942. 13″ × 10″. Wood-engravings by Reiner.
Editions Les Belles Feuilles

chromo-lithographed toy-book, more conventional than Fischer's but probably more popular with children. Carigiet's sense of colour is captivating.

SCANDINAVIA

One graphic artist of international fame lived in Norway during this period but unfortunately he illustrated no books. Edvard Munch, a wood-engraver, etcher and lithographer, owed a great deal to Gauguin and in turn his use of the natural grain of the wood had its effect on later engravers. The Jugendstil movement affected Scandinavia just as it affected Germany with perhaps even less benefit to the book-arts. The Norwegian Munthe illustrated in this style. Haavardsholm's illustrations for Holm's *Jonsok-natt* belong to this period although the book was not published until 1933. After the First World War Scandinavian illustration takes on an even stronger Germanic cast, especially noticeable in Swedish typography. Yngve Berg and Bull Hedlund are probably the best known Swedish illustrators of the older generation. Berg has always been influenced by the French engravers of the eighteenth century and his work is often pastiche. He has illustrated Ovid's *Ars Amatoria* and Goethe's *Roman Elegies*. Bull Hedlund has also produced pastiches for the works of Flaubert and Anatole France. The contemporary return to the woodcut is seen in Lennart Forsberg's illustrations for Almquist's *Ryska Minnet* (1956), bold designs which have actually been printed from the wood itself and not, as so often today, from electros. Another Swede, Eric Palmquist, was commissioned in 1953 to illustrate E. Tegner's *Frithiof's Saga* for the Limited Editions Club of America and produced a fine set of spirited pictures. But perhaps the most original Swedish draughtsman is Birger Lundqvist whose illustration for Jonsson's *Black Song* (1949) is here reproduced [392]. In Norway we have the painter Henrik Sörensen whose illustration for Bjornson's *Rusticales* must be mentioned; and also Olav Mosebekk who in 1956 provided some excellent lithographs for Kinck's *To Noveller*. The *Bible of Gustav V* edited in 1928 by O. Hjortzberg is a fine book, filled with vignettes, large illustrations and initials.

Most of the contemporary Danish book illustrators started work with the newspapers and their work has that technical proficiency that such training gives. The two best known are Ib Andersen who not only illustrated Walton's *Compleat Angler* in 1943 but also designed the whole book; and Axel Salto who produced some fine lithographs for Ovid's *Ars Amatoria*. But the contemporary fashion for woodcuts is also represented in books like *Scener af Adam Homo* (1956) which is illustrated by Jane Muus with cuts that have some of the rough vigour of linoleum.

HOLLAND AND BELGIUM

A. A. M. Stols, for whose Halcyon Press at Maastricht several books were illustrated by the English wood-engraver Buckland Wright, produced many other books notable for their classical typography. Often too these contained distinguished illustrations such as the aquatints by Alexeieff for Poe's *Fall of the House of Usher* which echo perfectly the eeriness of the story. In the trade book category Charles Eyck's coloured pen drawings for A. van Duinkerken's *Het Wereldorgel* are noteworthy for their chap-book style.

During the Second World War several presses were working illegally and one of these, the Unicorn Press, produced a delightful *Graphic A.B.C.* in 1943 illustrated by Rozendaal. Since the war the outline drawings of J. F. Doeve have appeared in many Dutch books, but they seem too often to lack the discipline required by the page. The publications of Stichting de Roos are among the best illustrated Dutch books of today, Wilde's *Salome* of 1950 with copper-engravings by J. P. Vroom and Bertrand's *Gaspard de la Nuit* in which M. T. Koornstra's fine lithographs gain an added effect by being placed low on the page. Of recent years the Dutch printer has been making for himself a great reputation but book illustration has lagged a little behind advertising art as it has in America. In Dick Elffer, however, Holland possesses an artist who has an equal reputation in both fields. Henry Miller's *The Smile at the Foot of the Ladder* (1953) is perhaps his best book so far.

Belgium possessed a fine graphic artist in James Ensor but unfortunately he has illustrated no books.[1] Her best-known illustrator is Frans Masereel who may be said to have invented

---

[1] *Arrêts Facultatifs* by G. Pulings, published in Paris in 1925, has however, a few unpublished designs by Ensor, reproduced by half-tone.

392. Jonsson: *Mörk Säng*, 1949. 8″ × 6¼″. Illustrations by Lundqvist

the woodcut novel without words, *Histoire Sans Paroles* (1920), *Visions* (1921), *Capitale* (1935—here the blocks are provided with legends) and so on. This idea was imitated by Nückel in Germany and Lynd Ward in America and in each case the object of the books is social satire. This has been the object too of other suites of plates from Hogarth and Goya to Kollwitz; and there is no doubt that pictures are often more telling than words in this context.

More important are Masereel's woodcuts for *The Creation* published by the Officina Bodoni in Italy in 1948, which afford an interesting comparison with Paul Nash's cuts for

393. *The Creation*, 1948. 15″ × 11″. Woodcuts by Masereel. Printed at the Officina Bodoni.
Pantheon Books

Genesis [393]. In Hagelstange's *Die Elemente* which the same press published in 1950 Masereel's illustrations take the form of mosaics reproduced by gravure.

SPAIN

There is not much to be said about Spanish illustration during the first thirty years of this century. An occasional book like Rusiñol's *L'Auca del Senyor Esteve* (1907) with illustrations by Ramon Casas reproduced in colour-line stands out. These are vigorous designs in chapbook style and brightly coloured, parallel to Nicholson's work in England. Poor paper and indifferent printing does not harm them. Like most of the later books of merit this one was published in Barcelona; and in 1932 that city was the scene of a commendable effort to produce well-illustrated books in limited editions under the title La Cometa. In that year appeared Calderon's play *La Vide es Sueño*, with engravings by E.-C. Ricart and in 1933 *El Alcalde de Zalamea* also by Calderon with lithographs by J. de Togores. In the next year Ricart also illustrated a *Don Quixote* for the Limited Editions Club of America. These three books are all well produced and typographically excellent. It is disappointing to find that their illustrations are mediocre.

Unfortunately the Civil War cut short this venture and Spanish publishing has only recovered slowly from that cataclysm. It also accelerated the flight from Spain to France of many of her best painters and illustrators, a migration which began with Vierge or earlier in the nineteenth century and continued with Gris, Picasso and Clavé in the twentieth. However one or two interesting books have appeared in recent years, among them Cervantes' *El Celoso Extremeño* in 1945 (another book more interesting for its typography than its pictures) with engravings by Andrés Lambert, and *Sevilla* (1949) with remarkable illustrations by Gregorio Prieto [394]. Lithography has not been neglected and F. G. Aguirre's big lithographs for Gil's *Jugar y Cantar* (1956) are noteworthy.

POLAND AND RUSSIA

Both these countries excel in two types of illustration, the one traditional with its roots far back in the Middle Ages, the other modern. The woodcut has always been a national mode of expression and some fine block books were being produced in Russia as late as the beginning of the seventeenth century. Until comparatively recently the woodcut suffered little competition from other media such as intaglio engraving or even from wood-engraving. The large chromo-lithographic children's book on the other hand dates from the middle of the nineteenth century in Western Europe. But it was Russia and Poland who revived and revitalized it early in this century.

No account of Polish illustration can afford to omit the name of the woodcutter Skoczylas, even though most of his work has been in separate prints. But he wielded great influence between the wars and even up to the present it can be seen in the woodcuts of Julius Kydrynski for the Polish translation of Steinbeck's *The Pearl* (1956). Here is the traditional cut, heavy for the page it is true, but with a quality all its own which consorts curiously with the American text. Chrostowski on the other hand produced engravings rather than cuts, with a corresponding gain in refinement and loss in strength. Among illustrators of children's books Olga Siemaszko stands out with her *Skarzypyta* by Jan Brzechwa and with many other books. Her childlike vision has been compared with Henri Rousseau's and there is no doubt that her books are amongst the finest being made for the children of any country [387]. W. Daszewski must be mentioned for his coloured linocuts (reproduced by lithography) in Pushkin's *Ksiazka i Wiedza* (1949) and H. Tomaszewski for his coloured lithographs in Kern's *First Verses* (1956). Le Witt and Him have already been mentioned in the English section but their Polish nationality must not be forgotten nor their first lithographic children's book, *Locomotive*, published in Warsaw in 1937.

The history of twentieth-century Russian illustration has yet to appear. Everything on the subject that is being written by Russians today (everything at least that is accessible to the West) is so spoiled by ideological nonsense that it is not worth reading. And yet Russian artists during the early years of this century produced some of the most exciting and original effects that have yet been extracted from wood; and if their lithographic children's books do not seem so original to us that is only because we have been imitating them so closely ever since they were introduced to us.

Among the masters of the Russian woodcut the names of V. A. Favorsky, A. I. Kravchenko and Andrew Goncharov stand out. Much of the best work in this medium was done in the period between the wars. By degrees, however, the realism that was imposed by the authorities killed the native genius and because the woodcut does not permit of realism its place was largely taken by representational water-colours reproduced by photo-processes for the huge editions that are now usual. Where the wood-engraving (more favoured than the woodcut because more realistic) is allowed to continue it still exhibits in the hands of these experts much of the old magic. In this category are Favorsky's illustrations for Pushkin's *Boris Godunov* (1956), Kravchenko's for Gorky's *Italian Stories* and *Short Stories* of Stefan Zweig [395], and Goncharov's for Grossman's *Roulettenburg*. More recently we find good wood-engravings by F. Konstantinov for *Tales and Stories of Ancient Egypt* (1956).

394. *Sevilla*, 1949. $13\frac{1}{2}'' \times 9\frac{1}{2}''$. Illustrations by Prieto

395. Zweig: *Short Stories*. Wood-
engravings by Kravchenko

Then there are occasional books like the old epic called *The Story of the Igor Regiment* which
was illustrated by peasant artists of Palekh in the traditional style.

Lithography has been coming into favour for adult books such as *Manon Lescaut* which
V. M. Koneshevich successfully illustrated in this way. But the best Russian lithographs are
to be found in the magnificent children's books which have preserved their originality and
their gaiety up to the present—and that in spite of official edicts against fairy tales and
'primitive art', which seem to have been little heeded in some quarters. The influence of
these books on the West has already been insisted on. Its special features are the large picture on the large page, sometimes bleeding but always without much margin; and an integral
part is the strong colouring which is also subtle, mainly from the darker end of the palette,
dark greens, reds, purples and so on. Nothing more different can be imagined from the
pastel shades favoured by Western illustrators for the young like Beatrix Potter. Coloured
papers are also used skilfully but generally the quality of the paper is poor.

In spite of their influence these books are little known and seldom seen outside Russia. It
is in fact not so much the influence of the books themselves as of an expatriate Russian
illustrator which has effected a minor revolution in the West. F. Rojankovsky worked in
France as we have seen, and is now at work in America. He is an extremely fine artist but

no finer than many who have never left Russia. V. Lebedev is represented here by a reproduction from *Usaty i polosatyi* (1930) which gives some indication of his brilliant technique [388], though not of the exquisite colouring which he employs and which even survives the poor printing and paper of a cheap little book like Marshak's *Tale of the Clever Little Mouse* (1956). But in Russia Lebedev is only one among many such artists; Charushin, Koneshevich, Staronossov, and Dobuzhinski have all illustrated delightful children's books, generally by colour lithography but in the case of Staronossov by wood-engraving.

Bibliography

This list does not include monographs on individual books or on individual illustrators

CHAPTERS I–III (MANUSCRIPTS)

Binyon, L. and others: Persian Miniature Painting (Oxford 1933)

Bibliothèque Nationale, Paris: Les plus beaux manuscrits français du VIIIᵉ au XVIᵉ siècle (Paris 1937)

— Les Manuscrits à peintures en France du VIIᵉ au XIIᵉ siècle (Paris 1954). Les Manuscrits à peintures en France du XIIIᵉ au XVIᵉ siècle (Paris 1955)

Birt, T.: Die Buchrolle in der Kunst (Leipzig 1907)

Boeckler, A.: Deutsche Buchmalerei vorgotischer Zeit (Koenigstein 1952)

Bradley, J. W.: Illuminated Manuscripts (London 1905)

Breasted, H.: Oriental Forerunners of Byzantine Painting (Yale 1924)

British Museum: Reproductions from Illuminated MSS (1907–28)

— Schools of Illumination (1914–30)

Diringer, D.: The Illuminated Book (London 1958)

Durrieu, P.: La Miniature Flamande (Brussels 1921)

Ehrenstein, T.: Das Alte Testament im Bilde (Berlin 1923)

Evans, Joan: Art in Medieval France (Oxford 1948)

Gayet, A.: L'Art copte (Paris 1902)

Gerstinger, H.: Die griechische Buchmalerei (Vienna 1926)

Goldschmidt, A.: German Illumination (English translation Florence 1928)

Gruyer, G.: L'Art ferrarais à l'époque des Princes d'Este (Paris 1897)

Henry, Françoise: Irish Art in the Early Christian Period (London 2nd edition 1947)

Herbert, J. A.: Illuminated Manuscripts (London 2nd edition 1911)

Harrison, F.: Treasures of Illumination (London 1937)

Huart, C.: Les Calligraphes et les Miniaturistes de l'Orient musulman (Paris 1908)

Huizinga, J.: The Waning of the Middle Ages (London 1937)

James, M. R.: The Apocalypse in Art (British Academy 1927)

Kitzinger, E.: Early Mediaeval Art in the British Museum (London 1940)

Kondakoff, N. P.: Histoire de l'art byzantin (Paris 1886)

Le Coq, A. von: Die manichaeischen Miniaturen (Berlin 1923)

Lejard, A. (ed.): The Art of the French Book (English translation London 1949)

Marteaux, G. and Vever, H.: Miniatures persanes (Paris 1913)

Mâle, E.: L'Art religieux du XIIIᵉ siècle en France (Paris 1902)

Martin, H.: Les Miniaturistes français (Paris 1906)

Millar, E. G.: English Illuminated Manuscripts (Paris 1926–8)

Morey, C. R.: Early Christian Art (Princeton 1941)

Oakeshott, W.: The Sequence of English Medieval Art (London 1950)

Pierpont Morgan Library, New York: Exhibition of Illuminated MSS (New York 1933–4). Illustrated catalogue of an Exhibition (New York 1940)

Rice, D. T.: Byzantine Painting and its Development in the West (London 1948)

Rickert, Margaret: Painting in Britain: The Middle Ages (London 1954)

Salmi, M.: The Italian Miniature (English translation 1957)
Saunders, O. E.: English Illumination (Florence 1928)
Swarzenski, Hanns: Monuments of Romanesque Art (London 1954)
Thompson, H. Y.: Illustrations of a Hundred MSS (London 1907–18)
Vagaggini, S.: La miniatura florentina (Florence 1952)
Weitzmann, K.: Illustrations in Roll and Codex (Princeton 1947)
Winkler, F.: Die Flaemische Buchmalerei (Leipzig 1925)
Wormald, F.: English Drawings of the 10th and 11th Centuries (London 1951)
Zimmermann, E. H.: Vorkarolingische Miniaturen (Berlin 1916)

CHAPTERS IV–VIII (PRINTED BOOKS)

GENERAL

Audin, M.: Histoire de l'imprimerie par l'image (Paris 1929)
Benesch, O.: Artistic and Intellectual Trends from Rubens to Daumier as shown in Book Illustration (Harvard 1943)
Bouchot, H.: The Book (English translation London 1887)
Crane, W.: Of the Decorative Illustration of Books Old and New (London 1896)
Dolphin, a journal (New York 1933–41)
Ede, C.: The Art of the Book (London 1951)
Ellis, R. W.: Book Illustration (Kingsport 1952)
Graphis, a journal (Zurich 1944–   )
Hind, A. M.: Introduction to a History of Woodcut (London 1935)
Hofer, P.: Baroque Book Illustration (Harvard 1951)
Ivins, W. M.: Prints and Books (Harvard 1927)
— The Artist and the Fifteenth Century Printer (New York 1940)
— Prints and Visual Communication (Harvard 1953)
Johnson, A. F.: One Hundred Title Pages, 1500–1800 (London 1928)
Kristeller, P.: Kupferstich und Holzschnitt in vier Jahrhunderten (Berlin 1922)
Jennett, S.: The Making of Books (London 1948)
Praz, M.: Studies in Seventeenth Century Imagery (London 1939)
Pennell, J.: Lithography and Lithographers (New York 1915)
— Modern Illustration (London 1895)
Pollard, A. W.: Fine Books (London 1912)
— Early Illustrated Books (Second edition London 1917)
Print Collector's Quarterly (Boston and London 1911–36)
Simon, H.: Five Hundred Years of Art in Illustration (New York 1942)
Schreiber, W. L.: Manuel de l'amateur de la gravure sur bois et sur métal au XV siècle (Berlin 1891–1911)
Strachan, J.: Early Bible Illustration (London 1957)
Sullivan, E. J.: The Art of Illustration (London 1921)
Weitenkampf, F.: The Illustrated Book (Harvard 1938)

ENGLAND

Abbey, J. R.: Life in England in Aquatint and Lithography 1770–1860 (London 1953)
— Scenery of Great Britain and Ireland in Aquatint and Lithography 1770–1860 (London 1952)
— Travel in Aquatint and Lithography, 1770–1860 (London 1957)
Alphabet and Image, a journal (London 1946–52)
Balston, T.: English Wood-Engraving, 1900–1950 (London 1951)
Book Collector, The, a journal (London 1952–   )
Darton, F. J. H.: Modern Book Illustration in Great Britain and America (London 1931)
Gray, B.: The English Print (London 1937)
Hardie, M.: English Coloured Books (London 1906)
Hodnett, E.: English Woodcuts, 1480–1535 (London 1935)
Muir, P.: English Children's Books (London 1954)

Reid, F.: Illustrators of the Sixties (London 1928)

Salaman, M. C.: British Book Illustration Yesterday and To-day (London 1923)

Signature, a journal (London 1935–54)

Sketchley, R. E. D.: English Book Illustration of To-day (London 1903)

Smith, J. A.: Children's Illustrated Books (London 1948)

Studio, a journal (London 1893–)

Thorpe, J.: English Illustration: the Nineties (London 1935)

Tooley, R. V.: English Colour Plate Books (2nd edition London 1954)

Typographica, a journal (London 1893–)

White, G.: English Illustrators: 'The Sixties', 1855–1870 (London 1897)

The *Ariel Books on the Arts* and the *Art and Technics* series of monographs called English Masters of Black and White were published in London between 1946 and 1950

FRANCE

Arts et Métiers Graphiques, a journal (Paris 1927–)

Bouchot, H.: Les Livres à vignettes, XVe au XIXe siècles (Paris 1891)

— Livres à vignettes du XIX siècle (Paris 1891)

Brun, R.: Le Livre français (Paris 1948)

— Le Livre illustré en France au XVI siècle (Paris 1930)

Calot, F. and others: L'Art du Livre en France des origines à nos jours (Paris 1931)

Champfleury: Les Vignettes romantiques (Paris 1883)

Claudin, A.: Histoire de l'imprimerie française au XVe et au XVIe siècle (Paris 1900–14)

Cohen H. and S. de Ricci: Guide de l'Amateur de livres à gravures du XVIIIe siècle (new edition Paris 1912)

Duportal, J.: Etude sur les livres à figures edités en France de 1610 à 1660 (Paris 1914)

Fürstenberg, H.: Das französische Buch im 18 Jahrhunderts (Weimar 1929)

Johnson, U.: Ambroise Vollard, Editeur. (New York 1944)

Hesse, R.: Le Livre d'art du XIXe siècle à nos jours (Paris 1927)

Lejard, A. (ed.): The Art of the French Book (English translation London 1949)

Lonchamp, F. C.: Manuel du bibliophile français 1470–1920 (Paris 1927)

Martin, A.: Le Livre illustré en France au XV siècle (Paris 1931)

Morin, L.: French Illustrators (New York 1893)

Mornand, P.: L'Art du Livre et son Illustration du XVe au XVIIIe siècle (Paris 1947)

Pichon, L.: The New Book Illustration in France (London 1924)

Portalis, R.: Les Dessinateurs d'illustrations au 18e siècle (Paris 1877)

Portalis, R. and Beraldi, H.: Les Graveurs du 18e siècle (Paris 1880–2)

Portique, Le, a journal (1945–51)

Sander, M.: Die illustrierten französischen Bücher des 19 Jahrhunderts (Stuttgart 1924)

Saunier, C.: Les Decorateurs du Livre (Paris 1922)

Singer, H. W.: Französische Buchillustration des achtzehnten Jahrhunderts (Munich 1923)

Skira, A.: Anthologie du livre illustré par les peintres et sculpteurs (Geneva 1946)

Strachan, W. J. Articles in *Typographica*, *Image* and *Vogue* on contemporary French illustration

Vaucaire, G.: Manuel de l'amateur de livres du XIX siècle (Paris 1894–1920)

Wheeler, M. (ed.): Modern Painters and Sculptors as Illustrators (New York 1936)

Les Artistes du Livre: a series of monographs published in Paris between 1928 and 1933

GERMANY, AUSTRIA, SWITZERLAND

Archiv für Buchgewerbe and Gebrauchsgraphik, a periodical (Leipzig 1899–)

Butsch, A. F.: Die Bucherornamentik der Renaissance (Leipzig 1878–81)

Fischer, A.: Die Buchillustration der deutschen Romantik (Berlin 1933)

Geisberg, M.: Die deutsche Buchillustration (Munich 1920–32)

Kristeller, P.: Die Strassburger Bücher-Illustration im XV und im Anfange des XVI Jahrhunderts (Leipzig 1888)

Kutschmann, T.: Geschichte der deutschen Illustration (Goslar 1899)

Lanckoronska, M. and Oehler, R.: Das Buchillustration des XVIII Jahrhunderts in Deutschland, Osterreich und der Schweiz (Berlin 1932–4)

Lang, O.: Die Romantische Illustration (Dachau 1922)
Ruemann, A.: Das deutsche illustrierte Buch des XVIII Jahrhunderts (Strassburg 1931)
— Die illustrierten deutschen Bucher des 19 Jahrhunderts (Stuttgart 1926)
Scheffler, K.: Die Impressionistische Buchillustration in Deutschland (Berlin 1931)
Schramm, A.: Der Bilderschmuck der Frühdrucke (Leipzig 1924–39)
Weisbach, W.: Die Basler Buchillustration des 15 Jahrhunderts (Strassburg 1896)
Worringer, W.: Die altdeutsche Buchillustration (Munich 1912)

OTHER EUROPEAN COUNTRIES

Adaryukov, V. Y.: Russkaya Kniga (Moscow 1924–6)
Conway, W. M.: The Woodcutters of the Netherlands in the Fifteenth Century (Cambridge 1884)
Delen, A. J. J.: Histoire de la gravure dans les anciens Pays Bas (Paris 1924–34)
D'Essling, Prince: Etudes sur l'art de la gravure sur bois à Venise (Florence 1907–14)
Goldschmidt, E. P.: The Printed Book of the Renaissance (Cambridge 1950)
Haebler, K.: Geschichte der spanischen Frühdrucke in Stammbäumen (Leipzig 1923)
Johnsen, N. J.: Døler øg Troll (Oslo 1935)
Kristeller, P.: Early Florentine Woodcuts (London 1897)
Lagerström, H.: Svensk Bokkonst (Stockholm 1920)
Lam, S.: Le Livre Polonais au XV et XVI siècle (Warsaw 1923)
Lippmann, F.: The Art of Wood Engraving in Italy in the XV century (London 1888)
Lyell, J. P. R.: Early Book Illustration in Spain (London 1926)
Marck, J. H. M. van der: Romantische Boekillustratie in Belgie (Roermond 1956)
Morazzone, G.: Il Libro Illustrato Veneziano del Settecento (Milan 1943)
Orcutt, W. D. (ed.): The Book in Italy during the 15th and 16th Centuries (London 1928)
Perrins, C. W. D.: Italian Book-Illustration and Early Printing. A Catalogue of Italian Books in the Library of C. W. D. Perrins (Oxford 1914)
Pirani, E. C.: Il Libro illustrato italiano: secoli XVII–XVIII (Rome 1956)
Renard, M.: L'Illustration, sa genèse, sa technique. Les illustrateurs belges (Brussels 1917)
Rooses, M.: Christophe Plantin, imprimeur anversois (Antwerp 1882–3)
Sander, M.: Le Livre à figures italien 1467–1530 (Milan 1942)
Sthyr, J.: Dansk Grafik 1800–1910 (Copenhagen 1949)
Tomov, E.: Bulgarian Graphic Art (English translation Sofia 1956)

AMERICA

American Artist, The: A Periodical (New York)
Burland, C. A.: Magic Books from Mexico (London 1953)
Linton, W. J.: The History of Wood-Engraving in America (Boston 1882)
Pitz, H.: A Treasury of American Book Illustration (New York 1947)
Smith, F. H.: American Illustrators (New York 1892)
Weitenkampf, F.: American Graphic Art (2nd edition New York 1924)

ORIENTAL ILLUSTRATION

Arnold, T. W. and Grohmann, A.: The Islamic Book (Paris 1929)
Brown, L. N.: Block Printing and Book Illustration in Japan (London 1924)
Binyon, L. and Sexton, J. J.: Japanese Colour Prints (London 1923)
Carter, T. F.: The Invention of Printing in China and its spread westwards (2nd edition 1955)
Exposition d'ouvrages illustrés de la Dynastie Ming (Peking 1944)
Fenollosa, E. F.: Makers of Ukiyo-ye (London 1896)
Strange, E.: Japanese Illustration (London 1897)
Tschichold, J.: L'Estampe chinoise ancienne en couleurs (Basle 1940)

Index

In the manuscript references, B.M. = British Museum, London, and B.N. = Bibliothèque National, Paris